Bilingual Minds

BILINGUAL EDUCATION AND BILINGUALISM
Series Editors: Professor Colin Baker, *University of Wales, Bangor, Wales, Great Britain* and Professor Nancy H. Hornberger, *University of Pennsylvania, Philadelphia, USA*

Recent Books in the Series
Power, Prestige and Bilingualism: International Perspectives on Elite Bilingual Education
Anne-Marie de Mejía
Identity and the English Language Learner
Elaine Mellen Day
Language and Literacy Teaching for Indigenous Education: A Bilingual Approach
Norbert Francis and Jon Reyhner
The Native Speaker: Myth and Reality
Alan Davies
Language Socialization in Bilingual and Multilingual Societies
Robert Bayley and Sandra R. Schecter (eds)
Language Rights and the Law in the United States: Finding our Voices
Sandra Del Valle
Continua of Biliteracy: An Ecological Framework for Educational Policy, Research, and Practice in Multilingual Settings
Nancy H. Hornberger (ed.)
Languages in America: A Pluralist View (2nd edn)
Susan J. Dicker
Trilingualism in Family, School and Community
Charlotte Hoffmann and Jehannes Ytsma (eds)
Multilingual Classroom Ecologies
Angela Creese and Peter Martin (eds)
Negotiation of Identities in Multilingual Contexts
Aneta Pavlenko and Adrian Blackledge (eds)
Beyond the Beginnings: Literacy Interventions for Upper Elementary English Language Learners
Angela Carrasquillo, Stephen B. Kucer and Ruth Abrams
Bilingualism and Language Pedagogy
Janina Brutt-Griffler and Manka Varghese (eds)
Language Learning and Teacher Education: A Sociocultural Approach
Margaret R. Hawkins (ed.)
The English Vernacular Divide: Postcolonial Language Politics and Practice
Vaidehi Ramanathan
Bilingual Education in South America
Anne-Marie de Mejía (ed.)
Teacher Collaboration and Talk in Multilingual Classrooms
Angela Creese
Words and Worlds: World Languages Review
Martí, P. Ortega, I. Idiazabal, A. Barreña, P. Juaristi, C. Junyent, B. Uranga and E. Amorrortu
Language and Aging in Multilingual Contexts
Kees de Bot and Sinfree Makoni
Foundations of Bilingual Education and Bilingualism (4th edn)
Colin Baker

For more details of these or any other of our publications, please contact:
Multilingual Matters, Frankfurt Lodge, Clevedon Hall,
Victoria Road, Clevedon, BS21 7HH, England
http://www.multilingual-matters.com

BILINGUAL EDUCATION AND BILINGUALISM 56
Series Editors: Colin Baker and Nancy H. Hornberger

Bilingual Minds
Emotional Experience, Expression and Representation

Edited by
Aneta Pavlenko

MULTILINGUAL MATTERS LTD
Clevedon • Buffalo • Toronto

Library of Congress Cataloging in Publication Data
Emotional Experience, Expression and Representation/Edited by Aneta Pavlenko.
Bilingual Education and Bilingualism: 56
Includes bibliographical references and index.
1. Bilingualism–Psychological aspects. 2. Emotions. I. Pavlenko, Aneta. II. Series.
P115.4.E46 2006
306.44'6'019–dc22   2005021290

British Library Cataloguing in Publication Data
A catalogue entry for this book is available from the British Library.

ISBN 1-85359-873-9/ EAN 978-1-85359-873-9 (hbk)
ISBN 1-85359-872-0 / EAN 978-1-85359-872-2 (pbk)

Multilingual Matters Ltd
UK: Frankfurt Lodge, Clevedon Hall, Victoria Road, Clevedon BS21 7HH.
USA: UTP, 2250 Military Road, Tonawanda, NY 14150, USA.
Canada: UTP, 5201 Dufferin Street, North York, Ontario M3H 5T8, Canada.

Typeset by Techset Composition Ltd.
Printed and bound in Great Britain by MPG Books Ltd.

Contents

The Contributors

Jeanette Altarriba (PhD in Cognitive Psychology, Vanderbilt University, 1990) is Professor of Psychology at the University at Albany, State University of New York, Albany, NY, United States. Her research interests include bilingual language processing, second language acquisition, emotion and cognition, and experimental paradigms that examine the intersection between language, perception, and memory. Her current work focuses on how monolingual and bilingual speakers represent emotion-related words in various contexts through the use of both implicit and explicit measures of cognitive processing. Her work has appeared in numerous scientific journals, including the *International Journal of Bilingualism, Journal of Memory and Language, Memory and Cognition*, and *Perception and Psychophysics*. She is the editor of *Cognition and Culture: A Cross-Cultural Approach to Cognitive Psychology* (Elsevier, 1993), and co-editor of *Bilingual Sentence Processing* with Roberto R. Heredia (Elsevier, 2002). A third volume with the same co-editor is now in preparation under the title *An Introduction to Bilingualism: Principles and Processes* (Lawrence Erlbaum, to appear).

Ayşe Ayçiçeği (PhD in Psychology, Marmara University, 1996) is Associate Professor of Psychology and Director of the Experimental Psychology Program at the Psychology Department at Istanbul University, Istanbul, Turkey. Her research interests include language processing, child development, parental styles, and personality disorders. Her work has appeared in numerous scientific journals, including *Applied Psycholinguistics, Clinical Psychology and Psychotherapy, Cognition and Emotion, The European Journal of Cognitive Psychology, European Psychiatry, Psychological Reports, Psychopathology*, and *Schizophrenia Research*.

Jean Berko Gleason (PhD in Linguistics and Social Psychology, Radcliffe–Harvard College, 1958) is Professor of Psychology at the Department of Psychology at Boston University, Boston, MA, United States. Her research examines child language development, language socialization, language processing, language disorders, language loss, and gender differences in parental communication styles. She is the editor of *The Development of Language* (Pearson/Allyn & Bacon, 2005, 6th edn) and *Psycholinguistics* (with N. Bernstein Ratner, Harcourt Brace, 1998, 2nd edn) and the author of numerous book chapters and articles that appeared in a variety of journals, including *Applied Psycholinguistics, Brain and Language, Contemporary Psychology, Discourse Processes, Language in Society,* and *Science.*

Mary Besemeres (PhD in English, Australian National University, 2000) is a Research Fellow at the Australian Research Institute, Division of Humanities, Curtin University of Technology, Western Australia. Her research interests include cross-cultural autobiography, bilingualism and immigrant experience, the cross-cultural family, and the relationship between culture and emotions. Her publications include *Translating One's Self: Language and Selfhood in Cross-Cultural Autobiography* (Peter Lang, 2002), and essays on bilingual and transcultural autobiography published in edited volumes and a variety of journals, including *a/b: Auto/Biography Studies, Biography, Canadian Slavonic Papers, Journal of Multilingual and Multicultural Development,* and *The Russian Review.* With Maureen Perkins she co-edits the journal *Life Writing.*

John D. Coley (PhD in Developmental Psychology, University of Michigan, 1993) is Associate Professor of Psychology at Northeastern University, Boston, MA, United States. His research examines the impact of culture and experience on categorization, reasoning, and conceptual development. His work has appeared in edited volumes and numerous scientific journals, including *Child Development, Cognition, Cognitive Psychology,* and *Memory and Cognition.*

Jean-Marc Dewaele (PhD in Romance Languages and Literature, Vrije University of Brussels, 1993) is a Reader in French and Applied Linguistics at Birkbeck College, University of London, London, United Kingdom. His research examines psycholinguistic, sociolinguistic, pragmatic, and psychological aspects of second language acquisition and multilingualism. His work has appeared in edited volumes and in numerous scientific journals, including *Applied Linguistics, Journal of Multilingual and Multicultural Development, Journal of Sociolinguistics,* and *Language Learning.* He is a co-editor of *Opportunities and Challenges of Bilingualism* (with Li Wei and A. Housen, Mouton De Gruyter, 2002) and *Bilingualism, Basic Principles and Beyond* (with A. Housen and Li Wei, Multilingual Matters, 2003), and the editor of *Focus on French as a Foreign Language* (Multilingual Matters, 2005).

Ramon Durazo-Arvizu (PhD in Applied Mathematics, University of Arizona, 1994) is Associate Professor at the Loyola University Stritch School of Medicine, Chicago, IL, United States. He is an expert in applied statistics, in particular in survival analysis, multivariate linear and logistic regression, and the computer intensive methods, and has ample experience in statistical consulting within the health sciences. His publications have appeared in a variety of journals, including *American Journal of Epidemiology, Annals of Epidemiology, Journal of the American Statistical Association (JASA)*, and *New England Journal of Medicine*.

Catherine L. Harris (PhD in Cognitive Science and Psychology, University of California, San Diego, 1991) is Associate Professor of Psychology at the Department of Psychology at Boston University, Boston, MA, United States. Her work examines the intersection between language, cognition, and emotions from a variety of perspectives, including skin conductance responsiveness. She has also studied the brain bases of psychopathology and normal personality variation, particularly the role of prefrontal cortex in impulse control, aggression, social cognition and executive processing. Her work has appeared in a variety of journals, including *Applied Psycholinguistics, Brain and Cognition, Cognition and Emotion, Journal of Experimental Psychology: Human Perception and Performance, Journal of Experimental Psychology: Learning, Memory and Cognition, Journal of Multilingual and Multicultural Development, Language and Cognitive Processes*, and *The Quarterly Journal of Experimental Psychology*.

Michèle Koven (PhD in Human Development, University of Chicago, 1999) is Assistant Professor in the Department of Speech Communication at the University of Illinois at Urbana-Champaign, IL, United States. Her work has addressed the relationship between language, identity, and emotion among bilinguals. In particular, she has been engaged in several long-term projects with the children of Portuguese migrants in France. She is currently completing a book-length monograph on these bilinguals' displays and experiences of identity and emotion in their two languages. Her work has appeared in *American Ethnologist, Ethos, Journal of Pragmatics, Language in Society*, and *Text*.

Alexia Panayiotou (EdD in Human Development and Psychology, Harvard Graduate School of Education, 2002) is a Lecturer in Management at the Department of Public and Business Administration at the University of Cyprus, Nicosia, Cyprus. Her research interests involve the relationship between bilingualism, emotion, and identity, emotions in the workplace, the production of discourse in/by organizations, and feminist theory. Her work has apeared in *Estudios de Sociolingüística* and the *Journal of Multilingual and Multicultural Development*.

Aneta Pavlenko (PhD in Linguistics, Cornell University, 1997) is Associate Professor at the College of Education, Temple University, Philadelphia,

United States. Her current research examines the relationship between language, emotions, and cognition in bilingualism and second language acquisition. Her work has appeared in edited volumes and numerous scientific journals, including *Applied Linguistics, Bilingualism: Language and Cognition, International Journal of Bilingualism, International Journal of Bilingual Education and Bilingualism, Journal of Multilingual and Multicultural Development, Language Learning, Multilingua,* and *Pragmatics and Cognition.* She is the author of *Emotions and Multilingualism* (Cambridge University Press, 2005) and co-editor of *Multilingualism, Second Language Learning, and Gender* (with A. Blackledge, I. Piller and M. Teutsch Dwyer, Mouton De Gruyter, 2001), *Gender and English Language Learners* (with B. Norton, TESOL, 2004) and *Negotiation of Identities in Multilingual Contexts* (with A. Blackledge, Multilingual Matters, 2004).

Ingrid Piller (PhD in English Linguistics, University of Technology, Dresden, Germany, 1995) holds the Chair of English Sociolinguistics and the Sociology of English as a Global Language at Basel University in Basel, Switzerland. Her current research focuses on linguistic aspects of globalization, specifically in the contexts of English language teaching and learning, romantic relationships and tourism. Her work appeared in a variety of edited volumes and journals, including *Annual Review of Applied Linguistics, International Journal of Bilingualism, Journal of Sociolinguistics,* and *Language in Society.* Her most recent book is *Bilingual Couples Talk* (John Benjamins, 2002).

Robert W. Schrauf (PhD in Medical Anthropology, Case Western Reserve University, 1995) is Associate Professor of Applied Linguistics at the Pennsylvania State University, State College, PA, United States. He completed postdoctoral work in the cognitive psychology of bilingualism at Duke University. His research concerns multilingualism and memory processes among cognitively healthy and cognitively impaired older immigrants. His work has appeared in edited volumes and in numerous scientific journals, including *Anthropological Theory, Culture and Psychology, Estudios de Sociolingüística, Ethos, Journal of Memory and Language, Journal of Multilingual and Multicultural Development, Memory,* and *Memory and Cognition.*

Olga Stepanova Sachs (PhD in Experimental Psychology, Northeastern University, 2004) is currently a postdoc at the university clinic for research on psychiatry and psychotherapy in Aachen, Germany. She also works for Warm Home, a Russian foundation that provides psychological and social assistance to refugee women and children from Chechnya. Her research interests are in the areas of language and cognition, bilingualism, and categorization and reasoning. Her work appeared in edited volumes and in the *Journal of Culture and Cognition*.

Kimie Takahashi is a PhD student in the Faculty of Education at the University of Sydney, Australia. Her research is a longitudinal ethnographic study of female Japanese sojourners in Australia, with a particular focus on their English language learning experiences.

Jyotsna Vaid (PhD in Experimental Psychology, McGill University, 1982) is Professor of Psychology at the Department of Psychology at Texas A&M University, College Station, TX, United States. Her research examines language processing, cognitive and neuropsychological aspects of bilingualism, and cognitive and psycholinguistic aspects of humor, literacy, and numeracy. Her work has appeared in edited volumes and in numerous scientific journals, including *Brain and Language, Journal of Pragmatics, Neuropsychologia*, and *Reading and Writing: An Interdisciplinary Journal*. She is the editor of *Language Processing in Bilinguals: Psycholinguistic and Neuropsychological Perspectives* (Lawrence Erlbaum, 1986) and co-editor of *Creative Thought: An Investigation of Conceptual Structures and Processes* (with T. Ward and S. Smith, American Psychological Association, 1997/ 2001).

Preface: Multilingualism and Emotions as a New Area of Research

ANETA PAVLENKO

What does it mean to open up a new area of research? Can an area ever be closed? Is the new thing simply a well-forgotten old one? Or is it a familiar idea that goes by a different name? Does it need to fit within research agendas in larger disciplinary fields? We face these questions every time we move into what we see as uncharted waters and working on this volume was no different. If we look at the precursors of the study of bi-/ multilingualism and emotions, it is clear that questions similar to ours were raised throughout the 20th century. At different points in time, Arsenian (1945), Weinreich (1953), Vildomec (1963), and Ervin-Tripp (1954, 1964, 1967) had all argued for the need to move beyond the issues of attitudes and motivation to the study of emotions and affective repertoires of bi- and multilingual speakers. In each case, however, the issues and questions raised by one researcher were not taken up by others.

What is different about the present situation is the *Zeitgeist* in which emotions became a legitimate and popular subject of inquiry in psychology, linguistics, and anthropology, thus opening ways for similar inquiries in the study of bilingualism. As a result, several of us became interested in issues of emotion representation, processing, and expression at about the same time. These inquiries went beyond the study of 'affective factors', with its focus on the interaction between single emotional states, such as anxiety, and the processes of second language learning and use. Rather, this new wave of research is concerned as much with understanding emotions as states, processes, and relationships, as it is with understanding second language acquisition and bilingualism, and as such has a lot to offer to the study of 'affective factors' where emotions have traditionally been undertheorized. The chapter by Piller and Takahashi, for instance, offers an intriguing argument for considering 'desire' in the study of motivation and language learning.

Furthermore, a better understanding of ways in which bi- and multilingual individuals represent, process, perform, and experience emotions can be valuable not just for the fields of bilingualism and second language acquisition, but also for the fields of linguistics, psychology, anthropology, and communication – the advantages of using speakers of two or more languages for cross-linguistic studies of emotion concepts and affective repertoires are demonstrated in several chapters, most prominently in that by Panayiotou.

Opening up a new area of inquiry is both a scholarly thrill and a great responsibility, as one cannot appeal to shortcuts, simply pointing to shared theories or naming well-known methodologies. Rather, all contributors try to make their theoretical, methodological, and analytical assumptions explicit, so that other scholars could replicate their work, build on it, and move the field in new directions.

For over four years now, several of us have continued to meet and to discuss our work in progress at the various colloquia on bilingualism and emotions that Jean-Marc Dewaele and I have organized at the Second University of Vigo International Symposium on Bilingualism,- Vigo, Spain, October 2002; at the Fourth International Symposium on Bilingualism, Tempe, Arizona, United States, May 2003; at the International Pragmatics Association Conference, Toronto, Canada, July 2003; and at the Fifth International Symposium on Bilingualism, Barcelona, Spain, March 2005. We are extremely grateful to the organizers and the audiences at these conferences for their feedback and support. It has also been wonderful to learn continuously of new studies of multilingualism and emotions and to see our core group expand over the years.

Several of the contributors also had an opportunity to comment on each other's work directly in the process of preparation of this volume and the two special journal issues that preceded it, *Estudios de Sociolingüística* (2004: 5, 1) and the *Journal of Multilingual and Multicultural Development* (2004: 25, 2/3). The multiple opportunities we all had to read and to comment on each other's work and to discuss directions for future research allowed scholars from different disciplines – psychology, anthropology, linguistics, literary theory, and human development – to learn from each other, to make imaginative and innovative interdisciplinary connections, and to establish common aims:

- to understand how emotion and emotion-laden words and concepts are represented and processed in the bi- and multilingual mental lexicons;
- to explore translatability of emotion concepts and thus contribute to the inquiry in linguistic relativity;
- to demonstrate that bi- and multilingualism, used as a unique lens, can illuminate new directions in the study of the relationship between languages and emotions, and thus to argue that cross-linguistic inquiry should not necessarily be limited to studies of

one language at a time or comparisons between monolingual speakers of different languages; and
- to put a human face on linguistic and psycholinguistic research, finding ways to bring speakers' lived experiences and concerns into our inquiry.

We hope that this volume will raise interest in and contribute to the understanding of ways in which emotions impact language choice and use, as well as ways in which bi- and multilinguals represent, process, and express emotions in their multiple languages. We also hope that it will contribute to a deeper understanding of the complexity of the bi- and multilingual experience. In fact, the original working title of the volume was *Language and Emotions of Bilingual Speakers*, but as the editing process proceeded it became increasingly clear that the incoming contributions involve something even more central than the role of emotions in our language choice and use, namely, bi- and multilingual minds and our experience of self.

In addition to changing the title, I also decided to forego the introductory overview of the field, because a detailed overview has already been accomplished elsewhere (Pavlenko, 2005). Instead, I opened up the volume with a chapter on bilingual selves that brings together introspective reports of bi- and multilingual speakers and empirical research and aims to show how studies of emotions in autobiographical memory, linguistic repertoires, and conceptual representations illuminate the experience of self. The next chapter, by Mary Besemeres, examines ways in which bilingual writers discuss their emotional experiences and identifies several areas of tension and untranslatability, where concepts from one language and culture do not easily fit within the other language. Ingrid Piller and Kimie Takahashi's chapter similarly transcends purely linguistic issues and considers emotional experiences of five Japanese women who arrive in Sydney, Australia, to learn English and search for Western men who can facilitate their entry into the 'glamorous English-speaking world'. Together, these chapters point to different ways in which some speakers experience their languages and cultures and to ways in which emotions mediate transitions between these experiential worlds.

The next three chapters shift the focus from emotional experience to expression and consider bi- and multilinguals' affective repertoires. Michèle Koven's chapter analyses affect performance in the two languages of a Portuguese–French bilingual and establishes that even childhood bilinguals may have somewhat different linguistic repertoires in their respective languages. She also shows that, in the case of her participant, the preferred language of emotional expression is the language learned in a public domain, not the one learned in the family. The issue of language choice is at the center of Jean-Marc Dewaele's chapter on anger expression. His analysis of answers from respondents to a web questionnaire identifies several factors that affect multilinguals' choice of language for anger expression in communication with other multilinguals. Jyotsna Vaid also uses a questionnaire to explore language choice, but in a different domain, that of humor. Her work inquires whether bilinguals have specific language preferences or whether they use their two languages indiscriminately for emotion management through the use of humor (e.g. to reduce tension or conflict, to express hostility). The findings point to some intriguing differences in participants' uses of English and Spanish and to ways in which their cultural and ethnic self-identification mediates their language preferences.

The following three chapters consider cognitive representation of emotion words and concepts. Alexia Panayiotou's chapter uses interviews with Greek–English and English–Greek bilinguals to question the cultural equivalence between English and Greek translation equivalents shame/*ntropi* and guilt/*enohi*. Olga Stepanova Sachs and John Coley use categorization tasks to compare representations of Russian and English translation equivalents jealousy/*revnost'* and envy/*zavist'* in monolingual and bilingual speakers. Jeanette Altarriba's chapter points to several dimensions on which emotion and emotion-laden words differ from abstract and concrete ones, and makes a convincing case for the study of representation and processing of emotion words as a unique category in the bilingual mental lexicon.

A somewhat different perspective on the processing of emotion-laden words is taken in the next chapter, by Catherine Harris, Jean Berko Gleason, and Ayşe Ayçiçeği, who examine bilinguals' psychophysiological reactions to various types of words in their two languages. Both this chapter and the next one, by Robert Schrauf and Ramon Durazo-Arvizu, point to ways in which language socialization experiences link languages, memories, and feelings of emotional arousal. In doing so, these chapters offer an excellent conclusion to the discussion in the volume, placing the findings, experiences, and self-perceptions discussed in the earlier chapters within the larger frameworks of autobiographical and emotional memory, and self-experience.

Having thus introduced the aims and the organization of the volume, I would like to end with a few words of thanks. For their insightful and productive feedback I thank all contributors who participated in the peer-review process, as well as other colleagues who generously donated their time and expertise to comment on the chapters: Nancy Bell, Martin Howard, Celeste Kinginger, Yumiko Ohara, Monika Schmid, Jenny Sia, and Elena Skapoulli. The contributions have also benefitted tremendously from thoughtful suggestions made by Colin Baker, our series editor. Working with such an amazing group of scholars was a wonderful learning opportunity and a great privilege, one I do not take for granted. Thank you for trusting me with your work. Jean-Marc Dewaele and I are also indebted to all bi- and multilinguals who contributed to our 'Bilingualism and emotions' questionnaire. Thank you for trusting us with your stories.

I am equally grateful for the unconditional support received over the years from the Multilingual Matters team, and in particular from Colin Baker and from Tommi, Mike, and Marjukka Grover, and Anna Roderick – by now all of you are more of a family than a publishing house. I am also very fortunate to have met Jenny Leeman, a linguist and a professional photographer, who knew exactly how my incoherent explanations might translate into a cover photograph that pays tribute to the first people who began the systematic examination of the relationship between bilingualism and emotions – bilingual psychoanalysts – and evokes the notions of multiple selves and the world of childhood irrevocably linked to our first learned language or languages.

For me, the world of childhood is forever linked to Russian and to the voices of my parents. This book is dedicated to the memory of my parents, Bella and Tadeush Pavlenko, who passed away in 2004, within four months of each other, bringing my life to a complete halt and creating a void that will be impossible to fill. I will miss you every day of my life, пусть земля вам будет пухом.

References

Arsenian, S. (1945) Bilingualism in the post-war world. *Psychological Bulletin* 42(2), 65–86.
Ervin, S. (1954, reprinted 1973) Identification and bilingualism. In A. Dil (ed.) *Language Acquisition and Communicative Choice. Essays by Susan M. Ervin-Tripp* (pp. 1–14). Stanford, CA: Stanford University Press.
Ervin-Tripp, S. (1964, reprinted 1973) Language and TAT content in bilinguals. In A. Dil (ed.) *Language Acquisition and Communicative Choice. Essays by Susan M. Ervin-Tripp* (pp. 45–61). Stanford, CA: Stanford University Press.
Ervin-Tripp, S. (1967, reprinted 1973) An issei learns English. In A. Dil (ed.) *Language Acquisition and Communicative Choice. Essays by Susan M. Ervin-Tripp* (pp. 62–77). Stanford, CA: Stanford University Press.
Pavlenko, A. (2005) *Emotions and Multilingualism*. New York: Cambridge University Press.
Vildomec, V. (1963) *Multilingualism*. Leyden: A.W. Sythoff.
Weinreich, U. (1953) *Languages in Contact: Findings and Problems*. New York: Publications of the Linguistic Circle of New York.

Chapter 1
Bilingual Selves

ANETA PAVLENKO

Do bi- and multilinguals sometimes feel like different people when speaking different languages? Are they perceived as different people by their interlocutors? Do they behave differently? What prompts these differences? These questions often pop up in conversations about bilingualism, but are rarely raised in the literature in the field (see, however, Grosjean, 1982; Heinz, 2001). Some scholars waive them away as naive and simplistic, others point out that we also perform different identities in the same language, when changing registers, contexts, interlocutors, or interactional aims. This is a valid point, because monolingualism is indeed a dynamic phenomenon. Even within the confines of one language, we continuously acquire new linguistic repertoires and behave and feel differently when talking, let's say, to our parents versus our children. At the same time, the argument that the study of bi- and multilingual selves is not worthy of scholarly attention or that it can be easily replaced with the study of multilingual identities is misleading and reductionist for at least two reasons.

The first problem with this argument is the sleight of hand by which it equates the notion of self-perception with that of performance, and the notion of self with that of identity. This substitution reveals a deep discomfort with the focus on something as intangible as 'feeling like a different person' and a preference for 'objective' identity performance data (conversations, texts, task performance) over 'subjective' self-perception data. I intend to show, however, that introspective data have both relevance and validity and can help us identify sources of bi/multilingual experience that are not directly observable in the study of identity performance.

The second problem with the argument is the framing of bi/multilingualism as an expanded version of monolingualism, rather than a unique linguistic and psychological phenomenon. In reality, acquisition of new registers in the same language is always facilitated by phonological, lexical, and morphosyntactic overlaps. In contrast, acquisition and use of a new language, in particular one that is typologically different from one's native language, is a much more challenging enterprise that may be further complicated by the need to negotiate new and unfamiliar surroundings. These differences are especially pronounced in late bilingualism, when speakers are socialized into their respective languages at distinct points in their lives, childhood versus adulthood, and in distinct sociocultural environments.

The goal of the present chapter is to legitimize the question about different selves, to examine whether bi- and multilinguals indeed perceive themselves as different people when using different languages, and to understand to what sources they attribute these self-perceptions. To do so, I appeal to answers from 1039 bi- and multilingual web questionnaire respondents, to reflections of bilingual writers, and to studies in psychology, psychoanalysis, linguistics, and anthropology. The triangulation of introspective data with the data from empirical and clinical studies of bilinguals' verbal and non-verbal behaviors will allow me to understand linguistic, psychological, and physiological processes that underlie the perception of different selves.

In line with the traditions of the field of bilingualism, I will use the term *bilingualism* to refer to research that examines both bi- and multilingualism. The term *bilingual* will be used to refer to speakers who use two languages in their daily lives, be it simultaneously (in language contact situations) or consecutively (in the context of transnational migration), regardless of respective levels of proficiency in the two. The term *late bilingual* will refer to individuals who learned their second language after puberty. The term *multilingual* will refer to speakers who use more than two languages in their daily lives. The term *bilingual* will, however, appear more frequently, because research to date has focused predominantly on bilinguals' selves.

Dual, Double, and Doubled Selves: Bilingualism and Schizophrenia

In bi- and multilingual communities, changes in verbal and non-verbal behavior that accompany a change in language are commonly taken for granted and do not elicit much interest. In fact, language boundaries can become quite blurred in contexts where code-switching and code-mixing prevail (cf. Auer, 1998). However, in traditionally monolingual societies, bilinguals are at times seen as people with two conflicting personalities whose shifting linguistic allegiances imply shifting political allegiances and moral commitments. Such views were particularly common in the first half of the 20th century. In the United States, during and after the First World War, language and educational policies targeted incoming immigrants and their children, forcing them to abandon their native languages in a show of loyalty to their new country (Pavlenko, 2002). A decade later in Germany, Nazi scholars began to equate bilingualism with Jews and other ethnic minorities and argued that bilinguals experience a pathological inner split and suffer intellectual and moral deterioration in their struggle to become one (Henss, 1931). They also referred to the 'bilinguality of feelings' and the 'mercenary relativism' of bilinguals who switch principles and values as they switch languages (Sander, 1934). Later on, North American scholars concerned with immigrant bilingualism linked continuing allegiance to one's primary ethnic community to the feelings of anomie, alienation, social isolation, nervous strain, and cognitive dissonance (Bossard, 1945; Child, 1943; Spoerl, 1943).

In the second half of the 20th century, the increased transnational migration, the revival of ethnic consciousness, and progressive educational scholarship contributed to the lessening of concerns and a greater understanding of the benefits of bilingualism. Nevertheless, the view of bilingualism as a problem of two incompatible identities, referred to here as the discourse of bilingualism as linguistic schizophrenia, has not vanished. In a treatise on bilingualism, Adler (1977: 40) warned that 'bilingualism can lead to split personality and, at worst, to schizophrenia'. Clarke (1976) likened foreign students in the United States to schizophrenic patients and argued that their learning of English is hampered by a clash of consciousness between the familiar traditional worlds they come from and modernity and progress they encounter in the United States. In bilingual psychoanalysis, schizophrenia persisted as a metaphor used to discuss problems brought on by culture shock, cognitive, linguistic, and cultural dissonance, and different social roles occupied by patients in their respective linguistic communities (cf. Amati-Mehler *et al.*, 1993). From time to time, this metaphor also pops up in political discourse. For instance, David Blunkett (2002), British Home Secretary, recently remarked that the use of English – rather than the native language – in Asian British households would help 'overcome the schizophrenia which bedevils generational relationships' in immigrant families.

Interestingly, the discourse of schizophrenia is not confined to negative descriptions of bilingualism by reactionary scholars or politicians. It also appears in bilinguals' own reflections and in particular in the work of translingual writers, that is, writers who write in more than one language or in a second language (Kellman, 2000). These writers display a unique sensitivity to intrinsic links between languages and selves and are painfully cognizant of the fact that in different languages their voices may sound differently even when telling the 'same' stories. For instance, a childhood French–English bilingual Julian Green recalls that when he decided to write about his early years in English, rather than French, his memoir took a whole different shape. Whereas the subject remained the same, the rhythm, the choice of words and details, the author's stance, and the pattern of disclosures and omissions varied between the two languages:

> I was writing another book, a book so different in tone from the French that a whole aspect of the subject must of necessity be altered. It was as if, writing in English, I had become another person. I went on. New trains of thought were started in my mind, new associations of ideas were formed. There was so little resemblance between what I wrote in English and what I had already written in French that it might almost be doubted that the same person was the author of these two pieces of work. (Green, 1941/1993: 62)

A similar experience is recounted by Tzvetan Todorov (1985, 1994) in his essay *Bilingualism, Dialogism and Schizophrenia*. Todorov arrived in France from Bulgaria as a young man and eventually became a prominent French scholar and intellectual. Eighteen years after his departure from Bulgaria, he was invited to come back for a conference on Bulgarian studies. In translating his conference paper about nationalism from French into Bulgarian he noticed the following:

> I had changed my imagined audience. And at that moment I realized that the Bulgarian intellectuals to whom my discourse was addressed could not understand the meaning I intended. The condemnation of attachment to national values changes significance according to whether you live in a small country (your own) placed within the sphere of influence of a larger one or whether you live abroad, in a different country, where you are (or think you are) sheltered from any threat by a more powerful neighbor. Paris is certainly a place that favors the euphoric renunciation of nationalist values: Sofia much less so. ... [the necessary modification] required that I change an affirmation into its direct opposite. I understood the position of the Bulgarian intellectuals, and had I been in their situation, mine probably would have been the same. (Todorov, 1994: 210)

Struck by this new awareness, Todorov no longer knew how to proceed. Should he act as if only his present opinion, informed by his French context, counted? Would that amount to a denial of his Bulgarian background? Or should he speak as a Bulgarian intellectual, although that would mean a denial of the past 18 years of his life? To theorize his experience, Todorov appealed to Bakhtin's (1981) notions of dialogism and polyphony that refer to the presence of several independent and often conflicting voices within a single text. These notions have often been used in positive descriptions of bi- and multilingualism.

Todorov challenged this unquestioning celebration of heterogeneity and drew attention to the darker side of immigrant bilingualism, which may also motivate internal conflict, mental distress and, ultimately, silence.

Todorov's (1985, 1994) essay, together with Hoffman's (1989) memoir about second language learning, *Lost in Translation*, offered a striking illustration of the drama of duality, embedded in bilingualism, and inspired scholars to examine how this experience is reflected in fiction, memoirs, and reflections of other translingual writers (Beaujour, 1989; Besemeres, 2002; De Courtivron, 2003a; Kellman, 2003a; Pavlenko, 1998, 2001, 2004a; Pérez Firmat, 2003; Stroińska, 2003; Valenta, 1991). These explorations reveal that the dominant metaphors and tropes that appear in bilinguals' reflections on language – tongue snatching, border crossing, borrowing, bigamy, betrayal, bifurcation, fragmentation, multiplicity, split, gap, alienation, dislocation, and double vision – reinscribe the feeling of duality and invoke the discourse of schizophrenia that also informs Todorov's (1985, 1994) and Hoffman's (1989) discussions of bilingualism. These metaphors convey an array of emotions: guilt over linguistic and ethnic disloyalties, insecurity over the legitimacy of a newly learned language, anxiety about the lack of wholesome oneness, angst over the inability to bring together one's incommensurable worlds, and sadness and confusion caused by seeing oneself as divided, a self-in-between, a self in need of translation. It is this painful and perhaps even violent facet of bilingualism that propelled a French-Spanish writer Claude Esteban to admit:

> ... having been divided between French and Spanish since early childhood, I found it difficult for many years to overcome a strange laceration, a gap not merely between two languages but also between the mental universes carried by them; I could never make them coincide within myself. (Esteban, 1980: 26; translated by Beaujour, 1989: 47)

It is important to note here that, whereas in the early 20th century the notion of inner split was used as an argument against bilingualism, Todorov and others do not argue against bilingualism per se. Rather, these writers discuss the split as a source of both anguish and creative enrichment, the latter stemming from the ever-present relativity of one's stance and perspective (cf. Hoffman, 1989). One can also legitimately ask whether the perception of a linguistic and psychological split is unique to translingual writers for whom the relationship with their multiple languages is by definition a challenge or whether individuals from other walks of life also feel that they have multiple selves?

Present Study

Research questions

The goal of the present study is to answer this question and to expand the scope of inquiry from experiences of immigrants and expatriates who learned their second language later in life (cf. Ervin-Tripp, 1954, 1964, 1967) to multilingual speakers with diverse learning trajectories, in particular those who learned two or more languages from childhood. Three questions are posited in the study: (1) do some bi- and multilinguals feel that they become different people when they change languages; (2) how do they make sense of these perceptions; and (3) what prompts some bi- and multilinguals to see their language selves as different, while others claim to have a single self. Notably, I do not aim to provide a definitive answer to the question of bi- and multilingual selves. In view of the richness and complexity of people's minds and diversity of their linguistic trajectories and experiences, a uniform answer is neither possible nor desirable. Rather, I want to understand the key influences that shape individuals' perceptions of the relationship between their languages and selves. In order to do so, I will look both at the attributed sources of self-perceptions and at discourses of bi/multilingualism and self the participants draw on in framing their answers.

Research design and participants

The data for the study were collected through a web questionnaire 'Bilingualism and emotions' created by Jean-Marc Dewaele and myself and maintained on the Birkbeck College website from 2001 to 2003 (Dewaele & Pavlenko, 2001–2003). The questionnaire contained 34 closed and open-ended questions and elicited the following sociobiographical information: gender, age, education level, ethnic group, occupation, languages known, dominant language(s), chronological order of language acquisition, context of acquisition, age of onset, frequency of use, and self-rated proficiency. In what follows, I analyze participants' responses to one open-ended question: 'Do you feel like a different person sometimes when you use your different languages?' Owing to limited space, I will not discuss the relationship between participants' answers and sociobiographical information, leaving this issue for future consideration.

The questionnaire was advertised through several listservs and informal contacts with colleagues around the world. It allowed us to gather an unprecedented amount of data from a large and diverse population of bi- and multilingual speakers of different ages and from a variety of linguistic backgrounds. A total of 1039 bi- and multilinguals[1] contributed to the database (731 females, 308 males). The ages of the respondents ranged between 16 and 70 years of age (mean = 35.6; SD = 11.3). The respondents were generally well-educated: high school diploma or less, 115 (11%); Bachelor's degree, 273 (26%); Master's degree, 308 (30%); Ph.D., 338 (33%); five participants chose not to answer the question. A majority ($n = 837$; 81%) reported working in a language-related area. In terms of the number of languages spoken by each individual, the sample consists of 144 bilinguals (14%), 269 trilinguals (26%), 289 speakers of four languages (28%), and 337 speakers of five or more languages (32%), with 157 people bilingual and 19 people trilingual from birth. Seventy-five first languages (L1s) are represented in the sample, with the number of speakers of each language as the L1 as follows: English = 303; Spanish = 123; French = 101; German = 97; Dutch = 76; Italian = 52; Catalan = 32; Russian = 29; Finnish = 28; Portuguese = 20; Greek = 15; Swedish = 15; Japanese = 11; Welsh = 10; and 61 other languages with fewer than 10 speakers, among them Arabic, American Sign Language (ASL), Basque, Bengali, Bosnian, Breton, Burmese, Cantonese, Danish, Duri, Farsi, Hebrew, Hindi, Hungarian, Indonesian, Latin, Latvian, Malay, Mandarin, Navajo, Norwegian, Nugunu, Oriya, Polish, Romanian, Serbo-Croatian, Sindhi, Slovak, Slovene, Tamil, Turkish, Ukrainian, and Vietnamese. More than half of the participants declared themselves to be dominant in L1 ($n = 561$), a smaller proportion reported dominance in two or more languages including the L1 ($n = 373$), and about 10% reported dominance in a language or languages other than the L1 ($n = 105$).

Clearly, these respondents are not representative of the general bi- and multilingual population. The overwhelming majority are well-educated 'elite bilinguals', people who have time and resources to invest in searching for information about and reflecting upon issues in bilingualism. The over-representation of well-educated professionals is explained by the advertising procedure (our informal contacts were other Ph.D.s who in turn knew other language professionals; similarly, the listservs we advertised on were most likely to be read by well-educated individuals who knew how to find these resources). The dominance of female respondents is perhaps best explained by the preponderance of women in education- and language-related professions.

Such pitfalls are inevitable with a web-based questionnaire whose distribution one cannot control and they need to be kept in mind when interpreting the patterns, as results might be different for a sample of working-class males without higher education. Nevertheless, statistical analysis of responses to a printed version of the questionnaire elicited from 50 multilinguals who did not finish high school did not reveal significant differences between this group and the rest of the sample (Dewaele, 2004). Furthermore, whereas it is possible that less metalinguistically aware participants would respond differently to the open-ended questions, I view the demographics of this sample as an advantage rather than a problem for the present inquiry. It is possible that people working in language-related professions may be more familiar with and open to the question about different selves than those working in other fields. They are also likely to have engaged in reflection on this issue at some point in their lives and to have formed an opinion. Finally, they may have more linguistic resources at their disposal to describe their perceptions and linguistic performances.

Analytical framework

Because the goal of the study is to understand participants' meaning-making systems, the study does not espouse a single theoretical perspective on bilingualism, emotions, or self. Rather, I want to explore how the respondents view these notions and what factors influence their views. Several approaches have been applied to analysis of this corpus, which consists of responses to a single question about different selves. First, I have conducted a descriptive quantitative analysis of the percentage of affirmative, negative, and ambiguous responses. Then, I examined all elaborated responses, that is, responses that went beyond a single word or a multiword phrase. Among these, I singled out responses containing attributions, that is, respondents' theories and interpretations as to why they might or might not feel like different people in their respective languages. These attributions were then sorted into thematic categories, and within each category I conducted two types of analysis. First, using a Bakhtinian approach described below, I attempted to identify discourses of bilingualism and self the participants drew on. Next, I appealed to triangulation of respondents' introspective answers with the data from empirical, clinical, and textual studies to understand the linguistic, psychological, and physiological processes that may inform bi- and multi-linguals' perceptions.

To analyze the discourses of bilingualism in participants' responses, I draw on Bakhtin's (1981, 1984, 1986) view of language as dialogic, where texts and utterances invariably bear traces and echoes of other texts and utterances, and on its elaborations by Kristeva (1969, 1986), Fairclough (1995, 2003) and Scollon and associates (1998). The assumption behind this approach is that for every text or type of texts, there is a set of other texts, discourses, and voices that are potentially relevant and potentially incorporated into the text (Fairclough, 2003):

> The living utterance, having taken meaning and shape at a particular historical moment in a socially specific environment, cannot fail to brush up against thousands of living dialogic threads, woven by socio-ideological consciousness around the given object of an utterance; it cannot fail to become an active participant in a social dialogue. (Bakhtin, 1981: 276)

In the true spirit of intertextuality, the definitions of analytical notions below are informed by the previous work but not constrained by it. Rather, they are adapted to the purposes of the present study. *Discourse* will refer to a particular world view, ideology, or perspective embodied in ways of talking about a particular phenomenon, in the present case the relationship between languages and selves (e.g. discourse of bilingualism as linguistic schizophrenia). *Heteroglossia* and *polyphony* refer to the presence of several distinct, and sometimes irreconcilable, discourses within a single text, signalled through lexical choices, shifts in style or register, or subordinating conjunctions. These discourses were traced through four discursive strategies, which I exemplify here in order to make clear the links made between particular wordings and strategies:

- *interdiscursivity*, that is, indirect references to particular discourses made through lexical or stylistic choices, for example, '... in a kind of linguistic schizophrenia';
- *intertextuality*, that is, the use of actual words from other sources or direct references to the sources, for example, 'As argued by Sapir and Whorf ...';
- *value assumptions*, that is, presuppositions about what is good or desirable, for example, 'that's the nice thing about it ...';
- *hidden polemic*, a particular type of interdiscursivity where the response is worded in opposition to an absent voice or discourse, for example, 'I do see changes in my personality but it is fun'.

The responses analyzed here represent Bakhtinian utterances par excellence. For Bakhtin, an utterance is always an answer, and web questionnaire responses are formal answers to specific questions, offering us easily identifiable addressees and immediately preceding texts. At the same time, the format of the web questionnaire responses, in particular their limited length and impossibility of follow-up questions, precludes any in-depth analysis of meaning-making systems of individual participants – thus the analysis below makes no claims to full understanding of the views of any single respondent. It would also be naive to posit that all of the recipients answered the same question – as will be shown below, their understandings of the question and of the required response did vary. On the other hand, the sheer number of responses and the diversity of respondents offer us a unique opportunity to create a composite picture of discourses of bilingualism and self circulating among elite bi- and multilinguals at the turn of the 21st century.

Results

Whereas other questions in the web questionnaire elicited matter-of-fact answers, the question about different selves elicited many emotional responses. The respondents signalled their approval and enthusiasm through lexical choices (absolutely, definitely, all the time!), the use of capital letters (YES; OOOOOOOOOh yes!; ABSOLUTELY), and punctuation (yes!). Some expressed their approval explicitly ('Ah now that's a good one'; 'This is a good question'; 'Very pertinent question for me'; 'Interesting thought'). This enthusiasm suggests that the question about different selves, often eschewed by the academic establishment, is nevertheless relevant to the lives of many individuals who speak more than one language.

Altogether, 675 participants (65%) offered an affirmative response to the question, 266 (26%) a negative response, 64 (6%) an ambiguous response, and 34 (3%) did not answer the question (31 left a blank space and 3 offered an irrelevant answer). Among the *affirmative responses*, 467 (69%) were elaborated responses of varying length and 208 (31%) were minimal responses that involved either a single word (yes, often, definitely, always, constantly, certainly, absolutely, of course, sometimes) or multiword phrases (yes I do; all the time). *Negative responses* contained 229 (86%) minimal responses (no, never, not really) and only 37 (14%) elaborated responses, which suggests that respondents saw more of a need to justify and explain positive answers than the negative ones (an issue I will return to later on). Some of these responses contained answers such as 'No, but I used to in the past'. Most of the *ambiguous responses*, 59 (92%), were given in the 'No but . . .' format, where a negative response was qualified in a number of ways.

What is most interesting about the responses, however, is not the numbers but the sources to which the respondents attribute their perceptions. A thematic analysis of the elaborated responses pointed to four main sources of perceptions of different selves: (1) linguistic and cultural differences; (2) distinct learning contexts; (3) different levels of language emotionality; (4) different levels of language proficiency. I will now discuss these sources and examine ways in which results of empirical studies can illuminate participants' self-perceptions.

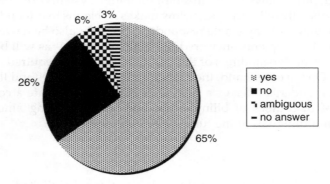

Figure 1.1 Types of responses to the web questionnaire

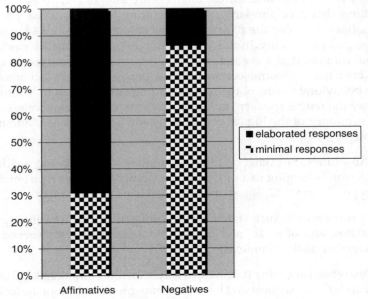

Figure 1.2 Elaborated vs. minimal responses

Linguistic and cultural differences and learning contexts

Self-perceptions

The first source of difference mentioned by the respondents are distinct verbal and non-verbal repertoires and cultural perspectives offered to them by their languages and cultures:

(1) Definitely! Speaking another language causes me to assume certain cultural perspectives that also entail certain behaviors. Language and culture are a package and true command of a second language requires extensive cultural knowledge and practice. (Louise, 25, English–German–French–ASL–Lakota)

(2) Yes because the use of a certain language demands that you act according to the behavioral norms of the corresponding culture. (Anastasia, 25, Greek–English–French–Italian–Chinese)

(3) Yes; it is difficult to explain but it's like you conform yourself to the way the native speakers talk and express themselves which is not necessarily the same as yours. For example the way the Greek people speak is very lively and very expressive. If I were to speak in the same way in English (or even German & French) people would misunderstand me and misinterpret my intentions – as it has happened many times. (Anna, 24, Greek–German–English–French)

What unites these and similar answers are categorical, non-modalized assertions that proclaim language and culture to be a unified 'package' that defines 'the way the native speakers talk' and thus links language/ culture and personality. In this one language–one personality discourse, a 'true' command of a second language requires conformity: non-native speakers have 'to assume certain cultural perspectives', to 'act according to the behavioral norms of the corresponding culture', and to 'conform to the way the native speakers talk'. Marina's statement below offers a succinct summary of the logical connections and assumptions made in this discourse:

(4)   Absolutely. Speaking a different language means being a different person belonging to a different community character type emotional type. (Marina, 42, Russian–English–Hebrew–Ukrainian)

Not surprisingly, such statements are most often made by immigrants, expatriates, and other bi- and multicultural speakers who learned their languages in distinct contexts:

(5)   Yes when I am using Italian especially. I am more emotional and use my hands more. My husband has also commented that I adopt the Icelandic attitudes when I am using Icelandic especially when speaking to officials. If you pick up the language from living in the country (a country) where it is spoken then you pick up the traits and habits of those people. (Wendy, 30, English–French–German–Italian–Icelandic)

(6)   Yes. I feel like I have a different personality in French. I learned most of my French on exchange and I feel like I was 'brought up' in French differently than I was 'brought up' in English. I notice that when I try to use English with my French-speaking friends in Quebec often the nature of the communication totally changes because I just don't speak the same way (i.e. as frequently) in English. (Sharlene, 27, English–French–German–Japanese–Inuktitut)

(7)   Yes. L1 is associated with all that I can't change in my life anymore for the better or for the worse: family childhood memories professional history up to a certain point etc. L2 (English) mostly and L3 (Spanish) are associated with my present and my dreamed future so they are kind of a bridge to this other person I might become. (Karen, 34, Brazilian Portuguese–English–Spanish–French–Italian)

(8)   Yes of course. I feel much more sophisticated when I speak English probably because I learnt it from sophisticated people in a private college in York some time ago. When I speak Dutch I feel like a more precise person. I learned to use it in a very precise and accurate way and for example never to mix up one word with another. (Clement, 18, French–Dutch–Italian–English)

These responses frame the perception of distinct selves through the discourse of language socialization visible in lexical and punctuation choices, such as the use of the term 'brought up' in quotation marks, which signals its status as a borrowing from another discourse, that of childhood socialization. Language socialization discourse is also visible in connections participants make between their perceived selves and the three trademarks of dual language socialization: distinct contexts ('on exchange', 'in a private college'), distinct time periods ('different periods', 'my present'), and distinct groups of people ('sophisticated people').

Both discourses, one language—one personality and language socialization, display a non-agentive view of the speaker, who does not speak the language but is rather spoken by it. This view harks back to the theory of linguistic relativity, also known as the Sapir—Whorf hypothesis, which argues that the language we speak influences the way we think. The corpus abounds in interdiscursive references to this theory, for example:

(9)   Yes when I am in the country were the language is spoken. I think differently. (Monica, 33, Italian–French–English–Spanish–Amharic)

The presence of such statements in the corpus is quite significant, because bilingualism has often been invoked to refute the theory of linguistic relativity. Macnamara (1970) argued that if the Whorfian hypothesis were true and languages created different worlds for their speakers, bilinguals would be doomed. If they were to think differently depending on what language is used, they would have difficulties communicating with themselves, and translating into one language what was said in another. More recently, Stubbs (1997: 359) stated: 'But languages are not incompatible. We can translate between them. And bilinguals speak different languages, but they do not perceive the world differently when they switch from one language to another'. And yet our respondents tell us that their thinking, behavior, and perception of the self and the world do change with the change in language. Let us examine then how their introspective statements square against the data from textual, experimental, and clinical studies.

Empirical data

Scholars who study translingual writing show that writers who write in more than one language often treat their languages as distinct instruments that require them to play different tunes (Beaujour, 1989; Besemeres, 2002; Kellman, 2000; Pérez Firmat, 2003; Trigo, 2003). For instance, for Rosario Ferré:

Writing in English is like looking at the world through a different pair of binoculars: It imposes a different mind-set. When I write in Spanish, my sentences are often as convoluted as a Baroque *retablo*. When

I write in English, I make my sentences straight and simple, because I want to be precise as well as practical. (in Kellman, 2003b: 138)

Self-translation is a painful task for such writers, and often they end up, like Todorov and Green, with a very different story in the other language (Besemeres, 2002; Pérez Firmat, 2003; Trigo, 2003). 'In every instance the "translation" becomes a rethinking, a recasting of the original in terms of the medium of the new language', states an Afrikaans–English writer André Brink (Kellman, 2003b: 206). Also, Gustavo Pérez Firmat, a literary scholar and a bilingual writer himself, astutely observes that 'what passes for balanced bilingualism is more often diglossia in disguise' (2003: 14), and thus the use of different voices for different purposes. Todorov (1994: 214) reaches the same conclusion reflecting on his own bilingualism – for him, diglossia, with its distinct functions for each language, is the only way out of oppressive 'silence and insanity looming on the horizon of boundless polyphony'.

Psychologists and psycholinguists have also addressed the issue of different selves. The pioneering studies of bilinguals' verbal behaviors were conducted by Susan Ervin-Tripp (1954, 1964, 1967), who employed an array of verbal behavior measures, including semantic differentials, word associations, sentence- and story-completion tasks, and the projective Thematic Apperception Test (TAT). To control for order effects, the sessions in the two languages in her studies commonly took place six weeks apart. The first of the studies examined Japanese and English responses of a Japanese–English bilingual, born in the United States in a Japanese-speaking family and educated in Japan between the ages of 8 and 14 years (Ervin, 1954). The researcher found that stories elicited by TAT pictures in Japanese were much more emotional than the ones told in English. In Japanese stories, people went mad with grief, cried aloud with pain, and wept over lost love, while in English a young man was robbed by a hypnotist, a woman came home drunk, and a girl was trying to complete a sewing project. The researcher explained these differences through distinct emotional relationships formed in the two languages of the participant.

Ervin-Tripp's (1964) second study examined responses of 64 French–English bilinguals, all of whom had lived in the United States for more than four years (mean $n = 12$) and learned English primarily from Americans. Forty of them were or had been married to Americans. The analysis showed that TAT stories elicited in French described more verbal aggression toward peers and more withdrawal and autonomy than the ones elicited in English. The author explained these results through speakers' language socialization experiences and in particular through the emphasis in the French culture and education on verbal argument and on withdrawal as a dominant mode of response after a disagreement.

Differences between responses in the two languages were also found in a study conducted with 36 Japanese–English bilingual women, war brides brought home by American servicemen (Ervin-Tripp, 1967). The most pronounced differences emerged in the word association and sentence-completion tasks, where Japanese associations dominated in Japanese and American ones in English. These findings were later replicated by researchers working with Tagalog–English bilinguals (Guthrie & Azores, 1968; Ventura, 1976).

The line of inquiry opened up by Ervin-Tripp was taken further by her student Hull (1990) in his dissertation entitled 'Bilingualism: Two languages, two personalities?' Hull set out to investigate the possibility that bicultural bilinguals may have distinct personalities associated with their respective languages and cultures. His first study examined the performance of three groups of late bilinguals, all of them immigrants to the United States, on a self-assessment instrument, the California Psychological Inventory (CPI). The participants completed the CPI twice, once in their first languages (L1), Spanish ($n = 74$), Chinese ($n = 57$), and Korean ($n = 17$), and once in their second language (L2) English, with 5 to 15 days between sessions. A within-group between-language analysis revealed significant differences between participants' responses in English and in their L1s. For instance, Spanish-speaking participants scored higher in English on the measures of self-acceptance, social presence, interpersonal prestige, emotional well-being, and achievement drive, which, in the author's view, reflects participants' identification with the individualistic Anglo culture. In the native languages, members of all three groups scored higher on the good impression scale, reflecting a greater cultural concern about other peoples' reactions to them. Hull (1990) attributed these results to language-related personality differences, as well as to translation inequivalence inherent in any translated instrument.

To examine whether self-ratings correspond to the ratings of bilinguals' behaviors by others, Hull's (1990) second study asked 35 Chinese–English and 24 Spanish–English bilinguals to participate in two sessions, one in English, and one in the native language, conducted five to seven days apart to control for language order effects. In each session, one bilingual participant interviewed the other about his or her childhood and adolescent life and experiences. Then, the 'interviewer' rated the 'interviewee', while the latter rated him/herself on personality scales supplied by the researcher. Then the roles were reversed and the procedure repeated. A between-language analysis revealed some differences in participants' ratings in the two languages. Spanish speakers rated themselves and their peers higher on extraversion and emotional stability in

English than in Spanish, while Chinese speakers rated themselves and their peers higher on conscientiousness and cultural sophistication in Chinese than they did in English. These findings show that, in some contexts, bilinguals may hold distinct frames of expectations when interpreting and assessing their own and others' behaviors in respective languages.

Other studies have replicated Hull's (1990) findings, showing that answers, self-reports, and narratives elicited from bicultural bilinguals may vary with the language of elicitation (Bond, 1983; Koven, 1998; Kuroda *et al.*, 1986; Marian & Kaushanskaya, 2004; Panayiotou, 2004; Ross *et al.*, 2002; Trafimow *et al.*, 1997). For example, Panayiotou (2004, see also the chapter by Panayiotou in this volume) elicited Greek–English and English–Greek bilinguals' reactions to the same story read to them in their two languages. The analysis of their responses showed that the participants interpreted and related to the 'same' events differently, depending on the language context; in Greek, the story elicited sympathy and concern for the protagonist, whereas in English it elicited indifference and disapproval. The two versions elicited not only different reactions, but also different imagery and cultural scripts, suggesting that the two languages were linked to distinct linguistic repertoires and cultural frames. At the same time, some participants code-switched, which suggests that bicultural bilinguals interacting with each other may draw on the full range of their cultural and linguistic repertoires, rather than switch them 'on' and 'off'.

Ross and associates (2002) compared self-ratings of Chinese-born Chinese–English bilinguals in Canada across language conditions. They found that participants responding in Mandarin and Cantonese exhibited higher agreement with Chinese cultural values than participants responding in English; they also reported lower self-esteem and offered more references to culture and more collective self-descriptions (i.e. descriptions of self in terms of group membership). Similarly, Marian and Kaushanskaya (2004) found that Russian–English bilinguals' memories from the Russian context contained more first person plural pronouns, whereas memories from the English context contained more first person singular pronouns. To explain their own and similar findings, Ross and associates (2002) argued that people's self-perceptions reflect currently accessible knowledge. A shift in language leads, in bicultural bilinguals, to the shift in cultural constructs and memories activated by that language and, consequently, to the shift in self-knowledge, self-perceptions, and self-descriptions.

The links between language and autobiographical memories were also found in studies conducted with Spanish–English (Schrauf & Rubin, 1998, 2000, 2004), Russian–English (Marian & Neisser, 2000), and Polish–Danish (Larsen *et al.*, 2002) bilingual immigrants who learned their languages at different times and in distinct environments (see also the chapter by Schrauf and Durazo-Arvizu in this volume). These studies show that, in immigrant bilinguals, L1 words commonly activate memories of events in the country of origin and L2 words activate memories of events that took place after immigration. These results suggest that the language of encoding is a stable property for linguistic memories, even though a memory can then be 'translated' into another language.

Studies by Ervin-Tripp (1964, 1967), Koven (1998), and Panayiotou (2004) also show that speakers socialized in distinct contexts may have distinct linguistic repertoires in their respective languages. A particularly convincing version of this argument appears in Koven's (1998) study of stories of personal experiences told by Portuguese–French bilinguals, children of Portuguese immigrants in France (see also Koven's chapter in the present volume). In addition to formal discursive analysis of Portuguese and French versions of the same event, the researcher interviewed participants about their experiences with the two languages (self-evaluation) and collected listener impressions of the tape-recorded stories (peer evaluation).

This triangulated approach uncovered systematic differences in bilinguals' presentations of self: the speakers were shown to use different lexical and morphosyntactic resources and registers in their two languages; they also perceived themselves differently and were differently described by the listeners. Peer evaluators noted that listening to the two sets of recordings of the same person they got the impression that they were dealing with different speakers, from different backgrounds, and with different reactions (e.g. rural versus urban, polite versus foul-mouthed). These impressions were also confirmed by the participants, who routinely mentioned to the researcher that they feel different in French and Portuguese, relate to people differently, and have a different perspective on the world. One woman stated, for instance, that Portuguese touches her more – speaking it she finds herself back in her childhood. At the same time, she does not have the same access to the language of youth in Portuguese as she has in French. The researcher explained her findings through distinct linguistic repertoires to which her participants had access; their Portuguese came from their rural parents and relatives, while French was the language of peer socialization in their urban setting.

Together, the studies in psychology and linguistic anthropology validate the introspective comments of the web questionnaire respondents and show that, when tested in their respective languages, bicultural bilinguals may perform differently on a variety of verbal tasks, from self-rating to storytelling, and may be differently perceived and evaluated by other individuals. These differences are commonly attributed to different semantic associations, linguistic repertoires, cultural scripts, frames of expectations, imagery, and memories activated by the respective

languages. At the same time, it is important to remember that these findings may be largely limited to individuals who had learned their
languages in distinct environments and who continue to use them in
relatively monolingual contexts. Individuals who live in multilingual
contexts and code-mix and code-switch on a daily basis may have a less
acute perception of linguistic and cultural boundaries.

Differences in language emotionality and proficiency
Self-perceptions
What is quite intriguing, however, is that the story of different selves
does not end with differences in linguistic and cultural contexts or perspectives. The respondents also invoke another source of different
selves that is much harder to interpret, namely, the feeling that the first
language is 'real' and 'natural', while later learned languages are 'fake',
'artificial', and performative:

(10)   I don't feel quite real in German sometimes – and formerly in
       French and Russian. I feel I'm acting a part. (George, 66, English–
       German–French–Russian)
(11)   Yes sometimes as a fake. Others it starts naturally and then I have
       that feeling of dissociation looking at myself from the outside
       especially when speaking in public in English. (Elisa, 57,
       Yiddish–Spanish–English)
(12)   Not entirely but a little bit. I feel less myself when speaking any
       language other than German but not in a bad sense. I feel more
       like I am acting a persona which can be good or bad. At the same
       time I tend to be more polite and self-conscious when speaking
       L2 to L5 I don't tend to consider as much what I say when speaking
       L1. But very often I feel like a better person when speaking L2 or L3.
       (Stefanie, 31, German–English–Spanish)

These comments set up the opposition between the first and the later
learned languages through a discourse that draws on Jungian psychoanalytic theory and differentiates between the private self and *persona*, an
image projected in public, often referred to as a mask, performance,
social role, or simply acting. The presence of this discourse is signaled
through intertextual strategies that invoke Jung's name directly;
for example,

(13)   Yes and I think it is natural because when you use your first
       language you are yourself with all of your acquired habits but
       using another language need to have a Mask (or Persona according
       to C.G. Jung) and it may give you a sense of being another Person.
       (Karim, 35, Farsi–English–German)

It is also signaled through interdiscursive strategies that do not invoke Jung directly but instead refer to personae, masks, or, as in the example below, 'classical psychological meaning':

(14)   Yes. A different persona in the classical psychological meaning. Your voice demeanour tone body language and role expectations change. The other party tends to be from a different culture you tend to adjust to it instantly. (Enrique, 48, Spanish–English–French–Italian–Portuguese)

(15)   ... Yes but more accurately a different persona not a different person ... (Alfredo, 38, Portuguese–English–Spanish–Japanese)

(16)   Yes definitely! I think there's a bit of acting involved when you speak a foreign language. (Darragh, 27, English–French–Spanish–Irish)

I suggest that the presence of this psychoanalytic discourse in the corpus is not accidental. A lot of theorizing about bilingualism and self came from the psychoanalytic literature and some of the respondents may be familiar with this work or at least references to it. Psychoanalytic theories also continue to be a major influence on Western conceptualizations of the self in general. For instance, Linde (1993) shows that Freudian theory is one of the key discourses Americans draw on in lifestorytelling. She argues that the simplified version of the theory is appealing because it offers storytellers analytical tools they can use to distance themselves from their own decision-making and behavior and to position themselves as authoritative experts. Jungian theory holds similar appeal to bi- and multilinguals – it offers convenient tools to theorize the detached, 'out-of-body' experience of using a language learned later in life.

But what are the linguistic and psychological underpinnings of this experience? It is possible that the feeling of ease and comfort attributed to speaking one's first language stems from superior mastery of the language, whereas the perception of artificiality stems from the need to manipulate less familiar repertoires of languages learned later in life. Several respondents refer to this possibility, framing an act of speaking a second language as a test and a performance that is observed and judged by others:

(17)   To a certain extent. I feel more at ease speaking in my mother tongue. It's like being at home with all the usual familiar worn and comfortable clutter around you. Speaking the second language is like being you but in someone else's house. (Ellen, 47, Welsh–English)

(18)   Yes. When speaking English I feel like my normal self (since I speak this language best). In Spanish I feel acutely 'Americanized' instead of balanced since I can't speak it as easily as English but I feel like

I really should be able to speak both fluently . . . (Jessica, 16, Spanish–English)

It is also possible that the perception of naturalness of the earlier learned languages and artificiality of the later learned ones stems from differences in emotionality experienced when using these languages. This possibility is indicated in attributions made by respondents who link acting metaphors to emotionality, for example:

(19)   Absolutely. I feel I can hide my emotions and myself a lot better in English. In Spanish I feel a lot more 'naked'. (Dolores, 31, Spanish–English–German–French)

To understand the sources of these self-perceptions, let us examine, once again, how the introspective statements square against data from textual, experimental, and clinical studies.

Empirical work

Translingual writers who write in their later learned language often argue that these languages are beneficial not only in practical terms, such as access to new and larger audiences, but also in psychological terms, offering writers new, 'clean' words, devoid of anxieties and taboos, freeing them from self-censorship, from prohibitions and loyalties of their native culture, and allowing them to gain full control over their words, stories, and plots (Kellman, 2000; Kinginger, 2004; Pavlenko, 2005; Pérez Firmat, 2003; Tannenbaum, 2003; Trigo, 2003). Kellman (2000) calls this distancing effect 'emancipatory detachment', and many writers concur with this assessment. For instance, Jerzy Kosinski, an immigrant from Poland and the first non-native speaker to win the most prestigious U.S. literary prize, the National Book Award, often said in his interviews:

English helped me sever myself from my childhood, from my adolescence. In English I don't make involuntary associations with my childhood. I think it is childhood that is often traumatic, not this or that war. (in Teicholz, 1993: 27)

Translingual writers also acknowledge that the use of the 'stepmother tongue' comes with a price: the ever-present nostalgia for the primeval emotionality of the selves linked to the mother tongue, the language that retains the incomparable ability to wound, to heal, and to caress:

Spanish certainly was the language of storytelling, the language of the body and of the senses and of the emotional wiring of the child, so that still, when someone addresses me as 'Hoolia' (Spanish pronunciation of Julia), I feel my emotional self come to the fore. I answer Sí, and lean forward to kiss a cheek rather than answer Yes, and extend my hand for a handshake. Some deeper or first Julia is being summoned. (Julia

Alvarez, American writer born in the Dominican Republic, in Novakovich & Shapard, 2000: 218)

Today, when someone addresses me as 'Luke' I respond without a second thought; when I hear 'lük' I jump as if I'd gotten an electric shock. Even though I know better, I feel as if someone had just looked down into my naked soul. (Luc Sante, American writer born in Belgium, in Kellman, 2003b: 160)

A Puerto-Rican writer, Rosario Ferré, argues that you don't have to be an immigrant to feel the distance between your two languages:

... Spanish still makes me suck faster at life's breast. ... I can roll on the ground and frolic in Spanish because I don't have to worry about anything; words always mean what they say. I love to make love in Spanish; I've never been able to make love in English. In English, I get puritanical. (in Kellman, 2003b: 137–38)

Similar comments are cited by Heinz (2001), who conducted in-depth interviews with eight bicultural bilinguals from a variety of linguistic backgrounds who had lived in the United States for between 3 and 28 years. The interviews focused on participants' experiences in their languages and revealed that the speakers were conscious of changes in their behavior and self-perceptions prompted by the change in language. They linked these changes to different cultural and conversational expectations into which they were socialized in respective linguistic contexts, and to greater emotionality and intimacy of the L1. Some participants underscored the importance of proficiency: those with lower proficiency in the L2 felt freer and more comfortable in the L1, whereas those whose L1 was undergoing attrition favored the L2 and felt able to express themselves freely in that language, liberated from the taboos and constraints of the mother tongue.

These perceptions are also borne out in clinical and experimental studies of bicultural bilinguals. Among the first to consider the relationship between bilinguals' languages, memories, and selves, were German-speaking psychoanalysts Buxbaum (1949), Greenson (1950), and Krapf (1955), who noticed that their bilingual patients commonly appeared more emotional and anxious when speaking their first language, German, and more detached in the later learned English or Spanish. Some patients simply refused to use the L1 in analysis even if they shared the language with the analyst. Greenson's patient, an immigrant from Austria, admitted: 'I am afraid. I don't want to talk German. I have the feeling that talking in German I shall have to remember something I wanted to forget' (1950: 19). Eventually, the use of German led her to recapture her feelings about her mother whom she found a 'loathsome creature' (1950: 19). This patient also linked her anxieties to her sense of a dual self: 'In German I am a scared dirty child; in English I am a nervous, refined woman' (1950: 19).

Recent studies in bilingual psychoanalysis confirmed these findings and established that in patients who learned their L2 in late childhood or adulthood, L1 words may function as triggers for painful, traumatic, and previously repressed memories and unacknowledged feelings (Amati-Mehler *et al.*, 1993; Aragno & Schlachet, 1996; Foster, 1996; Javier, 1995, 1996; Rozensky & Gomez, 1983). As a result, these speakers may associate anxiety and vulnerability with the L1 and favor the L2 as a mechanism of defense. They may also describe themselves as frightened, dependent, and vulnerable children in the L1 and as independent, strong, and refined individuals in the L2 (Aragno & Schlachet, 1996; Foster, 1992).

Studies of autobiographical memories discussed earlier (see also the chapter by Schrauf and Durazo-Arvizu) explain these findings through links made between a language and events experienced in this language. Studies by Harris and associates (2003, 2004, present volume) add another interesting layer to these explanations, pointing to connections between first language words, memories, and physiological responses. These studies show that different types of words elicit different physiological reactions in both monolingual and bilingual speakers, with taboo words eliciting the strongest responses. In late bilinguals, however, L1 taboo words commonly elicit a stronger response than L2 taboo words. Reprimands were shown to elicit strong responses only in the L1 of late bilinguals. Several Turkish–English bilinguals commented in the debriefing session that they could hear, in their mind, family members addressing reprimands to them. Together, the results and the comments suggest that the L1 effects stem from affective linguistic conditioning in childhood (Pavlenko, 2005), when languages are learned with the full involvement of the limbic system and emotional memory. In contrast, languages learned later in life may rely to a greater degree on declarative memory and thus produce weak responses and a feeling of detachment, disembodiment, and, in the words, of our respondents, 'artificiality'.

A closer look at the links between emotionality, proficiency, and second language performance was taken by Marcos and associates (1973a, b) in studies conducted with ten schizophrenic Spanish–English bilinguals. The studies demonstrated that these patients were consistently rated as showing more pathology when interviewed in L2 English. A comparative analysis of the Spanish and English interviews demonstrated that in English the patients often answered questions with a short sentence, a word, or even silence. At times, they misunderstood the questions – consequently, in many cases they offered different answers to the same questions asked in Spanish and English. Their L2 answers were also marked by language mixing, slow speech rate, hesitations, long pauses, and excessive use of the present tense where past tense would be used in Spanish. These markers of non-fluent L2 speech were often misperceived as signs of distress, depression, and incoherence. The studies also suggested that L2 users' increased concerns about the wording, pronunciation, and morphosyntax may lead to diminished attention to the affective component of the message and create an inconsistency between what is being said and how it is being communicated. This inconsistency and lack of visible affect may also contribute to an impression of emotional withdrawal and misinterpretation of the patients' responses. This groundbreaking work highlighted the contribution of language proficiency to the perception of dual selves, showing that effects of low proficiency may be misperceived by others as low affect, depression, or incoherence, appearing in one language only.

Together, the comments of the web questionnaire participants, reflections of translingual writers, and studies in psychology and psychoanalysis suggest that languages learned earlier and later in life may differ in experienced emotionality, with differences contributing to the perception of different selves. These conclusions, however, need to be qualified in a number of ways. To begin, the fact that the first language is often perceived as more emotional does not imply that this is also the language favored for emotional expression – in fact, some speakers feel much more comfortable discussing emotions in later learned languages, either because they grew up in a tradition of a 'stiff upper lip' or because they mainly live and interact in the realm of a second language (Heinz, 2001; Pavlenko, 2005). Similarly, a second language is not always a language of detachment – speakers who have low levels of proficiency and those who had negative experiences in the second language may associate it with increased levels of tension and anxiety, whereas those who negotiate relationships or raise children in the second language often view it as very emotional and meaningful (Pavlenko, 2004b, 2005).

Negative responses and evaluations

The discussion up to this point demonstrated that different respondents make different attributions with regard to the origins of their perception of dual selves. Some link it to linguistic and cultural differences, some to differences in levels of emotionality or proficiency, and others to distinct experiences in respective languages. Notably, however, changes in verbal and non-verbal behaviors may be interpreted differently by other respondents who see their selves as unitary and coherent, even when they do change ways of thinking or cultural perspectives:

(20) Not at all I feel I am the same person but speaking a different language and in a different way! I think you must change your

mentality when you are speaking a different language but it does not mean that you feel like a different person. (Marisol, 19, Spanish–English–French–Italian)

(21) I used to at first several years ago. Now I feel that the two cultures (i.e. French vs American) are so different that the language is just a way to express these cultural differences but using a different language doesn't change the core of who I am. I am americanized to a certain extent but only to fit North American cultural situations. I 'act French' so to speak as soon as I am back in France or speaking in French with French people. (Diane, 38, French–English–Spanish)

(22) Different languages allow me different thought structures and possibly different ways of feeling too. But these changes do not affect me deep within where I remain the same person. (Erica, 38, German–English)

These respondents draw on the discourse of a 'true' self, single and unitary, unaffected by the change in language. What is interesting, however, is that, as mentioned earlier, only 14% of the respondents chose to elaborate on the negative responses to the question about different selves, while 69% elaborated on the affirmative answers. It is possible that, in the respondents' view, the affirmative answer required more of an explanation and an elaboration than a negative one, treated as self-evident. One explanation for this is participants' awareness of the negative value often placed on duality and multiplicity:

(23) NO. I feel I am very lucky. (Marylin, 50, Italian–French–English–Dutch–Spanish)

(24) Yes. It is a good feeling tho. (Fiona, 27, English–French–German)

We can see that Marylin emphatically denies seeing her selves as different. She also presents herself as lucky because of that, thus implicitly agreeing with the view of double selves as a misfortune. Fiona, on the other hand, responds in the affirmative and evaluates the experience as a positive one. Then, however, she appeals to the subordinating conjunction 'though', which signals opposition and frames her evaluative comment as a hidden polemic with the negative assessment of duality. Hidden polemic can also be found in some of the attributions made by the respondents:

(25) Absolutely. Each language has its own cultural history and I have my own personal history in each. It is not a schizophrenia but definitely two different ways of being me. (Viktor, 45, Latvian–English)

(26) Definitely. Not in a schizophrenic sense. Usually simply because of context but sometimes strategically. (Thomas, 50, English–French–Japanese–German)

These and similar comments follow a pattern where a negative clause or denial ('not a schizophrenia'; 'not in a schizophrenic sense') is followed by a positive clause or assertion. According to Fairclough (2003), this type of denial implies that the assertion being denied had been made 'elsewhere'. The participants' lexical choices identify the 'elsewhere' as the discourse of bilingualism as linguistic schizophrenia, or the view of dual and multiple selves as causing an inner split. This discourse is clearly not treated with the same degree of seriousness as it would have been in some circles in the first half of the 20th century, yet the fact that 'schizophrenia' comes up time and again in this corpus, as it does in reflections of translingual writers, indicates that the discourse is still alive, if only as one to be opposed. The notion of inner split is a real concern for some respondents whose discomfort is visible in negative evaluations:

(27) Not really (but I have been anxious about this in the past). (Vivian, 36, English–Greek)
(28) somehow yes. i hate this! (Mihaela, 33, Romanian–Italian–French–English)
(29) yes. Sometimes I feel awfull. (Eduardo, 21, Spanish–English–French)
(30) Yes I do. Sometimes I feel like being two different persons or just a person with two incomplete languages. The worst moments are when I feel like not having a language identity. (Dorothee, 45, German–English–Swedish)

The first three responses offer a negative evaluation of the perception of distinct selves without much elaboration, thus implicitly presuming common ground with the addressees who should be able to understand why this perception invokes anxiety or discomfort. Comments by the fourth respondent offer more clues, linking the feeling of duality to fears of schizophrenia ('two different persons'), semilingualism ('two incomplete languages'), and illegitimacy ('not having a language identity') haunting those who do not neatly fit into the monolingual mold.

Yet the participants do not simply echo and reproduce various discourses, they also challenge and transform them. Responses (25) and (26) provide examples of a hidden polemic with the discourse of schizophrenia. Other respondents challenge this discourse through joking and ironic references:

(31) Yes. And come to think of it that is either the luxury of reflecting oneself in different language or maybe a worrisome component of multiple personality disorder? :-) I know that even my pitch changes. (Daniela, 40, German–English–Italian)

(32)   Maybe. But sometimes I feel like a different person when I use
       Lithuanian language too (I hope it is not clinical case :)). But it
       seem to me that when I use non-native language this feeling is
       more expressed. (Kastytis, 40, Lithuanian–Russian–English)

The first response juxtaposes two evaluative discourses, multilingualism as luxury versus multilingualism as personality disorder, but then
reduces the second discourse to an amusing joke both through the
wording and the use of the question mark and the smiley face. A
similar strategy is used by the second respondent who uses the smiley
face to signal that his reference to a 'clinical case' is nothing but a joke.

Direct and indirect challenges are not, however, the only form of resistance. Every threatening discourse eventually elicits counter-discourses
and the discourse of linguistic schizophrenia is not an exception. Some
participants challenge it through a counter-discourse of integration,
where integration functions as a powerful metaphor that acknowledges
linguistic and cultural differences, yet allows bilinguals to position
themselves discursively as whole:

(33)   Not really no. I feel I have integrated the French side of my character
       into my English side. (Kate, 49, English–French–German–Spanish)
(34)   A little also due to the fact that I am not the same person since I left
       Germany more than 10 years ago. But since I started talking
       German at home with my children again I guess I'm a linguistically
       more integrated person again. (Bertha, 32, German–English–
       Swedish–French)
(35)   I used to (between ages 20 and 40 as far as I can remember) but not
       any more. I think this is a matter of personality development – I
       know now that I am the same person whatever language I speak
       and I don't have to practice different personae. Before I wasn't so
       sure who I was and who I was seemed to change depending on
       outside circumstances – who I was talking to in what language. I
       suppose that now I have integrated the different personae into
       one??? (Alathea, 49, English–German–French–Arabic)

A similar role, as discussed earlier, is played by the Jungian psychoanalytic discourse that allows respondents to distance themselves from the
notion of linguistic schizophrenia by differentiating between the real
self, unthreatened by linguistic differences, and personae performed in
respective languages.

Discussion and Conclusions

Together, the interdisciplinary studies reviewed here offer intriguing
answers to the questions about bilingual selves. Reflections of bilingual

writers and explorations by linguists and psychoanalysts show that languages may create different, and sometimes incommensurable, worlds for their speakers who feel that their selves change with the shift in language. Studies in psychoanalysis, psychology, and linguistic anthropology demonstrate that bicultural bilinguals may exhibit different verbal behaviors in their two languages and may be perceived differently by their interlocutors depending on the language they use in a particular context. For these bilinguals, and in particular for immigrants and expatriates, the two languages may be linked to different linguistic repertoires, cultural scripts, frames of expectation, autobiographic memories, and levels of proficiency and emotionality. They may also be associated with conflicting allegiances, distinct imagined audiences, incompatible subject positions, and mutually exclusive arguments. Notably, these conclusions are particularly relevant for individuals whose respective languages are linked to – and used in – relatively monolingual environments. Those who live in bi- and multilingual contexts may not necessarily perceive such sharp differences between their linguistic selves.

The analysis of the present corpus offers several contributions to this body of scholarship and to our understanding of the relationship between language and self in bi- and multilingualism. To begin with, this analysis shows that the perception of different selves is not restricted to late or immigrant bilinguals, but is a more general part of bi- and multilingual experience. Secondly, the analysis of the corpus shows that similar experiences (e.g. change in verbal and non-verbal behaviors accompanying the change in language) may be interpreted differently by people who draw on different discourses of bi/multilingualism and self.

The presence of several alternative discourses of bilingualism and self constitutes perhaps the most interesting finding in the study, and to interpret it I will, once again, draw on Bakhtin's (1981) notion of dialogism. Bakhtin (1981) and his followers emphasize that texts and, for that matter, people do not simply draw on social and historic resources but transform them in meaningful ways. The notion of dialogue, in this view, points to the simultaneous connection and tension between the present and the past that shapes individual voices. It is this agentive view of human performance that informs my own understanding of the participants' answers.

To clarify what I mean by this, I turn to studies in which I compared language memoirs, that is, memoirs that deal with the learning and use of various languages, written by U.S. writers throughout the 20th century (Pavlenko, 2001, 2004a). An analysis of discourses of language and identity in these memoirs showed that the 20th century was marked by the ever-present tension between discourses that glorified belonging to one language and culture, even at the price of assimilation, and those that asserted the legitimacy of dual allegiances. In the early part of the century and particularly at the height of the Great Migration, immigrant writers were singing praises to the joys of assimilation. In contrast, the 1980s and 1990s saw an explosion of writing by those who were schooled in the 1940s and 1950s when Americanization was the only way. These writers challenged the imposition of monolingual ideologies and began to explore the painful splits and fissures of the bilingual condition. The older generation is now joined by the writers who grew up in the 1960s and 1970s, witnessing the revival of ethnic consciousness and experiencing the influence of postmodernist thought. The work of this younger generation challenges the essentialist notions of self, redefines the meaning and value of bi- and multilingualism, and suggests that anxieties over an inner split may stem from the lack of social acceptance of bilingualism and may disappear once bi- and multilingualism are accepted as the norm, rather than an exception. This work also proclaims that 'the distress of being double and somewhat homeless is overshadowed by the glory of being hybrid and open' (Dorfman, in De Courtivron, 2003b: 33).

I read the dialogue between the discourses in the present corpus in a very similar manner. The discourse of bilingualism as linguistic schizophrenia is still present in the corpus but mostly in the form of a voice from 'elsewhere' that is being mocked and resisted. The respondents engage in a number of counter-discourses, including the discourse of integrated identities and that of personae. More importantly, however, some participants no longer feel the need to reframe and justify their experiences – they make categorical assertions that their experiences are unique and enjoyable:

(36)   yes!!! and i love it . . . (Zarina, 27, Spanish–English–Portuguese)
(37)   yes definately – this is part of the fun of it. (Christina, 35, English–
        French)
(38)   Yes and that is a very pleasant feeling because it gives me choices
        that I wouldn't have if I were monolingual. (Stephan, 36, Italian–
        English–German–French–Russian)
(39)   Absolutely. It's a lot of fun. (Patricia, 48, English–French–German)

This framing normalizes bi- and multilinguals' experiences while underscoring their uniqueness. My chapter has pursued a similar goal: to legitimize and normalize bi- and multilinguals' experiences without trivializing them or equating them to a change in registers. On the contrary, the analysis of the present corpus suggests that as permeable and porous as they are, linguistic and cultural boundaries and entities exist and are real phenomena to be counted with. And as to the Sapir–Whorf hypothesis, in the words of yet another bilingual, Gustavo Pérez Firmat (2003: 13), its ultimate validity is irrelevant for understanding the bi/multilingual experience: 'what is crucial is that many bilinguals relate to their languages in ways that enact some version of this hypothesis. What may not be true for Spanish and English in any objectively demonstrable way may be true for an individual's apprehension of Spanish and English'.

The web questionnaire responses, reflections of translingual writers, and results of clinical and experimental studies place the locus of multiple selves in distinct contexts of language acquisition, and resulting differences in linguistic repertoires, cultural frames, autobiographic memories, and levels of experienced emotionality and proficiency. Undoubtedly, these differences also exist between various lexicons and registers within a single language, but they are much more pronounced between languages. As a result, bi- and multilingualism are similar to yet also distinct from, in important and meaningful ways, the mastery of multiple registers. François Grosjean (1982) has often argued that a bilingual is not two monolinguals in one body. Here I aimed to show that a bilingual is not exactly like a single monolingual either. Some bi- and multilinguals may perceive the world differently, and change perspectives, ways of thinking, and verbal and non-verbal behaviors when switching languages. Some may derive enjoyment from hybridity and relativity of their existence and others may feel that they inhabit distinct and at times incommensurable lifeworlds and experience pain and anguish over this condition. Yet this is not an aberration on their part but a part of what makes us human.

Acknowledgements

For their insightful comments on the earlier drafts of this paper, I would like to thank my anonymous reviewers, as well as Colin Baker, Mary Besemeres, Jean-Marc Dewaele, Alexia Panayiotou, Ingrid Piller, Monika Schmid, and Jenny Sia. I would also like to thank the audience of the SAUTE 2005 conference in Basel for their thoughtful comments and enthusiastic response to the plenary talk given on the basis of this paper. All remaining errors are exclusively mine.

Note

1. This chapter analyses an earlier version of the database, while Dewaele's chapter analyses a later version where the number of responses is somewhat higher ($n = 1454$). In both cases, prior to analysis, we deleted incomplete responses, doubled responses, and responses that looked less than serious.

References

Adler, K. (1977) *Collective and Individual Bilingualism: A Sociolinguistic Study.* Hamburg: Helmut Buske Verlag.

Amati-Mehler, J., Argentieri, S. and Canestri, J. (1993) *The Babel of the Unconscious: Mother Tongue and Foreign Languages in the Psychoanalytic Dimension* (J. Whitelaw-Cucco, trans.). Madison, CT: International Universities Press.

Aragno, A. and Schlachet, P. (1996) Accessibility of early experience through the language of origin: A theoretical integration. *Psychoanalytic Psychology* 13(1), 23–34.

Auer, P. (ed.) (1998) *Code-Switching in Conversation: Language, Interaction, and Identity.* London/New York: Routledge.

Bakhtin, M. (1981) *The Dialogic Imagination: Four Essays by M. Bakhtin* (M. Holquist trans.). Austin, TX: University of Texas Press.

Bakhtin, M. (1984) *Problems of Dostoevsky's Poetics* (C. Emerson, trans.). Minneapolis, MN: University of Minnesota Press.

Bakhtin, M. (1986) *Speech Genres and Other Late Essays* (V. McGee, trans.). Austin, TX: University of Texas Press.

Beaujour, E. (1989) *Alien Tongues: Bilingual Russian Writers of the 'First' Emigration.* Ithaca, NY: Cornell University Press.

Besemeres, M. (2002) *Translating One's Self: Language and Selfhood in Cross-Cultural Autobiography.* Bern: Peter Lang.

Blunkett, D. (2002) *Integration with Diversity: Globalisation and the Renewal of Democracy and Civil Society.* The Foreign Policy Centre. On WWW at http://fpc.org.uk/articles/182. Accessed June 17.05.

Bond, M. (1983) How language variation affects inter-cultural differentiation of values by Hong-Kong bilinguals. *Journal of Language and Social Psychology* 2, 57–66.

Bossard, J. (1945) The bilingual as a person – linguistic identification with status. *American Sociological Review* 10(6), 699–709.

Buxbaum, E. (1949) The role of a second language in the formation of ego and superego. *Psychoanalytic Quarterly* 18, 279–89.

Child, I. (1943) *Italian or American? The Second Generation in Conflict.* New Haven: Yale University Press.

Clarke, M. (1976) Second language acquisition as a clash of consciousness. *Language Learning* 26(2), 377–90.

De Courtivron, I. (2003a) Introduction. In I. De Courtivron (ed.) *Lives in Translation: Bilingual Writers on Identity and Creativity* (pp. 1–9). New York: Palgrave Macmillan.

De Courtivron, I. (ed.) (2003b) *Lives in Translation: Bilingual Writers on Identity and Creativity.* New York: Palgrave Macmillan.

Dewaele, J.-M. (2004) The emotional force of swearwords and taboo words in the speech of multilinguals. *Journal of Multilingual and Multicultural Development* 25 (2/3), 204–22.

Dewaele, J.-M. and Pavlenko, A. (2001–2003) Webquestionnaire *Bilingualism and Emotions.* London: University of London. On WWW at http://www.bbk.ac.uk/llc/biling + emotions/questionnaire.html.

Ervin, S. (1954, reprinted 1973) Identification and bilingualism. In A. Dil (ed.) *Language Acquisition and Communicative Choice. Essays by Susan M. Ervin-Tripp* (pp. 1–14). Stanford, CA: Stanford University Press.

Ervin-Tripp, S. (1964, reprinted 1973) Language and TAT content in bilinguals. In A. Dil (ed.) *Language Acquisition and Communicative Choice. Essays by Susan M. Ervin-Tripp* (pp. 45–61). Stanford, CA: Stanford University Press.

Ervin-Tripp, S. (1967, reprinted 1973) An issei learns English. In A. Dil (ed.) *Language Acquisition and Communicative Choice. Essays by Susan M. Ervin-Tripp* (pp. 62–77). Stanford, CA: Stanford University Press.

Fairclough, N. (1995) *Critical Discourse Analysis: The Critical Study of Language.* London: Longman.

Fairclough, N. (2003) *Analysing Discourse: Textual Analysis for Social Research.* London/New York: Routledge.

Foster, R. (1992) Psychoanalysis and the bilingual patient: Some observations on the influence of language choice on the transference. *Psychoanalytic Psychology* 9(1), 61–76.

Foster, R. (1996) Assessing the psychodynamic function of language in the bilingual patient. In R. Foster, M. Moskowitz and R. Javier (eds) *Reaching Across Boundaries of Culture and Class: Widening the Scope of Psychotherapy* (pp. 243–63). Northvale, NJ: Jason Aronson, Inc.

Green, J. (1941) An experiment in English. Reprinted in Green, J. (1993) *The Apprentice Writer* (pp. 47–62). New York/London: Marion Boyars.

Greenson, R. (1950) The mother tongue and the mother. *International Journal of Psycho-Analysis* 31, 18–23.

Grosjean, F. (1982) *Life with Two Languages: An Introduction to Bilingualism.* Cambridge, MA: Harvard University Press.

Guthrie, G. and Azores, F. (1968) Philippine interpersonal behavior patterns. In W. Bello and A. de Guzman (eds) *Modernization: Its Impact in the Philippines* (pp. 3–63). Quezon City, Philippines: Ateneo de Manila University Press.

Harris, C. (2004) Bilingual speakers in the lab: Psychophysiological measures of emotional reactivity. *Journal of Multilingual and Multicultural Development* 25(2/3), 223–47.

Harris, C., Ayçiçegi, A. and Gleason, J. (2003) Taboo words and reprimands elicit greater autonomic reactivity in a first language than in a second language. *Applied Psycholinguistics* 24(4), 561–79.

Heinz, B. (2001) 'Fish in the river': Experiences of bilingual bicultural speakers. *Multilingua* 20(1), 85–108.

Henss, W. (1931) Zweisprachigkeit als Pädagogisches Problem. *Ethnopolitischer Almanach* 2, 47–55.

Hoffman, E. (1989) *Lost in Translation. A Life in a New Language.* New York: Penguin Books.

Hull, Ph. V. (1990) *Bilingualism: Two Languages, Two Personalities?* Unpublished doctoral dissertation, University of California, Berkeley, CA.

Javier, R. (1995) Vicissitudes of autobiographical memories in a bilingual analysis. *Psychoanalytic Psychology* 12(3), 429–38.

Javier, R. (1996) In search of repressed memories in bilingual individuals. In R. Foster, M. Moskowitz and R. Javier (eds) *Reaching Across Boundaries of Culture and Class: Widening the Scope of Psychotherapy* (pp. 225–41). Northvale, NJ: Jason Aronson, Inc.

Kellman, S. (2000) *The Translingual Imagination.* Lincoln/London: University of Nebraska Press.

Kellman, S. (2003a) Preface. In *Switching Languages: Translingual Writers Reflect on Their Craft* (pp. ix–xix). Lincoln/London: University of Nebraska Press.

Kellman, S. (ed.) (2003b) *Switching Languages: Translingual Writers Reflect on Their Craft.* Lincoln/London: University of Nebraska Press.

Kinginger, C. (2004) Bilingualism and emotion in the autobiographical works of Nancy Huston. *Journal of Multilingual and Multicultural Development* 25(2/3), 159–78.

Koven, M. (1998) Two languages in the self/the self in two languages: French–Portuguese bilinguals' verbal enactments and experiences of self in narrative discourse. *Ethos* 26(4), 410–55.

Krapf, E. (1955) The choice of language in polyglot psychoanalysis. *Psychoanalytic Quarterly* 24, 343–57.

Kristeva, J. (1969) Le mot, le dialogue et le roman. In *Recherches pour une Sémanalyse*. Paris: Éditions du Seuil.

Kristeva, J. (1986) Word, dialogue, and the novel. In T. Moi (ed.) *The Kristeva Reader* (pp. 35–61). New York: Columbia University Press.

Kuroda, Y., Hayashi, C. and Suzuki, T. (1986) The role of language in cross-national surveys: American and Japanese respondents. *Applied Scholastic Models and Data Analysis* 2, 43–59.

Larsen, S., Schrauf, R., Fromholt, P. and Rubin, D. (2002) Inner speech and bilingual autobiographical memory: A Polish–Danish cross-cultural study. *Memory* 10(1), 45–54.

Linde, Ch. (1993) *Life Stories: The Creation of Coherence*. New York: Oxford University Press.

Macnamara, J. (1970) Bilingualism and thought. In J. Alatis (ed.) *Georgetown University 21st Annual Round Table, 23* (pp. 25–40). Washington, DC: Georgetown University Press.

Marcos, L., Alpert, M., Urcuyo, L. and Kesselman, M. (1973a) The effect of interview language on the evaluation of psychopathology in Spanish–American schizophrenic patients. *American Journal of Psychiatry* 130(5), 549–53.

Marcos, L., Urcuyo, L., Kesselman, M. and Alpert, M. (1973b) The language barrier in evaluating Spanish–American patients. *Archives of General Psychiatry* 29, 655–59.

Marian, V. and Kaushanskaya, M. (2004) Self-construal and emotion in bicultural bilinguals. *Journal of Memory and Language* 51, 190–201.

Marian, V. and Neisser, U. (2000) Language-dependent recall of autobiographical memories. *Journal of Experimental Psychology: General* 129(3), 361–68.

Novakovich, J. and Shapard, R. (2000) *Stories in the Stepmother Tongue*. Buffalo, NY: White Pine Press.

Panayiotou, A. (2004) Switching codes, switching code: Bilinguals' emotional responses in English and Greek. *Journal of Multilingual and Multicultural Development* 25(2/3), 124–39.

Pavlenko, A. (1998) Second language learning by adults: Testimonies of bilingual writers. *Issues in Applied Linguistics* 9(1), 3–19.

Pavlenko, A. (2001) 'In the world of the tradition, I was unimagined': Negotiation of identities in cross-cultural autobiographies. *The International Journal of Bilingualism* 5(3), 317–44.

Pavlenko, A. (2002) 'We have room for but one language here': Language and national identity in the US at the turn of the 20th century. *Multilingua* 21(2/3), 163–96.

Pavlenko, A. (2004a) 'The making of an American': Negotiation of identities at the turn of the twentieth century. In A. Pavlenko and A. Blackledge (eds) *Negotiation of Identities in Multilingual Contexts* (pp. 34–67). Clevedon, UK: Multilingual Matters.

Pavlenko, A. (2004b) 'Stop doing that, *ia komu skazala!*': Emotions and language choice in parent–child communication. *Journal of Multilingual and Multicultural Development* 25(2/3), 179–203.

Pavlenko, A. (2005) *Emotions and Multilingualism*. New York: Cambridge University Press.

Pérez Firmat, G. (2003) *Tongue Ties: Logo-Eroticism in Anglo-Hispanic Literature*. New York: Palgrave Macmillan.

Ross, M., Xun, W.Q.E. and Wilson, A. (2002) Language and the bicultural self. *Personality and Social Psychology Bulletin* 28(8), 1040–50.

Rozensky, R. and Gomez, M. (1983) Language switching in psychotherapy with bilinguals: Two problems, two models, and case examples. *Psychotherapy: Theory, Research and Practice* 20(2), 152–60.

Sander, F. (1934) Seelische Struktur und Sprache: Strukturpsychologisches zum Zweitsprachenproblem. *Neue Psychologische Studien* 12, 59.

Schrauf, R. and Rubin, D. (1998) Bilingual autobiographical memory in older adult immigrants: A test of cognitive explanations of the reminiscence bump and the linguistic encoding of memories. *Journal of Memory and Language* 39, 437–57.

Schrauf, R. and Rubin, D. (2000) Internal languages of retrieval: The bilingual encoding of memories for the personal past. *Memory and Cognition* 28(4), 616–23.

Schrauf, R. and Rubin, D. (2004) The 'language' and 'feel' of bilingual memory: Mnemonic traces. *Estudios de Sociolingüística* 5(1), 21–39.

Scollon, R., Tsang, W., Li, D., Yung, V. and Jones, R. (1998) Voice, appropriation, and discourse representation in a student writing task. *Linguistics and Education* 9(3), 227–50.

Spoerl, D. (1943) Bilinguality and emotional adjustment. *Journal of Abnormal and Social Psychology* 38, 35–57.

Stroińska, M. (2003) The role of language in the re-construction of identity in exile. In M. Stroińska and V. Cecchetto (eds) *Exile, Language, and Identity* (pp. 95–109). Frankfurt am Main: Peter Lang.

Stubbs, M. (1997) Language and the mediation of experience: Linguistic representation and cognitive orientation. In F. Coulmas (ed.) *The Handbook of Sociolinguistics* (pp. 358–73). Oxford: Basil Blackwell.

Tannenbaum, M. (2003) The narrative of language choice: Writers from ethnolinguistic minorities. *The Canadian Modern Language Review* 60(1), 7–26.

Teicholz, T. (1993) *Conversations with Jerzy Kosinski*. Jackson: University Press of Mississippi.

Todorov, T. (1985) Bilinguisme, dialogisme, et schizophrénie. In J. Bennani *et al.* (eds) *Du Bilinguisme* (pp. 11–26). Paris: Denoel.

Todorov, T. (1994) Dialogism and schizophrenia. In A. Arteaga (ed.) *An Other Tongue: Nation and Ethnicity in the Linguistic Borderlands* (pp. 203–14). Durham/London: Duke University Press.

Trafimow, D., Silverman, E., Fan, R.M.-T. and Law, J.S.F. (1997) The effects of language and priming on the relative accessibility of the private self and the collective self. *Journal of Cross-Cultural Psychology* 28, 107–23.

Trigo, B. (2003) The mother tongue. In D. Sommer (ed.) *Bilingual Games: Some Literary Investigations* (pp. 177–91). New York: Palgrave Macmillan.

Valenta, E. (1991) *Doubled selves and fractured childhoods: A study of the recit d'enfance in Nathalie Sarraute, Agota Kristof, and Claude Esteban.* Unpublished doctoral dissertation, Cornell University, Ithaca, NY.

Ventura, E. (1976) Ambiguity values of the Philippine Thematic Apperception Test. *Philippine Journal of Psychology* 9(1–2), 39–56.

Chapter 2

Language and Emotional Experience: The Voice of Translingual Memoir[1]

MARY BESEMERES

Speaking Russian, I tend to use diminutives because they are typical of the culture and somehow expected in the language. I suppose this makes me look more emotional and sentimental than I normally am. Am I misrepresenting myself? Surprisingly enough, I do feel somewhat emotional and sentimental when I'm speaking Russian. The very language I am using has changed me.

Christina Kotchemidova (2000: 130)

Introduction

This chapter takes as its point of departure a question recently posed by linguist Aneta Pavlenko, but rarely, if ever, asked in either literary studies or the social sciences:[2] 'what [do] bilinguals' own narratives contribute to the study of bilingualism?' (2001b: 321). More specifically, what might bilinguals' autobiographical writings have to say on the subject of bilingualism and emotion? Polish-born author Eva Hoffman, who emigrated at age 13 with her family from Europe to Canada, writes poignantly of the gap she recalls between her own and her mother's emotional worlds as immigrants: 'My mother says I'm becoming "English". This hurts me, because I know she means I'm becoming cold . . .' (1989: 146). Hoffman's words express some of the key concerns of a major contemporary genre of life writing – translingual memoir – which probes the emotional and psychological lives of migrants between languages and cultures. In this chapter, I explore ways in which several striking examples of the genre approach the questions of whether, and how, emotional experience is inflected differently in different languages.

The memoirs referred to in my discussion include Eva Hoffman's (1989) *Lost in Translation: A Life in a New Language*, Tim Parks's (1996) *An Italian Education*, Kyoko Mori's (1997) *Polite Lies: On Being a Woman Caught Between Cultures*, Peter Skrzynecki's (2004) *The Sparrow Garden*, and an autobiographical essay, 'La Double Vie de Veronica: reflections on my life as a Chinese migrant in Australia', by Veronica Zhengdao Ye (2003). I focus on the authors' treatment of the roles played in their experience by important forms of emotional expression in their two languages. These forms of expression range over several different categories of discourse, which do not presuppose precisely the same inter-relationship between speaker, emotion, and language. Some kinds of emotion words are used to describe what the speaker is feeling, for example, words like 'anxious' in English, or the Polish '*żal*' (something like sorrow); I call these 'emotion concepts'. These include phrases such as the Polish '*boję się*' ('I'm afraid', literally 'I am fearing'), as well as individual words, like the adjective 'anxious' and the noun '*żal*'. Diminutives like '*uccellina*' (little bird) in Italian are another kind of emotion word, which could be said to express the speaker's feeling more immediately. John Haiman (1989: 156) usefully distinguishes between the meaning of utterances such as 'Yuk!' and 'I feel disgust', linking the first type with linguist Karl Bühler's (1990) 'Ausdrucksfunktion' or expressive function of language, and the second with Bühler's 'Darstellungsfunktion' or representational function of language. Another way to define this difference would be to say that expressive words like diminutives and interjections *show* the speaker's emotion without being the subject of what is said. Moreover, they necessarily show the speaker's own feeling, rather than someone else's feeling; words like 'anxious' and '*żal*', by contrast, can be used to refer to anybody's feelings, either the speaker's or those of others. The memoirs considered here suggest that directly expressive forms like diminutives and more representational emotion concepts alike affect how people perceive and interpret what they feel.

Idioms, such as the Italian '*fare festa a qualcuno*', discussed in Parks's memoir, convey a certain attitude towards a display of feeling, an attitude for which there may be no ready counterpart in another language. '*Morai-naki*' in Japanese refers to the crying aroused by seeing someone else's tears, a kind of emotional behavior that, Kyoko Mori argues, is so common and familiar in Japanese cultural experience as to merit a special word. Bilingual writers' reflections on these diverse kinds of emotional vocabulary shed light moreover on cultural evaluations of emotional expression, and the related issue of the relative importance of verbal and non-verbal communication of feeling within different cultures.

Bilingual life writing offers a rare insight into the relationship between languages and emotions. Cognitive psychologist Merlin Donald's comments in the context of fiction are no less apposite where autobiographical literature is concerned:

The best writers have pushed the subjective exploration of the mind much further than would be permissible in clinical . . . psychology.

[Their] portrayals of it...are possibly the most authoritative descriptions we have.... [S]uch testimony constitutes our primary ethological database. (Donald, 2001: 78–85)

The methodology adopted in this chapter combines evaluative literary analysis with insights into the cultural meanings of emotions drawn from cultural psychology, linguistics, and the history of emotions (cf., for example, Kitayama & Markus, 1994; Stearns, 1994; Wierzbicka, 1999). I approach memoirs as representations of emotional experience that provide, potentially, no less valid a perspective on bilingualism and emotions than the data analysed in experimental and other kinds of empirical research.

The understanding of emotions implicit in these autobiographical texts lies somewhere between the positions of social constructionism (cf. Lutz, 1988) and a more traditional psychological view of emotions. For these authors, writing about their emotional experiences entails reflecting on states of feeling often not perceived by others, and thus experienced as *interior*, rather than located in the social domain. However, their writings also reveal how their feelings are shaped by concepts specific to a particular language, a medium they share with other speakers. Outside of that language, it becomes harder to talk about these feelings, to have them recognized. Emotions as seen by these authors, then, are both culturally shaped and individually experienced. Insofar as they write of the absence of direct counterparts in English to the emotion words they use in their other languages, their narratives lend support to a view of emotions as culturally relative, rather than universal.[3]

Literature Review

Before turning to the translingual memoirs themselves, I offer below a brief outline of the existing scholarly literature on bilingualism and emotion in Anglophone autobiography. Despite the proliferation of narratives of 'language migration'[4] in English since the publication of *Lost in Translation* (for discussions see Besemeres, 1998, 2002; Pavlenko, 2001a,b,c) and two earlier, landmark American autobiographies that explored psychological aspects of bilingualism,[5] the study of the relationship between language and emotion in these narratives is at a relatively early stage. Scholars who have written about emotions in bilingual life writing have focused on a range of aspects of the subject in different narratives; no single topic is addressed in all of the following studies.

In *Articulate Silences* (1993), King-Kok Cheung analyses memoir and fiction by three North American women writers – Maxine Hong Kingston, Joy Kogawa, and Hisaye Yamamoto – in the light of their concern with the roles played by speech and silence in Asian-American experience, and the different values attributed to silence within Japanese, Chinese, and Anglo-American cultures. Cheung discusses the phenomenon of 'emotional reticence' as manifested verbally through 'indirection' in Japanese culture and by means of silence in both Japanese and Chinese cultures. In the American cultural context, she argues, speech tends to be associated with freedom and empowerment, silence with inarticulateness and repression. Cheung challenges this valorization of speech and denigration of silence, which has led Anglo-American feminist critics to dismiss the Japanese and Chinese female protagonists of works by these three authors as weak and submissive. She argues that silence can itself be an articulate rhetorical strategy, and that it is often subtly and effectively deployed in these texts to communicate a character's feelings.

In her seminal essay 'On language memoir' – a term she herself coined for the genre I refer to as translingual memoir – Alice Kaplan writes of the emotions that motivate language learning, contending that they more often involve 'desire and fear and greed and the need to escape' than a wish to 'communicate' or to achieve 'empathy' with others (1994: 60). '[S]uch positive, altruistic motives', she writes, 'cannot possibly take into account the variety of contexts in which languages are learned' (1994: 60). She supports this point with suggestive readings of the memoirs of New York Jewish intellectual Alfred Kazin (1951), *A Walker in the City*, and Mexican American writer Richard Rodriguez (1982), *Hunger of Memory*, and with a memorable fragment from her own memoir of learning French, *French Lessons* (Kaplan, 1993). The passage recounts her meeting with the family of a speech pathologist in Bordeaux, Micheline, and later rivalry in French with a former patient of Micheline's, a Vietnamese refugee to France:

> Micheline was disgusted by my lack of generosity where Vu was concerned. '[Y]ou have no idea what he has been through, how he has rebuilt his life from nothing. Losing his mother and sister in a boat – we haven't a clue what that was like.' I was jealous of his success, his transcendence of the worst odds ... It was a measly feeling. (Kaplan, 1993: 68)

Kaplan's (1994) essay touches briefly on some other major authors of 'language memoir', including Elias Canetti, Eva Hoffman, and Vladimir Nabokov. The jealous hunger and ambivalence she ascribes to language learners, and brings out convincingly in the three narratives she discusses, is less evident, however, in Hoffman's *Lost in Translation*, which voices a strong desire to communicate: to 'translate' meanings without giving up too much of one's existing sense of self, yet to be open to a new reality and new interlocutors. Arguably, in Hoffman's case this is not so much the 'innocent' endeavor Kaplan dismisses as a hunger of another kind.[6]

Like Kaplan, in a recent article, Celeste Kinginger (2004) focuses on motivations for language learning as attested in bilingual memoir. She addresses the question of motivation through an in-depth reading of autobiographical works by a well-known bilingual, Canadian-born French author Nancy Huston. Kinginger's article sheds light on the emotional history of Huston's complex transition from English to French. She argues that Huston's autobiographical writings demonstrate that 'study of a foreign language can be driven by emotional investment and by richly nuanced imagination' and 'can also emerge from desire for new and more complex ways to live' (Kinginger, 2004: 160).

In an article on transformations of gender performance in language learning as portrayed in personal narratives, Pavlenko (2001a) investigates the cross-cultural negotiation of gender in friendships, intimate relationships, and those between parents and children. She notes that 'intimate relationships and friendships surface time and again as one of the most difficult areas for negotiation and an authentic performance of gender' (2001a: 151). Her discussion of passages from memoirs by Eva Hoffman, Dominican-American Julia Alvarez, Korean-American Helie Lee, and American travelers to Japan Karen Ogulnick and Cathy Davidson, as well as from a biography of Polish-born American writer Jerzy Kosinski, demonstrates how dependent perceptions of gender in intimate relationships are on a shared language and culture. To avoid being misinterpreted, second language users may be 'forced to abandon some speech acts they see as central to their performance of gender' (2001a: 154), and may have to 'internalize new expressions and speech acts, critical for full participation in gendered discursive practices of their new community' (2001a: 154–55).

My own book *Translating One's Self: Language and Selfhood in Cross-Cultural Autobiography* (Besemeres, 2002) examines the representation of culturally specific emotion terms in four cross-cultural narratives in English. In the case of Eva Hoffman's *Lost in Translation*, these terms are '*tęsknota*', a kind of yearning or nostalgia, and '*przyjaciółka*', a Polish word, which Eva experiences as non-equivalent with the English 'friend'. In Hungarian-born Australian author Andrew Riemer's memoirs, *Inside Outside* (Riemer, 1992) and *The Habsburg Café* (Riemer, 1993), the English emotion word 'embarrassment' is a prominent theme as well as (arguably) an underlying emotion giving impetus to the narrative. The recurrent, often idiosyncratic use of the word 'intimacy' in Richard Rodriguez's (1982) memoir *Hunger of Memory* indicates, I argue, semantic transference from the Spanish *intimidad*. Finally, in Kazuo Ishiguro's (1986) novel *An Artist of the Floating World*, the emotional world of the protagonist seems to combine an Anglophone awareness of guilt with a Japanese discourse of *haji* (a pervasive sense of shame) on the one hand and *sumanai* (an acutely other-oriented sense of guilt) on the other. The book concludes that these narratives show how moving between languages involves inhabiting significantly different conceptual and emotional worlds.

In the article in which the present chapter originated (Besemeres, 2004a), I consider Polish poet Stanislaw Baranczak's (1989) reflections on the gap between the English emotion concept 'happy' and the Polish '*szczęsliwy*', and examine the Cantonese interjection '*Aiyah*' and some forms of address in Italian (e.g. 'O Vittò!' for 'Vittorio') as significant types of emotional expression in two autobiographical novels not discussed here, Lilian Ng's (1994) *Silver Sister* and Nino Ricci's (1990) *The Book of Saints*. The current chapter includes new discussions of memoirs by Peter Skrzynecki and Kyoko Mori, and focuses additionally on the emotion words '*żal*' (Polish), and '*morai-naki*' (Japanese).

The studies cited above exemplify a number of different approaches to the inquiry into the relationship between bilingualism and emotions in cross-cultural autobiography. While not all of these works deal explicitly with issues such as the incommensurability of different languages' conceptualizations of emotion, they all affirm the centrality of emotional experience to narrative representations of lives between languages. This chapter offers a detailed account of how the relationship between language and emotions is explored across several kinds of emotion discourse in five contemporary translingual memoirs.

Translatability of Emotion Concepts

'anxious' versus '*boję się*'

Are specific ways of speaking conducive to particular ways of feeling? Does living 'in' a language, in the phrase of Eva Hoffman, help to engender certain emotions? In *Lost in Translation*, her memoir of migrating to North America from Poland at 13 years of age,[7] which explores her subsequent life 'in a new language', Hoffman portrays herself as being drawn in different directions when she thinks about her feelings in terms of the English word 'anxious' or the Polish for 'afraid':

> Between the two stories and two vocabularies, there's a vast alteration in the diagram of the psyche and the relationship to inner life. When I say to myself, 'I'm anxious,' I draw on different faculties than when I say, 'I'm afraid.' 'I'm anxious because I have problems with separation,' I tell myself very rationally when a boyfriend leaves for a long trip, and in that quick movement of self-analysis and explanation the trajectory of feeling is rerouted. I no longer follow it from impulse to expression; now that I understand what the problem is, I won't cry at the airport. By this ploy, I mute the force of the original fear; I gain some control. (Hoffman, 1989: 269)

When she identifies her feeling as one of anxiety, Hoffman finds herself responding with an attempt to quell it, as something harmful to her sense of self as an adult, someone in control of her own life. The Polish *'boję się'* (the verb she most likely has in mind here for 'afraid') has no such negative overtones; it is simply, ineluctably, the way she feels. Interestingly, *'boję się'* could equally well be used by a child or an adult, whereas the English term 'anxious' belongs to an adult register. Hoffman writes that her mother, who migrated to Canada from Poland in early middle-age, finds the notion of 'controlling' her feelings altogether alien, 'suffer[ing] her emotions as if they were forces of nature, winds and storms and volcanic eruptions' (1989: 269). Hoffman's account of thinking about her own feelings in terms of the words 'anxious' and 'afraid' suggests at once the advantage of the American vocabulary – a greater freedom from pain, a sense of empowerment – and the cost – a certain loss of spontaneity and expressiveness in the interests of appearing strong.

Shortly before she left Poland with her family, Eva (or Ewa as she was called then) passed around a notebook in class in which her schoolmates wrote 'appropriate words of good-bye' (1989: 78). Writing in a retrospective present tense, the author recalls:

> Most of them choose melancholy verses in which life is figured as a vale of tears or a river of suffering, or a journey of pain on which we are embarking. This tone of sadness is something we all enjoy. It makes us feel the gravity of life, and it is gratifying to have a truly tragic event – a parting forever – to give vent to such romantic feelings.
>
> It's only two years later that I go on a month-long bus trip across Canada and the United States with a group of teenagers, who at parting inscribe sentences in each other's notebooks to be remembered by. 'It was great fun knowing you!' they exclaim in the pages of my little notebook. 'Don't ever lose your friendly personality!' 'Keep cheerful, and nothing can harm you!' they enjoin, and as I compare my two sets of mementos, I know that, even though they're so close to each other in time, I've indeed come to another country. (1989: 78)

The contrast between her Canadian traveling companions' inscriptions, invoking fun, cheerfulness, and friendliness, and the plangent farewell poems of her Polish classmates, speaks volumes about the cultural distance Hoffman had traversed. The girlish injunction to 'keep cheerful', in particular, with its confidence in an ability to keep 'harm' at bay, connects clearly with the touchstone of 'control' so important to Eva's adult peers in New York, who tell each other frequently, 'I've got to get some control' (1989: 270). As Hoffman brings out, an 'insist[ence]' on 'cheerfulness' (1989: 271) is itself an approach to painful feelings and experiences, an attempt to overcome them by denying their force. At the same time, she pokes gentle fun at the element of romantic exaggeration in her own and her Polish classmates' luxuriating in the sorrow of lifelong parting, a trope that exalts the sadness people are fully permitted to feel.

Hoffman describes experiences of incommensurability between emotion concepts in her two languages. Her memoir suggests that individual emotion concepts are embedded in a particular cultural 'story': 'anxious' in modern English is part of a story influenced by popular psychology, according to which it is good to be in charge of one's own life, and consequently of feelings that could threaten such 'control'; *'boję się'* has no such story attached, but rather, as Hoffman writes about her mother, is part of a cultural outlook in which feelings are perceived as natural and the 'most authentic' part of a person. In addition, and perhaps most importantly from the point of view of the relationship between language and emotion, the passages from *Lost in Translation* affirm the impact of specific emotion concepts on emotional experience. In Hoffman's account, when someone uses a particular emotion word to describe a feeling, the word chosen helps to shape that feeling, affecting how the person perceives and interprets it, and hence how he or she experiences it.

'Żal': 'sadness', 'grief', 'sorrow'?

The second emotion concept I examine figures centrally in a new Australian memoir, *The Sparrow Garden* (2004), by poet Peter Skrzynecki, the son of Polish and Ukrainian immigrants to Australia. Skrzynecki's parents, deported to German forced labor camps during World War II, met in a Displaced Persons' camp after the war, and migrated to Australia in 1949, when Peter was four. *The Sparrow Garden* evokes Skrzynecki's years as a migrant child in working-class suburbs in Sydney, but the underlying theme of the narrative is the enduring closeness and strength of his bond with his parents. The language of their household appears to have been Polish; Skrzynecki's mother, Kornelia Woloszczuk, was from the Ukraine, but brought her son up speaking the language she shared with her Polish husband.[8] A Polish word that encapsulates at once the author's parents' sense of exile in Australia and his own sense of loss after their deaths[9] works almost as a *leitmotif* in the memoir. Writing of his emotions in the wake of his mother's death, Skrzynecki uses the Polish word *'żal'*, translating its meaning through images of his physical state, while suggesting the concept's fundamental untranslatability into English. He is filled with *żal* at the end of a visit to his parents' now vacant house, the home he grew up in:

> The voice in my head says, 'You're going away again', and a feeling like nothing else on earth comes over me, a heaviness, a laboured breathing,

slow, as if each breath might be my last, the physical experience of the word '*żal*'. It sounds like the house is speaking to me. (Skrzynecki, 2004: 10)

The same word appears in his account, towards the end of the book, of his delayed response to his father's death:

Something had been happening inside me; I can't say exactly when it entered my blood, but a terrible longing, *żal*, was building up in me, pulling me slowly but surely back to my father's death. I began to miss him like I hadn't missed him in the three weeks since he'd died. My body was hit with spasms as I walked, like I was having stomach cramps. I would sob, but the tears just wouldn't break. (2004: 216)

What strikes me in these passages, as a Polish-speaking reader, is Skrzynecki's forceful rendition of the sense of heaviness that characteristically accompanies the feeling of *żal*. This heaviness seems to be related to the fact that *żal* always entails a loss. Grammatically, *żal* takes the genitive and implies an object of one's feeling, '*żal mi czegos*', 'I [feel] *żal* for/about something'. Unlike 'grief' in English, *żal* is not used exclusively about the loss of a beloved person through death. It can be used about something as small as the loss of an object of sentimental value like a photograph, book, or pendant, no less than about bereavement. It can also be used about the loss of a friendship (*żal mi tej przyjaźni*). These examples show that in Polish, *żal* is thought of as an ordinary, omnipresent aspect of life, and yet, as Skrzynecki's memoir reveals, it is, potentially, a powerful feeling. The range of *żal*'s possible uses suggests that in Polish it is culturally acceptable to express strong feeling over the loss of something that in English would not warrant the use of a strong emotion word. The difference between '*żal*' and 'grief', then, points to different cultural attitudes to emotional expression reflected in Polish and English.

Of his *żal* for his father, Skrzynecki writes that it is 'a terrible longing' building up in him. 'Longing' is not part of the basic meaning of *żal* in Polish,[10] unless in the sense that feeling *żal*, one wishes deeply ('longs') that something were otherwise than as it is. However, it is perhaps a word that helps to translate *żal* into English, because it implies something stronger than 'be sorry for' or 'be sorry about', which could be used to translate *żal* in some contexts, for example, 'I'm sorry for him' (*żal mi go*). Doroszewski's *Polish Dictionary* (1958–1969) quotes uses of the word, which bear out the force of the emotion in Polish: '*serce krwawi, pęka, sciska się z żalu*', 'the heart bleeds, bursts, contracts with *żal*, and '*żal ogarnia*', '*żal* overwhelms'. These resonate with Skrzynecki's depiction of the 'spasms' and 'cramps' that assail him when he feels *żal* for his father.

In a passage about his parents' feelings of loss at having left Poland and the Ukraine, Skrzynecki attempts to capture how *żal* differs from English words for emotions that might seem related, such as 'grief', 'sadness' and 'sorrow':

> I failed to understand my parents' reluctance to accept the ocean as something beautiful, and in those early years of our migration I also failed to understand a deeper and more poignant reason to be drawn into associations with their exile; it had to do with their loss, with the word *żal*. Literally, it means 'sadness' or 'sorrow' or 'grief', but it has a depth to it that no English word can capture, certainly not in three letters. Anglo-Australians, especially literary critics and academics, often confuse it with sentimentality and a lack of irony in the work of European immigrants, failing to understand the deep psychological and emotional issues in the heart of the immigrant. In doing so, they reveal their own ignorance of the state of being of Europeans and sometimes display an inner fear of being demonstrative themselves, of exhibiting their own feelings, especially men, in public.
>
> *Żal* is more than a description of a physical feeling; it is a heartfelt reaction, carrying the notion of profound loss and yearning at the same time; it belongs to the language of the spirit or the soul, to an Absolute that is intangible. (Skrzynecki, 2004: 33–34)

This passage suggests the distinctive meaning of *żal*, while also conveying an impression of Australian attitudes to emotions as experienced by the child of non-English-speaking immigrants. Contrary to what Skrzynecki writes, as we have seen in the case of grief, *żal* does not 'literally' translate as 'grief', 'sadness', or 'sorrow'. Whereas sadness can be unspecified, as in the phrase, 'I feel sad, I don't know why', *żal* implies a real loss and a known cause. 'Sorrow' in English is slightly archaic and literary, where *żal* is contemporary and colloquial; while 'sorrow' can be used about an aspect of experience with which one lives in an ongoing way (e.g. a family member's illness), *żal* relates to a concrete loss that occurred in the past.

The word *żal* appears to be a central part of Skrzynecki's parents' immigrant experience as he understands it. His comment that Anglo-Australians – 'especially critics' – misunderstand the emotions expressed by European immigrants no doubt springs from experiences of having his evocation of such feelings in his poetry dismissed as sentimental.[11] It seems to imply that Anglo-Australians are, by virtue of their lack of knowledge of concepts like *żal*, less in touch with their true feelings than (East) Europeans. While Skrzynecki and Eva Hoffman are both sympathetic to Polish expressiveness and critical of the 'repressive' potential of Anglophone styles (Australian and American, respectively), Hoffman sees the gap as a difference in cultural values, whereas Skrzynecki tends to portray it as a fullness in Polish language and culture and a lack in English language/Australian culture. His awareness of the cultural dimension of *żals* untranslatability appears intuitive rather than analytical.

As the uses of it in *The Sparrow Garden* demonstrate, *żal* is not simply an emotion concept that is expressed somewhat differently in English as 'sadness', 'grief', or 'sorrow'. It is a category of emotion not recognized in English, and to that extent it is absent from Anglo-Australian culture, whether or not non-Polish-speaking Australians feel it (something hard to either prove or disprove). Without reflecting in depth, as Hoffman does, on the cultural contexts that inform these differing emotion concepts, Skrzynecki's writing conveys both the meaning and the untranslatability of *żal* through images, at times with intense lyricism. The very fact that the word recurs so often in his memoir points to how significant it is, in Skrzynecki's sense of his parents' lives, and in his own personal narrative.

Idioms: '*spettacolo*'/'*fare festa*' versus 'spectacle'/'fuss'

English translator and writer Tim Parks came to Italy in his twenties, eventually settling in Verona with his Italian wife Rita Baldassarre.[12] The second of his books about Italy, *An Italian Education* (1996), is dedicated to his 'foreign children', and it describes the life of his family from a bilingual and cross-cultural perspective. A distinctive quality of Parks's approach to Italian and English perspectives on emotion is the way in which he offers sharp insights into cultural differences yet half-jokingly, half-seriously persists in his own cultural bias. Early in *An Italian Education* he writes of the cultural salience of the notion of '*spettacolo*' in Italian, a word his neighbor Marta uses to express her admiration for his newborn daughter Stefania:

> *Un vero spettacolo!* It's worth noting what positive connotations that word attracts in Italian.... Whereas my mother always used to say: 'Tim, for heaven's sake, don't make a spectacle of yourself!' Meaning, don't draw attention to yourself. And meaning, little children should be seen and not heard, or better still neither seen nor heard. (Parks, [1996]2000: 97)

In a similar ironic vein, Parks explains the Italian concept of '*fare festa a qualcuno*' as it makes its appearance during a typical, unannounced visit from his wife's parents, who live many miles away:

> It would truly be hard to exaggerate the cooing and crying and sighing and kissing and nose-tweaking and exclamations and tears and tickles

and cuddles that now have to take place. The children must imagine they are the only people in the whole universe. Nonna lifts up Michele and dances round and round with him and '*O che bel bambino! O che ometto splendido! O che spettacolo!*' . . .

It's what the Italians enthusiastically call *fare festa a qualcuno*, which, literally translated, means 'to make a party for someone', and combines the ideas of welcoming them and smothering them with physical affection. Comparison of this expression with the slightly disapproving 'to make a fuss of' speaks worlds about the difference between Italian and English approaches to such occasions. ([1996]2000: 142–43)

Parks notes the disapproving tone implicit in both of the English phrases 'make a spectacle of' and 'make a fuss of', contrasting them with the entirely positive connotations of '*spettacolo*' and '*fare festa*'. As he suggests, the understanding underlying a phrase like 'make a fuss of' seems to be that expressing one's love for a child by exclaiming over her would encourage her in turn to express her own feelings on impulse – a bad thing, from an English point of view. Historian of emotions Peter Stearns (1994) has shown the link between the rise of the emotion of 'embarrassment' and the perceived childishness, in early 20th-century British and American societies, of showing one's emotions openly.[13] Parks does something similar in his humorous dramatization of the meetings between his children and their *nonni*. Yet he clearly retains some of that disapproval in the face of *fare festa* and of *spettacolo*, suspecting his in-laws (and even his wife) of insincerity in their displays of feeling, and wondering how effectively his children are imbibing this *modus operandi* from their milieu:

[M]other and father, sons and daughters, all criticise each other endlessly . . . [Y]et when they meet, when the Baldassarres are actually face to face, the gestures of affection, the extravagant *fare festa* . . . could not be more voluble or enthusiastic.

My wife embraces her mother rapturously. And her father. Michele watches them. Everybody does seem perfectly . . . delighted to see each other. The *nonni* are here! *Evviva*! Yet Michele is surely aware, even at five, that we complain a great deal about these [visits], . . . about not knowing how long Nonno and Nonna are going to stay . . . [N]o doubt the children take all this in, this wonderful *spettacolo* of affection, this carefully choreographed *festa*. And perhaps somewhere deep down they are learning to associate it with the fact that they must remember to say a huge and quite extravagant thank you to Nonno when he remembers to bring them a present . . .

I have often wondered, in this regard, whether Italians can really appreciate a story like *King Lear*. Why didn't Cordelia put on a bit more of a show for her foolish old father? Surely that was wrong of her. For there are times when a little falsehood is expected of you, and can be engaged in quite sincerely, because appearance has a value in itself. . . . (Parks [1996]2000: 146–48)

Rather than saying that he can't help suspecting his in-laws of insincerity, Parks confidently characterizes them as insincere. His amusement at his Italian family's expressiveness ('everybody will laugh themselves silly, hand-clapping, back-clapping, hugging and kissing'; p. 147) – and perhaps his awareness that his own restraint marks him as an outsider – translates readily into a cynical, ethnocentric reading. At the same time, his observation that a sense of *'spettacolo'* is important in Italian culture, that the visual element is significant when expressing one's feelings – making the expression seem theatrical from an 'Anglo' point of view – seems a strikingly insightful one. His children Michele and Stefi are, as he presents it, caught up in a dramatic excitement when their *nonni* arrive, a kind of performance into which they are drawn.

Feelings Embedded in Forms of Speech: Diminutives and Terms of Endearment (*'uccellina'*, *'ptaszku'*, *'córuchny'*)

Parks portrays himself as changing, however reluctantly, under the influence of the language and culture he now lives in, 'becoming a little bit more Italian' as he takes over, or gives in to, certain key idioms ([1996]2000: 165). When his little daughter Stefi excitedly runs into a desk, rather than scolding her as he might have done once, he responds with the idiomatic cry of *'che capitombolo'* ('what a tumble that was!') before gathering her up in his arms. However, he continues to find the diminutives with which strangers accost her when she trips on a sun-shade, excessive: *"'O che capitombolo! Che povera povera piccina!* Poor little thing!"' ([1996]2000: 125). A more literal translation of this exclamation – which is distinct in tone from the pitying 'poor little thing' – would be: 'what a poor, poor tiny one!'

Parks recalls the string of diminutives with which his wife greeted their daughter's birth with affectionate amusement:

Within five minutes of its birth the child has already been smothered in diminutives, many invented: *sinfolina, ciccolina, ciccina* . . . It must be one of the areas where Italian most excels: the cooing excited caress over the tiny creature, *uccellina, tartarughina* . . . Little birdie, little turtle. Rita is ecstatic. ([1996]2000: 68)

Like *fare festa*, these diminutives are eloquently revealing of a cultural gap between English and Italian approaches to expressing feelings. To emphasize the unsentimentality of his own approach in contrast to Rita's, Parks teasingly describes his newborn daughter soon after this as having 'dark eyes and an old man's face' (p. 82). Rita is 'ecstatic' – she makes no attempt to control her feeling, and this is a source of humor for her husband (and for us as readers).

I want to introduce here some autobiographical material of my own in order to highlight an aspect of the Italian use of diminutives discussed by Parks. When I compare *uccellina* and *tartarughina* with the Polish diminutives that I grew up with and now, in turn, use with my two-year-old daughter, I am struck – for all the warmth of each – by a difference in tone. Whereas *uccellina*, *ciccina*, and the others seem to express a delight, admiration, and celebration linked with the notion of the baby as *spettacolo* for all to see, the Polish '*ptaszku*' (little bird), '*kotku*' (little cat) or '*żabko*' (little frog) stress rather the speaker's close bond to and tenderness for the child, its tininess and hence a hint of pain and fear of loss in the love one feels for it (suggested also in the almost tearful word for tenderness in Polish, '*czułość*'). Additionally, where the Italian diminutives express the beholder's response to the child – Stefi's Nonna calls out '"*Oh la ciccinina!* . . . *Oh la civetta*, the little flirt!"' (p. 443) when Stefi promises Nonno a kiss in exchange for some chips' – Polish diminutives like '*ptaszku*' are intrinsically forms of address, because they are always used in the vocative case.

Some of the terms of endearment used by my Polish grandparents in their wartime letters to one another give a sense of how embedded feelings may be in the forms of speech of a particular language. Writing to my grandmother, who had been deported to a German labor camp with their two small daughters (my aunt and my mother) during the Warsaw Uprising in 1944, my grandfather would begin his letters full of longing with: '*Marysieńko przenajumiłowańsza i córuchny!*'.[14] The most literal approximation in English – albeit a hopelessly inadequate translation – would be: 'so-most-dearly-loved little Mary and sweet-daughters-of-mine!'. The coined adjective '*przenajumiłowańsza*' adds the superlative prefix '*prze-*' (like 'arch-' in English) to the already superlative prefix '*naj*' (like 'most' in English). '*Marysieńko*' is a diminutive from '*Marysia*', the informal version of '*Maria*'; the form '*córuchny*', from '*córki*' (daughters) is far more tender than the standard diminutive '*córeczki*'.[15] My grandmother would write back, '*Tadziuleczku kochany!*' (beloved little Tadzio). '*Tadziuleczku*', a form possible only in the vocative case, is a diminutive of a diminutive – '*Tadziulku*' – based in turn on another diminutive, '*Tadzio*', from the adult name '*Tadeusz*'. From an 'Anglo' perspective, these variants seem almost baroque, yet in Polish they are rich with feeling, more of it packed in with each added syllable. The difficulty of translating such words reveals the extent to which they shape individual speakers' feelings: because the meaning encoded in a word like '*uccellina*' cannot be directly translated into English, the feeling it expresses is peculiarly dependent on, or bound up with, the word itself; hence, Parks's use of it in his account in English of his wife's response to their daughter's birth. Speakers use these words to express their feelings, but by making such words available, languages take speakers' feelings in a particular direction.

Words for Emotional Behavior: Crying, *morai-naki*

Kyoko Mori moved from Japan to the United States for her studies when she was 20 years old, and made her home there, becoming a novelist and a college professor of creative writing. Her memoir *Polite Lies: On Being a Woman Caught Between Cultures* (Mori, 1997), written some 20 years later, reflects on how the cultures she has known construe the world and the self, and how different cultural perspectives combine, alternate, and sometimes conflict, in her own psyche and experience. From the point of view of languages and emotions, Chapter 9, 'Tears', is particularly illuminating. It begins with a startling illustration of the Japanese concept of *morai-naki*, which Mori translates as 'to receive crying', and defines as 'the way a person is moved to tears by watching others cry even though he or she has no personal reason to feel sad' (1997: 181). Her brother, Jumpei, tells her how, at their father's funeral, he 'got choked up' watching secretaries from the father's firm crying: '"It was *morai-naki* for me." He tipped his head back and laughed' (1997: 181). In the context of the memoir, Jumpei's characterization of his crying as a case of *morai-naki* is not so incongruous, because Mori has already conveyed something of how troubled their relations with their father were. Mori's mother took her own life when Mori was 12 years old, and we learn that she did so against the background of her husband's infidelity, intermittent emotional cruelty, and effective abandonment of her. Mori says of her father that to Jumpei and herself he 'was a scary character from our childhood' whom they avoided by living 'as far away from him as possible' (1997: 182) – in her own case, the United States.

In discussing *morai-naki*, Mori begins with a Japanese concept of communal crying in order to emphasize, ultimately, how narrowly delimited occasions for crying are in Japanese society:

> *Morai-naki* is acceptable because community is everything. If everyone is crying at a gathering, you should, too. Certain public rituals – funerals, grave visits, other Buddhist ceremonies related to death – are set aside as occasions for everyone's tears, for mass displays of emotions, while private, individual tears [...] are considered inappropriate and embarrassing. In Japan, you can cry all you want in a group. (1997: 182–83)

Through examples ranging from the public response in Japan to the suicide of writer Yukio Mishima to anecdotes from her life in Wisconsin, Mori analyses first how pain and its expression are viewed in the two cultures, and then how she herself engages with these different cultural modes of expression. She writes that her own feelings about crying are 'a confused mixture of values and behaviors I have learned and those I rebelled against' (1997: 186).

The clarity and dispassionate tone of Mori's analysis at times seem to belie her involvement with the emotions she is describing. Characteristic of her cool narrating style is her comment that what moves her in a novel like British author Kazuo Ishiguro's (1986) *The Remains of the Day* is 'not the butler and his situation' (the predicament of the main character) 'but the words and the sentences Ishiguro had written for him – how inevitably one word followed another as the narrator was forced to confront a painful revelation' (Mori, 1997: 188). She goes on: 'I cry because the writer's performance is as beautiful and perfect as [an] athlete's' (1997: 188). A little later, she writes about sharing with her friend Kate a 'practical' nature that would never see art as 'emotional catharsis': 'we are more concerned about bug sprays' (1997: 189) (Kate's sentiment when setting up her easel outdoors). When she writes like this, Mori seems to be overcompensating; rejecting sentimental clichés about art, she ends by denying that writing, hers included, can elicit and express feelings other than purely aesthetic ones, without being merely tear-jerking. Yet the glimpses she gives of her mother's despair, and of her own response to it as a child and an adult, create images and feelings in the reader with the power to haunt, an effect she no doubt intends. Clearly, Mori wants us to feel for her mother, not merely to admire the sentences she has written about her.

Mori's aestheticization of the emotional effects of writing may be related to the shame prescribed by Japanese culture, on her account, when personal feelings are exposed. It is of a piece with her own way of dealing with painful feelings, as she portrays it:

At different times in my life, I saw therapists and found them very helpful. I agree with them that talking is the first step to understanding and overcoming the negative events in our lives. But there are just a few things I don't ever expect to understand or overcome. The panic I feel about loss, the fear I have about dying, the love I feel for people or animals who are doomed to leave me – these feelings belong in that category. With feelings like these, talking doesn't do any good. [...] All I can do, to go on, is to treat these feelings as aberrations from my otherwise smooth life – to politely and stoically ignore them in the way I was brought up to do. (Mori, 1997: 204–205)

Mori refers here to the rules about emotional expression that she assimilated as a child who lost her mother in circumstances unspeakable for the culture. She describes herself as having been 'sealed' in her 'unhappiness' after her mother's death, because family members discouraged her from speaking about what she felt, and what her mother had gone through:

> My mother's suicide singled me out as a girl without a mother. [...] I felt sealed inside my unhappiness, unable to talk about it or ask for help. I had a problem nobody could understand, in a culture where nobody was supposed to talk about personal feelings. I could see no way out of my misery. Quiet suffering was all I could choose. (Mori, 1997: 193)

Her father and paternal grandfather warned Mori not to tell others of her mother's suicide as 'the disgrace' would prevent her and her brother from finding work or marrying in the future. Her mother's relatives, from loving motives, also disallowed talk of it (1997: 185). Each ban, overt and hostile or tacit and gentle, contributed to the 'sealing' of Mori's unhappiness in silence. Her sense of this silence as damaging coexists with her professed tendency as an adult to ignore deep fear and pain 'politely and stoically' – a case of the 'mixture' of (American) values in whose name she rebelled against her upbringing, and (Japanese) values by which she was brought up (1997: 186).

For Mori, there are two particularly salient ways of responding to a crying person that are available to her in the cultural environment she finds herself in, living in the Midwest of the United States. One is to offer a hug and to try to get the person to open up further about his or her feelings – an impulse sanctioned by popular psychology, with its emphasis on the healthiness of 'working through' one's emotions (as Mori suggests when she mentions 'therapists'). The other accepted response is to make light of the situation, to use humor to lift the other's spirits. Mori notes: 'Humor is a common Midwestern antidote to sadness. I often find myself resorting to it' (1997: 186).

At the funeral of a colleague's mother, one of her friends, who had recently lost both his parents, began to cry. She describes her response:

> My friend made light of his tears, calling himself a 'big wimp'. As I sat down next to him, I didn't lean over and hug him or encourage him to talk. I made some wisecrack about how churches should be equipped with boxes of Kleenex tucked between the hymnals and missals. [...] A note of cheerfulness is valued in the Midwest, just as quiet dignity is valued in Japan. (1997: 186)

It is hard not to read Mori's stated preference for the practice of cheering people up through humor and her discomfort with a response that encourages further tears and talking about the painful feelings as continuous, albeit in a translated way, with her childhood experience of being discouraged from speaking about her unhappiness. Her memoir raises the questions: What does the development of an emotional style owe to the cultural shapings one undergoes as a child? How far is such a style consciously chosen? And how dependent is it on the social context one is in?

The complexity of these questions is brought out when Mori writes that the habit of urging a crying person to say more about what they feel has, despite her general resistance to it, nevertheless ingrained itself at some level. When visiting Japan, she cannot stop herself from crying when she meets for the last time with a beloved aunt who is dying of cancer. Her relatives look away, not wanting to 'embarrass' her (1997: 196). Mori writes:

> Having adopted American ways, I can't always refrain from crying if I am with people I know well and trust. For a Japanese person to cry in a private situation, even in front of family, would indicate a suffering so great as to defy politeness, self-control, perseverance, and everything she has been taught. My relatives see my tears and conclude that I must be suffering from unspeakable hurt. (1997: 195)

While knowing that her relatives avert their eyes out of 'concern, respect, and love' for her, she finds herself wishing that, like her friends in Wisconsin, they would 'hug me and tell me everything would be OK – a meaningless thing to say, really', and 'tell me it was all right to cry' (1997: 197). Back in Wisconsin, on learning that a baby nighthawk she has been caring for will have to be put down, Mori is unable to refrain from crying in public, in front of some other volunteer bird rehabilitators. One of the volunteers, a stranger, offers Mori her phone number if she would like to talk about the loss of the bird. Mori comments: 'After wishing that my Japanese relatives would give me a hug and acknowledge my tears, I was wishing that this woman had left me alone and saved my dignity. I was completely inconsistent, but I didn't care' (1997: 203). Her reflections on crying and her reactions to people's responses in the different settings imply that emotional styles develop through habit and cultural osmosis, rather than through conscious choice; what is conscious is the self's observation and subsequent 'reading' of its emotional behavior.

The contrast drawn in *Polite Lies* between Japanese and American approaches to emotional expression compares interestingly with Eva Hoffman's comments on the concept of 'cheerfulness' in (American) English and the exaltation of sorrow she recalls in her Polish education (see the section on '"anxious" versus "*boję się*"'). Whereas Hoffman questions the creed of 'control' and 'insist[ence] on cheerfulness' that prevail among her New York peers, aligning herself more closely with her Polish Jewish mother's view of painful feelings as natural and beyond control, Mori appears to have embraced the value of cheerfulness, to have incorporated that cultural idiom over the alternative, therapeutic view of crying also available to her, while continuing to live out aspects of the emotional style she learned as a child in Japan.

Non-verbal Expression of Feeling and Cultural Attitudes to Emotion

As Mori's contrast between her Japanese relatives' and American friends' reactions to her tears demonstrates, culture impinges on language in more ways than those captured by the verbal. Arguably, non-verbal means of expression are part of a language as surely as lexicon or syntax, and insofar as someone's culture prompts them not to speak about something, the silence on that topic can itself be seen as part of the language. Veronica Zhengdao Ye's essay 'La Double Vie de Veronica: reflections on my life as a Chinese migrant in Australia' (2003)[16] shows how important certain silences remain for her, in her life between Chinese (Mandarin as well as Shanghainese) and English. Ye writes that the use of endearments and affectionate gestures in public would make her 'extremely uncomfortable'. Whereas some of her attitudes towards aspects of public interaction, like politeness, have gradually changed under pressure of Australian practice, she continues to avoid overt expression of her feelings:

> I remain fundamentally Chinese deep inside. My sense of *self* is Chinese. And I feel most at home when I can express myself, especially my feelings and emotions, in the Chinese way – subtle, implicit and without words.
>
> I smile to smooth over embarrassing situations. I wear big smiles even when my heart is crying and bleeding. Feelings are my self, and should only be known to me. I do not feel comfortable talking about my feelings, as doing so, my inner self feels stripped and vulnerable. (Ye, 2003)

Ye does not suggest, however, that the feelings that she equates with her 'inner self' are to be kept hidden from all other people. She portrays them not as private, but as vulnerable, to be shared without words, and only with '*zijiren*', a term she translates, tellingly, as 'oneself person; insiders'. If *zijiren* are 'oneself' people, not sharply distinguished from oneself, then one's feelings will not be so hard for them to read.

Ye clearly counts her parents and her husband among her *zijiren*. Whereas she regularly hears Australians saying 'I love you' on the phone or when parting, she and her parents have never said this to one another. She recalls leaving them for the first time to go to

Australia – ten thousand miles away – to live with her Australian husband:[17]

> [A]t the airport, we fought back our tears and urged each other repeatedly to take care; we wore the biggest smiles to wave good-bye to each other, to soothe each others' worries. Just like any other Chinese parting between those who love each other – there were no hugs and no 'I love you'. Yet I have never doubted my parents' profound love for me.

The cultural meaning of smiling instead of letting oneself cry is clearly not only to shield one's own feelings from scrutiny but also, and perhaps more so, to protect the feelings of others.

Ye remarks that it has taken some years for her to learn to be 'more communicative' in expressing her love and affection for her husband. She continues to believe that, fundamentally, love is expressed through acts of concern, such as 'forcing' her husband to eat (although she is aware that this would seem funny to many Australians, and restrains herself in public). With her mother, visiting her in Australia, she feels a 'bond that is beyond words'. She writes movingly of their walks together from the bus stop each day:

> I see her emerging from behind a bush, walking towards me across the street, and trying to take my bag, which is often heavily loaded with books. We walk side by side in silence toward the house. . . . I always wish that the road leading to the house would be longer so that I could prolong the moment, and the eternity contained therein. The picture of her face emerging from the hill is deeply etched in my memory. I know, emotionally, that I will remain Chinese in Australia.

It is important to acknowledge that Ye's is one voice, among the voices of other Chinese women, like those who speak on the pages of Xinran's book *The Good Women of China* (2002) – many of whom express unhappiness with the Confucian and Mencian-inspired injunctions against physical and verbal expressions of feeling. For Ye, 'honeyed words' such as 'I love you' still seem to be mere 'lubricants' in a relationship. This is her experience of what she finds in the new culture, an aspect of it that she baulks at making her own. Another immigrant might remain less faithful to the 'social reality' shaped by their upbringing. Ye writes that she has taken deeply to heart the traditional value of *jin xiaoxin* ('fulfil[ling] my filial duties and obligations'), and continues to feel guilt for having 'deprived' her parents of 'the *tianlunzhile* ("the happiness derived from natural bonds", "family happiness") of being with their only child'. Yet, she also writes, poignantly, of the decision she took, during the flight to China on her way to her father's funeral, to hug her mother when she arrived:

> All I could see in front of me was my father's silhouette enveloped in the mist of an early winter morning when the taxi taking me to the airport backed out of the driveway nearly two years before. I regretted deeply that I never hugged him. I decided that I would give my mother a big, long hug when I saw her, to abridge the physical separation. So I did when I saw her, a long and tight embrace; the first hug I have given to either of my parents.

Her words partly echo, after all, the very different experience of author Xinran, who writes that all her life she has 'longed to be held' by her mother: 'My mother . . . never once hugged or kissed me when I was a child; when I became an adult, any such display of affection between us was prevented by traditional Chinese reserve' (Xinran, 2002: 119).

Ye's comment that 'the Chinese way' to convey feelings is 'subtle, implicit and without words' highlights the issue of how the expression of feelings is viewed in different cultures: whether expressing one's feelings at all is considered a good thing, or not, and if so, then in what situations and in what ways. The translingual memoirs discussed here suggest that cultures can vary not only in the specific emotions they encourage, but also, and widely, in their attempts to regulate emotional behavior. As we have seen, in *An Italian Education*, British cultural norms emerge as cultivating a suspicion of open expression of feeling, judging it self-indulgent and intrusive. It sometimes appears as though emotions, in all their chaotic range, were a more accepted part of the fabric of Italian society, with Parks's own English-speaking culture broadly discouraging their expression. To conclude this so baldly, though, would be to ignore the distinctive emotional style of the book bound up with the concept of 'affection', perhaps particularly salient in British English. Parks's in-laws sometimes accuse him of '*la tipica freddezza anglo-sassone*' (Parks, 2002a: 444) ('typical Anglo-Saxon coldness'), but the tone that prevails in his book is one of affection, in which there is always a strong note of humor. Warm feelings are entirely acceptable – provided they are voiced tongue-in-cheek.

Skrzynecki's evocation of the feeling of '*żal*', his intuition of its absence in English and his impatience with Australian dismissals of it as 'sentimental' similarly point to a discomfort in Anglo-Australian culture with expressions of emotional intensity, and conversely to the perceived normalness of strong feelings in Polish culture. Hoffman's and Mori's different 'takes' on the American idiom of 'cheerfulness', one critical and the other appreciative, are also revealing of different cultural attitudes to the expression of painful feelings.

Conclusion

Hoffman, Skrzynecki, Parks, Mori, and Ye offer insights not only into the experience of bilingual immigrants but also more broadly into the relationship between language and emotions. Their narratives suggest that emotional vocabulary – expressive forms, emotion concepts, terms for emotional behavior – give a certain distinctive shape to a speaker's feeling. In particular, the emotion concepts that are available to us contribute to how we interpret what we feel, how we experience it, even how we act on it. The perspective of bilinguals like these suggests that the problem of which comes first, the person's feeling or the emotional freight of the word, might be, if not a chicken and egg proposition, practically irresolvable.

Equally, these authors' writings highlight the diversity of cultural approaches to emotional behavior, an area in which, as Ye's essay demonstrates, the non-verbal communication of feeling is as salient as emotion concepts, idioms, or expressive forms like diminutives. The experience of migrating into a new language often prompts the recognition that feelings that were previously felt to be purely personal are at least partly dependent on cultural forms. At the same time it may confront the bilingual with a struggle to choose between different ways of feeling and differing cultural norms of expression, and thus with the possibility of going beyond a particular emotional world.

Rather than imposing a set of questions formulated in advance, outside of the texts, research into the emotional dimension of bilingual life narratives necessarily engages with themes and questions arising from the narratives themselves. By their very nature, each of these texts reflects on aspects of emotional experience differently. It is difficult, then, to predict what kinds of questions in the field of language and emotions will be raised by other such narratives in the future. One area that could be fruitfully explored in more depth, however, is the kind of emotional styles that 'translinguals' are able to articulate in *writing* in their different languages. What is certain is that life writings of bilinguals offer a unique and important perspective on the relationship between language and emotions – one grounded in personal experience, and hence one that matters deeply to those raising the questions.

Notes

1. This chapter is a substantially revised version of an article published in the *Journal of Multilingual and Multicultural Development* (Besemeres, 2004a). See Literature Review for reference to the new material in this chapter and the discussions in the article that are not included here.
2. In linguistics, Pavlenko's own work, and that of Anna Wierzbicka, constitute two exceptions to the tendency to overlook bilingual life writing in researching language and emotion.

3. See Besemeres (2002: 9–35) for an account of the relationship between language, culture, and self that is neither deterministic nor positivistic, but sees the three as interconnected in complex ways. This account broadly underpins the approach to the nexus between language, culture, and emotions throughout this chapter.
4. Cf. Besemeres (2002: 10–11).
5. Maxine Hong Kingston's (1976) *The Woman Warrior* and Richard Rodriguez's (1982) *Hunger of Memory*.
6. See Besemeres (2004b) for a discussion of cross-cultural communication in Hoffman's narrative.
7. Hoffman, her younger sister, and her parents emigrated from Poland to Canada in 1959, three years after the Communist régime raised the ban on the migration of Jews. Her parents were survivors of the Holocaust. Hoffman completed her education in the United States and later worked as an editor for *The New York Times*.
8. Skrzynecki does not quote any Ukrainian words used by his mother, but recalls the longing she sometimes expressed for the land of her childhood, inaccessible to his imagination as a small boy in Australia (2004: 43–45).
9. Skrzynecki's father, Feliks, died in 1994, his mother in 1997.
10. No Polish word similar to 'longing' is listed among the several meanings of *żal* adduced in Doroszewski's *Polish Dictionary*.
11. It should be noted that Skrzynecki has won many awards for his writing. The power of the voice he gives to European immigrants in poems like those included in *Immigrant Chronicle* has in fact been recognized by Australian audiences, although this does not invalidate his point that emotions like *żal* are often read as sentimental by Anglo-Australians.
12. In his most recent book on Italy, *A Season with Verona*, Parks mentions that he was 25 when he first came to Verona, earning a living as a private English teacher (2002a: 104). In *Italian Neighbours* (Parks, 1992/2001: 123), he writes of having been appointed as a lecturer after several years of freelance translating. He lectures at IULM University, Milan (*The New York Review of Books*, 25 April 2002b: 3).
13. See Stearns (1994: 147).
14. *Listy rodzinne Marii i Tadeusza Smoleńskich z lat 1944–46 (po powstaniu warszawskim)*. Unpublished collection of letters, transcribed by Marta Bichniewicz.
15. The suffix '*uchna*' occurs with only four nouns (other than proper names): *córuchna*, *matuchna* (from *matka*, mother), *babuchna* (from *babcia*, grandmother), *ciotuchna* (from *ciocia*, aunt). Presumably they are based on the model of adjectives like *mięciuchny* (soft little), *miluchny* (dear little), *maluchny* (small little), *bieluchny* (white little), which all suggest something delicate and lovable. These are the only adjectives with this suffix listed in Doroszewski's (1959–1968) *Słownik języka polskiego*.
16. Ye's essay appeared in *Mots Pluriels No. 23* (http://www.arts.uwa.edu.au/motspluriels/MP2303vzy.html). All references are to this web page.
17. Ye migrated to Australia to join her Australian husband Tim in 1997, at the age of 23.

References

Baranczak, S. (1989) *The Weight of the Body: Selected Poems*. Evanston, IL: TriQuarterly Books.

Besemeres, M. (1998) Language and self in cross-cultural autobiography: Eva Hoffman's *Lost in Translation. Canadian Slavonic Papers* 40(3–4), 327–44.

Besemeres, M. (2002) *Translating One's Self: Language and Selfhood in Cross-Cultural Autobiography.* Oxford: Peter Lang.

Besemeres, M. (2004a) Different languages, different emotions? Perspectives from autobiographical literature. *Journal of Multilingual and Multicultural Development* 25(2–3), 140–58.

Besemeres, M. (2004b) Lost in translations? Eva Hoffman and Tim Parks. In P. Wagstaff (ed.) *Border Crossings: Mapping Identities in Modern Europe* (pp. 125–43). Oxford: Peter Lang.

Bichniewicz, M. (n.d.) (transcribed). *Listy rodzinne Marii i Tadeusza Smolenskich z lat 1944–46 (po powstaniu warszawskim)* (Family letters of Maria and Tadeusz Smolenscy from 1944–1946, after the Warsaw Uprising). Unpublished correspondence.

Bühler, K. (1934/1990) *Theory of Language: The Representational Function of Language.* Amsterdam: John Benjamins.

Cheung, K.-K. (1993) *Articulate Silences: Hisaye Yamamoto, Maxine Hong Kingston, Joy Kogawa.* Ithaca, NY: Cornell University Press.

Donald, M. (2001) *A Mind So Rare: The Evolution of Human Consciousness.* New York: W.W. Norton & Co.

Doroszewski, W. (ed.) (1958–1969) *Słownik języka polskiego* (11 vols). Warsaw: PWN.

Haiman, J. (1989) Alienation in grammar. *Studies in Language* 13, 129–70.

Hoffman, E. (1989) *Lost in Translation: A Life in a New Language.* London: Vintage.

Ishiguro, K. (1986) *An Artist of the Floating World.* London: Faber.

Kaplan, A. (1993) *French Lessons: A Memoir.* Chicago: The University of Chicago Press.

Kaplan, A. (1994) On language memoir. In A. Bammer (ed.) *Displacements: Cultural Identities in Question* (pp. 59–70). Bloomington: Indiana University Press.

Kazin, A. (1951) *A Walker in the City.* New York: Harvest/Harcourt.

Kinginger, C. (2004) Bilingualism and emotion in the autobiographical works of Nancy Huston. *Journal of Multilingual and Multicultural Development* 25(2–3), 159–78.

Kingston, M. (1976) *The Woman Warrior: Memoir of a Girlhood Among Ghosts.* New York: Vintage Books.

Kitayama, Sh. and Markus, H. (1994) *Emotion and Culture: Empirical Studies of Mutual Influence.* Washington, DC: American Psychological Association.

Kotchemidova, Ch. (2000) Looking for the God of language. In K. Ogulnick (ed.) *Language Crossings: Negotiating the Self in a Multicultural World* (pp. 127–30). New York: Teachers College Press, Columbia University.

Lutz, C. (1988) *Unnatural Emotions: Everyday Sentiments on a Micronesian Atoll and Their Challenge to Western Theory.* Chicago: Chicago University Press.

Mori, K. (1997) *Polite Lies: On Being a Woman Caught Between Cultures.* New York: Henry Holt.

Ng, L. (1994) *Silver Sister.* Port Melbourne, Victoria: Mandarin Australia.

Parks, T. (1992/2001) *Italian Neighbours.* London: Vintage.

Parks, T. (1996/2000) *An Italian Education.* London: Vintage.

Parks, T. (2002a) *A Season with Verona.* London: Vintage.

Parks, T. (2002b) Biographical note. *The New York Review of Books*, 25 April, 3.

Pavlenko, A. (2001a) 'How am I to become a woman in an American vein?': Transformations of gender performance in second language learning. In A. Pavlenko, A. Blackledge, I. Piller and M. Teutsch-Dwyer (eds) *Multilingualism, Second Language Learning and Gender* (pp. 133–74). Berlin: Mouton de Gruyter.

Pavlenko, A. (2001b) 'In the world of the tradition, I was unimagined': Negotiation of identities in cross-cultural autobiographies. *The International Journal of Bilingualism* 5(3), 317–44.

Pavlenko, A. (2001c) Language learning memoirs as a gendered genre. *Applied Linguistics* 22, 213–40.

Ricci, N. (1990) *The Book of Saints*. New York: Picador.

Riemer, A. (1992) *Inside Outside*. Pymble, NSW: Angus & Robertson.

Riemer, A. (1993) *The Habsburg Café*. Pymble, NSW: Angus & Robertson.

Rodriguez, R. (1982) *Hunger of Memory: The Education of Richard Rodriguez*. New York: Bantam.

Skrzynecki, P. (2004) *The Sparrow Garden*. St Lucia, Queensland: University of Queensland Press.

Stearns, P. (1994) *American Cool: Constructing a Twentieth-Century Emotional Style*. New York: New York University Press.

Wierzbicka, A. (1999) *Emotions Across Languages and Cultures: Diversity and Universals*. Cambridge: Cambridge University Press.

Xinran (2002) *The Good Women of China*. London: Vintage.

Ye, Veronica Zhengdao (2003) La Double Vie de Veronica: Reflections on my life as a Chinese migrant in Australia. *Mots Pluriels* No. 23. On WWW at http://www.arts.uwa.edu.au/motspluriels/MP2303vzy.html.

Chapter 3

A Passion for English: Desire and the Language Market

INGRID PILLER and KIMIE TAKAHASHI[1]

Introduction

In this chapter we explore the discursive construction of the desire to learn another language, specifically Japanese women's desire to learn English. We aim to make a sociolinguistic contribution to the literature on motivation and language learning, which all too often continues to consider 'motivation' as a trait learners have (or do not have). However, motivation, or the 'desire to learn', as we see it, is a complex multifaceted construction that is both internal and external to language learners, and is not linked to success in a straightforward fashion – as we will show in this chapter, the link may even be negative. In our ethnographic study of five highly motivated Japanese learners of English-as-a-second-language (ESL) in Sydney, Australia, we try to provide a detailed description of (1) what it means to 'desire English', (2) how that desire for English is situated within wider discourses about Japanese women on the one hand, and English on the other, and (3) how that desire for English was played out in the lives of the participants – particularly their emotional lives and their love lives – during their overseas experience in Sydney.

The chapter is organised as follows: in the next section we introduce our theoretical framework, which views desire as dialectically constituted in the relationship between the macro-domains of public discourses and the micro-domains of individual experience. We will then introduce our participants in the methodology section, before presenting a brief review of the construction of *akogare* [desire] in Japanese media discourses, particularly promotional materials for English-language schools and overseas study programs. Then we will move on to describe how five young Japanese women living in Sydney, Australia, position themselves vis-à-vis the *akogare* discourse, and how their romantic and sexual choices inflect their language-learning opportunities and vice versa.

Theoretical Framework

In our understanding of 'desire' we follow Cameron and Kulick's (2003a,b) call to move the study of language and desire beyond theories of 'inner states' to investigations of the ways in which a variety of desires are discursively accomplished. If desire is discursively accomplished, it is obviously context-specific, and in this paper we focus on the *akogare* or 'desire' that Japanese women sometimes feel for the West and Western men. Japanese women's desire for the West and Western masculinity is 'common-sense knowledge' in Japan, and has been widely discussed in sociology, anthropology, and in popular media (e.g. Dower, 1999; Igata, 1993; Kelsky, 1999, 2001; Kimura & Yamana, 1999; Ma, 1996; Miyazaki, 1997). The 1980s and 1990s, in particular, saw a significant level of public anxiety about Japanese women's occidental longings and their sexual explorations with *gaijin* [foreigner] men, both domestically and internationally (Toyoda, 1994). Japanese women who actively sought the company of *gaijin* men, in locations such as Yokosuka, Hawaii, and New York, were given the notorious nickname of 'yellow cabs', suggesting that they were as (sexually) available as taxis. While the 'yellow cab' discourse has somewhat faded, other discourses of *akogare* for the West and Western men remain.

However, researchers in English Language Learning (ELL) and English Language Teaching (ELT), or second language acquisition (SLA) more generally, have paid scant attention to Japanese women's romanticization and eroticization of the West. Conversely, ELL has, if at all, only been treated as a marginal aspect of sociological and anthropological investigations of the occidental longings of Japanese women. By contrast, we will argue in the following that *akogare* for three discursive spaces – the West, Western men, and ELL – inextricably links these. By doing so, we also hope to make a contribution to the understanding of the continued spread of English.

Critical linguists have produced incisive analyses of the macrosocietal power relationships within which the spread of English-as-an-international-language (EIL) occurs (e.g. Pennycook, 1998, 2001; Phillipson, 1992; or, specifically with reference to Japan, Kubota, 1998, 2002; Tsuda, 1990, 1993). However, while we have a good understanding why and how English is promoted, that is, 'the supply side', there is still a lack of analysis of 'the demand side' of ELT as Robert Phillipson, one of the foremost scholars in the field, admitted in a recent interview (Karmani, 2003). In other words, analyses of why and how people around the world desire to learn English are largely lacking to date (but see, e.g. Bailey, 2003; Piller, 2002, in press; regarding the desire to learn languages other than English see, e.g. Kinginger, 2004; Piller, 2001).

This is a serious omission if we follow Foucault (1977, 1980) in assuming that the mechanisms of power operate at every level of social life, including the level of individual life. The workings of power include the inculcation of desires that lead individuals to modify their own bodies and personalities. This means that individuals' desires may work against themselves, or, as Lukes (1974: 34) puts it, individuals' 'wants may themselves be a product of a system which works against their interests'. Thus, we see our paper as a contribution to critical linguistic approaches to ELT and EIL. As such, it goes significantly beyond earlier work by Piller (2002), where the term 'language desire' was coined to describe the attraction for speakers of English, and, in a few cases, German, that the participants in her study on bilingual couples reported. In that work, the term 'language desire' was used descriptively and no link between 'desire' and 'power' was made. An analysis of the interplay between power and desire in the data reported in Piller (2002) has been undertaken in Piller (in press).

Given our assumption that power and desire must be conceptualized jointly, structures of desire must be constitutive of the ways in which desire is enacted in the micro-domain. Such an understanding of the relationship between language and desire is similar to the Bakhtinian (1981, 1986) concept of heteroglossia. Bakhtin and his collaborators use the concept of heteroglossia to model the interrelationship between the macro-level of ideologies and the micro-level of conversation. For them, language use in the micro-domain cannot be understood without reference to larger discourses. In this view, individuals' desires and expressions thereof are structured by the discourses of desire, the values, beliefs, and practices circulating in a given social context. Therefore, and in keeping with our view that desire is constituted in public and private discourses, this research combines a discourse-analytic approach to public data with a critical ethnography of private data (see also Piller, 2002).

Methodology

Both micro-domain and macro-domain data were gathered between 2001 and 2004 from a variety of sources, as part of an ongoing ethnographic project.[2] The micro-domain data were collected from five main participants – Japanese women living in Sydney: Ichi (21 years old at the time of joining the study), Yoko (29 years old), Yuka (22 years old), Eika (30 years old), and Chizu (39 years old). These are pseudonyms and the participants are listed in the order in which they joined the study. These participants were approached by Takahashi through their then educational provider (Ichi), her social networks in Sydney's Japanese community (Yoko, Yuka, and Chizu), or her personal connection from Japan (Eika). We will now briefly introduce each woman.

At the age of 20, Ichi arrived in Sydney in 2000 for her tertiary education. She chose to study in Australia because she had a positive image of Australia through her handsome Australian high-school teacher of English, and had previously visited Australia for a month during her high-school years. After a year in an English language intensive course for overseas students (ELICOS) program, she became an arts student with a sociology major. Her university education was to be funded by her parents until graduation in early 2005. She lives in a university dormitory and has gone back to Japan for visits on a yearly basis. After graduation, she plans to go to the United States, to join her American boyfriend, with whom she has an online relationship.

Yoko arrived in Sydney in 2002 at the age of 29. She had recently been divorced from her Japanese husband and felt that she wanted to change her life, and finally act on her life-long desire for the West. In Sydney, she initially attended a language school and then pursued a hospitality degree. Throughout her stay she had to support herself financially, and worked in various roles in the hospitality industry. In late 2004 she had to leave Sydney for visa reasons and, at the time of writing (12/2004) is back in Japan to pursue a visa to a French Polynesian island where she has been offered a job in the tourism sector.

Yuka was a *hikikomori* [a recluse who avoids interacting with others] in her junior high school years and came to Australia in 1996 at the age of 17 to start a new life. She completed high school in Sydney and then enrolled in an arts degree with a combined major in gender studies and Chinese and was due to graduate in early 2005. Throughout her time in Australia she has been financially supported by her family in Japan. For visa reasons she will have to leave Australia after graduation. As she does not want to return to Japan and has become increasingly invested in learning Chinese, she is currently pursuing job opportunities in China.

Eika was a successful career woman in Japan and arrived in Australia in 2003 on a working-holiday visa just before she turned 30. The timing of her overseas stay was dictated by visa restrictions, which limit working-holiday visas to under-30-year-olds. Eika had previously spent time in the United States and the purpose of her stay was to reacquaint herself with the English language and to consider her future. Eika's stay was possible because of the savings she had accumulated during her career. None of her pursuits in Sydney, including an English language course and a human resources degree, proved satisfactory, and she left Australia in late 2004 for a round-the-world trip, which has since taken her to the United States.

Chizu arrived in Australia in 1999 at the age of 36. Since her early childhood in a remote rural area, she had a strong *akogare* for English and the West. In Japan she had an Australian boyfriend and their break-up led to her decision to come to Australia for three months. Since then, she has studied at various institutions in Sydney including, most recently, a diploma course on natural therapy. Chizu has lived with a Japanese family most of her time in Australia and has become a key family member. She has no intention of returning to Japan on a permanent basis and has been exploring different visa options for staying in Sydney other than as a permanent student, with little success.

All participants arrived in Sydney with the express purpose of improving their English, and all of them started out as ESL students. Although that changed over the duration of their stay and they became involved in other forms of education, they maintained that their main purpose of living and studying in Sydney was to improve their English and their tertiary courses were seen as a chance to practice English, particularly to master academic English.

Data are also drawn from secondary participants; these included individuals both in Australia and Japan. The largest group of secondary participants is similar to the primary participants in that they, too, are Japanese women aged between 20 and 40 years, who are either studying at an English-language school (either in Japan or overseas), or studying in Australia, at institutions such as private colleges, Technical and Further Education (TAFE) colleges, or at university. Some have entered Australia on a working-holiday visa, which permits holders to remain in Australia for up to one year and pursue part-time work during that period. Only people below 30 years of age from a selected group of countries (mostly developed nations such as Germany, Japan, United States) are eligible for a working-holiday visa.

The micro-domain data comprised more than 40 formal and informal interviews, field-notes from direct observations of their daily social interaction with others, and records of telephone conversations, e-mails, and MSN messenger exchanges. Having a similar background (a single Japanese woman in her thirties living overseas) enabled Takahashi to establish rapport with the participants and allowed relatively easy access to their communities of friends and partners, their private spaces and narratives. From these data, we focused on the participants' personal accounts of their attempts to learn and use English across various contexts; for example, what was their goal or ideal method in ELL? With whom did they want to socialize and why and how were they doing so?

The macro-domain data consisted of discourses of *akogare* for the West and for Western sexual and romantic partners, and of ELT and ELL, circulating in Japanese media during the period of data collection (2001–2004). The media in question are mainly magazines, particularly women's magazines and ELL magazines, ELT and ELL websites, and advertisements and other promotional materials for English-language schools. All the participants were familiar with these discourses.

For this chapter, we identified two types of references from these data: (1) *akogare* references and narratives; and (2) comments about ELL, including learning strategies, opportunities to practice and use English, and social interactions in English. These references were analyzed thematically to model the relationship between desire(s), power, and ELL.

The Glamour of ELL and *ryugaku* 'Studying Overseas'

'Dare datte nanimono ka ni nareru' [you can become who you want to be] (*Yappari Kaigaie Ikoo*, December 2000); *'isshuukan no jibun hakken ryugaku* in Australia' [one week *ryugaku* to find yourself in Australia] (*Natsu no Ryugaku*, Summer 2003); *'naze nyuuyooku wa yume ni kikuno ka? Naritai jibun ni naru tame no ryugaku'* [why is New York good for dreams? *ryugaku* that enables me to become who I want to be] (*Ryugaku Journal*, May 2003) blare the headlines. Another one says *'kaigai seikatsu de mitsukeru atarashii jibun: ryugaku de jinsei wo kaeyoo* in Australia' [Finding a new self overseas: Change your life through *ryugaku* in Australia] (*Ryugaku Journal* May 2002); and the slogan of *Wish* (2002, no. 8), one of the major *ryugaku* magazines [note the title], reads *'oosutoraria & nyuujiirando: atarashi ikikata hajimeyoo'* [Australia and New Zealand: Let's start a new life]. As in these examples, women's magazines and other media texts, routinely connect ELL and *ryugaku* with *ikikata* [life-style]. English is portrayed as a glamorous means of reinventing and empowering one's womanhood, as a woman's indispensable weapon to cope in chauvinistic Japan (see also Bailey, 2003; Kelsky, 2001).

Indeed, English-related topics are an indispensable feature of Japanese women's magazines, and as many as 80% of Japanese women in their twenties profess an interest in learning English (*'Baggu ya akusesarii to issho kana? eigo bijin'* [The same as bags and accessories? English beauty], *Asahi Evening*, 23 February 2004: 5). This focus piece on ELL in Japanese women's media published in *Asahi*, one of the major broadsheets in Japan, also cites Kimura, a media development manager with ALC, a leading language-study publishing house based in Tokyo, as saying that a special feature on an English-related topic often leads to an increase in sales. ALC is trying to capitalize even further on this demand with its recent introduction of a glossy English-study magazine for women (see Figure 3.1).

English Language Learning and *ryugaku* features serve to define the meaning of ELL for Japanese women by stating and disseminating what is proper, successful, and desirable. Desirable characteristics of the successful English teacher are consistently presented in terms of gender, race, and looks. Figure 3.1, for instance, shows an excerpt from a portrait feature about English teachers from four major private English-language schools (*eikaiwa*) in Japan. All of the teachers photographed are good-looking (as marked by their suits and 'clean' smiles) white men, presumably native speakers of English. The accompanying text claims that female students' English will improve faster with teachers such as these because the female student will be anxious to see her good-looking, white, male teacher again soon. The social relationship expressed between the teachers in the photographs and their viewers is close personal, that is, head and shoulders (Kress & van Leeuwen, 1996), in all cases. This focus on the personal relationship with the teacher is reinforced in the texts, which provide ample information about the teachers' personal lives, rather than, say, their educational backgrounds or teaching careers. Indeed, the texts resemble personal ads for a romantic partner much more than professional bio statements. Kevin Black of the GABA English conversation school, for instance, is introduced as follows:

> Teacher Kevin Black. Kevin frequently visits Hakone because he loves Japanese history and hot springs. 'My policy is to change my teaching method depending on my students. I try to get rid of their fear of using English'. He likes going to karaoke, and what's more, he likes singing Japanese pop songs like those of *Chemistry* [*Chemistry* is a popular male duo and their fans are mainly women in their teens and twenties; http://www.chemistryclub.net/pc/top.jsp, last accessed on 16 April 2004]. It's a real surprise.

The portrayal of these English teachers constructs and reinforces the myth of White men as lady-first gentlemen that is prevalent in Japanese women's magazines (Russell, 1998). White men are often associated

Figure 3.1 Images of English teachers in Japan (*Source*: *an-an*, 19 July 2002: 37)

with sophistication, sensitivity, and refinement. They are portrayed as handsome, often with blond hair and blue eyes, well-educated, well-dressed, understated and kind, not so different from the ways in which Hollywood stars and Western musicians are represented in the same media.

The romantic and sexual innuendo, expressed in the statement that women will learn English faster with teachers such as these because they will be keen to return to the teacher, is pervasive in media discourses (see also Ma, 1996). A recently launched English-study magazine for women, published by *ALC*, for instance, is entitled *Virgin English*. It is the unique selling proposition of *Virgin English* that women can beautify themselves through English. Their philosophy is expressed by the marketing manager as follows: *'eigo to iu tsuuru ga minitsuku to naimen ni jishin ga waku. Sorega "utsukushisa" to naru'* [When she acquires English as a tool, she becomes more confident inside. That creates 'beauty'] (*Asahi Evening*, 23 February 2004: 5). Furthermore, success in ELL is consistently linked with relationships with Western men. For instance, one section of the magazine offers several linguistic strategies for developing relationships with *ikemen gaijin* [good-looking, desirable foreigners] and for rejecting *damenzu gaijin* [bad, ugly foreigners] (*Virgin English*, March 2004: 48–51).

Virgin English also features ways to 'learn love and sex through [Hollywood] movies'. Learners are advised to memorise romantic and provocative phrases such as 'I will have poetry in my life, and adventure, and love. Love above all' (Gwyneth Paltrow in *Shakespeare in Love*, 1998), 'You know what's going to happen? I'm gonna fall in love with you. Because I always, always do' (Marilyn Monroe in *The Prince and the Showgirl*, 1957), 'Oh, yeah, right there' (Meg Ryan in *When Harry Met Sally*, 1989), 'To hell with Brett, you know? I've got a vibrator' (Cameron Diaz in *There Is Something About Mary*, 1998), or 'We had a great weekend, Leo. And that's that. Now, it's Sunday. And it's over.' (Meg Ryan in *Kate and Leopold*, 2001). These are printed in pink, presented as effective and sexy, and each phrase is recommended differently depending on the outcome desired. Desired outcomes include seduction as in the Marilyn Monroe phrase, which is described as irresistible because of the force of 'gonna'. Other learning objectives are the ability to talk sexy, and the ability to end a relationship without causing bad blood (*Virgin English*, March 2004: 52–57). Indeed, Hollywood movies have widely become new ELL 'textbooks', teaching not only English, but also providing guidance in matters of love and sex. It is the implication of Hollywood movies in the girlhood and adolescence dreams of the participants to which we will turn in the next section.

In sum, women's magazines consistently make a link between learning English and changing one's life, including in matters of romance and sex.

Indeed, all the primary participants found *ryugaku* articles in women's magazines such as *an-an* and *Cosmopolitan* inspirational for learning English and going overseas. Yoko, for instance, says:

Yoko: nihon de yoku koo iu zassi karite ta n desu yo ne [pointing at Japanese women's magazines in my office]. yoku sono ki ni natte masita yo. kekkoo soo iu zyosei zassi de ryugaku toka eigo no seikoo zyutu tokatte yonde te atasi mo dekiru n zya nai katte omottari site masita mon. tatoeba *an-an* tokatte yoku eigo no yatte ru zya nai desu ka? kosumoporitan toka kinzyo no tosyokan kara karite mite masita mon @@

Yoko: in Japan, I used to read magazines like those [pointing at Japanese women's magazines in KT's office]. they often inspired me. I used to read these articles on *ryugaku* for women and strategies for successful English study, and I used to think, 'I can do this, too!' 'an-an', for example, often features English related topics, don't they? in Japan, I used to borrow Cosmopolitan magazines from the local library @@ (f14may03yoko)[3]

Dreaming of Tom Cruise and Brad Pitt

All the primary participants and most of the secondary participants report a fascination with Hollywood stars and Western musicians during their girlhood and adolescence. Whereas this seems to have been a general admiration for the West in their childhood, it became rapidly gendered and romanticized as they entered adolescence. For instance, Eika had a romantic obsession with Tom Cruise, particularly as the star of *Top Gun* (1985), in her secondary school years. Chizu fell in love with Christopher Atkins from the *Blue Lagoons* (1980), and Yoko has been obsessed with Brad Pitt for a number of years. Whereas the specific object of their *akogare* (i.e. a specific star) differs, all these movie stars and musicians are white Western men, from or based in the United States, and acting or singing predominantly in English.

During the participants' adolescence, their romantic *akogare* for Western stars was increasingly conflated with a desire for learning English, resulting in an immediate or future increase in their contact with English. For example, in order to express their admiration, some of the women in our study wrote a fan letter in English to the stars they were obsessed with, as Eika and her classmate did. After seeing *Top Gun*, they decided to send a fan letter to Tom Cruise. However, their English was not advanced enough to compose such a letter. This did not diminish their enthusiasm. On the contrary, they used a number of resources to achieve their goal: a template letter provided in the teenage magazine *Screen* formed the basis of their composition. Further, they sought help from their high-school English teacher, who proofread and edited the letter. Eika recalls that, as they continued to work on the letter, they began to imagine the possibility of receiving a personal invitation from Tom Cruise:

Eika: ano toki are datta yo~, bikku doriimaa datta yo ne @ atasitati kaite ru toki sa~ ukkiuki zya nai, de kare [Tom Cruise] ga sa~ nihon no zyosi koosei no zyoonetu wo sittara hyotto site hariuddo ni gosyootai toka ne ~ kangaete te sa ~ !@@@

Eika: you see, we were big dreamers at that time@ when we were writing the letter, we were so excited about the whole thing, and we thought if he [Tom Cruise] found out about our passion for him ... from Japanese high school girls ... we might get invited to Hollywood!@@@ (i4june03eika)

Although neither a personal response nor an invitation was likely, fantasizing about meeting him as a young woman in love was powerful enough to make them work on their English. They rehearsed their self-introduction in English in preparation for this imaginary occasion:

Eika: de sa~, mosi hontoo ni soo iu koto ni nacchattara doo suru ~ toka itte te. sonna toki ni zyaa tomu ni doo yatte zikosyookai suru mitai na? kanozyo to atasi sa~ @

Eika: we were talking about what if it really happened. how should we introduce ourselves to Tom? she and I @

Kimie: @@

Kimie: @@

Eika: issyo ni rensyuu site ta yo @

Eika: we were practicing together@

Kimie: e, eigo?

Kimie: what, English?

Eika: un, eigo no rensyuu

Eika: yeah, practicing English.

Kimie: @zyoodan desyo?@

Kimie: @are you kidding me?@

Eika: kare ga me no mae ni iru sootei de sa~, 'how do you do?', 'my name is Eika' [with deliberate intonation and higher pitch of her voice] @@@. hontoo ni baka datta yo ne~. atasitati sa~ @@@

Eika: imagining him in front of us, *'how do you do?'*, *'my name is Eika'* @@@. we were so stupid then, really. we were @@@(i4june03eika)

The participants' romantic desire for Western stars thus was the first in a series of links created between ELL and romantic attraction. In practicing how to introduce themselves in English to Tom Cruise, Eika and her friend created an imaginary relationship between the Western actor as their object of *akogare* and themselves. English emerges as a powerful tool to construct a gendered identity and to gain access to the romanticized West. Surrounded by the multiple discourses of English as a desirable and powerful language, most of the informants report having had *akogare* for the English language and Western culture since their childhood. However, during their adolescence, this *akogare* for the English language and the West became increasingly gendered and romanticized.

Following One's Dreams: *ryugaku* in Sydney

Ichi and Yuka followed their adolescent *akogare* straight out of their teens to Australia. Eika, Chizu, and Yoko resurrected their youthful dreams when they became increasingly disillusioned with life in Japan, after Yoko's divorce, and when Eika and Chizu felt trapped in a job that seemed to lack direction. All of the primary participants spent a minimum of 21 months in Sydney. After the original period they had planned to stay (a few months to a year in most cases) had expired, they had decided to stay on because they felt their progress in English was nowhere near enough. They also began to fear that they would forget their English back in Japan. They either lived off their savings or were supported by their parents.

In order to make sense of their interactional and emotional experiences in Sydney, it is imperative to begin by looking at the ways in which their *akogare* discourses shaped their personal measures of success. Such measures are multiple, changeable, and contextual, with some being more foregrounded than others depending on the context in which the participants found themselves. For most informants, however, the ultimate personal measure of success was socially based. The acquisition of grammar or vocabulary, even as expressed in test scores, did not matter as much as their access to and social acceptance by Australian native speakers in the forms of friendship or romance. *'Gaijin ni kakomareta mainichi no seikatsu'* [Everyday life surrounded by *gaijins*] was what they had typically imagined for themselves before arriving in Sydney and that sort of life was thought of as a 'natural' means and ends to learning English, as *ryugaku* magazines had led them to believe prior to departure.

Yoko's reflection on her imagination prior to her arrival in Sydney is a case in point:

Yoko: oosutoraria ni kuru mae, yoku koo sidonii no dokka no kafe de~ suteki na hakuzin tomodati ni kakomarete @@, RYUUTYOO koo eigo de tyatto site waratte ru zibun wo soozou sitari site masita yo @@

Yoko: before coming to Australia, I used to imagine myself surrounded by many beautiful white friends in a café, somewhere in Sydney @@, chatting and chuckling with them in my FLUENT English @@ (i30april 02yoko)

However, once in Sydney, the 'everyday life surrounded by *gaijins*' image quickly lost its validity. All of the participants felt unable to either understand native speakers or make themselves understood by them in social encounters, finding it impossible to move beyond the initial greeting level. In a matter of weeks, the forming of friendships and intimacy with Australians proved to be extremely hard and challenging, if not impossible, without an excellent command of English. Hence, relationships with native speakers became a signifier of their symbolic success in ELL and successful identity transformation from a monolingual Japanese to a bilingual cosmopolitan.

Shortly after their arrival, all participants experienced a deeply felt disappointment because of their inability to interact in English. They spoke about their lack of grammar, which they felt made speaking difficult, if not impossible, and their 'untrained ear', which prevented them from understanding what had been said, particularly in *oojii* [Aussie] English. However, they diligently worked at overcoming those shortcomings with the means they could access – they bought additional monolingual English textbooks in Sydney, or had bilingual textbooks sent from Japan; they dutifully spent hours and hours watching TV and listening to the radio in order to 'train their ear' to the sound of (Australian) English. Despite their efforts, these conventional learning strategies did not only prove ineffective, but also dull. Many cried over their excruciatingly slow progress and the gap between their earlier dreams of *ryugaku* life and their realities. In contrast to their dreams of becoming fluent easily and 'naturally' in interactions with native speakers, they found that they had very few opportunities to meet non-Japanese people or other (Asian) ESL students. At the same time that their dreams of 'picking up' English easily were shattered, the participants were increasingly exposed to success stories that linked fluency with a romantic relationship. At school and in their social circle of ESL friends, everyone spoke with admiration of women who had become fluent rapidly once they had secured a native speaker boyfriend. In the next section, we will turn to the ways in which a Western boyfriend came to be seen as a 'master strategy' for successful ELL.

'I Need a Man': *akogare* for Western Men

The intensity of the participants' *akogare* for Western men varies (across participants but also over time) from an unachievable dream, a sheer fantasy, to one of their explicit goals, or even an absolute necessity for their success in ELL. However, what emerges as a common theme is the assumption that a Western romantic partner is the ultimate 'method' to improve one's English. After months of diligent 'conventional' ESL study, Eika reached the following conclusion:

Eika: [...] de, omotta n da yo ne~, mosi koo konsutanto ni eigo wo ne tyanto syabereru kikai wo tukuru to sitara ... otoko da! tte. neitjibu no kare ga hituyoo ka na tte sa.

Eika: [...] then I thought, if I need to create a more constant opportunity to actually speak English ... a man! I need a native speaker boyfriend. (f22oct03eika)

A native speaker partner is seen as good for ELL because romance creates a relaxed atmosphere for the use of English on a regular basis. Furthermore, while their self-esteem suffered as a result of their perceived failure at achieving English fluency, the power dynamics of a relationship, where they knew themselves to be desired and loved could restore their self-confidence:

Eika: yappari kono kare ga zibun wo suki datte sitte ru to yuuri da yo ne. nanka uwate ni dereru tte iu no. aite ga sa~ zibun ni toku-betu na kanzyoo ga aru tte sitte ru to motto zibun no koto hanasitaku naru yo ne. de eigo de yaru no mo sonna ni kowaku nai mitai na.

Eika: I think it's really advantageous when you know that this man wants you. you kind of have the upper hand. when you know that he has a special interest in you, you kind of feel like talking more about yourself. taking risks in English doesn't seem so threatening. (f17mar03eika)

However, Western men are much more than just a linguistic resource. They are also a symbol of romance and chivalry. English terms of endearment are seen as a particular expression of Western heterosexual relationships. Many participants confessed their desire to be called 'darling', 'honey', or 'sweetheart':

Ichi: seiyoo no hito wa yoku *'darling'* toka *'sweetie'* toka *'babe'* toka iu yan [...] mukasi kara soo iu no yowai n yo @@@ de ne, nikaime no deito no toki ni, Sean ga *dinner* tukutte kureta n yo. de kaimon itta toki, ano kare wo yonda n yo~ *'hey Sean'* tte, sositara kare, *'yes, darling?'* tte. Soo iu no suggoi akogarete ta kara. nanka aa, kare no onna ni natta n ya na tte kanzi sita wa @@@

Ichi: Westerners often say 'darling', 'sweetie' and 'babe' [. . .] I have a soft spot for these words @@@ well, on the second date, Sean cooked dinner for me. when we went shopping, and I called out to him, like, 'hey Sean', he said to me, 'yes, darling?' I had so much *akogare* for it. it really made me feel like I was his girl @@@ (i30sep03ichi)

These terms of endearment allow the participants a transformational experience from their Japanese world to the Western world because they feel that romantic nuances and Prince-Charming-associations of Japanese terms of endearment are non-existent. Eika recalls feeling drawn into another world when she was called 'honey' by her Australian boyfriend:

Eika: saisyo wa, bikkuri sita yo . . . kore ka ~ uesutan no sekai! mitai na kanzi de ne. hazime wa bikkuri site tyotto muzukayukatta to omou yo, de tyotto hitogoto datta kanzi ga suru. demo uresikatta yo tasika ni ne, aa, aziazin zya nai hito to renai site ru n da na tte. nihongo de wa nai nyuansu de syo, dakara tigau sekai ni kityatta na ~ to omotta shi. uresikatta no wa hibiki da yo. daarin no kotoba no hibiki.

Eika: at first, I was surprised . . . I thought 'wow, this is the Western world!' in the beginning, it was ticklish and felt like it was happening to someone else. but, I was happy, and it made me feel that I was really with a non-Asian man. the Japanese language does not have the same nuances and so it made me feel like I had been drawn into a different world. what made me happy about it most really was the sound . . . the sound of 'honey, darling'. (m28mar04eika)

Conversely, attempts by English-speaking boyfriends to use Japanese terms of endearment or expressions of love are considered a real turn-off. Ichi, for instance, reports how disgusted she felt when her Australian boyfriend, who knew some Japanese, tried to use Japanese during sexual intercourse:

Ichi: yatu ga beddo de nihongo tukatta n yo~, moo sinziraren gurai iya yatta wa~. 'suggoku nurete ru ne!' tte nihongo de itta n yo [with a frown on her face and frustration in her voice]. moo saitei yatta wa!

Ichi: you know he was using Japanese in bed and it was a major turn-off! he said to me, 'wow you are so wet!' in Japanese [with a frown on her face and frustration in her voice]. it was so disgusting! (f31july02ichi)

It is clear from Ichi's statement, and the fact that she stopped seeing this man soon after, that the participants exert a number of choices in relation to native-speaker boyfriends. Whereas it may seem from our discussion so far that the participants would take any native-speaking man they could get, nothing could be further from the truth. Two themes emerge in the choices they exerted with regard to potential partners, namely race and knowledge of Japanese.

Akogare and Race

As discussed in the sections on 'The Glamour of ELL' and 'Dreaming of Tom Cruise and Brad Pitt', media discourses present the desirable English-speaking man as White. Not surprisingly then, Whiteness in potential partners is highly prized by the participants, as for instance in this statement from Chizu:

Chizu: yappari hakuzin da yo. datte kodomo no koro kara no akogare dakara hakuzin igai kangaerarenai yo ne. @mou sonna koto itte ru tosi zyaa nai n da kedo, imada ni hakuzin to hanasu to koofun sityau mon @@, nanka zibun de kawaiku syabettyattari, koe ga takaku nattyattari suru no wakaru n da yo ne @@@!

Chizu: I like white men. well, it's my childhood *akogare*, so I can't think of any other option but white. @ I know that I am too old to fancy them like this, but I still tend to get excited when I talk with white men @@, and I find myself speaking more cutely and using a higher-pitched voice @@@! (t15mar04chi)

Similarly, the race of one of Ichi's boyfriends, and his British nationality, were a cause of celebration even for her mother:

Ichi: okaasan kare no koto yorokonde ru n da yo ne @@@

Ichi: my mother is really happy with him @@@

Kimie: @@@

Kimie: @@@

Ichi: dokkara kita no~ tte. yuukei kara da yo tte ittara, suggoi yoro-konzyatte, 'wa ~ zyaa, igirisuzin zya nai!' toka itte @@

Ichi: she asked me where he came from. I told her that he was from the UK, and she was so excited, like, 'wow, he is ENGLISH!' @@

Kimie: @@@

Kimie: @@@

Ichi: maa, tenkeiteki na hakuzin igirisuzin da yo tte ittara yokatta ne
           tte itte kurete sa @@

Ichi: she was excited for me when I told her that he is a classic white
           English man @@ (i21nov03ichi)

Their *akogare* for White men often had a positive effect on their agency
and led them to seek out interactional opportunities, as in the case of Ichi,
who frequently went out 'man-hunting' with an Australian girlfriend on
weekends. In some cases, the desire to meet a White man was stronger
than the desire to meet a native-speaking partner; in other cases, and at
other points in time, the desire for a native-speaking partner, proved
stronger than race considerations. Yoko's story provides a case in point.
When she first came to Australia, she did not even consider Asian-
Australian men as potential romantic partners, or even as linguistic
resources. She regarded a party where she had an opportunity to mix
with Asian-Australian men, who were all native speakers of English, as
a waste of time:

Kimie: paatjii doo datta no?

Kimie: so, how was the party?

Yoko: tyotto kii te kudasai yo~, baabekyuu paatjii ni wa ippai oosutor-
           ariazin kuru tte tomodati ga itte ta tte itta zya nai desu ka? de,
           suggoku tanosimi ni site ta n desu yo. demo, ano, maa takusan
           hito wa, aa, hotondo wa, atasi no tomodati no furattomeito no
           tomodati datta n desu kedo, moo, minna azian oosutorarian
           datta n desu yo! maa minna neitjibu ka eigo perapera na hitotati
           bakkari datta n desu kedo, iya ~ kimie-san, atasi wa koo iu
           otoko tati to asonde iru hima wa nai na tte. hontoo ni, yooku
           wakari masita yo, aa atasi wa hakuzin no kare ga hosii n date.

Yoko: listen, I told you that my friend told me that there would be
           many Australians at the BBQ party? so I was really looking
           forward to it. Well, there were a lot of people, mostly my
           friend's flatmate's friends, but they were all Asian-Australian!
           they were all native speakers or spoke English really well. but
           I felt, 'they aren't my type of men'. Kimie, I am not here to
           waste my time mixing with men like these guys. once again I
           had this self-confirmation that what I want is a white boyfriend.
           (f25july02yoko)

However, gradually Yoko's reasoning changed and she considered it
more important to find any native-speaker partner to practice her
English rather than to waste time pursuing a native-speaker partner

who might also be White. Eventually, John, a Chinese-Australian, became her first *gaijin* boyfriend in Australia:

Yoko: maa hakuzin otoko ga doono koono to zutto itte masita kedo, kek-kyoku aziazin tukamae tyai masita. tyotto keisan tigai desita yo ne. demo, kare neitjibu nande, doonika naru to omoi masu @@

Yoko: I was going on and on about white men for a long time, but in the end, I got an Asian. it's a bit of a miscalculation, but really he is a native speaker, so I will survive @@ (f21dec03yoko)

His native-speaker identity was what encouraged Yoko to get romantically involved with him in the first place, and to remain in their rocky relationship for longer than she would otherwise have. As her ambivalent comment 'I will survive' implies, however, John's racial background remained at the forefront of her experience of him, and did so as a problem. During their relationship, she stressed any aspect of John that enhanced his legitimacy as an Australian whenever possible:

Yoko: kare wa aziazin nan desu kedo, neitjibu zya nai desu ka. kare no hii oziisan ga oosutoraria ni kite, kare no otoosan mo okaasan mo tyainiizu syaberenai n desu yo. John mo tyainiizu zenzen syaberenai si. dakara, hontoo ni nakami wa oojii na n desu yo ne … […] aruhi, kare ga sigotoba no koriigu ni '*G'day mate*' tte itte ru no kiita n desu yo. atasi sorede kandoo sityatte, aa, kare tte hontoo ni oojii nanda ∼ tte omoi masita.

Yoko: he is Asian, but, he is a native speaker of English. his great grandfather came to Australia, so neither his father nor his mother can speak Chinese. John can't speak Chinese at all either. so he is really an Aussie inside … […] the other day, I heard him say, 'G'day mate' to his colleagues at work. that really impressed me and got me to realize again that he was a real Aussie. (f21dec03yoko)

Even despite the fact that White men dominated the participants' desires, not all White men were automatically desired as potential partners, or even as linguistic resources.

'Sleazy Japanese Speakers'

Whereas there can be no doubt that Whiteness is treated as the norm, and the most desirable racial identity of their interlocutors, White men who speak Japanese were rejected by all the participants. Such men are often referred to as 'sleazy Japanese speakers' or simply *ruuzaa* [loser].

When they first arrived in Australia, most participants had easier access to people with connections to Japan, and their bilingualism and associated interest in befriending Japanese people, especially women, were considered an advantage. For Eika, the bilingualism of White people who had studied Japanese meant a window of opportunity for friendship and romance. Despite this positive assessment of bilingual Western men, Eika's relationship with such a man in the first few months of her stay in Sydney was a constant struggle over language choice. According to Eika, Andrew paid very little attention when she talked in English, but became much more attentive when she spoke in Japanese. Consequently, Eika often felt she had no choice but to speak Japanese, which in turn made her feel guilty because the main objective of her life in Sydney was to master English. Using Japanese on a daily basis seemed like an act of betraying her determination to improve her English. Despite her protests, Japanese remained the main language in the relationship, and Eika felt doubly betrayed as she had dreamed of a chivalrous Westerner who would take her needs and concerns seriously. So, even before their romance ended, Eika started to long for a monolingual *gaijin* boyfriend:

Eika: moo, tugi no kare wa zettai ni nihongo siranai hito ni suru!

Eika: for my next boyfriend, I am going to choose someone who doesn't know Japanese language! (f19june03eika)

Language choice is not the only problem that bilingual Western men present for the participants. Much more crucially, White men with any level of fluency in Japanese are assumed to be interested in Japanese women mainly for their supposed sexual 'easiness'. As we pointed out in the introduction, there is a pervasive sexist and nationalist stereotype of Japanese women as 'yellow cabs', as having blind *akogare* for Western men and sleeping with anyone who is White and English-speaking. Given the pervasiveness of this discourse in Japan, anyone who has any knowledge of Japan can be expected to be familiar with statements such as these, from a Japanese travel website:

[...] In sum, the reason why Japanese women are so willing to have sex with *gaijin* men is their abhorrence of Japanese society and their desire to escape. This easily explains contemporary Japanese women's passion for learning English, popularity of English schools, and English teachers' unlimited access to sex. Sex with *gaijins* is the same as speaking English with *gaijins,* and is one step towards escaping from Japan. What is more, sex is not as difficult as studying English. It is in fact so easy. (http://member.nifty.ne.jp/worldtraveller/enjo/gaijin.htm; last accessed on 26 March 2004; KT's translation).

Consequently, *gaijin* men who have more than high-school fluency in Japanese[4] immediately raise alarm bells with the participants. They suspect that they are sexual predators who are after easy sex with 'stupid' Japanese women, who would be so dazzled by their Whiteness as not to see through their real intentions. Yoko provides an example:

Yoko: nihongo hanaseru gaizin ni auto suguni, 'iyaa, kono hito zyapaniizu kiraa dakara ki wo tukenai to' tte omoi masu mon. nihonzin zyosei suki de ite kureru no wa ii n desu kedo ne. demo, nanka, kantan ni sekkusu yattyau toka iu imeezi motarete ru to omou to iya ni nattyau n desu yo ne. dakara, soo iu hito to auto, moo furaatte inaku nattyai masu. wazawaza soo iu hitotati to aitai to omoi masen ne ... soo iu hitotati to tomodati ni naru no tte kantan da to wa omoi masu kedo.

Yoko: when I meet *gaijin* men who can speak Japanese, I immediately think, 'ok, this guy must be a Japanese killer' and that I have to be careful. I guess it's kind of nice that they like Japanese women. but it is their image of Japanese women as sexually easy which turns me off. so when I meet one, I just walk away; I don't go out of my way to go find guys like them ... even though it may be easier to be friends with them. (t17mar04yoko)

Bilingual men are also assumed to be interested in Japanese women because they consider them as passive, submissive, feminine, and obedient – stereotypes about Japanese women that all participants reject. Yuka, for instance, complained of a bilingual Westerner in her social circle:

Yuka: zibun ga itumo asonde ru nihonzin no onnanokotati tte baka bakkari da si eigo syaberenai kara, atasi ga eigo SYABERERU TTE sinzirarenai n desu yo. dakara kare atasi no koto iya na n desu yo datte eigo SYABERERU si iitai koto datte IETYAU kara. saisyo ni atta toki nante, hontoo ni baka de eigo no syaberenai nihonzin no onna mitai na kanzi de. atasi ga eigo syabereru tte wakatta ra bikkuri site sinzirarenai tte kanzi @@

Yuka: he can't believe that I CAN speak English because most of the girls he goes out with are stupid and can't speak English. that's why he can't stand me because I CAN speak English and CAN express my opinions. when we first met, his attitude to me was obvious; he treated me as if I was a dumb Japanese girl who can't speak a word of English. when he found out that I was able to speak English, he looked stunned and could not believe it @@ (t15mar04yuka)

Lastly, bilingual men are not even considered as a way into Australian society as they often exclusively socialize with Japanese (women):

Yoko: anoo soo iu hitotati tte nihonzin to bakkari turumu zya nai desu ka. soo iu hito no paatji toka iku to nihonzin bakkari na n de nani kore tte kanzi de. daitai mukasi no onna wa nihonzin dattari mo suru n desu yo. dakara ne eigo ga mokuteki da si soo iu nihongo hanasu gaizin to turundemo syooga nai tte omoi masen?

Yoko: you know, these guys only hang out with Japanese people. you go to their party and it will be full of Japanese people, and I feel like, what the hell? most of their ex-girlfriends are Japanese, too. so what's the point in getting to know Japanese speaking *gaijins* when my goal is to improve my English? (t17mar04yoko)

Avoiding Japanese-speaking *gaijins* can be seen as a refusal to be positioned in any of the stereotypes that circulate about Japanese women: sexually easy, submissive, or linguistically deficient English speakers. At the same time, the participants position these men as cheap, unintelligent, and unworthy of their attention. In a related development, a women-only English study agent, *Go-Girls*, has rapidly gained popularity in Japan's competitive EFL industry in recent years, and this may be so because it provides an environment where female English learners can feel 'safe' and do not have to concern themselves with the sexual and power politics inevitably involved in interactions with Western male teachers (see McMahill, 2001, for a similar description of feminist English classes in Japan).

Conclusion

Akogare refers to a bundle of desires – for a 'Western' emancipated lifestyle, for a 'Western' prince charming and ladies' man, for mastery of English – all of which entail and inflect each other. Media discourses paint a black-and-white picture of the world in which these desires matter; on the one hand, there is the *ryugaku* illusion of finding oneself and one's *ikikata* in Sydney, New York, or some other mythical place in the West, that is promoted in women's magazines, *ryugaku* magazines, and the like. On the other hand, there is the misogynist and nationalist scare discourse of Japanese women as unthinking slaves of their fantasies. The participants in this study are well aware of both discourses, and try to find a way to realize their dreams without falling victim to them – even if not always successfully. Their stories are full of contradictions, disappointments, and rejections. The same women who idealize the West and idolize Western men ridicule some of them as losers. Yoko, for instance, who sees it as her life's mission to turn herself into a 'White' native speaker like Cameron Diaz and to find a White native-speaker boyfriend like Brad Pitt, has rejected several romantic and sexual invitations by White native-speaker men. On the one hand, the practices of the participants reflect and reproduce the hegemonic *akogare* discourse for English and the West. On the other hand, they also challenge the essentialist dichotomy between White native speakers as desired and powerful, and non-native speakers as desiring and powerless. The participants exercise tremendous agency in fulfilling their *akogare*, with the structures of *akogare* in turn constraining their agency, which we take as their 'socioculturally mediated capacity to act' (Ahearn, 2001: 112).

For instance, in order to establish and maintain a relationship with a male native speaker, the informants dynamically drew on their gendered and sometimes sexual attraction. The most explicit example comes from a secondary participant, 34-year-old Miri. A decade earlier, Miri had studied English in the United States, and she reported having had no shortage of interactional opportunities in English at her dormitory as her racial and sexual identity magnetized post-adolescent college males:

Miri: dame na kotati wo tukatte eigo rensyuu site ta no omoi dasu to nanka mune ga itamu no yo ne~. ippai deeto wa sita kedo~ eigo zyootatu sitakatta dake nan de tukatte ta ne. ima wa warui na tte omou kedo @@

Miri: my heart aches with guilt when I remember how I used to use these poor guys to practice English. I went on many dates, but I was just taking advantage of them to improve my English. I feel really bad about it now @@ (f15aug02miri)

She considered male residents in her dormitory as 'free practice partners' and while she was happy to chat with them, she never let down her guard as she knew their 'real' intentions:

Miri: nani yaritai ka nante hontoo moro bare. yaritai dake. sekkusu sitai dake nan da yo ne. nanka koo odeko ni 'yarasete!' tte kaite atte, 'onegaisimasu' ttsuu no ga koo tjiisyatu no mune no tokoro ni kaite atta ri @ hotondo no kotati wa busaiku datta kara maa, hanasita kedo hyoomen teki na koto dake ne.

Miri: what they wanted was sooo obvious; they just wanted to get laid. sex was all they were after. It said 'yarasete (let me do you)!' on their forehead or 'I am begging you' on their T-shirt across their chest @ most of them were fairly ugly, so I would chat with them to practice English, but only on a superficial level. (f15aug02miri)

Miri understood the racial and sexual politics in her dormitory and capitalized on them. There are numerous cases where the informants draw on their identity as the desired Asian Other to get access to linguistic resources. In countless social contexts, they report feeling utterly deficient and powerless due to their limited linguistic and social capital. Nevertheless, it is also possible for them to position themselves as the desired Other and to negotiate the power balance to their advantage.

However, it would be misleading to end with the suggestion that the participants are successfully renegotiating the power imbalance inherent in the emotional relationship that sets up the West as object of desire and Japanese women as the desirers. For the women in this study, the lives they aspire to are powerfully associated with English. There can be no doubt that this relationship is constructed and maintained in media discourses that serve powerful market interests – be it the language school and *ryugaku* market, or, on a broader level, the consumption of all the branded goods and services associated with *ikikata*. As they have stayed on in Sydney beyond the originally intended period, the women are financially less secure than they were before they came here: Chizu, Eika, and Yoko gave up their careers in Japan and their life-savings are dwindling away, and Ichi and Yuka continue to rely on financial assistance from their parents. As the expected rewards of these sacrifices – fluency in English, full participation in Sydney's fashionable society, an *ikemen* [handsome, desirable] boyfriend – have not been forthcoming, desire may even give way to depression.

A striking example comes from Eika. In April 2004, it emerged that Eika had been harassed by one of her TAFE lecturers, and all this former competent career woman, who was confident in her English before she came to Australia, could do was to keep it to herself for a long time. Eventually, she experienced a series of nervous breakdowns. When she finally talked about it to Kimie Takahashi, she said:

Eika: toozen nanda yo ne hontoo datte atasi no eigo dame da si kare no iu toori. soreni sa~ zenzen eigo nobasu doryoku toka mo site kite nakatta si . . . demo hontoo moo nannimo dekinai tte omottyau si kore izyoo wa muri kana tte ne koo doonika genzyoo wo yoku suru ni attate sa nannimo dekinai tte kanzi.

Eika: I deserve it, you know, because my English is not very good, and he is right about me. besides I haven't been trying hard to improve my English either . . . but it's just that I feel so hopeless and helpless myself that I can't begin to do anything to get better. (t14april 04eika)

Thus, the Lukes' (1974) quote cited in the 'Theoretical Framework' section fully applies to the participants. While *akogare* does turn on their agency and makes them pursue the object/s of their desires, the failure that is built into the system – that is, it is impossible to become a White native speaker – also makes them turn themselves into victims: silenced, incompetent, and depressed. In terms of the often-made connection between desire – or 'motivation' as it is called in most research papers – and success in second language learning, it is important to point out that the most fluent participant, Yuka, was also the one who had the least amount of *akogare*.

Notes

1. Our names appear in alphabetical order. The research reported in this chapter is part of Kimie Takahashi's Ph.D. project, conducted under the supervision of Ingrid Piller. We would like to record our thanks to the co-supervisor, Gerard Sullivan. Special thanks are to Nerida Jarkey for her help with the Romanization of the Japanese.
2. The study received ethics clearance from the University of Sydney Human Ethics Commission.
3. The following transcription conventions are used:

.	short pause
. . .	long pause
~	extended ending typical of Japanese
CAPS	emphatic stress
@	laughter
@laughter@	the statement between the two @s is made laughingly
[. . .]	analyst's omission
'yarasete!'	change in voice quality when another voice is imitated or quoted
(sitting down)	research notes

   Type of data and date of data collection can be found in the brackets at the end of each quote. For instance, (f17april04eika) indicates that the specific quote is drawn from the field-note written on 17 April 2004, about Eika. Other types of data are represented as follows: e = e-mails; i = interview; m = MSN messenger; and t = telephone conversation.
   Data are provided in the Japanese original first, followed by a translation into English. The 99 style recommended by the Society for the Romanization of the Japanese Alphabet is used (http://www.roomazi.org/top.html, last accessed on 19 April 2004).
4. Japanese is the most frequently learned foreign language at school level in New South Wales (Department of Education and Training NSW, 1998).

References

Ahearn, L. (2001) Language and agency. *Annual Review of Anthropology* 30, 109–37.
Bailey, K. (2003) *Living in the* eikaiwa *wonderland: English language learning, socioeconomic transformation and gender alterities in modern Japan*. Unpublished PhD dissertation, University of Kentucky.
Bakhtin, M. (1981) *The Dialogic Imagination: Four Essays*. Austin: University of Texas Press.
Bakhtin, M. (1986) *Speech Genres and Other Late Essays*. Austin: University of Texas Press.
Cameron, D. and Kulick, D. (2003a) Introduction: Language and desire in theory and practice. *Language and Communication* 23, 93–105.

Cameron, D. and Kulick, D. (2003b) *Language and Sexualtiy.* Cambridge: Cambridge University Press.

Department of Education and Training NSW (1998) *Statistical Bulletin: Schools and Students in New South Wales.* Sydney: Department of Education and Training, NSW.

Dower, J. (1999) *Embracing Defeat: Japan in the Wake of World War II.* New York: Norton.

Foucault, M. (1977) *Discipline and Punish: The Birth of the Prison.* New York: Pantheon.

Foucault, M. (1980) *Power/Knowledge: Selected Interviews and Other Writings, 1972– 1977.* New York: Pantheon.

Igata, K. (1993) *Itsuka igirisu ni kurasu watashi [Someday I Shall Live in England].* Tokyo: Chikuma Shobo.

Karmani, S. (2003) 'Linguistic imperialism 10 years on': An interview with Robert Phillipson. On WWW at http://www.tesolislamia.org/articles/interview_ rp.pdf. Accessed 13.12.04.

Kelsky, K. (1999) Gender, modernity, and eroticized internationalism in Japan. *Cultural Anthropology* 14(2), 229–55.

Kelsky, K. (2001) *Women on the Verge: Japanese Women, Western Dreams.* Durham and London: Duke University Press.

Kimura, Y. and Yamana, A. (1999) *Nihon josei no jittai [What Japanese Women are Really Like].* Tokyo: Hiratai Books.

Kinginger, C. (2004) Alice doesn't live here anymore: Foreign language learning and identity reconstruction. In A. Pavlenko and A. Blackledge (eds) *Negotiation of Identities in Multilingual Contexts* (pp. 219–42). Clevedon: Multilingual Matters.

Kress, G. and van Leeuwen, T. (1996) *Reading Images: The Grammar of Visual Design.* London: Routledge.

Kubota, R. (1998) Ideologies of English in Japan. *World Englishes* 17(3), 295–306.

Kubota, R. (2002) The impact of globalization on language teaching in Japan. In D. Block and D. Cameron (eds) *Globalization and Language Teaching* (pp. 13–28). London: Routledge.

Lukes, S. (1974) *Power: A Radical View.* London: Macmillan.

Ma, K. (1996) *The Modern Madame Butterfly.* Rutland, VT, and Tokyo: Charles E. Tuttle.

McMahill, C. (2001) Self-expression, gender, and community: A Japanese feminist English class. In A. Pavlenko, A. Blackledge, I. Piller and M. Teutsch-Dwyer (eds) *Multilingualism, Second Language Learning and Gender* (pp. 307–44). Berlin and New York: Mouton de Gruyter.

Miyazaki, C. (1997) Hansamu na gaikokujindansei wa hontouni 'risou no darin' ka? [Is a handsome foreign man really your 'ideal sweetheart'?]. In S. Ohira and T. Kato (eds) *Marugoto onna no tenki: Itsukara demo yarinaosou [The Complete Women's Turning Point: It's Never Too Late to Get Your Life in Order]* (pp. 134–45). Tokyo: Aspecto.

Pennycook, A. (1998) *English and the Discourses of Colonialism.* London: Routledge.

Pennycook, A. (2001) English in the world/the world in English. In A. Burns and C. Coffin (eds) *Analysing English in a Global Context: A Reader* (pp. 78–89). London: Routledge.

Phillipson, R. (1992) *Linguistic Imperialism.* Oxford: Oxford University Press.

Piller, I. (2001) Identity constructions in multilingual advertising. *Language in Society* 30(2), 153–86.

Piller, I. (2002) *Bilingual Couples Talk: The Discursive Construction of Hybridity.* Amsterdam: Benjamins.

Piller, I. (in press) 'I always wanted to marry a cowboy': Bilingual couples, language and desire. In T.A. Karis and K. Killian (eds) *Cross-Cultural Couples: Transborder Relationships in the Twenty-First Century.* Binghamton, NY: Haworth.

Russell, J. (1998) Consuming passions: Spectacle, self-transformation, and the commodification of blackness in Japan. *Positions* 6(1), 113–77.

Toyoda, S. (1994) *Kokuhatsu! Ieroo kyabu – masukomi koogai wo utsu* ['*Yellow cab' Accused! – Criticism of Corruption in the Mass Media*]. Tokyo: Sairyush.

Tsuda, Y. (1990) *Eigo-shihai no koozoo* [*The Structure of the Hegemony of English*]. Tokyo: Daisan Shokan.

Tsuda, Y. (1993). *Eigo-shihai e no iron* [*Objections to the Hegemony of English*]. Tokyo: Daisan Shokan.

Chapter 4

Feeling in Two Languages: A Comparative Analysis of a Bilingual's Affective Displays in French and Portuguese[1]

MICHÈLE KOVEN

Do bilinguals express feelings differently in their two languages? This is a question that many bilinguals have anecdotally reported. This matter has also been explored by bilingual writers (Green, 1985; Hoffman, 1989; Rodriguez, 1982; Steiner, 1975), scholars discussing these authors (Beaujour, 1989; Pavlenko, 1998; see also Besemeres, this volume), patients in psychotherapy (Amati-Mehler, *et al.*, 1993; Schrauf 2000), and experimentalists (Ervin, 1964; Koven, 1998; Pavlenko, 2002a) who have noted the different quality of bilinguals' affective expressions in their two languages.

This chapter addresses this question both conceptually and empirically. I first investigate this matter by situating bilinguals' language-specific affective expression within larger issues of sociolinguistic diversity. I then describe empirical methods used to analyze how one French–Portuguese bilingual displays affect differently in her two languages.[2] To explore systematically how people perform and experience affect with multiple sets of sociolinguistic resources, I examine how Linda (a pseudonym), the French–Portuguese bilingual daughter of Portuguese migrants in France, performs different kinds of affective displays in her two languages.

This chapter is organized in the following manner. I first review scholarship on the relationship between language and affect. I then present the specific biographical and ethnographic contexts in which Linda has lived. Subsequently, I describe and then apply a set of methods used to elicit and analyze Linda's affective performances in French and Portuguese. I then argue that it is not structural differences between French and Portuguese that account for Linda's French versus Portuguese affective displays, so much as the range and kinds of discursively enactable affective performances and personas to which she has access in each language. Ultimately, this chapter contributes to an understanding of bilinguals' language-specific 'emotional' expressions, by appealing to an understanding of the relationship between language and emotion as socio-pragmatic in nature.

Sociolinguistic Perspectives on Bilingual Displays of Affect

Following Wierzbicka (1999: 271) and Pavlenko (2002a,b), what do the experiences of bilinguals tell us about the culturally constructed nature of emotion more generally? Scholars with an interpretive approach to the study of emotion have regularly asked about the comparability of emotional idioms across cultures (Doi, 1974; Harré, 1986; Lutz, 1988a,b; Lutz & White, 1986; Rosaldo, 1980; Shweder, 1994; Wierzbicka, 1999). However, such scholarship has typically not been applied to bilinguals or accounted for sociolinguistically complex situations. Instead, it has compared the contexts and meanings of emotions in single populations. This has often been done as if each culture were a unified whole, with one major idiom in which to display emotion.

Some scholars, however, have recognized the importance of sociolinguistic diversity, both within communities, and for individual speakers. A number of linguistic anthropologists have explored the range of available styles and contexts within particular communities, through which social actors may perform affect differently (Abu-Lughod, 1986; Besnier, 1995; Errington, 1984; Heider, 1991; Irvine, 1990; Kulick, 1992). The issue of sociolinguistic diversity and affect was also examined in earlier studies of codeswitching, where a code switch could mitigate or intensify the affective force of an utterance (Gal, 1979; Gumperz, 1982). Other variable elements of language, such as pronominal choice, were also shown to convey affective meanings (Friedrich, 1972).

In this light, social actors in many communities may regularly have access to multiple, verbally mediated ways of performing affect. One can then systematically compare the forms and meanings of affective display within the same community across contexts and ask not only how speakers of different languages and cultures differ in their affective expression and experience, but how the same social actor displays and experiences affect differently across multiple ways of speaking. Discursively oriented analysis can further comparative analyses of affect by asking how to 'calibrate' (Silverstein, 1993; Whorf, 1956 [1940]), 'transduce' (Silverstein, 2000), or decontextualize and then recontextualize (Bauman & Briggs, 1990) different performances of the 'same' affective display both across and within groups. By examining the consequences of different ways of speaking for the performance of affect, such an approach becomes a way to re-engage what Lucy (1992, 1997) and Hymes (1966) have called functional or discursive relativity.

Studying Affective Displays

To explore a bilingual's affective displays in her two languages, one must first specify which aspects of the verbal expression of affect to compare. There is a diversity of approaches among scholars, who focus on the relationship between verbal language and affect, a complete review of which is beyond the scope of this article (see Besnier, 1990). Many scholars have studied how people talk about emotion (Heider, 1991; Moore *et al.*, 1999; Wierzbicka, 1999), frequently with a focus on lexical semantics. Others have studied how people engage in emotional talk, independently of explicit reference to emotion (Besnier, 1990; Burger & Miller, 1999; Irvine, 1982, 1990; Ochs, 1988; Ochs & Schieffelin, 1989; Rosenberg, 1990). Scholars from the second orientation argue that one can better understand the role of speech in affective expression by going beyond a referential to a more indexical understanding of language (see Silverstein, 1976/1995). Furthermore, language forms that index affect may do so multifunctionally and non-exclusively (Ochs, 1990). In other words, the same devices that index affect may also index social identity and interpersonal rapport. In this way, to look at the verbal indexing of affect, one should look at aspects of discourse that may simultaneously index identity and interactional stance. In this chapter, I draw from this second approach, and examine how Linda implicitly communicates her affective stances through French and Portuguese indexical strategies. More specifically, I focus here on Linda's affective displays in narratives of personal experience (Besnier, 1992; Burger & Miller, 1999; Hill, 1995), by comparing the different intensities and locally recognized affective stances in stories she tells in her two languages, as well as what other bilinguals infer about her affect from those tellings.

Linda's Ethnographic and Sociolinguistic Contexts

The sociolinguistic and biographical contexts in which any bilingual has learned and spoken his/her two languages are critical to understanding the role of bilingualism in affective experience. Linda's relationship to her two languages has taken shape in the context of her family's circulation between urban France and rural Portugal. When I met her, she was a 20-year-old university student of Portuguese, living in a suburb of Paris. She was born in France of parents from a village in the northeastern region of Portugal, Trás-os-Montes. She and her family spend at least one month every year in her parents' village of origin, where they have built a house. I had known her for over six months and had already observed her in a variety of contexts before she participated in the semi-controlled portion of this study.

Linda is a relatively balanced bilingual, who spends a good deal of time in French and Portuguese bilingual and monolingual contexts. French is a language of public and private interactions for Linda. Many of her friends in France are monolingual French speakers. Having grown up and gone to school in France, her French is indistinguishable from that of a French monolingual of her age group and social background.

Portuguese is Linda's first language and it continues to play a major role in her life. She was raised by her parents and grandmother in a Portuguese suburb of Paris, where many activities, including religious practices, are conducted in Portuguese. Her parents continue to speak mostly Portuguese with her. Her live-in grandmother does not speak French. When she is in Portugal, most of her social contacts occur in Portuguese. Her current long-term boyfriend has always lived in Portugal and speaks no French. After she completes her university studies, she plans to move to Portugal to marry him and to work. In this way, Portuguese is not only her family's immigrant language spoken in the home, but also the language of the romantic and professional future she has planned for herself.

Linda herself evaluates her speech against French and Portuguese monolingual norms. Because she is aware that each language is the only native tongue for many in France and Portugal, Linda strives for monolingual-like skill in both languages, even if she may not command as full of a register range in Portuguese as in French. She is not pleased that her Portuguese is at times influenced by French. As she puts it, 'it's true that Portuguese, if I could master it like Portuguese Portuguese people [in Portugal], I'd be really happy, y'know' (here and further on all interview quotes are in the author's translation). Her goal is to speak Portuguese like someone who has lived only in Portugal. She is glad that she 'passes' in Portugal as a monolingual Portuguese, not as the daughter of émigrés. As she puts it, 'In Portugal, well, people who don't know me, if I don't tell them I'm an émigré, they can't tell'.

Linda does not necessarily value bilingualism, if it detracts from monolingual-like performances (Koven, 2004). She envies monolinguals for their (imagined) lack of confusion about their identities and languages. For example, she does not want her boyfriend to become bilingual or even to learn any French. She wants him to stay 'really one hundred percent Portuguese, no French, no mixing... He doesn't stress out. He's Portuguese. Period... We [Luso-descendants] don't know if we are Portuguese, if we are French because... we are always in-between, and I dunno, I think it's a pain in the ass to have a mix in your head ... when you're Portuguese or when you're French, you only have one language, hop, you're there, you have your language in your head, and that's it. . . . if he was mixed . . . maybe we wouldn't have the same relationship . . .' For Linda, each language is supposed to be an autonomous system that can meet all of a speaker's social and expressive needs. In this respect, she does not see each language as part of a larger repertoire of complementary expressive resources, but rather as ideally equivalent, potentially competing sets of resources. Linda's striving toward monolingual ideals and experiences in monolingual contexts is significant, for she frequently finds herself restricted to the expressive resources of only one of her two languages.

Despite her belief that she should be able to express herself in the same way in her two languages, she acknowledges that she has a different persona and affective style in French and in Portuguese. 'Translating' or failing to 'translate' affective performances across cultural and linguistic boundaries is an issue that Linda discusses at length. Speaking Portuguese and French does not give her the same 'sensation'. 'It's not the same personality in French and in Portuguese . . . when I speak French and I switch to Portuguese, there's something that's different'. She also reports that others, in particular her cousins, have often pointed out this difference to her, 'They look at me, "that's not the same Linda . . . there's something when you speak, it's not the same thing . . . shit, it's not the same cousin"'. She thinks that in Portuguese she comes across to people as more timid, calm, and reserved, whereas in French she comes across as more wacky (*fofolle*). The difference in her affective displays in the two languages, she suggests, is both a matter of intensity and of style. More specifically, Linda says that she has a harder time getting mad in Portuguese than in French. This difference in her French and Portuguese affective styles has come up in her relationship with her boyfriend.

> I get angry more easily in French. It comes out more . . . For example, with my boyfriend, when I fight with him, it gets in the way and I want to tell him tons of things . . . once I told him, 'you're lucky that you don't understand French'. He's like, 'why?' I'm like, 'because I'd have so many things to tell you . . .' I was mad and in Portuguese it didn't come, y'know. I said a couple little things, but it didn't come with the same force as in French. In French I had everything ready to unleash and in Portuguese I had to control myself, to calm down . . . otherwise it would have been, 'oh you piss me off, you bug the shit out of me, don't stress me out',[3] all that, whereas in Portuguese, I don't have that vocabulary . . . in French it's direct it's, 'you're a pain in my ass. You piss me off'. It's simple.

She also reported that she often wishes that she could 'get angry' at him in the same way in Portuguese that she would in French, 'Because I tell myself that like that when I feel like screaming, sometimes when I feel like telling him something and it doesn't come to me in Portuguese, I tell myself, "if only I could tell him in French so that he'd understand, I'd like that"'.

Therefore, she reports that she assumes a persona with greater restraint in Portuguese, one who does not and/or cannot use profanity. However, when she quotes what she would have said to her boyfriend in French (above), she presents it as a caricature of extremely colloquial French. She presents this quotation to illustrate what would not get translated into a Portuguese account. One could argue that this discrepancy comes from her ignorance of comparably vulgar Portuguese expressions. However, Linda may also not feel entitled to use equivalent Portuguese (see also Koven, 2001). According to Linda, she knows Portuguese swear words, but her family has always objected to her using them, as if they do not belong in her mouth. 'My mother doesn't like us to use bad words...it's really old people who use those...' In other words, she may not merely be unaware of Portuguese obscenities. Rather, there may be taboos against her using them that do not exist for her in French. These taboos may be related to the gendered personas she feels entitled to assume in each language. Other bilingual Luso-descendant women also seem to enact different kinds of female personas in each language, associated with their non-equivalent placements in rural Portugal and urban France (Koven, 1998). The two women described in Koven (1998) come across as more assertive and irreverent in French, and more reserved and deferential in Portuguese. Linda's reported experience may thus be related not only to her different competencies, but to the different gendered norms and personas she enacts in French and Portuguese contexts.

As described above, Linda does not only display affect with other bilinguals – she has regular monolingual interactions with peers and kin in both countries. In such contexts, she is confined to displays in either French or Portuguese. Thus, for example, although she is pleased that her boyfriend is a 'pure' monolingual, she also acknowledges that she can only enact a subset of her verbally mediated personas with him. He may never 'know' her through French, but only through her more 'contained' Portuguese. In this way, she may sometimes have to show how she feels exclusively in one language, where only some of her affective ways of speaking are accessible.

Data/Method

Moving from Linda's own explicit talk about her affective styles, one should ask how these actually manifest themselves in her discourse. As part of a larger semi-controlled study in which Linda participated, I had people tell a series of stories of personal experience twice, once in each language (for a detailed discussion see Koven, 1998). The disciplinarily hybrid method of the controlled portion of this study is informed by the sociolinguistic interview as understood by Labov (1972b), and by ongoing ethnographic work that let me set up recordable situations conducive to engaged, informal story-telling. I sought to approximate informal conversation between peers, as close as possible to real peer-group story-telling, yet still maintain control to make within- and across-person comparisons possible. In this regard, what one loses by using elicited data, one gains by being able to make more systematic comparisons, within and across people.

Participants told stories separately to two different listeners, so that each time speakers would have an unprimed audience, unfamiliar with the stories. Each time the interviewer was a different female French–Portuguese bilingual of the same age, also the daughter of Portuguese migrants. Linda told stories first in Portuguese to one of the interviewers. This interviewer asked Linda questions such as 'Can you tell me about a bad experience you may have had with someone you knew well?' As Linda began telling a story, the interviewer listened appreciatively, and jotted down a key word that captured the general topic of the story. Following this first session, Linda then met alone with the second interviewer in French. This second interviewer re-elicited the same stories with the list of key words made by the first interviewer, asking, 'You told the other interviewer a story about X. Can you tell me what happened?' Although any individual speaker, such as Linda, only told stories in a single order, across my larger sample of 23 speakers (Koven, in preparation), the order in which interviewees told stories, French–Portuguese, or Portuguese–French, was varied. In my full corpus of 23 speakers, no consistent order effects have been observed for the phenomena reported below for Linda.

Analysis

Comparing discursive strategies for affective performance across languages and cultures presents challenges, whether it involves a comparison of how two groups of people experience/perform the 'same' emotion, or of the same person's affective performances across two contexts. The analyst must decide how to make different performances and contexts analytically comparable. Below, I discuss tools for analyzing and comparing affective stance in narratives of personal experience in two languages. I use two complementary approaches: (1) formal analysis of the discursive strategies speakers use to communicate affect in French and Portuguese narratives; (2) others' reactions to audio-recordings of the original speakers' affective performances. These listeners were also bilinguals from a similar background, unacquainted with the recorded speaker. Together, these two approaches show how Linda consistently performs different affective intensities and different affective personas in French and Portuguese, which are formally describable, and that produce a tangible effect for listeners.

Formal analysis

The approach I adopt involves identifying the strategies through which speakers display or index their affective stances in colloquial French and Portuguese narratives. Rather than compare the functions of individual indexical devices in the two languages, I compare the larger *speaker role perspectives* that such devices help to instantiate. In this way, I compare the combinations of speaker role perspectives present in narratives told in speakers' two languages.

This notion of speaker role combines aspects of Labov's notion of evaluation (Labov & Waletzky, 1967, Labov, 1972a), Goffman's (1981a) idea of footing and production format, and Bakhtin's (1981) notion of voicing, as well as more recent applications (Hill, 1995; Koven, 2002; Wortham, 2001). From these different perspectives, I adopt the notion that people do not express a unified, monolithic subjectivity when they talk. A study of discursively displayed affect should thus examine the multiple roles through which any individual may talk, including how that individual can simultaneously animate and evaluate perspectives of others or of earlier versions of him/herself, distinct from his/her perspective in the 'here and now'. A coherent sense of a speaker's affective stance thus emerges from an overall orchestration of different 'here and now', 'there and then', 'self and other' speaker roles. Below (and as discussed at greater length in Koven, 2002), I identify three primary speaker roles in the first-person narratives of personal experience told by French–Portuguese bilinguals – narrator, interlocutor, and character:

(1) There is the event of narration itself, in which the speaker takes on the role of storyteller, obtaining an extended turn at talk in which he/she narrates. Here the relevant speaker role is that of *narrator*.

(2) There is the larger context of the interview or conversation in which the stories are told. Here the relevant speaker roles are those of co-conversationalists or *interlocutors*.

(3) There is the narrated speech event, which is presupposed and invoked in the event of narration. Here the relevant speaker roles are those of the narratable and performable *characters*.

Often a stretch of speech involves more than one speech event frame and speaker role, resulting in double voiced utterances (Bakhtin, 1981). These roles are described below, and summarized in Table 4.1.

Table 4.1 Six speaker role perspectives

Speaker role	Indexical devices and strategies in French and Portuguese that instantiate the stance
Narrator Unmarked, neutral narration	• Imperfect, • Pluperfect, • Preterite/passé composé, • Historical present Ex. *tinha-le comprado uma prenda* *I'd bought her a present*
Interlocutory Commentary that breaks from and/or comments on the narrative; metanarration (Babcock, 1977; Bauman, 1986)	(1) Parenthetical or here-and-now remarks that break from the advancement of plot (Babcock, 1977; Bauman, 1986) (2) Shifts to a marked register that non-referentially index speaker affect and/or social identity above and beyond the referent they pick out (Silverstein, 1976/1995). (3) Quantifying intensifiers that do not merely refer to quantity or size, but rather index speaker affect (Labov, 1984) (4) Discourse markers that do not show logical connections within the story that are not used to show logical, propositional relations between referential components (Dickel Dunn, 1999; Maynard, 1989; Schiffrin, 1987) (5) Shifts to a second-person pronoun in otherwise first-person narration (O'Connor, 1994) (6) Laughter (Jefferson, 1984) (7) Gasps (8) Interjections that contribute only to indexing affect and contribute nothing to reference (Jakobson, 1960; Goffman, 1981b) (9) Sighs Ex. **et puis j'sais plus c'que, trop**^+ *c'qu'elle m'a dit* **and then I don't remember what, too much**^+ *what she said to me*[5]
Narrator/interlocutory Narration with embedded interlocutory commentary	Ex. *e ela chega-se* **só**+ *ao pé de mim, e* **cada uma**+, **levei*** **tantas**+ *naquele dia* *and she comes* **right**+ *up to me, and* **each one**+(*blow*), *I* **really**+**got it*** *on that day*
<u>Character</u> Performance of characters in direct quotation; deictics no longer point to reporting, but to reported event	Ex. *puis, j'* **fais**,* '<u>Ouais chuis allée t'acheter ton cadeau</u>' *then, I'm* **like**,* '<u>Yeah, I went to buy you your present</u>'

(continued)

Table 4.1 *Continued*

Speaker role	Indexical devices and strategies in French and Portuguese that instantiate the stance
Narrator/character Indirect quotation/free indirect discourse; deictics point to reporting event	Ex. *elle m'a demandé où j'étais allée* *she asked me <u>where I'd gone</u>*
Interlocutory/character Fusion of current stance with quoted character segments for which one could attribute speech to both 'here-and-now' speaker and to performed character	Ex. *e depois ela,* '<u>Onde é que tu foste,</u> **não sei o quê,** ∧* **ganana** ∧* '. *and then she [said]',* <u>where were you,</u> **blabla,** ∧* **blabla.** ∧* '

Italics = narrator; **bold = interlocutor**; <u>underline = character</u>
For a list of transcription conventions see p. 113.

Narrator role

The first speaker role perspective is that of *narrator*. This role is instantiated when a speaker gets an extended turn at talk, taking responsibility to an audience for telling a story (Bauman, 1977, 1986). In this role, the speaker uses deictics that situate her as a participant in both the narrating and narrated events. The narrator role typically involves past tense (or historical present) narration, in which the speaker describes events through a series of 'temporally ordered past-tense clauses' (Labov & Waletzky, 1967). In French and Portuguese, these devices typically include a past tense or historical present verb. In colloquial French and Portuguese, these tenses include the *passé composé* (French) or the preterite (Portuguese), the imperfect (French and Portuguese), the pluperfect (French and Portuguese), and the historical present (French, and to some extent Portuguese).

Interlocutory role

As noted by Labov (Labov & Waletzky, 1967; Labov, 1972b, 1997), personal storytellers very rarely talk about their experiences from an exclusively narrator role perspective. A story emerges from, responds to, and alters an ongoing interaction – the larger context of the interview or conversation in which the story is told. Thus, the second role perspective is that of current, 'here-and-now' *interlocutor*. It is in this role that speakers engage in what Bauman (1986: 98–101) and Babcock (1977) have called metanarration, the 'overtly and explicitly social interactional elements of ... discourse ... have the effect of bridging the gap between the narrated event and the storytelling event by reaching out phatically to the audience, giving identificational and participatory immediacy to the story' (Bauman, 1986: 99–100). It is in this role that speakers display inter-personal rapport and affect, conveying their attitudes toward the narrated events and the ongoing interaction. This interlocutory role may continue to either interrupt or intersect with other roles.

Within the interlocutory role, speakers use a combination of language-specific indexical devices. To determine the French and Portuguese speech forms that may index the speaker's inhabitance of the interlocutory role, I coded over 700 stories of personal experience in French and Portuguese for devices through which speakers marked their current stance, and thus deviated from strict expository narration. Such deviations are evident when the speaker uses forms that allow her to either break from the advancement of plot or add something to her narrative that accomplishes more than the development of plot (Labov, 1972a; Polanyi, 1979). A full list of devices appears in Table 4.1. Although this list includes a larger set of devices than is frequently given in discussions of the pragmatic effects of discourse forms, it is not exhaustive. In particular, beyond laughter, gasps, and sighs, other prosodic and paralinguistic markers or contextualization cues (Gumperz, 1982), such as pitch, stress, lengthening, and volume are not included, nor are visual elements such as gaze, gesture, or facial expressions. Attention to other vocal and non-vocal cues that accompany and are an integral part of these role performances may complement or complicate this framework in future work.

Character role

Finally, the third speaker role is that of *characters*. Here, speakers replay the thoughts, feelings, words, deeds of characters from the narrated event, through various modes of reported speech. The role of reported speech has been discussed as having the same 'involvement creating' (Tannen, 1985) function as the interlocutory strategies described above. Some scholars have talked about reported speech as a strategy through which speakers may communicate their current affective stance in less semiotically 'transparent' and therefore perhaps more potent ways (Berman, 1999; Besnier, 1992). In the current model, reported speech does not directly index the current speaker's affect per se, but presents characters from the narrated event in a way that invites participants to identify with or judge characters in a particular light. Speakers use the deictics of verb tense, spatio-temporal adverbs, and pronouns to indicate whether an utterance is being presented primarily from the perspective of the quoted character or from the perspective of the narrator. In this way, the speaker can make come alive a context different from that of the immediate interaction.

Although character role speech may also function to advance plot, like interlocutory role speech, character role speech tends to accomplish its semiotic effects nonreferentially (Silverstein, 1976/1995). Specifically, character role speech derives its pragmatic effects through social iconicity and indexicality (Koven, 2001). In this way, characters may be made to come alive as locally imaginable types of people, speaking in ways that contrast with the interlocutor's style. To capture the manner in which characters were presented, I also coded each clause of direct discourse for one of five registers/styles in which the quoted character was made to speak in each language: (1) unmarked, (2) more familiar than conventional for the reported speech situation, (3) higher than conventional for the reported speech situation, (4) more vulgar than conventional for the reported speech situation, or (5) other language (French if surrounding speech is in Portuguese, Portuguese if surrounding speech is in French). A stretch of character speech was coded as familiar, high, vulgar, or other language, if quoted characters were made to use a speech register that gradiently challenges or departs from local sociolinguistic norms and expectations of co-occurrence and alternation (Ervin-Tripp, 1972/ 1995), for the kind of speech event represented. In this way, no form is familiar, formal, or vulgar in and of itself, but is judged as such depending on the character in whose mouth and in which situations it is used.

Double voicing

Each of these three roles can of course be performed alone, or simultaneously with the other two roles. For example, in indirect discourse, the narrator perspective is combined with that of the quoted character (Voloshinov, 1973). If a speaker combines plot advancement and current commentary, this is an example of interlocutor–narrator double voicing. Character and interlocutor speech can be simultaneous, if the speaker talks in such a way that her current interlocutory attitude has become fully collapsed or superimposed upon with that of a character (Silverstein, 1993; Wortham, 2001).

Summary of framework

With this framework, one can look for similarities and differences in the relative presence of these speaker roles in stories Linda told in each language. By seeing how Linda performs, moves between, and combines these roles, this framework allows one to analyze and compare affective stances across storytellings, across languages. As described, one can predict that stories with higher proportions of interlocutory and character role speech are likely to come across as more affectively engaged, relative to stories presented primarily in narrator role speech. Table 4.1 summarizes the devices that instantiate each speaker role perspective. To talk about Linda's different affective displays in narratives in her two languages, we will then be looking for consistencies and differences in patterns of narrative alignments and re-enactments in stories told in each language. In the transcripts in the appendix, narrator speech is italicized, interlocutory speech is bolded, and character speech is underlined.

Systematic coding

All of Linda's corpus was coded using the above framework. First, speech was parsed into clauses. A clause was defined as any segment with a conjugated verb or infinitive. Discourse markers (Schiffrin, 1987) or interactional particles (Maynard, 1989) and interjections that do not show logical connections were also counted as a clause. Each clause was then assigned to one of the six speaker role categories. Each clause of character speech was then also assigned to one of five registers: unmarked, familiar, high, vulgar, other language. To make stories of different lengths comparable, quantitative results for speaker role inhabitances are reported as percentages of total clauses (e.g. the percentage of all clauses rendered in narrator role).[4]

Local interpretations

Formal analysis of the frequencies and relative proportions of speaker roles and the indexical devices that instantiate them reveals little about what their presence means to people. After comparing the speaker roles people occupy in each language, we may ask what effects their coordinated use has to participants. Following Lucy (1992) and Besnier (1994), it is circular to assert that linguistic forms have certain 'psychological', 'interpersonal', or 'cognitive effects', if one relies exclusively on linguistic data. It is preferable to seek a broader ethnographic context to understand what seemingly affective performances actually index for participants (Besnier, 1994). Thus, rather than just compare formal differences between French and Portuguese narrations of a story, I enlisted local judgements of speakers' affective displays. I asked listeners a series of open-ended questions about how recorded speakers seemed to feel and react. With listeners' reactions to and interpretations of the stories, we tap into the socioculturally informed affects speakers conjure up when they talk, what others infer about what and how a speaker 'feels' from how he/she talks. This methodology is inspired by Lambert (1967), Gumperz (1982), Schieffelin (1990), and Urciuoli (1998), whose use of participants' reactions to recordings of speech samples lets one learn how people link the form of an utterance with its social and psychological functions. By appealing to others' reactions to tellings of the 'same' story in two languages, one gets a better sense of whether the indexical strategies a speaker uses in each performance succeed in displaying coherent, conventionally recognized affective stances.

Summary of analytic tools

Together, these two approaches (formal analysis and others' reactions), along with Linda's earlier noted reports about her affective experiences in French and Portuguese, allow one to identify and compare the formal indexical, largely non-referential devices a speaker uses in each language – and also to get a sense of what conventional affective displays the use of those forms indexes for participants.

Data Presentation

Linda told 12 different stories of personal experience twice – first in Portuguese, then in French, each time one-on-one, to a different female French–Portuguese bilingual of her age. She had not met either interviewer before, but knew that each was also a bilingual Luso-descendant. I will present two tellings of the 'same' story, formal analyses of the tellings, as well as five bilingual listeners' commentaries on recordings of each telling of the story. To determine whether she consistently used the same kinds of strategies in her two languages throughout the interview, beyond this individual story pair, I will then present results from a larger corpus of narratives Linda told in each language.

Two tellings of fight with mother

In the appendix, one can view the full transcription and English translations of a story Linda told of a fight she had with her mother on Mother's Day. She told this story in response to a request to tell about a bad experience with someone she knew well. In both versions, Linda reported that her mother had nagged her about where she had been. This annoyed Linda, so she threw the gift at her mother, at which point her mother slapped her. In the transcripts in the appendix, one can see how I coded each clause of both renditions, using the framework described above. Insofar as was possible, stories have been aligned so that comparable segments lie next to each other.

There are many noteworthy differences between these two tellings, only some of which I have space to explore here (Table 4.2). In both languages, Linda shifts back and forth between speaker roles. In both versions, the percentage of the pure narrator role, the most neutral storytelling mode, is relatively low (16.1% in French and 27.7% in Portuguese). In

Table 4.2 Proportion of all clauses in the narrative in each speaker role: French telling versus Portuguese telling

Language	N	NI	I	C	NC	IC	Total
Mother's Day French	16.1 $n=14$	21.8 $n=19$	35.6 $n=31$	23.0 $n=20$	1.1 $n=1$	2.3 $n=2$	100 $n=87$
Mother's Day Portuguese	27.7 $n=13$	21.3 $n=10$	25.5 $n=12$	14.9 $n=7$	2.1 $n=1$	8.5 $n=4$	100 $n=47$

N, narrator; I, interlocutor; C, character.

Table 4.3 Ninth segment of the narrative

Portuguese	English translation of Portuguese	English translation of French	French
e eu, peguei na prenda que eu le tinha oferecido e **botei**-*a* pro chão,*	*and I, I took the gift that I'd given her and* **I put it*** *on the ground,*	*then I* **flung*** *the gift at her,* **you know,***$ *I* **flung*** *it on the ground,*	*puis je lui ai* **balancé*** *le cadeau,* **quoi,***$ *j'l'ai* **balancé*** *par terre,*

(*italics, narrator role;* **bold, interlocutor role**)

both, Linda engages in a good deal of interlocutory commentary, alone and combined with narrator and character roles. In both, she quotes the different characters. One could expect that listeners might have the impression of an 'affective' presentation in both. However, Linda tells a much higher proportion of the Portuguese narrative as a neutral narrator (N), and a much higher proportion of the French narrative as an interlocutor (I). Similarly, she performs a higher proportion of character speech (C) in French. These differences may yield an impression of greater affective intensity in the French telling than in the Portuguese. These trends are striking in particular segments, for example, the ninth segment of the narrative (Table 4.3).

The Portuguese is primarily in narrator mode, with only one clause in narrator–interlocutor role because of the shift to the more familiar '*botei/* put'. In French, it is far more interlocutory, with three tokens of lower register use (*balancé*/flung x2, *quoi*/you know). '*Quoi*' also functions as a discourse marker. One might speculate that this profile of role occupancies might create an impression of more intense 'reliving' in the French version, with the greater presence of the character role and more performance of the interlocutory role.

Interlocutory strategies

As discussed above, one challenge of this coding scheme is that it compares stance across two different languages, claiming equivalent functions for different (kinds of) indexical devices. In Table 4.4, I present the repertoire of interlocutory devices that Linda uses to present her current stance in both languages, and the proportions of those devices. Each indexical device in the interlocutory mode has also been coded on the transcripts. As one can see, she uses somewhat different combinations of devices to accomplish the roles in the two languages.

Table 4.4 Mother's Day story: Interlocutory device repertoire (percentages)

Interlocutory device	Mothers's Day in French	Mother's Day in Portuguese
Shifts to familiar	27.4% ($n = 17$)	22.5% ($n = 9$)
Shifts to high	4.8% ($n = 3$)	2.5% ($n = 1$)
Shifts to vulgar	3.2% ($n = 2$)	2.5% ($n = 1$)
Shifts to other language	0%	0%
All shifts	35.5% ($n = 22$)	27.5% ($n = 11$)
Intensifiers	12.9% ($n = 8$)	22.5% ($n = 9$)
Second person	1.6% ($n = 1$)	0%
Interjections	3.2% ($n = 2$)	2.5% ($n = 1$)
Discourse markers	24.2% ($n = 15$)	10.0% ($n = 4$)
Parentheticals	21.0% ($n = 13$)	17.5% ($n = 7$)
Laughter	1.6% ($n = 1$)	20.0% ($n = 8$)
Sighs	0%	0%
Gasps	0%	0%
Totals	100% ($n = 62$)	100% ($n = 40$)

All interlocutory devices were summed, and proportions of each kind of device are given in Table 4.4. Across these two stories, in Portuguese she uses more quantifying intensifiers to show her current stance (Portuguese 22.5% versus French 12.9%). In French she uses more shifts to a marked register (35.5% versus 27.5% of all interlocutory devices). Of those shifts, a higher proportion involves shifts to a familiar or vulgar register in French than in Portuguese. She also uses many more discourse markers in the French version than the Portuguese (24.2% versus 10.0%). To further illustrate these trends, one can compare several equivalent segments in the two narratives (Table 4.5).

Table 4.5 Comparison of equivalent segments

Portuguese		French	
e ela chega-se **só+** ao pé de mim, e **cada uma+**, levei* **tantas+** naquele dia ((laughs))#	and she comes **right+** up to me, and **each one+** (blow), I **really+ got it*** on that day ((laughs))#	so euh, **so$**, **well$** she gave me(vulg.)* a **good+** smack/ licking(fam.)*, you know,*$	donc euh, **bon$,ben$,** elle m'a foutu*une bonne+ râclée*, quoi,*$

In both segments, Linda uses multiple devices that I have coded as interlocutory on the transcripts in the appendix. In Portuguese she says, *'levei (fam) tantas naquele dia'*, roughly equivalent to colloquial 'I really got it' with an intensifier and accompanying laughter. In French, this same event is rendered as *'bon, ben, elle m'a foutu (vulg) une bonne râclée (fam)'* [well, you know, she nailed (vulg) me a good smack (fam.)] where *foutre* is in a vulgar register, and *râclée* in a familiar register, preceded and followed by discourse markers. In French, in this single stretch she uses more shifts to a lower register and more discourse markers; in Portuguese, most of her stance is communicated through quantifying intensifiers, *só, cada uma, tantas*.

Throughout the two tellings, she uses more colloquial (familiar and vulgar) terms in French, where in Portuguese she uses relatively neutral terms. Compare *zangou-se comigo* [she got mad at me] with *on s'est engueulé* [we bawled (vulg.) each other out] (Segment 4 in the transcript). At times she does use a marked register in Portuguese, for example, in the segment discussed earlier, *botei a prenda* [I put the present]. This is marked not for its vulgarity, but for its unschooledness/rurality; it stands as a marked register alternate to the more standard *deitar* [place] or *pôr* [put]. In French, to present this same action, she says *'je lui ai balancé le cadeau, quoi'* [I flung the gift at her, y'know] with *balancer*, a more familiar term, that also connotes more force and anger, follwed by the familiar discourse marker, *quoi*. 'Balancer' contrasts with the more neutral *donner* (give) or even *lancer* (throw) (see Segment 9).

This divergent register usage is also apparent in how she frames quoted speech. In French, she uses the familiar metapragmatic verb of speaking *faire*, *'je fais'*, roughly equivalent to 'I go', or 'I'm like', marked for its familiarity, and associated with 'young', urban, less educated speakers. In Portuguese, she frames quotes with the relatively neutral presentation of the subject pronoun, *ela, eu* (she, I) without an explicit verb of speaking. This is a relatively neutral form of quote presentation.

As we see, the qualitative comparison is supported quantitatively, with her greater use of shifts to a lower register in French, and greater use of quantifying intensifiers in Portuguese.

Performance of character roles

Linda not only speaks as a current interlocutor, but also through quoted characters. In French, she consistently makes quoted characters speak in 'extreme', marked styles. The Portuguese quotes appear in a comparatively neutral, unmarked register. In French, her quoted retort to her mother is quite familiar relative to local norms of teenage child–parent speech. It is marked with the contraction of *oui* to *ouais*, the presence of the familiar discourse marker *quoi*, and the use of the blunt

Table 4.6 Percentages of clauses of direct quotation in each relative style

	Unmarked	_Familiar_	_High_	_Vulgar_	_Other language_
French	25.0%	65.0%	10.0%	0%	0%
	$n=5$	$n=13$	$n=2$	$n=0$	$n=0$
Portuguese	71.4%	28.6%	0%	0%	0%
	$n=5$	$n=2$	$n=0$	$n=0$	$n=0$

imperative _tiens ton cadeau_/take your present, in speech to an elder. This trend is supported quantitatively (see Table 4.6).

Listener reactions

Having noted these different strategies qualitatively and quantitatively, one can now proceed to ask how listeners judged the use of these strategies – how they inferred Linda's affect from both tellings. Listeners noted both a difference in the affective intensity and persona evoked in these two tellings.

Intensity

The five listeners each spontaneously and independently commented on how upset Linda was in each telling. They talked about intensity in more holistic terms than the quantitative analyses alone reveal. Each reported that Linda seemed less upset in the Portuguese telling than in the French telling. They heard her as more currently moved by her own storytelling in French. As one said about the French, 'we feel more the atmosphere of nervous tension.... In Portuguese it's lighter, it's less tense... in French this was a hard experience for her, she hasn't digested it'. Another put it, 'she invests herself less in it [in Portuguese] ... she relives it less'. Another situated the difference between the two tellings in the 'strength' of her words, 'it's lighter in Portuguese, there isn't the same force, there isn't the same, there isn't the same violence... the words she uses are less expressive'. Another listener commented more about her impression of the narrated event, how the original argument with her mother must have been, based on Linda's French telling, 'I see the scene very clearly (.) a fight/chewing out uh (.) for nothing/ bullshit... it must have been pretty virulent. She must have been real mad, real frustrated, totally hurt'. She then goes on to describe that Linda is totally absorbed in the telling: 'It's the conflict that (.) that lasts, that's difficult to manage'. Whereas in Portuguese she has 'tons of distance'. The last listener described the French as coming from someone who isn't calm but very highly strung. There is thus a consensus among the five listeners that the French version displays greater affective intensity, or more precisely, that the speaker re-enacts the event more fully in the French telling, displaying that this event is more 'present' for her. With these listeners' reactions, we see that the coding scheme presented above is supported by listeners' perceptions of affective stance. Listeners respond to the pragmatic force of certain clusters of devices in the speaker roles, hearing them as indexes of Linda's affective stance.

Affective performance and persona

Listener reactions allow us to talk about 'intensity' in more differentiated terms than could the quantitative analysis. They reveal more about the kind of affective performances Linda enacted in each language. Following Irvine (1982, 1990), Rosaldo (1980), and Lutz (1988a,b), cultural performances of affect typically presuppose and creatively enact local notions of different kinds of personhood and social relations. Indeed, when listeners heard Linda speak, they spontaneously commented not only on the extent and nature of Linda's stance, but made the link between that reaction and the kind of person Linda must be. From the French recording, listeners argued that they heard Linda as more 'upset' and 'angrier' in the here and now of the telling, but also interpreted the manner of her display in perduring, characterological terms: Linda comes across as a more rebellious, disrespectful, and provocative person in French. These listeners thus describe the multiple indexical foci of Linda's talk about a bad experience – how her talk indexes both intensity and persona for listeners.

One listener said that she saw Linda as 'a girl who won't let herself be taken advantage of but who at the same time is looking for trouble ... even the tone of her voice, it's it's got, pff, a little vulgarity ... and at the same time provocation, even if, even if, she's is basically not mean'. This listener reported that she heard Linda as less vulgar and provocative in Portuguese. Another listener described Linda in very similar terms, saying that she seemed less aggressive and violent in Portuguese. Another said about the French, 'well, better not piss her off ((laughter))'. Another also described her as more worked up, aggressive, and rebellious in French. She later said, 'She's not a nice little girl, eh, in French. Not in Portuguese either ... she's much more aggressive when she speaks French than when she speaks Portuguese. Her Portuguese doesn't show her desire to say to her mother, "stop it, you're making me mad" ... in French she says more to her mother, "you're driving me nuts ... "'. From these comments we see that Linda's French performance evoked a very particular, locally recognizable image, not just of angry affect, but of a type of angry person.

Results from Linda's Entire Corpus

From only one story pair, one should not draw conclusions about how this speaker regularly performs affect in her two languages. I thus present the patterns of speaker role inhabitance across the 24 stories Linda told (12 stories told in each language). If indeed the quantitative patterns of speaker role inhabitance are consistent across her corpus, one can speculate that listeners might form similar impressions of her from listening to other stories.

Again, it is interesting to note how infrequently she engages in simple narration (N) in either language – just 13.6% of clauses in French and 19.4% in Portuguese (Table 4.7). As with analyses of the story pair described above, these numbers show that Linda is engaged in much interlocutory and character role performance in both languages. In other words, in both languages, she is doing something beyond simply narrating – either demonstrating her current stance or presenting the perspective of a character. In both languages she is performing the voices of characters in direct quotes at similar rates (13.2% versus 12.6%). In some sense, Linda is able to mobilize discursive resources to present somewhat comparable sets of speaker role perspectives. In both languages, this lends further empirical support to the notion that narrative discourse involves much more than the elaboration of plot (Bakhtin, 1981; Koven, 2002; Wortham, 2001).

However, these similarities are relative. Across her 12 story pairs, Linda still speaks more often in the narrator role (N) in Portuguese than in French (19.4% versus 13.6%), more stepping entirely outside of the narrative in French, as an interlocutor (I), to display her current assessment (51.4% versus 44.4%). In other words, from these materials, it seems that she may consistently display greater affective intensity in French than in Portuguese narratives.

We can also ask about the proportions of different devices and strategies Linda consistently uses to present interlocutory and character stances. As seen in Table 4.8, she continues to use a greater proportion of quantifying intensifiers in Portuguese than in French (23.9% versus

Table 4.7 Percentage of French and Portuguese narrative corpus in each speaker role

	N	NI	I	C	NC	IC
French	13.6% $n=161$	13.3% $n=158$	51.4% $n=610$	13.2% $n=157$	4.7% $n=56$	3.8% $n=45$
Portuguese	19.4% $n=122$	15.9% $n=100$	44.4% $n=279$	12.6% $n=79$	3.5% $n=22$	4.3% $n=27$

N, narrator; I, interlocutor; C, character

Table 4.8 Linda's profile of interlocutory devices (percentages)

	French	*Portuguese*
Shifts to familiar	18.0% $n = 204$	18.0% $n = 110$
Shifts to high	8.0% $n = 91$	8.1% $n = 50$
Shifts to vulgar	1.1% $n = 12$	0.2% $n = 1$
Shifts to other language	0.0% $n = 1$	0.7% $n = 4$
All shifts	27.2% $n = 308$	27.0% $n = 165$
Quantifying intensifiers	16.2% $n = 183$	23.9% $n = 146$
Second person	1.6% $n = 18$	0% $n = 0$
Interjections	1.1% $n = 12$	3.9% $n = 24$
Discourse markers	24.6% $n = 278$	9.8% $n = 60$
Parentheticals	28.6% $n = 323$	33.2% $n = 203$
Laughter	0.8% $n = 9$	2.1% $n = 13$
Sighs	0% $n = 0$	0% $n = 0$
Gasps	0% $n = 0$	0% $n = 0$
Total	100% $n = 1131$	100% $n = 611$

16.2%). Similarly in French, she uses a greater proportion of discourse markers (24.6% versus 9.8%). She uses more shifts to a vulgar register in French than Portuguese (1.1% versus 0.2%). This indicates that she consistently uses a different, and perhaps a wider set of interlocutory strategies in French. One could argue that this difference demonstrates that Linda similarly has access to and uses a more complex, developed set of interlocutory devices in French. Whether this comes from Linda's linguistic ability in each language, her sense of entitlement to adopt equivalent affective stances in each language, or broader French and

Table 4.9 Proportion of styles in which direct quotes are performed

	French	*Portuguese*
Unmarked	51.0% $n = 80$	68.4% $n = 54$
C familiar	42.0% $n = 66$	26.6% $n = 21$
C high	3.8% $n = 6$	5.1% $n = 4$
C vulgar	0.6% $n = 1$	1.3% $n = 1$
C other language	3.8% $n = 6$	0.0% $n = 0$
Total	101.2% $n = 157$	101.4% $n = 79$

Percentages exceed 100%, as coding was not exclusive. Clauses could fall into more than one register.

Portuguese norms of affective display, it nonetheless has consequences for the discrepancy in affective stance that she reported and others perceived.

Although she generally performs similar proportions of direct quotation in each language, she is more likely to perform exaggerated quoted voices in French, putting more familiar and vulgar speech in the mouths of quoted characters in French, regardless of the 'actual' language any particular character may have used (Table 4.9). Perhaps, following Besnier (1992), this may be a less 'transparent', but nevertheless potent way of communicating affect.

Given that listeners heard a story pair with patterns that are relatively representative of her larger corpus, one might predict that listeners would form similar impressions of her after hearing her other story pairs in two languages.

Discussion of Limitations of Current Study

Although this chapter has focused heavily on elicited materials, it has drawn from multiple sources that each provides convergent evidence: Linda's own reports of her experience in each language, narrative performances in the context of interviews with two Luso-descendants, and others' reactions to recordings of those performances. These different sources of data confirm that Linda has embodied something experientially real, both to her and to listeners.

Of course, whether the two interviews actually simulate Linda's affective displays in two languages outside of the interview context is an important methodological question. As both tellings were elicited in France, by interviewers whom she knew to be bilingual, one could even speculate that her two tellings would yield a less marked difference between French and Portuguese affective displays than would two tellings in naturally occurring French and Portuguese monolingual contexts. In the interviews, if she had wanted access to the affective associations of the other language, she could have code switched. In her everyday monolingual settings, however, Linda may not have that option and may be confined to the resources of one language at a time.

Similarly, one wants to exercise caution before claiming that Linda's case generalizes to other French–Portuguese bilinguals, or to bilinguals in general. In ongoing work (Koven, in preparation), I am investigating these issues with materials from 22 other speakers from this same population. It should not be surprising to find other populations of speakers who also have access to multiple, verbally mediated, context-specific ways of displaying affect, as sociolinguistic diversity is the rule rather than the exception.

Furthermore, before replicating a similar study with a different bilingual group or individual, one should also determine ethnographically how the different linguistic contexts and affective idioms are distributed within a community and/or for a particular person. In other contexts, people may not necessarily experience the presence of multiple idioms of affective display as occurring in distinct, separate settings. For example, bilinguals who spend most of their time with other bilinguals may perhaps not manifest the same degree or kinds of differences as did Linda. They may be able to activate with each other the affective associations of both languages. However, as Rampton (1995) has argued, much work on the social meanings of language use in multilingual populations has adopted an 'in-group' bias. From such an 'in-group' perspective, one might assume that bilinguals would most frequently interact with other bilinguals, and thus that they would normally share the same combinations of affective idioms with those around them. However, it should first be empirically demonstrated which languages speakers share with their different intimate and less intimate interactional partners. In this instance, Linda does not share a bilingual repertoire with many of the people whom she regularly talks to, including some of her family members and her boyfriend. In this sense, unlike a bilingual whose intimates are also bilingual, Linda's French and Portuguese contexts of affective display with intimates may be relatively segregated. Therefore, it may not be the case that Linda, other bilinguals, or perhaps anyone, necessarily shares an entire overlap of verbal repertoire with those with whom they are most likely to display affect, no matter how intimate. No single interaction or relationship permits expression of an actor's whole range of styles of affective display. Most people are regularly 'confined' to a subset of their repertoire, in any given interaction. In this regard, that Linda seems to perform distinct French and Portuguese affective displays may be related to the fact that she does, in large measure, occupy two monolingual worlds. As a result, she must regularly limit herself to the resources, intensities, and personas available to her in one or the other language.

Conclusion

This analysis has suggested approaches and tools for comparing the same speaker's affective performances in two sociolinguistic contexts. Linda speaks less as an interlocutor and more as a neutral narrator in Portuguese than in French. Similarly, she performs the voices of quoted characters in more extreme, marked styles in French than in Portuguese. Supporting this formal analysis, both listeners and Linda also reported that they 'felt' that she is more forceful/intense in French than in Portuguese. Futhermore, it is not just that she performs 'more' affect in French than Portuguese. Both Linda and listeners perceive her as enacting a different kind of affect, from a different kind of social actor. She is perceived in French not just as angrier in the here and now, but as an angrier person. On the other hand, in Portuguese she comes across as someone who uses less profanity, restrains herself, and is thus a more 'calm, reserved' person. As she displays similar patterns of speaker role inhabitance across her corpus, one could predict that listeners would consistently notice the same kinds of differences in her French and Portuguese displays.

What accounts for these differences? These languages are grammatically very similar, and from a Whorfian point of view are both examples of 'Standard Average European' languages (Whorf 1940/1956). There may be slight differences in the grammatical resources available to speakers in French and Portuguese. However, these structural differences alone cannot account for why Linda experiences herself and the evaluators experience her as angrier, more forceful, and more aggressive in French. It is doubtful that there is some inherent property of French or Portuguese that constrains the kind or degree of affective performance speakers can perform in each language. Rather than grammar, it may be a question of the styles of affective performance to which Linda has access in French and Portuguese contexts. Recall Linda's remark that she 'contains' herself in Portuguese, but not in French. This speaks to her own sense of the intensities and kinds of displays that she is either able to or entitled to perform, not to what each language grammatically permits. There may indeed be people who swear freely in Portuguese to display affect; yet Linda recognizes she is not and cannot be one of 'them'. Recall how she put it, she doesn't 'have' that vocabulary. Perhaps it is not just that that she cannot but that she would not feel as free to use it. It may be unacceptable for Linda to quote herself talking back to her mother in such familiar terms in Portuguese as she did in French, where she does have access to a 'back-talking' persona. Linda may not be free to perform an aggressive persona in Portuguese. Whether a question of what she is able or entitled to do in Portuguese, this difference matters for the available range of affective displays, intensities, and gendered personas she can perform in each language.

This work contributes to discussions of bilingualism and emotion methodologically and conceptually. Methodologically, this chapter has gone beyond looking at how bilinguals talk *about* emotion, by instead emphasizing how one bilingual discursively 'does' or displays emotion/affect. It has then looked at the complex, indexical connections between such discursive displays and people's interpretations of (their own and others') affect. By using these multiple strategies, one reduces the limitations of both approaches. As discourse-oriented scholars have long noted the limitations of asking people directly about their verbal practices, one does not rely exclusively on speakers' talk about their own affective experiences, similarly one does not rely exclusively on comparative percentages of discursive devices as indexes of some affective stance or identity, without recourse to local interpretations of particular ways of talking. Future research into bilingualism and emotion should continue to distinguish between how bilinguals use linguistic forms to *show* feeling, and how they talk *about* feeling. The relationships between these two levels of emotional 'meaning' can then be determined empirically.

Furthermore, this work has highlighted the centrally sociolinguistic dimensions of the relationships between bilingualism and emotion. One should expect to find relationships between sociolinguistic diversity and affective expression for most people in locally specific ways, whether bilingual or not. Future work should investigate how and to what extent the nature of particular bilinguals' between-language differences in their affective expression is comparable to other cases of sociolinguistic diversity associated with different types of affective display, for the same speaker or as distributed within a community. To draw such comparisons, each case should first be situated ethnographically, to determine which linguistic resources and affects are available to people. Such scholarship can then illuminate how different ways of talking shape the same people's feelings across contexts.

Acknowledgements

I would like to thank Aneta Pavlenko for very helpful feedback as well as Niko Besnier and Michael Silverstein. Funding was provided by a Châteaubriand fellowship from the French Government, a funded exchange between the École des Hautes Études en Sciences Sociales and the University of Chicago, and a Beckman Fellowship from the University of Illinois Reseach Board. All remaining errors are my own. A more extended version of this paper appears in *Text* 24(4), 471–515.

Notes

1. A different version of this paper appears in *Text* (2004), 24(4), 471–515.
2. Scholarship in linguistic anthropology has privileged the term 'affect' over 'emotion', to describe the range of socially recognizable feelings, attitudes, and stances that people may experience, display, and recognize across a number of different cultural contexts (Besnier, 1990; Irvine, 1982; Ochs & Schieffelin, 1989). In this tradition of scholarship, 'emotions' have sometimes been understood as assuming Western folk understandings of personhood, or implying a defined set of psychologically located states, such as anger, sadness, disgust, and so on (Besnier, 1990: 421). Drawing more from this first tradition with its more general approach to the study of 'feeling', I nevertheless use affect and emotion interchangeably.
3. This self quote is translated from the original,'ah, tu m'fais chier, tu m'emmerdes, m'prends pas la tête'.
4. As part of the larger study based on materials from 23 speakers, intercoder agreement was established by having two coders independently code 20% of the entire corpus, including Linda. Reliability was computed separately for both French and Portuguese. In French, coders agreed about clause boundaries 92.9% ($n = 4950$) of the time, and in Portuguese 93% ($n = 3948$) of the time. For speaker role inhabitance, I used Cohen's (1960) Kappa as my formula for computing intercoder agreement. Cohen's Kappa allows one to correct for rates of agreement due purely to chance. Kappa was 0.83 in Portuguese ($n = 3441$) and 0.89 ($n = 4680$) in French. Cohen's Kappa for register was 0.76 ($n = 3750$) for Portuguese and 0.75 ($n = 2870$) for French. Fleiss (1981) describes Kappa over 0.75 as excellent.
5. Because of space limitations, I provide here an example of only one interlocutory device. Please see Koven (2002) for examples of each device.
6. Although the interviewers clearly play an important role in the elicitation and co-narration of the story, for the purposes of this article, only interviewee speech has been counted.

References

Abu-Lughod, L. (1986) *Veiled Sentiments: Honor and Poetry in a Bedouin Society.* Berkeley: University of California Press.

Amati-Mehler, J., Argentieri, S. and Canestri, J. (1993) *The Babel of the Unconscious: Mother Tongue and Foreign Languages in the Psychoanalytic Dimension* (J. Whitelaw-Cucco, trans.). Madison, CT: International Universities Press.

Babcock, B. (1977) The story in the story: Metanarration in folk narrative. In R. Bauman (ed.) *Verbal Art as Performance* (pp. 61–80). Prospect Heights: Waveland.

Bakhtin, M. (1981) *The Dialogic Imagination.* Austin: University of Texas Press.

Bauman, R. (1977) *Verbal Art as Performance.* Prospect Heights: Waveland.

Bauman, R. (1986) *Story, Performance, and Event.* New York: Cambridge University Press.

Bauman, R. and Briggs, C. (1990) Poetics and performance as critical perspectives on language and social life. *Annual Review of Anthropology* 19, 59–88.

Beaujour, E. (1989) *Alien Tongues: Bilingual Russian Writers of the First Emigration.* Ithaca: Cornell University Press.

Berman, L. (1999) Dignity in tragedy: How Javanese women speak of emotion. In G. Palmer and D. Occhi (eds) *Languages of Sentiment* (pp. 65–106). Philadelphia: John Benjamins.

Besnier, N. (1990) Language and affect. *Annual Review of Anthropology* 19, 419–51.

Besnier, N. (1992) Reported speech and affect on Nukulaelae Atoll. In J. Hill and J. Irvine (eds) *Responsibility and Evidence in Oral Discourse* (pp. 161–81). New York: Cambridge University Press.

Besnier, N. (1994) Involvement in linguistic practice: An ethnographic appraisal. *Journal of Pragmatics* 22, 279–99.

Besnier, N. (1995) *Literacy, Emotion, and Authority: Reading and Writing on a Polynesian Atoll.* New York: Cambridge University Press.

Burger, L. and Miller, P. (1999) Early talk about the past revisited: Affect in working-class and middle-class children's co-narrations. *Journal of Child Language* 26(1), 133–62.

Cohen, J. (1960) Coefficient of agreement for nominal scales. *Educational and Psychological Measurement* 20, 37–46.

Dickel Dunn, C. (1999) Public and private voices: Japanese style shifting and the display of affective intensity. In G. Palmer and D. Occhi (eds) *Languages of Sentiment* (pp. 107–30). Philadelphia: John Benjamins.

Doi, T. (1974) *The Anatomy of Dependence.* New York: Kodansha International.

Errington, J. (1984) *Language and Social Change in Java.* Athens: Ohio University Center for International Studies.

Ervin, S. (1964) Language and TAT content in bilinguals. *Journal of Abnormal and Social Psychology* 68, 500–507.

Ervin-Tripp, S. (1972/1995) Sociolinguistics. In B. Blount (ed.) *Language, Culture, and Society: A Book of Readings* (pp. 300–65). Prospect Heights: Waveland.

Fleiss, J. (1981) *Statistical Methods for Rates and Proportions.* New York: Wiley.

Friedrich, P. (1972) Social context and semantic feature: The Russian pronominal usage. In J. Gumperz (ed.) *Directions in Sociolinguistics* (pp. 270–300). New York: Holt, Rinehart, and Winston, Inc.

Gal, S. (1979) *Language-Shift: Social Determinants of Linguistic Change in Bilingual Austria.* New York: Academic Press.

Goffman, E. (1981a) Footing. In *Forms of Talk* (pp. 124–59). Philadelphia: University of Pennsylvania Press.

Goffman, E. (1981b) Response cries. In *Forms of Talk* (pp. 78–123). Philadelphia: University of Pennsylvania Press.

Green, J. (1985) *Le Langage et son Double.* Paris: Éditions de la Différence.

Gumperz, J. (1982) *Discourse Strategies.* New York: Cambridge University Press.

Harré, R. (1986) *The Social Construction of Emotions.* New York: Basil Blackwell.

Heider, K. (1991) *Landscapes of Emotion: Mapping Three Cultures of Emotion in Indonesia.* New York: Cambridge University Press.

Hill, J. (1995) The voices of Don Gabriel: Responsibility and self in a Modern Mexicano narrative. In D. Tedlock and B. Mannheim (eds) *The Dialogic Emergence of Culture* (pp. 97–147). Chicago: University of Illinois Press.

Hoffman, E. (1989) *Lost in Translation.* New York: Penguin.

Hymes, D. (1966) Two types of linguistic relativity. In W. Bright (ed.) *Sociolinguistics, Proceedings of the UCLA Sociolinguistics Conference, 1964* (pp. 114–67). The Hague: Mouton.

Irvine, J. (1982) Language and affect: Some cross-cultural issues. In H. Byrnes (ed.) *Contemporary Perceptions of Language: Interdisciplinary Dimensions. Georgetown University Roundtable on Languages and Linguistics* (pp. 31–47). Washington, DC: Georgetown University Press.

Irvine, J. (1990) Registering affect: Heteroglossia in the linguistic expression of emotion. In C. Lutz and L. Abu-Lughod (eds) *Language and the Politics of Emotion* (pp. 126–63). New York: Cambridge University Press.

Jakobson, R. (1960) Closing statement: Linguistics and poetics. In T. Sebeok (ed.) *Style in Language*, pp. 350–77. Cambridge: MIT Press.

Jefferson, G. (1984) On the organization of laughter in talk about troubles. In J. Atkinson and J. Heritage (eds) *Structures of Social Action: Studies in Conversation Analysis* (pp. 346–69). New York: Cambridge University Press.

Koven, M. (1998) Two languages in the self/the self in two languages: French–Portuguese bilinguals' verbal enactments of self in narrative discourse. *Ethos* 26(4), 410–55.

Koven, M. (2001) Comparing bilinguals' quoted performances of self and others in tellings of the same experience in two languages. *Language in Society* 30(4), 513–58.

Koven, M. (2002) An analysis of speaker role inhabitance in narratives of personal experience. *Journal of Pragmatics* 34(2), 167–217.

Koven, M. (2004) Transnational perspectives on sociolinguistic capital among Luso-descendants in France and Portugal. *American Ethnologist* 31(2), 270–90.

Koven, M. (in preparation) *Enacting Selves in Two Languages.*

Kulick, D. (1992) *Language Shift and Cultural Reproduction: Socialization, Self, and Syncretism in a Papua New Guinean Village.* New York: Cambridge University Press.

Labov, W. (1972a) *Language in the Inner City.* Philadelphia: University of Pennsylvania Press.

Labov, W. (1972b) *Sociolinguistic Patterns.* Philadelphia: University of Pennsylvania Press.

Labov, W. (1984) Intensity. In D. Schiffrin (ed.) *Meaning, Form, and Use in Context. Georgetown University Roundtable on Languages and Linguistics* (pp. 43–70). Washington, DC: Georgetown University Press.

Labov, W. (1997) Some further steps in narrative analysis. *Journal of Narrative and Life History* 7(1–4), 395–415.

Labov, W. and Waletzky, J. (1967) Narrative analysis: Oral versions of personal experience. In J. Helm (ed.) *Essays in the Verbal and Visual Arts* (pp. 12–44). Seattle: University of Washington Press.

Lambert, W. (1967) A social psychology of bilingualism. *Journal of Social Issues* 23, 91–109.

Lucy, J. (1992) *Language Diversity and Thought: A Reformulation of the Linguistic Relativity Hypothesis.* New York: Cambridge University Press.

Lucy, J. (1997) The scope of linguistic relativity: An analysis and review of empirical research. In J. Gumperz and S. Levinson (eds) *Rethinking Linguistic Relativity* (pp. 38–69). New York: Cambridge University Press.

Lutz, C. (1988a) *Unnatural Emotions: Everyday Sentiments on a Micronesian Atoll and Their Challenge to Western Theory.* Chicago: University of Chicago Press.

Lutz, C. (1988b) Ethnographic perspectives on the emotion lexicon. In V. Hamilton, G. Bower and N. Frijda (eds) *Cognitive Perspectives on Emotion and Motivation* (pp. 399–419). Dordrecht: Kluwer Academic Publishers.

Lutz, C. and White, G. (1986) The anthropology of emotions. *Annual Review of Anthropology* 15, 405–36.

Maynard, S.K. (1989) *Japanese Conversation: Self-Contextualization Through Structure and Interactional Management.* Norwood: Ablex.

Moore, C., Romney, A., Hsia, T. and Rusch, C. (1999) The universality of the semantic structure of emotion terms: Methods for the study of inter- and intra-cultural variability. *American Anthropologist* 101(3), 529–46.

Ochs, E. (1988) *Culture and Language Development.* New York: Cambridge University Press.

Ochs, E. (1990) Indexicality and socialization. In J. Stigler, R. Shweder and G. Herdt (eds) *Cultural Psychology: Essays on Comparative Human Development* (pp. 287–308). New York: Cambridge University Press.

Ochs, E. and Schieffelin, B. (1989) Language has a heart. *Text* 9, 1, 7–25.

O'Connor, P. (1994) 'You could feel it through your skin': Agency and positioning in prisoners' stabbing stories. *Text* 14(1), 45–75.

Pavlenko, A. (1998) Second language learning by adults: Testimonies of bilingual writers. *Issues in Applied Linguistics* 9, 3–19.

Pavlenko, A. (2002a) Bilingualism and emotions. *Multilingua* 21(1), 45–78.

Pavlenko, A. (2002b) Emotions and the body in Russian and English. *Pragmatics and Cognition* 10(1–2), 201–36.

Polanyi, L. (1979) So what's the point? *Semiotica* 25(3–4), 207–41.

Rampton, B. (1995) *Crossing: Language and Ethnicity Among Adolescents.* New York: Longman.

Rodriguez, R. (1982) *Hunger of Memory.* Boston: Godine.

Rosaldo, M. (1980) *Knowledge and Passion: Ilongot Notions of Self and Social Life.* New York: Cambridge University Press.

Rosenberg, D. (1990) Language in the discourse of the emotions. In C. Lutz and L. Abu-Lughod (eds) *Language and the Politics of Emotion* (pp. 162–85). New York: Cambridge University Press.

Schieffelin, B. (1990) *The Give and Take of Everyday Life: Language Socialization of Kaluli Children.* New York: Cambridge University Press.

Schiffrin, D. (1987) *Discourse Markers.* New York: Cambridge University Press.

Schrauf, R. (2000) Bilingual autobiographical memory: Experimental studies and clinical cases. *Culture and Psychology* 6(4), 387–417.

Shweder, R. (1994) 'You're not sick, you're just in love': Emotion as an interpretive system. In P. Ekman and R. Davidson (eds) *The Nature of Emotion: Fundamental Questions* (pp. 32–45). New York: Oxford University Press.

Silverstein, M. (1976/1995) Shifters, linguistic categories, and cultural description. In B. Blount (ed.) *Language, Culture, and Society: A Book of Readings* (pp. 187–221). Prospect Heights: Waveland Press.

Silverstein, M. (1993) Metapragmatic discourse and metapragmatic function. In J. Lucy (ed.) *Reflexive Language: Reported Speech and Metapragmatics* (pp. 33–58). New York: Cambridge University Press.

Silverstein, M. (2000) Tra(ns)ducing the (co(n))text(ure) of culture: Naming and the necessarily transformative nature of 'translation'. Paper presented at the conference on *Translation*, University of Leipzig, Lepizig, Germany, September 2000.

Steiner, G. (1975) *After Babel.* New York: Oxford University Press.

Tannen, D. (1985) *Talking Voices.* New York: Cambridge University Press.

Urciuoli, B. (1998) *Exposing Prejudice: Puerto Rican Experiences of Language, Race, and Class.* Boulder: Westview Press.

Voloshinov, V. (1973) *Marxism and the Philosophy of Language.* New York: Seminar Press.

Whorf, B.L. (1940/1956) *Language, Thought, and Reality: Selected Writings of Benjamin Lee Whorf*, J. B. Carroll (ed.). Cambridge: MIT Press.

Wierzbicka, A. (1999) *Emotions Across Languages and Cultures*. Cambridge: Cambridge University Press.

Wortham, S. (2001) *Narratives in Action: A Strategy for Research and Analysis*. New York: Teachers' College Press.

Appendix: Transcription and Translation of Two Tellings of Fight

A: interviewer 1
B: interviewer 2
L: Linda
<u>Underlining, character role</u>
Italics, narrator role
Bold, interlocutory role

Interlocutory devices placed after their occurrence:

- Parenthetical/here-and-now remarks, ^
- Marked register usages that non-referentially index speaker affect and/or social identity above and beyond the referent they pick out, *
- Intensifiers that do not merely refer to quantity or size, but rather index speaker affect, +
- Discourse markers, $
- Shifts to a second-person pronoun to invite the audience to identify with the teller, @
- Laughter, #
- Gasps, &
- Interjections, %
- Sighs, ~

Portuguese	English translation of Portuguese		English translation of French	French
A⁵: 'tá bem, e euh, em França, aconteceu-te alguma coisa de similar, uma situação difícil com um amigo ou com, com a tu- com a tua família L: mmh$ é com a mi(h)nha mã(h)e#^ A: com tua mãe? L: porque foi, ba- $ é sempre+ assim^, é muit'+ pertinho + *^, foi, houve duas, houve uma para, para a festa da mãe,	A: okay, and uh, in France, did something similar happen to you, a difficult situation with a friend or with, with you-, with your family L: mmh$, it's with m(h)y mo(h)ther#^ A: with your mother? L: because it was, ba-$ it's always+ like that^, it's very+ real + * close^, it was, there were two, there was one for mother's day,	1	B: Oh yeah (...) okay now, we're talking about, in France, ptt, your mother, on Mother's day, she got angry with you, she gave you a a L: a good + * smack/ licking*(fam.), yeah$ B: a smack,* yeah$ L: ((laugh))# yeah,$	B: ah ouais (...) okay, maintenant, on parle euh, en France, ptt, ta mère, au moment de la fête des mères, elle se serait euh fâchée avec toi, elle t'aurait donné une une L: une bonne+ * râclée,* ouais$ B: une claque,* ouais$ L: ((laugh))# ouais,$
tinha-l'e comprado uma prenda,	I'd bought her a present,	2		
		3	but it was because uh, I'd waited for her all+ afternoon, we were supposed to run errands, and then okay$, really + it must have been six o'clock, y'know,$* okay,$ I didn't want to go out anymore, 'why are we going and all$*, neuneuneu'^*	mais c'était pa'ce que euh, j' l'avais attendu toute + l'après-midi, on devait aller faire des courses, et puis bon$, dev- vraiment + il devait être six heures, quoi$*, bon,$ j'avais plus envie de sortir, pourquoi, on y va et tout$$ neuneuneu,'^*
'pois ela não sei como é^ que le dou naquele dia, 'tava chateada*, e zangou-se comigo, e por isto e por aqui:lo, e porque tu és assim, e porque tu és assado,*	then she I dunno^what was wrong with her on that day, she was peeved*, and she got angry at me, for this and for tha:t, and because you're like this, and because you're like that,*	4	and then we had it out *,	et puis on s'est engueulé,*

5	and okay$, I went out anyway+ to buy her the mother's day gift, and then I went home,	et bon,$ chuis quandmême + allée lui acheter le cadeau de la fête des mères, puis chuis rentrée,
6	she asked me where I'd gone, and blabla bla^*.	elle m'a demandé où j'étais allée, et patati et patata^*.
7	then I'm like,*'Yeah* I went to buy you your gift,'	puis, j' fais,* 'Ouais* chuis allée t'acheter ton cadeau,'
8	and then I don't remember what, too well^ + what she said to me,	et puis j'sais plus c'que, trop^ + c'qu'elle m'a dit,
9	then I flung* the gift at her, you know,*$ I flung* it on the ground,	puis je lui ai balancé* le cadeau, quoi,$ j'l'ai balancé* par terre,
10	I said to her,' yeah, well,* if that's how it is, take* your gift, you know,* I, I went out to buy it for you with so much so much pleasure,*' I'm like,*'but hold on* you talk to me like that,*' I'm like,* Okay, well *take *your present, you know,*' I'm like,* but hold on* I'll give it to you the same way * you're talking back to me,'	j'lui ai dit,' ouais bah', mais si c'est comme ça, tiens* ton cadeau, quoi,* je, chuis allée te l'acheter avec tellement de, tellement de, de plaisir*', je fais,*' mais attends*', tu m' parles comme ça,*' j' fais,* bon, ben *tiens *ton cadeau, quoi,* je fais,* mais attends* je te l'offre de la même manière que tu me réponds',

e eu, peguei na prenda que eu le tinha oferecido e **botei-a*** pro chão,

and I, I took the gift that I'd given her and **I put it** * on the ground,

Continued

Portuguese	English translation of Portuguese		English translation of French	French
e ela chega-se só + ao pé de m(h)im#, e cada uma + , levei* tantas + naquele dia ((laughs))#	and she comes right + up to me(h)#, and each one + (blow), I really + got it* on that day ((laughing))#	11	so euh, well,$ okay $ she nailed me* a good+ licking*, you know,*$	donc euh, bon$ ben$ elle m'a foutu*une bonne+ râclée*, quoi,*$
A: mandaste a prenda pro chão L: mandei, mesmo + por ca'sa* dela, porqu'eu fui le comprar aquilo com tanta+ coisa *,	A: you threw the present on the floor L: I did, really + 'cos* of her, because I went to buy that for her with so much+ stuff/ love*,	12		
		13	after you@ got my brother who got there in the mean time and all,* okay$, who took my si(h)de, as (h)usual#	après t'as@ mon frère qui est arrivé entretemps et tout,* bon$, qui a pris ma dé(h)fense, comme d'habitu(h)de#
		14	and uh, but it's true ^that that went really+ badly, I mean^, it's^,^pff% we've had a couple like that, at any rate, + now it's calmed down ^now that I'm 18,^well,$ since I turned 18,^ B: mm L: 18, okay$ now for two years, it's over,^ it's fine^, it's cool.^* but before it was, uh, more, she's very+ prot-, protrec- B: mh L: protective,*^ so it doesn't work-^, but there's stuff*^ that doesn't work* with her^, so uh$, ppff.%	et euh, mais c'est vrai^ que ça s'est très + mal passé, je veux dire,^c'est,^ pff,% on en a eu quelques unes comme ça, quand même, + maintenant ça s'est calmé^ depuis qu'j'ai dix-huit ans,^ fin,$ que j'ai eu mes B: mm L: dix-huit ans, bon$, maintenant depuis deux ans c'est bon,^ c'est bien^, c'est cool,^* mais avant c'était, euh, plus, elle est très+ prote- protrec B: mh L: protectrice,*^ donc ça va

		pas-^, mais y a des trucs*^'qui passent* pas avec elle^, donc euh$, ppf %
15	*and after she [says],* 'Where were you, **bla bla**,^* **ganana**^*'	*e depois ela,* 'Onde é que tu foste, **não sei o quê**,^* **ganana**,^*'
16	*and me, 'so, I went with so much (love),* to buy the gift.'*	*e eu 'atão, fui com tanta coisa* a comprar a prenda.'*
17	A: *and you got it* that day?* L: **ah $, I got it.* man*%** A: *a slap* L: **well$,** *then not a few +,*	A: *e levaste* alguma nesse dia?* L: **ah,$ levei.* fogo*%** A: *uma boffetada* L: **bah$** *aí, não foram poucas +,*
18	*then m-my brother got there,* **well,$** *my brother also + started making noise* there', 'you're always beating up on the girl,* **bla bla bla,**^^***	*'pois chegou o mo o meu irmão,* **pois,$** *o meu irmão começou também + lá,pra lá a berrar,* ''tas sempre a bater na rapariga,* **não sei quê**,^*'**não sei quê mais**^*',

Chapter 5

Expressing Anger in Multiple Languages

JEAN-MARC DEWAELE

Introduction

The study of expression of emotion by second language (L2) users raises a number of specific questions. Would emotional discourse of less fluent L2 users sound 'robotic' in the ears of native speakers (or in their own ears)? Could L2 learners be taught to recognize and communicate emotions in the L2 using paralinguistic cues? Do L2 users have a preferred language for angry outbursts? Can they 'channel' angry feelings into any language they are proficient in with equal ease? Bilinguals' autobiographies suggest that there are constraints on language choice for the expression of anger. One such author, Nancy Huston, a Canadian from Alberta who emigrated to France as a young adult, notes the following about the expression of anger in a foreign language:

> (...) il y a toujours quelque chose de ridicule à s'emporter dans une langue étrangère: l'accent s'empire, le débit s'emballe et s'achoppe ... on emploie les jurons à tort et à travers – et, du coup, on doit s'ingénier à trouver des moyens plus raffinés pour exprimer sa colère. (*Lettres Parisiennes*, 1986: 23)
>
> [there is always something ridiculous about getting carried away in a foreign language: the accent gets worse, the rhythm runs off and stumbles ... you use the wrong swearwords in the wrong way – and, as a result, you have to work at finding more refined ways to express your anger.] (the quote and its translation come from the study on Huston by Kinginger, 2004: 172)

I share Huston's views on the difficulty of expressing anger in a foreign language after the following personal experience. Coming back from the Second International Vigo Conference on Bilingualism in 2002, where I had presented a paper on swearing in multiple languages (Dewaele,

2004a), I was confronted with the phenomenon I had described at the conference. Flights out of Vigo were delayed because of the fog. In order to catch a connecting flight to Madrid, a colleague and I were bundled into a taxi and driven at breakneck speed to the nearest airport, Porto, across the Portuguese border. Arriving at the gate a few minutes before take-off, my colleague rushed through unhindered after waving his ticket. I was not so lucky. A missing validation code on my ticket meant that I could not board the plane. Feeling really angry, I went to the airline counter to complain. After a few halting sentences in Spanish (which I had been using a lot in the previous days), I realized that I could not express anger adequately in Spanish. My boiling frustration and indignation could not be channeled into Spanish sentences. I then switched to English, and although it is my third language (L3), I felt I could express anger in it much better than in Spanish.

When I later analyzed what had happened, I realized that a number of factors had contributed to my preference for English to express anger. I lacked the anger repertoire in Spanish and I lacked the fluency needed to gain the upper hand. When engaging a linguistic confrontation, one needs to be quite sure of oneself. Rusty armor with chinks is worthless, and listening to my wooden Spanish, I felt like a beginner karate student facing a black belt. I realized that grammatical, lexical, or socio-pragmatic errors would undermine the perlocutionary effects[1] I was seeking, that is, an apology and an offer for help to catch a different flight. Stumbling or hesitating would make me look like an angry fool, swearwords were out of bounds, in other words, my tongue was tied.

This personal anecdote serves to illustrate my argument that, in interaction with other multilinguals, multilingual individuals may have preferences for specific languages for expression of strong emotions. Researchers have found that the preferred language for expression of strong emotions, including anger, is often the speaker's first language (L1) (cf. Pavlenko, 2002). Memories of emotional events in the L1 have been reported as feeling more vivid and intense (Schrauf, 2000), and physiological responses to reprimands in the L1 heard from parents in childhood are stronger than their translation equivalents in languages learned later in life (Harris *et al.*, 2003). Altarriba (2003) suggests that emotion words in the L1 benefit from multiple traces in memory, which strengthen their semantic representation. Emotion words in a less frequently used language lack these connotations and are less deeply encoded. This might explain why the L2 has sometimes been described as being more detached, more distant than the L1.

It is important to keep in mind that a multilingual's dominant language is often the first language to have been acquired. There are indications that when a multilingual is subsequently socialized into a second or third language and becomes dominant in that language, this language may become the preferred one for communication of anger (Dewaele, 2004d; Pavlenko, 2004).

In the present study, I will use the database on bilingualism and emotions (Dewaele & Pavlenko, 2001) to examine multilinguals' language choice for expression of anger in a variety of situations. I will begin by defining 'emotion' and 'anger' and present a brief overview of approaches and levels of analysis in the study of anger. Then I will survey the research on emotion and anger in the LX (i.e. any language other than the L1, that is, L2, L3, L4, etc). This discussion will be followed by a rationale and methodology of the present study. Next, I will present the quantitative analyses and link them to participants' views. Finally, I will consider what the findings add to the existing body of knowledge on anger expression among multilinguals.

Emotions, Anger, and its Expression

A neuropsychological approach

What exactly is an emotion? We may have an intuitive understanding of emotions, but their sheer complexity makes them difficult to define. Neuroscientists attempt to answer this question by focusing on the neuropsychology of emotion, and the neural and neurochemical mechanisms underlying emotional processing (Borod, 2000). They try to distinguish emotional from cognitive processes, arguing that to make progress in understanding the neurobiological nature of emotions, experimental strategies need to be used that are different from those common in cognitive science (Panksepp, 2003). In a review of the research in the field, Panksepp (2000) suggests that the neurobiological systems that mediate the basic emotions (anger, fear, surprise, sadness, joy, disgust) are constituted of genetically coded, but experientially refined executive circuits situated in subcortical areas of the brain (specifically the prefrontal dorsolateral cortex), which can coordinate the behavioral, physiological and psychological processes that need to be recruited to cope with a variety of survival needs and that provide the individual with fundamental values for the guidance of behavior. Research on the conceptualization and expression of emotion has revealed that descriptions of emotional experience correspond with physiological changes (i.e. autonomic and somatic activity levels) associated with emotional arousal. Harris (2004) argues that this 'brain-based' perspective has a heuristic value as incongruence between psychophysiological measures and the subjective reports 'would falsify the brain-based perspective or would force one to develop an explanation for why subjective and physiological reports differed' (2004: 225). The present study is based on the assumption that a physiological link exists between basic emotions and the language that codes and expresses them.

A cognitive linguistic approach

Cognitive linguists Wierzbicka and Harkins (2001) accept that technological advances allow researchers to identify with increasing detail the areas of the brain and the specific wave patterns that are linked with emotional states. Yet they express concern about the fact that the outcomes of this research, carried out in predominantly English-speaking research environments, are often applied to human brains in general, not just to speakers of a particular language or members of a particular cultural group. The authors do not deny that emotions are linked to physiological processes, but stress that the study of emotions needs input from a variety of languages. Language plays a crucial role because 'whatever the conditions that produce an emotion like anger, whether or not it is visibly expressed, and whatever physiological responses accompany it, it is only through language (if at all) that we can know that what is experienced *is* anger' (Wierzbicka & Harkins, 2001: 2–3).

In other words, cognitive linguists do not reject the idea that emotions have a physiological substrate. Rather, they argue that despite the degree of technical sophistication in research into the neuropsychology of human emotion, researchers seem unaware of absolutizing their own language (with its built-in culture and concepts). As a consequence, writes Ye (2001), they are like frogs in a well (*jingdiziwa*, a Chinese idiomatic expression), unable to jump out and seeing only 'the little circle of sky above [their] well, imagining it to be the whole world' (2001: 359). These anglophone researchers tend to forget that the walls of the well are built with the bricks of specifically Anglo values and judgements.

Wierzbicka and Harkins (2001) accept that there may be a basic human experience of something like 'anger', yet argue that it would be problematic to claim that such an experience would be precisely equivalent to the English 'anger', or to its translation equivalents or synonyms in other languages. They also point to the inherent variability in emotional responses between people in similar contexts; what one person might find harmless could be perceived as offensive by another person. Even a single individual might react differently at different moments in time.

Moreover, the way emotions are displayed is highly variable: 'one may turn red with anger, glower and shout in one situation and appear white-faced, expressionless and icily polite in another' (Wierzbicka & Harkins, 2001: 2). This variation in display of emotions is also linked to social and cultural factors. Markus and Kitayama (1991) argue that the view of the self is radically different in Western and Eastern cultures. In the West the self is viewed as independent, self-contained, and autonomous, while it is considered interdependent ("composed primarily of relationships with others instead of inner attributes" p. 236) in Asian, African, Latin-American and many southern European cultures (p. 225).

Assumptions about the etiology of emotional expressions for ego-focused emotions are therefore quite different in these different cultures:

> For those with independent selves, emotional expressions may literally "express" or reveal the inner feelings such as anger, sadness, and fear. For those with interdependent selves, however, an emotional expression may be more often regarded as a public instrumental action that may or may not be related directly to the inner feelings. (Markus & Kitayama, 1991: 236).

While in the West "some emotions, like anger that derive from and promote an independent view of the self" can be displayed, in societies where the self is considered interdependent, overt expression of anger is avoided: "Anger may seriously threaten an interdependent self and thus may be highly dysfunctional" (Markus and Kitayama, 1991: 236).

The arguments of cognitive linguists strike a cord with bilingualism researchers, who are fully aware of the role of cross-linguistic differences in cross-cultural communication and miscommunication.

A socioconstructivist approach

In his seminal book *Anger and Aggression: An Essay on Emotion* (1982), James Averill wonders 'how can justice be done to the complexity of behavior without violating the need for simplicity on a conceptual or theoretical level' (1982: 4). Averill criticizes oversimplified definitions of emotions as patterns of arousal or cognitive appraisals. To address their complexity, he adopts a systems approach that places emotions within the hierarchy of behavioral systems, and allows for analysis at social, psychological, and/ or biological levels: 'at each level, it is also possible to distinguish broader systems of behavior, of which emotions are a part. Thus, we can analyze emotions in relation to social systems, psychological systems and biological systems' (1982: 19). Consequently, Averill defines emotions

> as socially constituted syndromes (transitory social roles) which include an individual's appraisal of the situation and which are interpreted as passions, rather than as actions. (Averill, 1982: 6)

Averill does not use the word 'syndrome'[2] in a pathological sense, but rather with the meaning of 'subsystem of behavior'. These subsystems are composed of such elements as physiological changes, expressive reactions, instrumental responses, and subjective feelings. He distinguishes emotions from other transitory social roles on the basis of the cognitive appraisals involved: 'each emotion is based on a particular set of appraisals or evaluative judgments' (1982: 19).

Averill also distinguishes between three broad (and idealized) classes of emotion: impulsive, transcendental, and conflictive emotional states.

Anger belongs in the last category. He warns, however, that an emotion is not just the sum of its parts and that, as a consequence, the grounds are never sufficient in themselves for attribution of emotion: 'The attribution of emotion also depends on the nature of the appraised object and on the meaning of the emotional role (i.e. how the emotional role relates to broader systems of behavior, primarily at the social level of analysis)' (1982: 19). Averill further argues that emotions reflect 'the thought of an epoch, the secret of a civilization. It follows that to understand the meaning of an emotion is to understand the relevant aspects of the sociocultural system of which the emotion is a part (subsystem)' (1982: 24). Following his general definition of emotion, Averill rejects the assumption that anger is a subjective experience or simply a state of physiological arousal and defines anger as

a socially constituted syndrome (i.e., a transitory social role), the relevant rules are the social norms related to anger, and the functions are to be found primarily on the social level of analysis. (1982: 30)

Summary

The purpose of this short overview of the three different approaches to the phenomenon of anger is not to discuss the merits and drawbacks of each, but rather to present some of the theoretical and methodological issues in the field and to highlight the contributions of each approach. Because my level of analysis is sociolinguistic (language choice for the expression of anger in social interaction), the framework provided by Averill (1982) is ideally suited, especially as it acknowledges other possible levels of analysis. The fact that the data for the present study were gathered through an online research instrument in English presupposes that participants had a fair understanding of the language, and sufficient knowledge of the concept of anger in English, possibly influenced by overlapping concepts in their L1(s), to provide information on habitual language choice to express this emotion. The potential discrepancy in the conceptual representation of 'anger' does not affect the validity of the data, because anger expression is not seen here as a single speech act, but rather as a loose constellation of speech acts, some highly conventionalized and some quite creative and imaginative, reflecting the unique multicompetence of the speaker.

Expression of 'Anger' in a Second Language

A study by Rintell (1984) is one of the seminal works in the area of Second Language Acquisition (SLA) and emotion. She discovered that L2 users find it hard to judge the degree of emotional intensity of speech in L2 English. Chinese, Arabic, and Spanish participants, enrolled in an intensive English program, experienced greater difficulty than English native speakers in identifying and rating the intensity of different emotions (including anger) in taped conversations. The participants' performance was linked to their linguistic and cultural background and language proficiency. Beginners had the lowest scores, intermediate learners had slightly higher scores, advanced students performed better but scored nonetheless well below the native speakers. A comparison between groups revealed that L1 Chinese speakers had lower scores than L1 Arabic speakers, who in turn had lower scores than L1 Spanish speakers. Rintell's (1984) findings indicate that the amount of time spent studying the target language (TL), and the time spent in the TL country do not necessarily result in similar levels of socialization in the TL. Research into language socialization in multilingual settings shows that the process of acquisition of new interpretative frameworks occurs throughout the lifetime of multilingual speakers (Bayley & Schecter, 2003).

Pavlenko (2004) looked at the effects of second language socialization on language choice for the expression of anger and other feelings in parent–child communication within multilingual families. She found that whereas a majority of parents reported a preference for the L1 for praising and disciplining their children, a number of parents reported that as a result of the socialization process their LX had acquired strong affective connotations. Their LX was perceived to be highly emotional and had become the preferred language for praising and disciplining their children. Pavlenko (2004) concludes that adult second language socialization in the private domain of the family may make other languages seem as emotional as the first.

The context of acquisition of a TL may also play a role in users' choice of that TL to express anger. Toya and Kodis (1996) considered the use of swearwords and the pragmatic use of rudeness in English in a small sample of native speakers (NSs) of Japanese with advanced English proficiency. They point to the specific difficulty that their learners face, that is, having to 'master two different norms of expressing emotions, especially Western and Oriental norms' (Toya & Kodis, 1996: 280). The researchers used oral discourse completion tests and introspective interviews. Participants were presented with five situations in which anger was expected and were asked (1) how they would feel in each situation, (2) how they would or would not express their emotions verbally and/or non-verbally, and finally (3) why they would or would not express themselves in those ways. The results demonstrated that frequency of use of rude expressions was linked to the length of stay in English-speaking countries and the confidence of the L2 users. A control group of NSs of English was found to be more expressive than the non-native speakers (NNSs), although the difference in reactions was smaller than expected. The authors suggest that the lower degree of expressiveness in the L2 could be linked to the more restricted input to which the learners had been exposed (there is little display of anger in the foreign language classroom) and the fact that learners have little confidence in using angry words: 'The acquisition of rude language appeared to be an extremely sensitive issue because of the possible danger and misunderstanding involved in using such expressions, of which NNSs were well aware' (Toya & Kodis, 1996: 293).

Dewaele (2004c) analyzed individual differences in the use of colloquial words (including swearwords) in a cross-sectional corpus of advanced L2 French of L1 speakers of Dutch and English. One of the striking findings was that the frequency of contact with the TL and proficiency levels in the TL were positively correlated with proportions of colloquial words. Dewaele and Pavlenko (2002) came to similar conclusions concerning the effects of frequency of contact and proficiency levels in the TL on the use of emotion words in interlanguage (IL) corpora of advanced oral French of Dutch L1 speakers and advanced oral English of Russian L1 speakers. Higher proportions of colloquial and emotion words in the L2 could therefore be indicative of higher levels of L2 socialization.

Harris, Ayçiçegi, and Gleason (2003) analyzed the emotional impact of words in the L1 and L2 through their effect on autonomic reactivity. The researchers used electrodermal monitoring to compare reactivity for reprimands, taboo words, aversive, positive, and neutral words presented visually and auditorily in the L1 and the L2 of Turkish−English bilinguals. Physiological reactions to taboo words presented auditorily in the L1 Turkish were found to be much stronger than their translation equivalents in the L2 English. Childhood reprimands in the L1 were found to be the most physiologically arousing, whereas similar expressions in their L2 had little effect. A final exploratory analysis was carried out to verify whether sociobiographical variables predicted skin conductance responses. Neither age, gender, age of exposure to English, age of arrival in the United States, length of stay in the United States, self-rated proficiency, nor English verbal proficiency significantly predicted skin conductance responses.

In a follow-up study, Harris (2004) found that reprimands presented in the L1 of Spanish−English bilinguals who had grown up in the United States (early learners) elicited larger skin conductance responses than comparable expressions in the L2. No such difference was obtained for those who were first exposed to English during middle childhood (late learners), indicating that age of acquisition of the second language and proficiency modulate speakers' physiological reactions to emotional language. The author argues that the reason the first language is often experienced as more emotional than the second language is because the first language is learned in a context that is the most consistently emotional (see also the chapter by Harris *et al.* in this volume).

This explanation could also account for the patterns I uncovered in a number of studies on swearing. In Dewaele (2004a) I investigated self-reported language choice for swearing among more than 1000 multilinguals, using a part of the corpus on which the present study is based. The results suggest that swearing happens most frequently in the multilinguals' dominant language. Mixed instruction, an early start in the learning process, and frequent use of a language were found to predict the choice of that language for swearing.

In Dewaele (2004b) I used the same corpus to analyze variation in perceived emotional force of swearwords in the multilinguals' different languages. Participants reported that emotional force is highest in the L1 and gradually lower in languages learned subsequently. Participants who learned their language(s) in a naturalistic – or mixed – context gave higher ratings on emotional force of swearwords in that language than instructed language learners. Perception of emotional force of swearwords was also positively linked to self-rated proficiency in a language and frequency of use of that language. Age of onset of learning was found only to predict perception of emotional force of swearwords in the L2. A strong correlation appeared between perception of emotional force of swearwords and frequency of use of swearwords, which suggests that learners may avoid the use of linguistic 'nuclear devices' if they are unsure about their yield. The general preference for swearing in the L1 and the stronger emotional resonance of swearwords in that language did not prevent participants from occasionally using their other languages depending on the intended perlocutionary effects and the linguistic competence of the interlocutor. Dewaele (2005), again using the same corpus, focused specifically on the effect of context of acquisition on the self-reported use and perceived emotional force of swearwords. The effect was significant for both dependent variables, but generally stronger for self-reported language choice for use of swearwords than for perception of their emotional force.

To sum up, the existing body of research suggests that a number of interacting variables affect language choice for expression and interpretation of anger. The L1 seems to be the obvious choice for many multilinguals as it usually has the strongest emotional connotations due to early and prolonged socialization in that language. However, this language preference may not be set in stone.

Rationale for the Present Study

The present study rests on the assumption that anger, a neurologically based emotion, originates in social interaction and that its expression is shaped by a wide variety of cultural, linguistic, and individual variables. The interaction of these variables affecting anger expression of monolingual speakers is undoubtedly complex. Yet the complexity of factors affecting the expression of anger by multilingual speakers is of a different order altogether, due to multilinguals' rich and varied linguistic trajectories. The objective of the present study is to begin identifying factors affecting language choice for anger expression in multilingual speakers. Can second language socialization, for instance, affect language preference for the expression of anger or does the L1 forever remain the preferred language for this specific speech act? What other independent variables are linked to language choice for expression of anger among multilinguals? To answer these questions satisfactorily, a large corpus of quantitative and qualitative data is needed. The statistical analysis of 'hard' quantitative data allows the researcher to identify patterns of variation in the data, and these patterns can, in turn, be linked to participants' own views. These views add valuable nuances, especially in cases where participants report views or behaviors that go against general trends and would be erased if the sole focus was on 'averages'. Wierzbicka observes on this topic:

> I am not saying that every opinion of every bilingual person should be regarded as authoritative, or that testimonies of bilingual persons should replace all other methods of studying human emotions. Rather, I am saying that such testimonies need to be taken into account, and that they complement semantic (and other) objective approaches. (2004: 95)

Method

Participants

A total of 1454 multilinguals (1033 females, 421 males) contributed to the web questionnaire database used in the present study. The participants spoke a total of 77 different L1s. Anglophone native speakers represent the largest group ($n = 433$), followed by native speakers of Spanish ($n = 162$), French ($n = 159$), German ($n = 131$), Dutch ($n = 96$), Italian ($n = 66$), Finnish ($n = 38$), Catalan ($n = 36$), Russian ($n = 35$), Portuguese ($n = 34$), Swedish ($n = 24$), Greek ($n = 21$), Chinese ($n = 18$), Afrikaans ($n = 14$), Danish ($n = 14$), Japanese ($n = 14$), Welsh ($n = 11$), and Polish ($n = 10$). The remaining 138 participants share another 57 languages: Albanian, Arabic, Armenian, Basque, Bengali, Boobe, Bosnian, Bulgarian, Cheyenne, French Creole, Croatian, Czech, Esperanto, Estonian, Faroese, Farsi, Frisian, Galician, Gujarati, Hebrew, Hindi, Hungarian, Ibo, Icelandic, Indonesian, Irish, Korean, Latvian, Lingala, Lithuanian, Luganda, Lugwara, Luxembourgish, Macedonian, Malay, Malinke, Marathi, Norwegian, Oriya, Punjabi, Romanian, Rwandan, Serbian, Serbo-Croatian, Sindhi, Slovak, Slovene,

Sundanese, Tagalog, Taiwanese, Tamil, Turkish, Ukrainian, Vietnamese, Wobe, Yiddish, and Zulu.

The most frequent L2 is English ($n = 607$), followed by French ($n = 303$), Spanish ($n = 143$), and German ($n = 96$). French is the most frequent L3 ($n = 322$), followed by English ($n = 318$), German ($n = 190$), and Spanish ($n = 123$). The same languages are the most frequent L4s: German ($n = 192$), French ($n = 160$), and Spanish ($n = 124$). The most frequent L5s are Spanish ($n = 81$), German ($n = 66$), and Italian ($n = 63$).

The mean age of onset of learning was 8.5 years (SD = 6.4) for the L2; 13.7 years (SD = 6.7) for the L3; 17.8 years (SD = 6.9) for the L4, and 21.6 years (SD = 7.9) for the L5. The L2 was defined as the second language to have been acquired, the L3 the third, and so on. Participants were generally highly educated, with 155 having a high school diploma, 418 a Bachelor's degree, 452 a Master's degree, and 424 a doctoral degree. Age ranged from 16 to 73 years (mean = 35.5; SD = 11.2).

The questionnaire elicited information about the participants' language choice for broad categories of interlocutors. Table 5.1 illustrates the patterns of language choice across these categories. The L1 is the usual choice for the expression of anger with family members (66.2%). The L2 and L3 are used most frequently to express anger at colleagues, while the expression of anger in the L4 and L5 is mostly directed at strangers.

I am aware that these data represent very broad generalizations of habitual language choice in certain situations with very broad categories of interlocutors. Yet the choice to make the categories broad was a conscious one – I was concerned that it might be too time-consuming for participants to provide information on specific interlocutors, and that the resulting information would have been too unwieldy to handle.

Table 5.1 Distribution of participants according to language choice for the expression of anger and the categories of interlocutors

	L1		*L2*		*L3*		*L4*		*L5*	
	n	*%*	*n*	*%*	*n*	*%*	*n*	*%*	*n*	*%*
Interlocutor										
Colleagues	151	11.2	474	34.7	369	34.2	197	26.7	89	22.0
Family	891	66.2	281	20.6	93	8.6	63	8.5	45	11.1
Friends	186	13.8	382	28.0	290	26.9	202	27.3	106	26.2
Strangers	36	2.7	164	12.0	318	29.5	273	36.9	163	40.2
All	81	6.0	65	4.7	9	0.8	4	0.5	2	0.5
Total	1345	100	1366	100	1079	100	739	100	405	100

I am also fully aware that the format of the questionnaire may have given inordinate importance to the order of acquisition, whereby, for instance, the L5 (language learned fifth in chronological terms) is effectively the speaker's L2, with L2, L3, and L4 studied and forgotten. One could in fact argue that assigning categorical values (L1, L2, L3) to languages negates the intrinsically dynamic character of multicompetence in multilinguals' minds. The present labeling of languages according to the order of acquisition is used for convenience purposes.

Research design

In addition to gender and education level, four main independent variables were selected in the present design: (1) degree of socialization in the LX (i.e. any language other than L1), (2) acquisition context, (3) age of onset of learning the language and, (4) self-perceived oral proficiency. The dependent variable is a frequency score reflecting habitual language choice for the expression of anger. Variables will be presented in more detail in the following sections. Internal consistency[3] was measured for the data collected for the five situations in the L1, L2, L3, L4, and L5 using the Cronbach alpha coefficient. Sample sizes may vary across the analyses because some participants did not provide data for all the dependent variables. Quantitative results are supplemented by qualitative data provided by the same participants. These responses, elicited by means of open-ended questions, have a purely illustrative value in the present study.

Independent variables

Socialization in the LX. The variable 'socialization in the LX' is a second-order variable based on the difference in the general frequency of use of the L1 and an LX (either the L2, L3, L4, or L5). The information had been collected through the following question: *How frequently do you use each of the languages?* Possible answers on a five-point Likert scale included: (1) yearly (or less), (2) monthly, (3) weekly, (4) daily, (5) all day. The subtraction of the score for the LX from the score for the L1 gives a value that reflects the difference in frequency of use of the L1 and the LX. For example, if a participant indicated that s/he used the L1 'all day' (score 5) and the L2 'weekly' (score 3), the L2 socialization score would be 2, indicating a 'very weak' degree of socialization in the L2. If, on the other hand, the L2 was used 'all day' (score 5) and the L1 'weekly' (score 3), the L2 socialization score would be −2, indicating a 'moderate' degree of socialization in the L2.[4] The distribution across categories can be seen in Table 5.2. The category 'very weak' socialization represents over half the participants in the L2 and it rises to three-quarters of the participants for the L3, and an even higher proportion for the L4 and L5. Inversely, those in the categories 'moderate' to 'strong'

Table 5.2 Distribution of participants according to degree of socialization in the LX

	L2		L3		L4		L5	
	n	%	*n*	%	*n*	%	*n*	%
LX socialization								
Very weak	745	51.2	965	78.5	743	85.4	451	88.3
Weak	376	25.9	123	10	70	8.0	37	7.2
Moderate	176	12.1	83	6.7	38	4.4	13	2.5
Strong	157	10.8	59	4.8	19	2.2	10	2.0
Total	1454	100	1230	100	870	100	511	100

socialization represent about a fifth of the participants in the L2 and this drops to 10% and less in the subsequent languages.

Context of acquisition. The variable 'context of acquisition' distinguishes between three types of contexts: (1) naturalistic context (i.e. no classroom contact, only naturalistic communication outside school), (2) mixed context (i.e. classroom contact + naturalistic contact), and (3) instructed context (i.e. formal classroom contact only). No further distinction was made between types of formal instruction, such as, for instance, 'immersion classrooms', where the TL serves as the medium for teaching non-language subject matter and 'non-immersion classrooms', where the TL is the instructional target. Similarly, the notion of 'naturalistic context' as used here is a cover term for a wide range of ways in which a language can be learned without guidance from a particular teacher or program, but developed gradually or spontaneously through interaction with speakers of the TL. Clearly, the variable 'context of acquisition' cannot be easily disambiguated from the 'context of use'. One could argue that the instructed learner whose only contact with the TL was in the classroom would rarely be compelled to express anger in that language.

Table 5.3 presents the distribution of the participants according to context of acquisition for the L2, L3, L4, and L5. The most striking difference occurs between the L2 and the other languages: the L2 was learned solely through formal instruction in less than 40% of the cases, while this rose to more than 65% of the cases for the L3, L4, and L5.

Age of onset of learning. Research into age of onset of learning effects has usually focused on linguistic accuracy, that is, error-free production or native-like pronunciation (Birdsong, to appear). DeKeyser (2000) suggests

Table 5.3 Distribution of participants according to context of acquisition of the LX

	L2		*L3*		*L4*		*L5*	
	n	%	*n*	%	*n*	%	*n*	%
Context of acquisition								
Instructed	560	39.1	811	67.1	596	69.1	316	66.4
Mixed	653	45.6	322	26.7	186	21.6	100	21.0
Naturalistic	219	15.3	75	6.2	81	9.4	60	12.6
Total	1432	100	1208	100	863	100	476	100

that exposure to a language at a young age increases the probability of reaching high levels of proficiency. Onset of puberty is often quoted as a crucial age, after which the learning of languages becomes more arduous, although late learners can attain native-like levels (Birdsong, to appear).

For the purpose of the study, I grouped our participants in three categories for age of onset: those who started learning the language between birth and age 2,[5] those who started before puberty (ages 3–12), and those who started as teenagers (age 13+). The data in Table 5.4 show a gradual decrease in young learners between the L2 and the L5.

Self-perceived oral proficiency. Self-report measures were shown to correlate highly with linguistic measures of proficiency (Kroll *et al.*, 2002; Mettewie, 2004). They have the added advantage of being easy to collect, enabling researchers to consider larger sample sizes than in research based on production data.

Table 5.5 shows that, whereas more than 96% of participants judge themselves to be highly to maximally fluent in their L1, only three-quarters rate themselves as highly for the L2, and the proportion

Table 5.4 Distribution of participants according to age of onset of learning the LX

	L2		*L3*		*L4*		*L5*	
	n	%	*n*	%	*n*	%	*n*	%
Age of onset (years)								
0–2	265	18.3	34	2.8	0	0.0	0	0.0
3–12	924	63.8	577	47.1	161	18.6	35	7.4
13+	260	17.9	614	50.1	704	81.4	440	92.6
Total	1449	100	1225	100	865	100	475	100

Table 5.5 Distribution of participants according to self-perceived proficiency

	L1		L2		L3		L4		L5	
	n	%	*n*	%	*n*	%	*n*	%	*n*	%
Proficiency										
Minimal	20	1.4	52	3.6	165	11.3	228	26.5	170	36.1
Low	7	0.5	77	5.3	237	16.3	212	24.7	122	25.9
Medium	19	1.3	208	14.3	334	23	220	25.6	94	20.0
High	92	6.3	430	29.6	322	22.1	142	16.5	61	13.0
Maximal	1311	90.2	677	46.6	162	11.1	58	6.7	24	5.1
Total	1449	100	1444	100	1220	100	860	100	471	100

drops to a third for the L3, a quarter for the L4, and less than a fifth for the L5. Self-perceived proficiency scores appeared to be very highly correlated with frequency of general use of language: (L1: rho = 0.21, $n = 1438$; L2: rho = 0.61, $n = 1434$; L3: rho = 0.63, $n = 1190$; L4: rho = 0.59, $n = 848$; L5: rho = 0.59, $n = 466$; all $p < 0.0001$). In other words, participants who used a language frequently also rated their oral proficiency in that language higher.

Dependent variable

The present study focuses on the self-reported language choice for expression of anger in five different contexts. The question was formulated as follows: 'If you are angry, how frequently do you typically use a language to express your anger?' Possible answers on a five-point Likert scale included: never = 1, rarely = 2, sometimes = 3, frequently = 4, constantly = 5. The contexts included anger directed to oneself, to friends, to family, to strangers, and anger expressed in letters or e-mails.[6] Information was collected for the L1, L2, L3, L4, and L5. The dependent variables are thus the numerical values reflecting frequency of habitual language choice for the expression of anger in the five contexts. A series of one-sample Kolmogorov–Smirnov tests revealed that the values for frequency of language choice for expression of anger in the five contexts in up to five languages are not normally distributed (Kolmogorov–Smirnov Z values vary between 6.3 and 13.2, all $p < 0.0001$). The distribution of participants across five frequency categories (ranging from 'never use this language' to 'use this language all the time') are strongly skewed towards the positive end of the continuum for the L1, and are strongly skewed towards the negative end of the continuum for the L3, L4, and L5 (see Figure 5.1). The

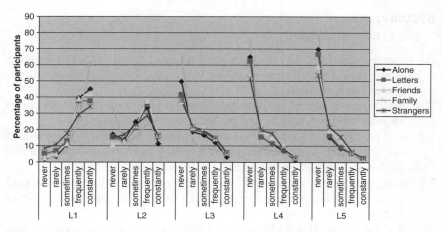

Figure 5.1 Distribution of participants according to their frequency of use of a language for the expression of anger

distribution for the L2 comes closest to a normal distribution, but the Kolmogorov–Smirnov Z values are still significant. As a consequence, Kruskal–Wallis tests were used as non-parametric equivalents to one-way ANOVAs; Wilcoxon Signed Ranks Tests and Mann–Whitney tests were used instead of *t*-tests.

Before I proceed to discuss the results, I would like to acknowledge that language choice for expression of anger is determined by many more variables than the broad categories of interlocutors and mode of communication included in the present design. This is the dilemma facing any researcher using questionnaires; a compromise needs to be reached between the level of detail and the overall length of the questionnaire. The questionnaire inquired about different aspects of bilingualism and emotion, eliciting information for every language in the participants' repertoire. The question on anger was only one of 34. Had we asked for more detail, we might have faced a problem of fatigue, which would have compromised the quality of the feedback, as well as the number of participants completing the questionnaire.

To partly remedy these limitations, I have analyzed answers to open-ended questions that inquired about: (1) linguistic preferences for emotion terms and terms of endearment; (2) language of the home and language of argument; and (3) ease or difficulty of discussing emotional topics in languages other than the L1. Comments about anger made in responses to these questions will be used to illustrate the quantitative findings.

Hypotheses

It was hypothesized:

(1)   that the speakers' L1 would be the preferred language for expression of anger and that there would be a monotonic decline in languages learned subsequently;
(2)   that as the result of socialization into an LX, that specific LX could become the preferred language for expression of anger;
(3)   that participants who learned their LX in an instructed setting would use it less frequently to express anger than participants who learned the LX in a mixed or naturalistic environment;
(4)   that participants who started learning an LX at a younger age would use it more frequently to express anger than participants who started learning the LX later;
(5)   that participants who feel more proficient in a language would also use it more frequently to express anger than participants who feel less proficient;
(6)   that gender and education level could affect language choice for the expression of anger.

Results

This section is divided into six parts reflecting the six hypotheses. The first part looks at language choice for expressing anger in the five contexts across the five languages. It compares frequency of language choice for expressing anger in the different languages using paired Wilcoxon Signed Ranks Tests. The second part proposes a non-parametric analysis of the effect of socialization into LX on the frequency of choice of the LX for expression of anger in the five contexts, with illustrations drawn from participants' comments. Similar approaches are used in the following parts concerning the effects of acquisition context, age of acquisition, self-reported proficiency, and gender and education level.

Testing hypothesis 1: Language choice for expressing anger in five contexts

Mean scores for language choice for expressing anger in the five contexts are presented in Figure 5.2. It shows that multilinguals use the L1, on average, *frequently* to express anger (the mean scores range between 3.7 and 4.2 for the different contexts). The L2 is used, on average, *sometimes* (with scores ranging between 2.8 and 3.4). The L4 and L5 are, on average, *never* or *rarely* used (score range 1.5–1.9, and 1.4–1.8, respectively). This means that, whereas the analysis of the data for the L4 and the L5 is perfectly possible from a statistical point of view, it is based on very small variations. A quick look at the differences in mean

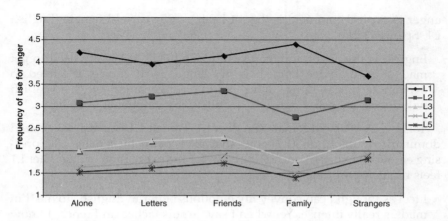

Figure 5.2 Mean scores for language choice for expressing anger in the L1, L2, L3, L4 and L5 in the complete database

scores between the five contexts reveals that the L1 is used relatively more frequently with family members. Other languages are used less frequently within the family. Wilcoxon Signed Ranks Tests confirm that the frequency of use of a language to express anger decreases highly significantly from the L1 to the L4. The difference between the L4 and L5 is less significant (see Table 5.6). Mean scores are presented in Figure 5.2.

The respondents' comments reflect the patterns presented in Figure 5.2. Most participants report a preference for the L1 to express

Table 5.6 Pairwise Wilcoxon Signed Ranks Tests in frequency of language use across languages

		L1/L2	*L2/L3*	*L3/L4*	*L4/L5*
Alone	Z	−19.9	−16.6	−7.7	−2.5
	Asymp. Sig.	0	0	0	0.013
Letters	Z	−13.2	−15.0	−9.0	−3.7
	Asymp. Sig.	0	0	0	0
Friends	Z	−15.4	−16.5	−8.2	−3.8
	Asymp. Sig.	0	0	0	0
Parents	Z	−22.4	−13.8	−4.1	−2.3
	Asymp. Sig.	0	0	0	0.023
Strangers	Z	−9.3	−13.7	−8.6	−3.1
	Asymp. Sig.	0	0	0	0.002

anger. A typical comment is that of Leah,[7] a 25-year-old female (English L1, Spanish L2):

> English is my anger and 'counseling' language. If I really need to get mad or give advice English is my language of choice. If I need to explain technical things have neutral conversation etc. ... Spanish will do just as well. English is definitely my emotional language.

KTH, a 28-year-old female (English L1, French L2, Spanish L3, shared dominance in the L1 and L2) notes that she is perfectly capable of expressing emotions in her L1 and L2, but that for the expression of anger her L1 feels more appropriate:

> I feel as though I can convey my emotions better in English. To me 'I'm mad' is really intense. Yet when I say 'Je suis fâchée' in French, I know that I am mad but it feels different. (...) I think this all comes from the fact that I learned to be angry (...) first in English and then in French. For me English is more appropriate for my anger. French I am able to use for other emotions: sadness and extreme joy for example.

Other participants opt for the L1 to express anger because of its perceived seriousness:

> I see English as my stronger 'more serious' language in terms of expressing anger or 'serious matters'. (...) However Spanish is more valuable to me when expressing endearment or feelings of love or affection. (ALG, a 28-year-old female, English L1, Spanish L2)

The following participant, Johan, a 24-year-old male (Afrikaans L1, English L2, Dutch L3, Zulu L4) reports that angry reproaches in the L2 do not seem to have the same perlocutionary effect as similar reproaches in the L1:

> Critique in English (...) is usually not taken personally at all. In Afrikaans for example I would ponder on it more and take it more personally if applicable. E.g. 'You are late!' – I'll think 'Oh what the heck traffic'. 'Jy is laat!' – I'll think 'I may seem tardy...'

SG (a 24-year-old female, Greek L1, English L2, French L3, Italian L4) reports that she may discuss emotions in her foreign languages, but that for extreme emotions the L1 is the preferred channel of communication:

> From experience when being in a romantic or friendly relationship using other languages I try to use the language of my partner/friend trying to express feeling in his/her language. Nevertheless for strongest emotions – anger, extreme annoyment, passion, lust – my first instinct is L1 as it comes more naturally.

Barbara, a 33-year-old female (German L1, English L2, Latin L3, French L4) also uses her partner's L1 to express emotions because of his lower proficiency in her L1, but she reverts to her L1 when the anger takes over:

> In our relationship we use English for two reasons. My English is far better than his German and although his German is quite good by now he can always PREFER not to understand. We also argue in English which feels really really fake to me and I feel so helpless when there is anger building up inside me and I just can't express it. It feels so sterile arguing in English like I'm not actually getting rid of any of the emotional pressure and I sometimes just burst out in German to let off some steam. That's quite a bizarre situation then but it helps and sometimes makes both of us laugh.

The same participant also points out that she resorts to swearwords in her L2 when arguing in that language to make up for the lack of emotional resonance:

> And it's tempting to try and make up for what I perceive as lack of oomph in my expression of i.e. anger by the use of swearwords since they sound great but don't have any emotional consequence for me but that doesn't usually go down too well with my surroundings.

These comments show that the majority of the respondents prefers the L1 for expression of anger because of its perceived superior emotional force. The L1 is preferred if 'I really need to get mad'; the expression of anger in the L1 is described as 'more serious', 'more intense', 'more appropriate', 'more natural', 'less effortful', and 'having a stronger effect'. The LX, on the other hand, 'lacks oomph', feels 'fake' or 'sterile'. Similar terms and arguments were presented by the participants to explain their code-switching to the L1 to praise or discipline their children (Pavlenko, 2004).

Testing hypothesis 2: Socialization into LX

A series of Kruskall–Wallis tests showed that socialization into LX had a highly significant effect overall ($p < 0.0001$) on the self-reported language choice for anger expression (see Table 5.7 for the complete results). A look at the mean scores for the L1 shows that intense socialization into the L2 is linked to a significant drop in the use of L1 for anger expression (see Figure 5.3). Not surprisingly, strong socialization in the L2 is linked to a more frequent choice of that language for the expression of anger. Similar patterns emerged for strong socialization in the L3, L4, and L5.

These statistical results are also backed up by participants' comments. Those with moderate socialization into LX report feeling comfortable in

Table 5.7 Overview of the effects of the independent variables on self-reported frequency of the L1, L2, L3, L4, and L5 for the expression of anger in five contexts (Kruskal–Wallis tests)

Language	Situation	Socialization in LX (df = 3)		Context of acquisition (df = 2)		Age of onset of learning (df = 2)		Self-perceived oral proficiency (df = 4)	
		Value of chi²	Asymp. sig.	Value of chi²	Asymp. sig.	Value of chi²	Asymp. sig.	Value of chi²	Asymp. sig.
L1	Alone	170.3	***	n/a	n/a	n/a	n/a	89.2	***
	Letters	173.0	***	n/a	n/a	n/a	n/a	94.7	***
	Friends	227.2	***	n/a	n/a	n/a	n/a	79.7	***
	Family	107.1	***	n/a	n/a	n/a	n/a	54.9	***
	Strangers	208.6	***	n/a	n/a	n/a	n/a	63.1	***
L2	Alone	294.2	***	85.1	***	11.0	**	330.4	***
	Letters	244.0	***	54.7	***	3.2	ns	342.7	***
	Friends	336.6	***	68.7	***	3.6	ns	366.4	***
	Family	271.7	***	101.0	***	61.6	***	230.5	***
	Strangers	236.7	***	37.8	***	0.5	ns	250.4	***
L3	Alone	231.2	***	69.3	***	8.0	*	333.2	***
	Letters	175.8	***	46.7	***	9.6	*	335.7	***
	Friends	227.3	***	87.1	***	7.6	*	361.8	***
	Family	210.3	***	47.4	***	16.8	***	167.6	***
	Strangers	159.8	***	54.0	***	13.8	**	287.2	***

(continued)

Table 5.7 *Continued*

Language	Situation	Socialization in LX (df = 3)		Context of acquisition (df = 2)		Age of onset of learning (df = 2)		Self-perceived oral proficiency (df = 4)	
		Value of chi²	Asymp. sig.	Value of chi²	Asymp. sig.	Value of chi²	Asymp. sig.	Value of chi²	Asymp. sig.
L4	Alone	125.8	***	72.1	***	4.7	*	191.4	***
	Letters	100.0	***	45.4	***	10.4	**	218.9	***
	Friends	110.8	***	75.5	***	3.0	ns	237.5	***
	Family	164.0	***	67.5	***	0.8	ns	123.3	***
	Strangers	85.4	***	47.0	***	4.8	*	187.5	***
L5	Alone	63.0	***	31.4	***	0.8	ns	132.2	***
	Letters	47.2	***	28.0	***	0.6	ns	122.0	***
	Friends	49.9	***	32.6	***	0.7	ns	137.1	***
	Family	62.3	***	36.6	***	2.4	ns	79.3	***
	Strangers	36.7	***	22.8	***	1.3	ns	102.3	***

*$p < 0.05$, **$p < 0.001$, ***$p < 0.0001$

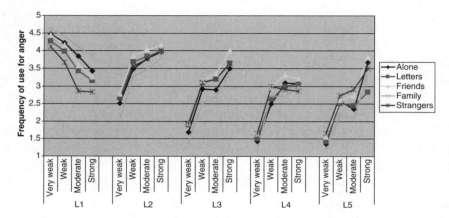

Figure 5.3 The effect of socialization on language choice for the expression of anger

both languages to communicate anger. Marigold, a 41-year-old female (French L1, English L2, German L3, Italian L4, Norwegian L5) reports using her L1 and L2 equally to express emotions:

> I discuss emotions with family and friends in both languages and express my feelings (positive or negative) to myself or others in both.

Some multilinguals apply principles of economy in their anger performance, using short, strong swearwords from the L2 in L1 speech:

> It's [English] the language I swear in too! Most appropriate to use for short outbursts ('damn!' versus German 'verdammt' – a mouthful compared to the former one; does not lend itself well to one-vowel outbursts. See also 'shit' 'fuck' 'darn' 'blast' etc.). German therefore to be used for well-expressed anger. (HV, a 29-year-old female, German L1, English L2, Spanish L3, French L4)

Another participant, ML, a 39-year-old male (Portuguese L1, French L2, English L3, Greek L4, Dutch L5) wrote that language choice for the expression of anger is solely dictated by the languages known by the interlocutor:

> I express my anger and deepest feelings in the language that the person I'm talking to will understand better.

Several participants report a gradual shift in language choice for the expression of anger after a prolonged and intense use of that language with partners. In the case of KM, a 35-year-old female (English L1, French L2, German L3, Chinese L4, Italian L5), the preferred language for arguments with her partner has shifted back from her L2 to the L1 (i.e. her dominant language) because it is less effortful for her and because her partner has gained proficiency in her L1:

Initially we argued in French but as his English improved I find myself arguing more and more in English; it feels like I'm no longer 'making the effort' but just expressing my anger.

Bruce (a 48-year-old male, English L1, Chinese L2, French L3, and living in China) has completely adopted the language of his host country to express anger:

Definitely argue in Chinese! I have had several native speakers of Chinese as girlfriends/lovers/spouse and some of them spoke English quite fluently. But when you argue English goes by the wayside. Three reasons I think: (1) A native Chinese speaker would prefer to revert to her first language when arguing because arguing in English would put her at a disadvantage with me a native English speaker; (2) Even though I learned Chinese as an adult my ability to express myself in 'extreme' situations – under threat in great anger – is quite strong; (3) To me Chinese is like 'Black English' in America. It may not be a 'high-class' or 'academic' language in the eyes of westerners but it is bloody good for expressing feelings.

RD is a 41-year-old male (English L1, French L2, Japanese L3) who has been living with a Japanese partner in Japan for the last six years; they communicate in Japanese. His constant exposure to Japanese allowed him to notice important cultural differences between the English and Japanese emotion scripts regulating negative emotions and to develop appropriate emotion scripts in Japanese:

I've come to believe that most Japanese people refrain from discussing their emotions with other people (of course there are exceptions). It seems to be considered selfish or ungentlemanly to discuss your emotions unless you are pleased or happy about something. Even then comments are restricted to a minimum. Feelings of irritation, frustration, anger, fear or sorrow can be communicated verbally or non-verbally but they appear to be more commonly communicated without words.

The formulation of our question about expressing anger may in fact have been confusing for Japanese L1 or L2 users, as more frequent use and exposure to Japanese would lead to a realization that some emotions are best expressed non-verbally. This is confirmed by Kumiko, a 40-year-old native speaker of Japanese (with English as L2) who stated:

It is easier to scold someone in English because the expressions are more direct. In Japanese scolding may be done through distance-creating acts rather than verbal scolding.

Other Asian participants reported that they in fact do appeal to English to escape the social taboo on the open expression of anger in their native languages. Quipinia, for example, a 24-year-old female from Hong Kong (Cantonese L1, English L2 – learned in instructed context at the age of 5) reported:

> my family kind of suppress the expression of emotion at home, therefore I feel a lot easier to use another language to express the feelings and the different personality inside me.

She recalls an incident in which she burst out in English at her parents who know English but with whom she usually speaks Cantonese:

> But I remember one time when they were arguing with me and I was sooooooooooo angry that I shouted out 'IT'S UNFAIR!!!!' I guess it's regarded quite impolite if I shouted at my parents (you know Chinese Traditional family) but at that point I feel that I had to express my anger and let myself just do it in another language; perhaps I feel I'm another person if I say that in English.

Deborah's comments below suggest that some of her languages simply lend themselves more easily to emotion talk. Her L5 Italian seemed to offer her a wider emotional range than her L4 Finnish, despite the fact that she was socialized into both languages. She does report swearing in both languages:

> I currently only use English and Finnish. When I was living in Italy and speaking Italian everyday, I found it quite easy to talk about emotional topics in Italian, sometimes even with relative strangers like the lady I bought my milk from and the mothers whose children played with mine in the park. I also learned to swear quite fluently in Italian (and learned to drive a car in Italian so that even today when driving I sometimes swear in Italian at Finnish drivers). I have never found it easy to speak in Finnish about how I feel. (Deborah, a 53-year-old female, English L1, French L2, German L3, Finnish L4, Italian L5, and currently living in Finland)

This does not stop her from using Finnish swearwords, however, and she cites emotional as well as pragmatic reasons for doing so:

> I tend to swear slightly more often in Finnish than in English because Finnish has a trilled 'r' that I find emotionally very satisfying. Also swearing in English to a Finn is sometimes counterproductive because they find it comic.

These comments suggest that LX can become the preferred language for anger expression, once emotion repertoires and scripts have been acquired in the process of language socialization. We will now explore this issue in more depth looking at contexts of acquisition.

Testing hypothesis 3: Context of acquisition

The Kruskall–Wallis tests revealed that acquisition context had a highly significant effect overall ($p < 0.0001$) on the self-reported language choice for expression of anger (see Table 5.7). An inspection of the mean scores for different languages shows that instructed learners use the language less frequently to express anger as compared to mixed and naturalistic learners (see Figure 5.4).

A number of instructed language learners point out that anger repertoires in the TL were not part of the curriculum, hence their difficulties to express anger or irritation in authentic communication in the TL. PS, a 30-year-old male (Catalan L1, Spanish L2, English L3) and instructed learner of English explained that getting angry in English was very difficult for him: 'I wasn't taught anger at school'. In a similar vein, Bart, a 24-year-old male (Dutch L1, French L2, English L3) and instructed user of French writes:

> in school we learn how to use French in a polite and friendly way but when I am calling to the Customer Service of a French company to complain about something and want to sound a bit more severe irritated angry ... then it is difficult to find that severe irritated angry tone because you are concentrating on French grammar and vocabulary ... I wouldn't have to do that in Dutch.

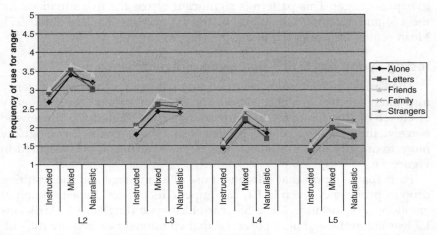

Figure 5.4 The effect of context of acquisition on language choice for the expression of anger

Participants' comments help to shed light on the reason why the effect of context of instruction, as reflected in Chi-square values, is not as powerful as socialization or self-perceived oral proficiency. The length of exposure to a particular language, and the socialization into that language, after the initial 'acquisition' phase might dramatically reduce the effect of the context of acquisition in adult multilinguals. For example, MP, a 31-year-old female (English and Greek L1s, French L2, Albanian L3) reports:

> I was born in Greece and spent my formative years there. I remember a point at the age of 16 when I came to live in England with my parents. Although I've always gone to an English school I found it very difficult to find the words to express emotions in English (...). Now after 15 or so years the situation is the exact opposite. My mother was born and bred in Greece with Greek parents. English was a language she was taught in school. She emigrated at around the age of 35 and has been living in England for the last 15 years. She now finds it extremely difficult to express herself in Greek and interestingly she also finds it more difficult to relate to Greek people.

Testing hypothesis 4: Age of onset of learning

The Kruskall–Wallis tests showed that the effect of age of onset of learning on language choice for the expression of anger is quite robust for the L2 and L3, and somewhat weaker for the L4. It fails to reach significance in any situation in the L5. The general pattern is that a lower age of onset corresponds to a higher frequency of use of the language to express anger. This pattern is significant across the five situations for the L3, and for three situations in the L2 and the L4 (see Table 5.7). Mean scores are presented in Figure 5.5.

Testing hypothesis 5: Self-perceived oral proficiency

The Kruskall–Wallis tests revealed that self-perceived oral proficiency in a language has a highly significant effect overall on the frequency of choice of that language to express anger (see Table 5.7). Those who perceive themselves to be very proficient in a language use that language more frequently to communicate anger. Mean scores are represented in Figure 5.6.

Participants report that infrequent use of a language and the resulting drop in proficiency, even in L1, can impede its use for the expression of emotions. For instance, DF, a 55-year-old female (English L1, Afrikaans L2 learned at the age of 5) observed that emotional talk is more difficult in Afrikaans, which she spoke fluently as child 'mainly because I don't have the opportunity to speak it frequently and struggle to "access" old vocabulary and learn new vocabulary'. Also, Christina, a 36-year-old

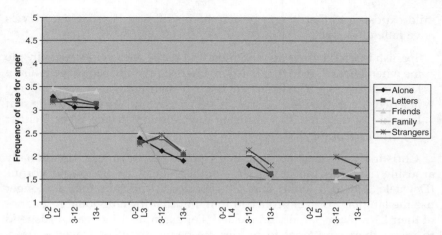

Figure 5.5 The effect of age of onset of learning on language choice for the expression of anger

female (Spanish and German L1, English L2, Italian L3, French L4), comparing the emotional weight of her five languages, noted that one of her L1s, German, has lost its emotional resonance. She also raises another important point, namely that to express emotions in a language,

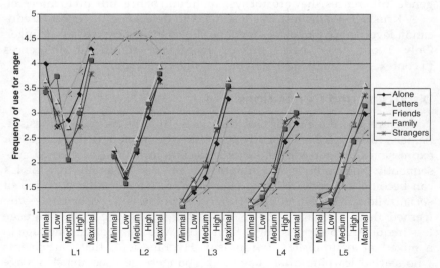

Figure 5.6 The effect of self-perceived proficiency on language choice for the expression of anger

mild exposure to that language may be insufficient if proficiency levels have fallen too low:

> Spanish is what I grew up with most and really feels very special inside me when I hear it, read it or speak it. English my third language is also a favourite because I married an English man and have spent all my married life in the UK. German is very rusty and I use it so little that I could not describe it as arousing any emotions in me when I either hear it or speak (try) it.

Christina's observation that her German is no longer emotionally arousing is quite intriguing. In another study of the same corpus (Dewaele, 2004d), I found that self-reported L1 attriters may no longer use the language or feel proficient in it, but that the emotional resonance of their L1 remains largely unaffected. For example, L1 swearwords tend to retain their emotional force, despite being rarely – if ever – used. Christina's case is notably different – it is possible that the loss of affective reactions points to complete attrition of the language.

Testing hypothesis 6: The effects of gender and education level

The effects of gender were tested using a Mann–Whitney test. The results show significant differences in 7 out of 25 cases (5 contexts × 5 languages). Females reported a more frequent use of the language for the expression of anger in four cases, while males reported more frequent use in three cases. One can thus conclude that although there are some gender differences, they are not systematic and hence difficult to interpret.

A Kruskall–Wallis test was also used to determine the effect of education level on frequency of language choice for the expression of anger. Only 2 out of 25 cases showed marginally significant differences (5 contexts × 5 languages), defying any interpretation.

Discussion and Conclusions

To sum up, the findings of the study fully support hypothesis 1, namely, that speakers' L1 is generally the preferred language for expression of anger with monotonic decline in languages learned subsequently. The findings also support hypothesis 2, namely that the LX can become the preferred language to express anger after a period of socialization. The results fully support hypothesis 3: participants who learned their language(s) in an instructed setting used that language less frequently to express anger than those who learned the language in a mixed or naturalistic environment. Hypothesis 4, that participants who started learning a language at a younger age used that language more frequently to express anger than those who started later, is supported only partially. Hypothesis 5, namely that participants who feel more proficient in a language use that language more frequently to express anger than those who do not feel as proficient, is fully supported. Finally, the data did not allow to either confirm or disconfirm hypothesis 6 – in the absence of a clear pattern, one can simply say that there is no sufficient data to claim the influence of either gender or education on language choice for anger expression.

The present findings show that events at the beginning (age of onset) and during the language learning process (context of acquisition) reverberate for years in multilinguals' linguistic behavior. The effect may be weak but remains perceptible. Harris and associates (this volume) suggest that the effect of age of onset of learning may be linked to the fact that emotional regulation systems and language develop in parallel in early childhood. At the same time, they discuss cases where strong emotional reactions were exhibited in languages learned later in life. In the present study, the effect of age of onset is present but it is weaker than that of the other independent variables. One possible reason for the slight discrepancy between the two sets of results (stronger versus weaker effect) is that language choice for the expression of anger is probably guided more by a person's social environment than by that person's psychology. The participants in the Harris *et al.* study reacted physiologically to stimuli presented to them. They had no conscious control over their reactions, and the patterns that emerged could be interpreted as indicators of their psychological make-up. In contrast, in the present study the dependent variable is a self-reported frequency scale for habitual language choice. This choice might be mediated by a set of situational variables, but it remains largely a conscious decision of the speaker to pick a particular language with a particular interlocutor in a specific situation. There was no way of measuring whether participants felt more or less angry using different languages to express anger.

The second background variable, context of acquisition, had a slightly stronger effect on language choice for anger expression. Here, too, one can imagine several reasons why this effect is not stronger. One source could lie in the timespan between the acquisition phase and the moment the data were gathered: different events such as non/use of the language may have intervened, either reinforcing or annulling the effect of the context of acquisition on language choice. Some participants reported never to have used an instructed language again after school, others reported picking it up again much later and becoming highly proficient in the language. In other words, the effect of some more recent life-events may quickly overwhelm the effect of variables linked to the genesis of the language learning experience.

The fact that context of acquisition does resonate for so long is remarkable, however. Maybe this is because context of acquisition roughly equates with type and intensity of exposure to an LX and the opportunity to use that LX in authentic interactions. If contact with an LX had been limited to the classroom, stylistic range and emotion repertoires would inevitably be more limited compared to those of the L2 users who had experienced and used the language in a wider variety of situations. Anger scripts and repertoires rarely figure in second-language textbooks. When they are, they tend to be too polite. Angry words or expressions, especially if they are vulgar or slang, are banned from the classroom because of their offensive character. The participants reported experiencing difficulties in expressing anger in languages they were solely or mainly taught at school. This may not be a problem if the interlocutor is equally proficient in the languages of the speaker, where code-switching offers a way of 'letting of steam' as Barbara reported, but it is more difficult if the speaker has to remain in a monolingual mode. The data of the present study offer support for the 'emotional contexts of learning' hypothesis put forth by Harris and associates in their chapter, which posits that a language learned, or habitually used, in an authentic context may acquire a stronger emotional resonance than languages learned in the classroom only.

The fact that most of the participants used their L1 most frequently to communicate anger, could lead to the hasty conclusion that this constitutes support for 'the popular and oversimplified assumption that in late bilingualism, L1 is always the language of emotions and LX the language of distance or detachment' (Pavlenko, 2004: 200). However, this view is put in perspective by the finding of strong LX socialization effects. These suggest that there is nothing intrinsically different between the L1(s) and the LXs. The fact that early socialization usually happens in the L1(s) means that a multilingual will develop rich and varied memories with strong emotional connotations in that language. However, LX socialization – a variable that reflects a trajectory rather than an event in the participant's life – can alter language preference for emotional expression. In other words, the LX can become the most emotional language, and this was the case for participants like Deborah in the present study, who reported shifts in language preference linked to new partners or simply to the fact of having moved to a different country and, subsequently, having acculturated.

The results of the present study show that self-perceived proficiency, probably linked to the recent linguistic history of the multilingual, exerts a much stronger pull on his/her language choice for anger expression than linguistic experience in the more distant past. The reason for this is probably that the expression of anger in an LX entails a confrontation with an adversary that is likely to possess superior linguistic skills. As the anecdotes in the beginning of the paper illustrated, the use of anger scripts in confrontations with native speakers is limited to those L2 users who have had the time and opportunity to acquire the nuances and the linguistic and conceptual fluency to carry it off. They must perceive themselves to be close enough to the 'in-group' of native speakers to be credible and effective when expressing anger and to produce the intended perlocutionary effects. The absence of consistent effects for gender and education suggests that language choice for the expression of anger operates independently from sociolectal variation patterns.

There is finally also a potential effect that was not discussed in the present paper, namely the personality of the speaker. Indeed, extraverts were found to use colloquial words and emotion words more frequently than introverts in the LX (Dewaele, 2004d; Dewaele & Pavlenko, 2002). It can be assumed that extraverts might also be less reticent to express anger in an LX, even if they realize that they do not master that particular emotion repertoire completely. Introverts may be less willing to risk loss of face by using an inappropriate anger repertoire. Participants' comments suggest that the expression of anger covers a wide range of speech acts, which vary according to the home culture: yelling can be acceptable for the expression of anger in Southern Europe, but it is taboo in Asia. Having to focus on vocabulary and grammar, L2 users may ignore paralinguistic variables, such as intonation and prosody, to express their anger. This mismatch between the verbal content and the non-verbal aspects may confuse the interlocutor, and the speaker's communicative intentions may not be decoded accurately. The problem of miscommunication is less likely to occur in a multicultural environment. Multilinguals can use their multicompetence to develop multilingual speech acts and emotion scripts that are quite unique to them, or shared by their partner, family, or ethnic group. These speech acts and scripts for the expression of anger are not static, but reflect the changes in the user's linguistic environment. It is also likely that a growing awareness of sociocultural and sociopragmatic norms in the LX contributes to an evolution in the user's repertoire for expressing anger in the LX. To conclude, I would describe the expression of anger in an LX as the verbal equivalent of performing ballet: it requires a lot of practice, and a lot of what the French call *doigté* (in English: skill and tact).

Acknowledgements

I would like to thank the anonymous reviewers and the volume editor, Aneta Pavlenko, for their insightful comments and suggestions on previous versions of this chapter.

Notes

1. The perlocutionary force describes the effect the speaker's utterance has on the hearer (Austin, 1962).
2. 'a syndrome is a set or population of responses that covary in a systematic fashion' (Averill, 1982: 7).

3. Internal consistency refers here to the homogeneity of the items making up the five 5-item scales within the questionnaire (Dörnyei, 2003).
4. The values were recoded in five categories: all positive values were grouped in the category 'very weak' socialization, zero values constituted the category 'weak' socialization, values from -1 to -2 constituted the category 'moderate' socialization, and values between -3 to -5 were grouped in the category 'strong' socialization.
5. The usual boundary between bilingual first language acquisition and bilingual second-language acquisition (Hamers & Blanc, 2000).
6. Internal consistency reliability was quite high for the five-item scales in the L1 (alpha = 0.87), L2 (alpha = 0.88), L3 (alpha = 0.89), L4 (alpha = 0.91), and L5 (alpha = 0.90).
7. Participants who indicated that they preferred to remain anonymous in the questionnaire will be referred to by their initials, in other cases I will use the participant's first name.

References

Altarriba, J. (2003) Does *cariño* equal 'liking'? A theoretical approach to conceptual nonequivalence between languages. *International Journal of Bilingualism* 7(3), 305–22.

Austin, J. (1962/1975) *How to Do Things with Words: The William James Lectures Delivered in Harvard University in 1955* (2nd edn). Cambridge: Harvard University Press.

Averill, J. (1982) *Anger and Aggression: An Essay on Emotion*. New York: Springer-Verlag.

Bayley, R. and Schecter, S. (2003) Introduction: Towards a dynamic model of language socialization. In R. Bayley and S.R. Schecter (eds) *Language Socialization in Bilingual and Multilingual Societies* (pp. 1–6). Clevedon: Multilingual Matters.

Besemeres, M. (2004) Different languages, different emotions? Perspectives from autobiographical literature. *Journal of Multilingual and Multicultural Development* 25(2/3), 140–58.

Birdsong, D. (in press) Nativelike pronunciation among late learners of French as a second language. In O.-S. Bohn and M. Munro (eds) *A Festschrift for Jim Flege*. Amsterdam: John Benjamins.

Borod, J. (2000) *The Neuropsychology of Emotion*. London: Oxford University Press.

DeKeyser, R. (2000) The robustness of Critical Period effects in Second Language Acquisition. *Studies in Second Language Acquisition* 22(4), 499–533.

Dewaele, J.-M. (2004a) Blistering barnacles! What language do multilinguals swear in?! *Estudios de Sociolinguistica* 5(1), 83–106.

Dewaele, J.-M. (2004b) The emotional force of swearwords and taboo words in the speech of multilinguals. *Journal of Multilingual and Multicultural Development* 25(2/3), 204–22.

Dewaele, J.-M. (2004c) Individual differences in the use of colloquial vocabulary: the effects of sociobiographical and psychological factors. In P. Bogaards and B. Laufer (eds) *Learning Vocabulary in a Second Language: Selection, Acquisition and Testing* (pp. 127–53). Amsterdam: John Benjamins.

Dewaele, J.-M. (2004d) Perceived language dominance and language preference for emotional speech: The implications for attrition research. In M.S. Schmid, B. Köpke, M. Kejser and L. Weilemar (eds) *First Language Attrition: Interdisciplinary Perspectives on Methodological Issues* (pp. 81–104). Amsterdam: John Benjamins.

Dewaele, J.-M. (2005) The effect of type of acquisition context on perception and self-reported use of swearwords in the L2, L3, L4 and L5. In A. Housen and M. Pierrard (eds) *Investigations in Instructed Second Language Acquisition* (pp. 531–59). Berlin: Mouton De Gruyter.

Dewaele, J.-M. and Pavlenko, A. (2001) Web questionnaire *Bilingualism and Emotions*. University of London.

Dewaele, J.-M. and Pavlenko, A. (2002) Emotion vocabulary in interlanguage. *Language Learning* 52(2), 265–324.

Dörnyei, Z. (2003) *Questionnaires in Second Language Research: Construction, Administration, and Processing*. Mahwah, NJ: Lawrence Erlbaum.

Hamers, J. and Blanc, M. (2000) *Bilinguality and Bilingualism* (2nd edn). Cambridge: Cambridge University Press.

Harris, C. (2004) Bilingual speakers in the lab: Psychophysiological measures of emotional reactivity. *Journal of Multilingual and Multicultural Development* 25(2/3), 223–47.

Harris, C., Ayçiçegi, A. and Gleason, J. (2003) Taboo words and reprimands elicit greater autonomic reactivity in a first than in a second language. *Applied Psycholinguistics* 24, 561–79.

Kinginger, C. (2004) Bilingualism and emotion in the autobiographical works of Nancy Huston. *Journal of Multilingual and Multicultural Development* 25(2/3), 159–78.

Kroll, J., Michael, E., Tokowicz, N. and Dufour, R. (2002) The development of lexical fluency in a second language. *Second Language Research* 18, 141–75.

Markus, H. and Kitayama, S. (1991) Culture and self: Implications for cognition, emotion, and motivation. *Psychological Review* 98(2), 224–53.

Mettewie, L. (2004) *Attitudes en motivatie van taalleerders in België* (Attitudes and motivation of language learners in Belgium). Unpublished PhD dissertation, Vrije Universiteit Brussel, Brussels, Belgium.

Panksepp, J. (2000) The neuro-evolutionary cusp between emotions and cognitions: Implications for understanding consciousness and the emergence of a unified mind science. *Consciousness and Emotion* 1(1), 15–54.

Panksepp, J. (2003) At the interface of the affective, behavioral, and cognitive neurosciences: Decoding the emotional feelings of the brain. *Brain and Cognition* 52(1), 4–14.

Pavlenko, A. (2002) Bilingualism and emotions. *Multilingua* 21, 45–78.

Pavlenko, A. (2004) 'Stop doing that, ia komu skazala!': Language choice and emotions in parent–child communication. *Journal of Multilingual and Multicultural Development* 25(2/3), 179–203.

Rintell, E. (1984) But how did you *feel* about that? The learner's perception of emotion in speech. *Applied Linguistics* 5, 255–64.

Schrauf, R. (2000) Bilingual autobiographical memory: Experimental studies and clinical cases. *Culture and Psychology* 6, 387–417.

Toya, M. and Kodis, M. (1996) But I don't want to be rude: On learning how to express anger in the L2. *JALT Journal* 18(2), 279–95.

Wierzbicka, A. and Harkins, J. (2001) Introduction. In J. Harkins and A. Wierzbicka (eds) *Emotions in Crosslinguistic Perspective* (pp. 1–34). Berlin: Mouton De Gruyter.

Wierzbicka, A. (2004) Bilingual lives, bilingual experience. *Journal of Multilingual and Multicultural Development* 25(2/3), 94–104.

Ye, V. (2001) An inquiry into 'sadness' in Chinese. In J. Harkins and A. Wierzbicka (eds) *Emotions in Crosslinguistic Perspective* (pp. 359–404). Berlin: Mouton De Gruyter.

Chapter 6

Joking Across Languages: Perspectives on Humor, Emotion, and Bilingualism

JYOTSNA VAID

Introduction

Humor, a pervasive element of social interaction, expresses and elicits a variety of emotional states from joy and surprise to sarcasm and hostility. This chapter addresses the relationship between bilingualism and emotion through the lens of humor and related speech acts (e.g. joking). Although much has been written about its nature, forms, and functions, surprisingly little empirical work has been directed at how humor operates in users with multiple linguistic and/or cultural identities (see Vaid, 2000, 2003). Yet, research on humor use in multiple language users would greatly enrich our understanding of bilingualism, as well as our understanding of humor. For students of bilingualism, the study of humor would broaden the study of language from decontextualized, representational aspects of language to contextualized, performative aspects. For students of humor, the study of humor use among multiple language users would deepen awareness of the ways in which humor comprehension depends on shared, tacit linguistic and cultural knowledge.

Questions of potential interest in the interface of humor, emotion, and bilingualism include the following: How is humor used by members of linguistically and/or culturally diverse speech communities to convey or, for that matter, disguise, various emotional states? What is the role of code-switching in relation to humor in bilingual discourse? What novel linguistic constructions have emerged as bilinguals play with and through language? How do perceptions of their humor use differ for minority versus majority culture respondents? How does the nature of dual cultural identity affect bilinguals' beliefs about the prevalence and nature of humor use across languages? In what follows, we will examine these and related questions.

The chapter is organized in three parts. The first part considers the phenomenon of humor and relates it to discourse, emotion, and language competence. The second part considers different manifestations of bilinguals' word play and explores possible functions associated with humor as it is used by members of diverse speech communities. The third part presents empirical data from two recent survey studies conducted by the author on perceptions of humor uses by Anglo-American versus Mexican-American individuals, and on the influence of cultural identity on bilinguals' humor beliefs and practices. The chapter concludes by suggesting some directions for further research on humor and bilingualism.

Humor as a Mode of Discourse

In defining humor it is important to refer to the mode of discourse. A humorous mode is playful and often irreverent. Although these qualities stand in sharp contrast to qualities that characterize serious discourse, humor's apparent lack of seriousness does not mean that it is inconsequential. Indeed, humor has been said to be adaptive for the human species in providing a way of coping with adversity (Vaid, 1999). In a serious mode of discourse, a single, objective reality is presupposed and any disagreements about how reality is to be interpreted are sought to be minimized and resolved. Ambiguity and paradox are seen as hindrances to communication and, as such, have no place in serious discourse. In contrast, a humorous mode of discourse portrays reality more whimsically as having multiple versions. In a humorous mode, the normal rules of logic and of discourse are temporarily suspended. Rather than striving for a single, conventional view of reality, humorous discourse serves, instead, to unsettle existing conceptions by playfully exposing the underlying beliefs and values that underlie dominant social constructions of reality. In a humorous mode, ambiguity and absurdity play a central role and are cultivated rather than avoided (Mulkay, 1988; Nehrlich & Clarke, 2001). Under the guise of humor, normal conversational maxims can be violated, socially unspeakable topics can more easily enter the discourse, and power relations can be inverted (Crawford, 2003). For these reasons, a humorous mode has been characterized as ambiguous, indirect, decommitted, multivocal, and transgressive (Gilbert, 2004; Sommer, 2004).

Taxonomies of humor

Several taxonomies of humor have been put forth. Some focus on the form and structure of humor, others on its content, others on techniques that arouse laughter, and still others on the communicative functions of humor.

With regard to different forms of humor, one can distinguish between jests, quips, gags, humorous anecdotes, and jokes, to name the most common forms. Of these, jokes have received particular attention. Jokes are structured in such a way that they establish certain expectations in the listener's mind and then abruptly thwart those expectations with the presentation of the punchline (Attardo, 1994; Koestler, 1964). That is, jokes create schemas only to skew them (Norrick, 1986). Violation of expectations is, thus, a key ingredient of joke structure. Jokes thrive on violations of the ordinary ways of seeing the world, violations of the ordinary ways of using language, and violations of the ordinary ways of expressing emotions.

Different techniques may be enlisted to induce humor. These include the use of mimicry or impersonation, exaggeration, mockery, understatement, unexpected twists of logic, irony, disguise, punning, and appeals to the reader's superiority (Thomas, 2001). The choice of technique may in turn depend on the intended use of humor. Humor may be intended to have a therapeutic effect or a subversive effect. It may be self-deprecatory or it may mock others in order to expose human frailties such as self-exaltation, self-righteousness, self-deception, greed, pride, envy, or dishonesty.

Taxonomies focusing on functions of humor have pointed to the multifaceted uses of humor in social interaction, including humor to enforce social norms (Martineau, 1972), to publicly expose disapproved behavior (Al-Khatib, 1999), to express one-upmanship, to stereotype others, to create or maintain group solidarity (Hay, 2000; Holmes & Hay, 1997), to emphasize power differences, and to provide a means to cope with adversity (Graham *et al.*, 1992; Thomas, 2001).

Humor as emotion management

Whereas humor expresses and elicits feelings of amusement, joy, or elation, the emotions that give rise to humor need not be positive. In fact, humor is often fuelled by negative events or by experiences that are, or were at some point, emotionally upsetting. Such emotions as fear, anger, shame, or even grief may find expression in humor and, in the process, are transformed by it, for being able to laugh about something implies that one has achieved some distance from it and put it in some perspective. However, humor may not always unmask one's true feelings, it may also be used to disguise or even deny one's feelings. The very distancing that makes it possible for something to be rendered as funny may make it possible to discount or dismiss the depth or intensity of an underlying sentiment.

Chafe (2003) argues that laughing expresses an emotion of its own, a pleasant feeling that he terms 'the feeling of nonseriousness'. This feeling shares certain characteristics with other emotions, including not being entirely under voluntary control, fading slowly, being contagious, occurring in degrees, and occurring universally. Laughter, according to Chafe (2003), mitigates the seriousness of an unpleasant experience, which may account for why it tends to occur when something is experienced as awkward, confusing, disastrous, disgusting, embarrassing, illegal, insulting, stupid, threatening, or unethical. By laughing, we are temporarily disabled or distracted from taking seriously, and from taking action with respect to, experiences that it would be inappropriate to take seriously, or to act on (Chafe, 2003).

Related to the above notion is the view of humor as the interpersonal management of emotions, both one's own emotions as well as those of others. Humor is particularly prevalent in settings where emotions may need to be regulated, such as in negotiation interactions in the workplace (Adelsward & Oberg, 1998) or in hospital settings. Based on observations by health care providers of the occurrence of humor in medical interactions, Francis (1999: 171) proposed the following general model of humor as interpersonal emotion management: 'Humor intended to manage the emotions of others is (1) a culturally-based sensitivity to context, including [sensitivity to] the status of the actors present as well as the setting and timing, (2) which strengthens or restores the feeling norms of the situation and creates amusement in the self and others, (3) generating positive emotions among members of an interacting group by bonding them and/or reducing an external threat, (4) often at the expense of some excluded person(s), event(s), or object(s), and (5) must be recognized by at least two participants in the interaction'. This plausible and inclusive account of humor as it is actually used in interaction will be adopted in the present overview as a working definition of humor.

Humor competence and language/cultural competence

Whereas learners and users of a second language may be able to express themselves with little difficulty when using their second language, they often find expressing themselves affectively through humor in that language more daunting. This ability is especially difficult for adult learners of a language. A noted American applied linguist who had taught for several years at the university level in one of his many languages, Hebrew, made the following observation: 'Even after so many years, I had not learned how to play with the language, whether through puns, innuendoes, or other forms of humor' (Cohen, 2001: 94–95). The ability to understand and use humor appropriately has been seen as a hallmark of attaining native-like proficiency in a language (Hall, 1959). The reason for the difficulties experienced by even advanced users of a second language may be because humorous word play requires knowledge of the linguistic and cultural conventions of a speech community, which prescribe what can be talked about and how.

One may speak of humor competence as a form of mastery not merely of the rules of a language, but also of the unwritten cultural norms of the speech community (Chiaro, 1992; Laurian, 1992; Nilsen, 1989). To the extent that joking involves a violation of norms, knowledge of linguistic and cultural norms is essential in order to know what would constitute a transgression.

In the next section we turn to a consideration of the various forms of humor produced by speakers of more than one language and the functional significance of humor for members of linguistically and culturally plural societies.

Creativity in Humor and Word Play Across the Bilingual's Languages

The ability to be creative and play with language is a pervasive aspect of everyday language use and is not confined to literary language (Cook, 2001; Scherzer, 2002). As members of a shared speech community, native speakers of a language can and indeed are expected to bend and break its rules and patterns and be seen to be playful and creative with language. By contrast, non-native speakers are usually not accorded the same freedom to transgress. If they choose to do so anyway, their productions are, more often than not, regarded by others as mistakes (Prodromou, 2003: 46). However, as shown in recent ethnographic accounts, both beginning language learners (Davies, 2003) and advanced learners (Bell, 2002) engage in humor with native language users. The humor may very often arise from a recognition of errors made when using the target language, such as borrowing cognates that turn out to be 'false friends' or taking literally what was meant to be taken figuratively.

However, some 'errors' made by second language users may not be actual errors, but semantic extensions from the native language. Nilsen (1981) suggests that, instead of referring to these as errors, they might be better described as bilingual folk poetry. It may be particularly inappropriate to equate 'difference' with 'deficiency' when confronting deviations from standard usage on the part of English speakers from countries constituting the 'expanding outer circle' of users of English (Kachru, 1985). Among members of linguistically plural communities, playing with the sounds and the rules of language is, in fact, a widespread practice and one that might even be accentuated by having access to more than one language and culture. Haugen (1986) maintained that bilinguals have all kinds of fun from which monolinguals are excluded. Not only can they shift to and from their languages or mix languages within a single sentence, they can also exploit associations across languages, and 'be two different persons and live in two different worlds when the one of these becomes too boring or troublesome' (Haugen, 1986: 119).

Indeed, several examples have been documented of bilingual humor, or the comic effect arising when words in two languages are juxtaposed in certain ways using mimicry, mispronunciation, or misunderstanding to exploit sound similarities or ambiguities at various levels of language (e.g. Nilsen, 1981). Bilingual humor may either be intended by the speaker to be humorous or may arise inadvertently.

Inadvertent humor

One example of inadvertent humor is when the meaning of words in one language is mistakenly interpreted from the perspective of their meaning in the other language. An example of such humor is given by Leeds (1992: 133), who describes a six-year-old boy living in France who came from his French father who was gardening to ask his American mother in the kitchen the following question:

'Dad wants to know where to plant the streetbeard'. She replied: 'What do you mean "street beard"? Say it in French!' The boy retorted, 'La rhubarbe'.

Many other instances of inadvertent humor arise from not realizing that certain ways of phrasing something lend themselves to other interpretations in that language that, although not intended, serve as a playful metacommentary on the intended message. These forms of humor exploit the polysemy and ambiguity that is rife in normal language use. Some examples are given below in the form of signs in English found in hotels or stores in parts of the world where English has the status of a non-native language. At a Bucharest hotel lobby: 'The lift is being fixed for the next day. During that time we regret that you will be unbearable'. Outside a Hong Kong tailor shop: 'Ladies may have a fit upstairs'. At a Bangkok dry-cleaners: 'Drop your trousers here for better results'. (See http://www.digi-taldreamdoor.com/pages/quotes/funny_signs.html.)

Accent humor

Many forms of linguistic humor, such as malapropisms or spoonerisms, are based on deliberately exposing and laughing at a linguistic deviation from the norm. One form of humor that uses defective performance as its basis is so-called accent humor, that is, humor that exaggerates mispronunciation and incorrect use of grammar and vocabulary.

Dialect humor is one form of accent humor, where the accent of speakers of a dialect exploits ambiguity and misunderstanding for humorous effect. The following example is illustrative:

American in an Australian hospital asks the nurse:
Did I come here to die?
'No', responds the nurse, 'it was yesterdie'.

Not surprisingly, non-native speakers of a language, who are most likely to show mispronunciations and errors in their speech, are often the butt of such humor. There are several examples of statements that are inadvertently humorous if spoken in a Spanish accent by Mexican-American non-native speakers of English (Nilsen, 1981):

I'm studying law at Jail [Yale].
Now that she had new glasses she was better able to wash [watch] the children.
I mate [met] him more than once.
They were feeding father [fodder] to the cows.

Non-native users may themselves engage in language play and humor that exploits accent and misunderstanding of word meanings. The Mexican immigration experience in Texas has given rise to several jokes based on word play between English and Spanish. These jokes either rely on a deliberate phonetic confusion between English and Spanish to produce humor or on the protagonist misreading words or phrases, as in the following example (Reyna & Herrera-Sobek, 1998: 218):

A group of Mexicans was arrested for breaking into a vacant house. When they went to court, they told the judge that they were merely obeying a sign that read 'For Sale' which they read as 'Forzale' (force it open).

Intentional humor

There are several examples of innovative uses of Spanish and English (and Spanglish) by Latino bilinguals from immigrant communities in New York City. Loan words or names may be rendered in literal translation, yielding such expressions as 'July Churches' and 'Placid Sunday' for the names of the singers Julio Iglesias and Placido Domingo.

Bilingual puns

Bilingual punning may be considered a unique form of humor produced or enjoyed by bilingual users. Bilingual punning in Germany is ubiquitous in advertising and journalistic writing. In an analysis of 100 English–German puns compiled from billboard ads, print ads, and Internet sources, Stefanowitsch (2002) observed that the majority of the puns involved a syllable of a German or English word being replaced with a word from the other language. One example quoted by Stefano-witsch is particularly apt: the German word *Kultur* (culture) has given rise to a whole array of puns, including (1) *Kul-Tour*, which is used by travel agents to refer to tours focusing on the culture of a country, (2) *Cool-tur*, used in an ad seeking to get young people interested in their cultural heritage, and (3) *cool-tour*, used as a title of a webzine that seeks to offer its readers a 'tour' of 'cool' popular culture. For these and other bilingual puns to work, that is, to be recognized and appreciated, Stefanowitsch argued, the puns require a strong linguistic frame, defined as a recognizable, entrenched chunk of language. The chunk of language can be a word or a well-known phrase, such as a proverb, a pragmatic routine, or a song title.

Code-switching

A widespread device for style shifting in bilingual communities involves the use of code-switching. Switching complicates meanings, intentionally or otherwise. Code-switching can be a device to frame something as humorous (Cromdal & Aronsson, 2000). The use of a particular code in discourse can signal not only how the utterance is to be interpreted but also information about the context and social identities of the interlocutors. Describing code-switching into Hindi among Fijians, Siegel (1995: 101) noted: 'Hindi is not normally used for communication among Fijians; so when a Fijian switches to Hindi among other Fijians, it is a marked choice. For the listener(s), it is almost always a clear signal that the speaker is joking. For the speaker, it is a means of indicating the informality of the context and emphasizing solidarity with the listener(s). It also affirms that the speaker is in a social relationship with the listener(s) that allows joking – and, with certain relatives, that the speaker is fulfilling kinship obligations'.

The act of code-switching itself may be humorous in the creative or unusual way in which language is used (see Vaid, 2004). The creativity may arise from word play that deliberately exploits structural similarities (as in the case of bilingual puns) or it may arise from the fact of engaging in code-switching itself where the norm involves a strict separation of languages.

Code-switching may also lead to humor when the variety switched into is considered funny. In most societies, a particular variety of language is designated as the object of humor. This is usually the informal variety, or the low variety in diglossic cases (Apte, 1985). In bilingual societies, a particular language may be identified as more appropriate for joking, for example, Guarani rather than Spanish in Paraguay, or Punjabi rather than Hindi among north Indians. This situation may arise from a desire to parody speakers of that language, who are often the butt of humor whether because of the way they speak or the way they behave, or for some other reason.

Humor Performance, Ethnicity, and Resistance

Recent theorizing within the psychological literature has begun to examine the psychological impact of straddling two cultures

(LaFromboise *et al.*, 1993; Schrauf, 2002). Vivero and Jenkins (1999) propose that bicultural experience confers a sense of cultural home-lessness and marginality. However, this marginality may contribute to a potentially heightened cognitive and social awareness because of the multiple frames of reference associated with participating in several cultures. One could expect then that humor, which has been characterized as the performance of marginality (Gilbert, 2004), may attain a prominent status among members of marginalized groups. Inasmuch as joking can be seen as being essentially an attack on control, or a subversion of the dominant structure of ideas (Douglas, 1968), humor performed by members of marginalized groups may be viewed as a powerful form of resistance to dominant discourses about ethnicity or about language itself.

Within the field of folklore, the study of jokes that persist in a community has been used to illustrate ways in which members of the community psychologically manage anxieties produced by social problems and channel them into structured expressive forms. This view of jokes is particularly applicable to the Texas–Mexican community. Americo Paredes (1968) developed a set of three categories of Texas–Mexican jokes that took a critical psychological account of the social domination that characterized the relationship between the Anglo-Texan and the Mexican immigrant population. The categories of humor Paredes outlined included jokes in which the Anglo-American is duped by a Texas–Mexican trickster figure, jokes of a self-satirical nature in which the Texas Mexican appears to accept certain stereotypes held by Anglos, and jokes that blend elements from the other two categories.

To these categories Jose Limon (1977) added a new category consisting of jokes in which the Anglo-American is confronted through a surrogate figure, namely, the Anglicized Mexican, or the *agringado*. *Agringados* emerged as the result of internal differentiation in Texas–Mexican society in direct response to the presence of Anglo-Americans. They are characterized as individuals who overtly reject the Mexican-American way of life and identify instead with Anglo culture. In describing instances of joking performance directed at *agringados*, Limon counters claims that Texas–Mexican joking is an exercise in self-hatred or envy of those who have successfully crossed the boundary to the dominant culture (see also Zenner, 1970) and suggests that such joking behavior derives instead from 'a position of historically derived cultural awareness' (Limon, 1977: 48). Sommer (2004: 14) notes in this regard that '[c]oncern about the self-deprecation of migrants who both incite and enjoy ethnic humor sounds paradoxical and paternalist, as if the under-privileged newcomers didn't take pride in the wisdom of self-irony, as if they didn't know better than to laugh at themselves'.

Indeed, the linguistic virtuosity of bilinguals in immigrant communities may be seen as a response to the racializing discourse they are subjected to by guardians of the white public space and as a challenge to the notion of bounded languages and identities. As Zentella (2003: 62) notes, 'Latin@s have a good deal of fun at the expense of gringos, and language play is at the heart of their defense against their marginalization, exploitation, and stigmatization'. The use of Spanglish, calques, loans, loan translations, puns and dialect jokes by Latinos in New York City and immigrant communities elsewhere reveals the various ways in which humor is used to perform marginality and express resistance to dominant discourses.

Performance by stand-up comics of different ethnicities provides the newest form of portrayal, and subverting, of cultural stereotypes through humor. Comedic representations delivered by ethnic minority comics to predominantly white, majority culture audiences have been on the rise. Such performances raise questions about whether humor reproduces and perpetuates racist stereotypes or subverts them. One New York-based Latino comedian, John Leguizamo, of Puerto Rican and Colombian descent, does not regard his comedy as perpetuating racist stereotypes, but as a form of social exorcism of negative self-images of Latinos (Chirico, 2002).

Research on ethnic humor has typically portrayed ethnic identity as fixed and static and has all but ignored multi-ethnic peoples as active creators of humor. However, for individuals of mixed ethnicity, humor can be a positive affirmation of multi-ethnicity, one that transforms previously alienating experiences. Darby Li Po Price (2000), a stand-up comic of mixed ethnicity, notes that stand-up comedians of varying or mixed ethnicities routinely subvert dominant expectations by expressing their identities as shifting, transgressive, and socially constructed. Whereas the dominant expectations are that ethnic humor will involve stereotypical or disparaging references, stand-up comics, according to Price, use multi-ethnicity as grounds for humor by reducing it to a social absurdity. This is illustrated in the following interchange between Bo Irvine, a comic with Portuguese, Filipino, and Hawaiian heritage, and a Caucasian moderator, Lynn Waters, during a televised discussion about ethnic humor (cited in Price, 2000: 181):

Lynn: Okay, someone has to tell an ethnic joke.
Bo: Okay, I'm Portuguese and Hawaiian, so if you believe the stereotypes, I'm dumb but too lazy to find out why.

The strategy of embracing ethnic humor to expose prejudices and disparaging stereotypes is particularly characteristic of the stand-up routines of Muslim comedians, who are enjoying a new prominence in the post-September 11 climate, performing for non-Muslim audiences in the West and occasionally for immigrant audiences as well. Here, for example, is the signature opening statement of the British Muslim comic Shazia Mirza: 'Hi, my name is Shazia Mirza – at least that's what it says on my pilot's license' (quoted in Del Negro, 2004). In a similar vein, the website of Tissa Hami, an Iranian-born comic in Boston, quipped that 'people who disapprove of her act will be taken hostage' (quoted in Murphy, 2004). Playing on the West's current preoccupation with terrorism, Canadian filmmaker Zarqa Nawaz produces 'terrodies' or comedies about terrorism, for her film company aptly named FUNdamentalist Films.

In summary, members of linguistically and culturally plural communities use humor to play with and through language, to construct shifting identities, to affirm their linguistic and cultural hybridity, and to express resistance to discourses of social domination.

Humor Use in Bilingual Communities: An Empirical Exploration

In this final section, I present two empirical studies of the uses of humor by members of a Spanish–English bilingual community in Texas. Questions underlying this research included the following: What is humor used for by members of majority versus minority communities? Is humor used similarly or differently for emotion management across the bilingual's languages? Is humor produced more often in one of the bilingual's languages or is it produced equally across languages? Do bilinguals react to humor differently if it is presented in one language rather than the other? Do bilinguals view their own humorous personae as invariant when they shift from one language to another or from one cultural setting to another? Does humor come more naturally to multiple language users? Do such users find humor in more things, or appreciate more kinds of humor than single language users? In what ways are bilinguals' beliefs about humor and their actual humor practices shaped by their perceptions of their own cultural identity?

Study 1: Perceptions of humor uses by Mexican-Americans and Anglo-Americans

Little is currently known about the extent to which humor, used in the service of different psychological and social functions including emotion management, varies across cultures. The present study was part of a larger study of how members of different minority groups as compared to Anglo-Americans perceive their frequency of humor use in a variety of interactional contexts (see Vaid *et al.*, 2004). The study aimed to determine which functions would be rated similarly and which differently by Mexican-American versus Anglo-American college students. Participants were to judge their own use of humor for a range of contexts followed by that of typical members of their cultural group. The items chosen included affiliative and non-affiliative aspects of humor, and humor uses that pertained primarily to the level of the individual, the interpersonal level, or the societal level (see Table 6.1 for the list of items and their classification). The items were developed by consulting previous published reports of humor uses in conversation (e.g. Graham *et al.*, 1992; Hay, 2000).

Method

Participants. Eighty-eight students from Texas A&M University, ranging in age from 18 to 23 years, participated in the study. They were classified into two groups – Anglo-Americans and Mexican-Americans – on the basis of their self-identification on a brief questionnaire. Forty-seven participants were Mexican-American (24 males and 23 females) and 41 were Anglo-American (14 males and 27 females). Half of the participants also completed a detailed language and cultural background questionnaire presented between the two testing conditions. The questionnaire indicated that the vast majority of respondents were born in the United States, felt comfortable in their two cultures, knew Spanish and English, but reported better comprehension of English.

Humor uses instrument and procedure. A 19-item humor uses instrument developed specifically for this study was administered. Participants were tested in two conditions. In the first condition, they were to rate the frequency of their own humor use (Self Condition), whereas in the second condition they rated the frequency of humor use for typical members of their culture. The same set of 19 items was used across conditions. Ratings were made using a five-point scale, where 1 indicated 'almost always' and 5 'almost never' [use humor for the particular function indicated].

Data analyses. Several analyses were performed on the survey data. First, a measure of relative distribution of the rankings was obtained for each group and condition (see Table 6.1). This measure illustrates which uses of humor were ranked most frequent and which were ranked least frequent, and suggests where the groups responded similarly and where they differed. Secondly, each of the 19 items was individually analyzed in a three-way ANOVA as a function of Condition (i.e. self versus culture), Group (i.e. Mexican-American versus Anglo-American), and Gender. Finally, two 4-way ANOVAs were performed on mean ratings of the items: one examined humor ratings as a function of Affect Type (positive versus negative affiliative), Condition, Group, and Gender, whereas the other examined humor ratings as a function of Dimension (individual, interpersonal, societal), Condition, Group, and Gender.

Table 6.1 Classification of humor use items in Study 1

	A. Affiliative	*B. Non-affiliative*
Individual	To be absurd	To manage one's anxieties or fears
	To be playful	To be self-mocking
	To be creative with language	
Interpersonal	To be affectionate	To tease someone
	To be a good sport	To express hostility or aggression
	To share funny personal experiences	To let others know one's likes or dislikes
	To show romantic interest in someone	
Societal	To reduce tension or conflict in a situation	To put others in their place
	To create solidarity	To enforce social norms
	To increase liking by others	To disrupt or undermine the social order
		To expose injustices and right social wrongs

Results

Relative ranking of humor items by perceived frequency of use. Table 6.2 lists the relative frequency rankings of the 19 humor items per group and condition in descending order (the higher the numerical value, the lower the frequency of use).

For the items ranked highest and lowest in frequency, rankings were comparable across groups and conditions. Both groups gave 'to share funny personal experiences' the highest ranking for Self and Culture. Further, both ranked 'to be playful' the second highest across conditions. The groups ranked 'to express hostility or aggression' lowest across conditions and gave 'to create solidarity' and 'to expose injustices and right social wrongs' the next lowest rankings. For two other items, 'to reduce tension or conflict in a situation' and 'to increase liking by others' both groups gave comparably high rankings (within the top eight) across conditions.

The rankings differed by group for certain items. For example, in the Self condition, Anglo-Americans ranked 'to be self-mocking' higher than did Mexican-Americans (4 versus 9, respectively). In contrast, the

Table 6.2 Ranking of relative frequency of Self versus Culture in humor use by Mexican-Americans and Anglo-Americans (1 = almost always use humor, 5 = almost never use humor)

Rank	MexAm Self		MexAm Culture		AngloAm Self		AngloAm Culture	
	Item	Rating	Item	Rating	Item	Rating	Item	Rating
1	Share funny experiences	1.53	Share funny experiences	1.79	Share funny experiences	1.73	Share funny experiences	1.66
2	Be playful	1.79	Be playful	1.83	Be playful	1.83	Be playful	2.12
3	Be creative	2.26	Tease	2.13	Tease	1.93	Tease	2.17
4	Increase liking	2.30	Be creative	2.28	Be self-mocking	1.95	Increase liking	2.24
5	Reduce tension	2.30	Increase liking	2.34	Increase liking	2.20	Be self-mocking	2.37
6	Tease	2.40	Be affectionate	2.47	Reduce tension	2.32	Be absurd	2.41
7	Be affectionate	2.43	Be self-mocking	2.47	Be creative	2.46	Be creative	2.46
8	Be a good sport	2.43	Be a good sport	2.57	Be absurd	2.59	Reduce tension	2.51
9	Be self-mocking	2.45	Be absurd	2.74	Be a good sport	2.73	Manage anxieties	2.93
10	Romantic interest	2.57	Romantic interest	2.85	Romantic interest	2.95	Be a good sport	3.00
11	Be absurd	2.77	Reduce tension	2.96	Show likes/dislikes	2.98	Be affectionate	3.02
12	Enforce norms	2.96	Enforce norms	2.98	Be affectionate	3.00	Put others in place	3.02
13	Show likes/dislikes	3.04	Show likes/dislikes	3.04	Manage anxieties	3.20	Show romantic interest	3.10
14	Manage anxieties	3.06	Manage anxieties	3.11	Enforce norms	3.37	Show likes/dislikes	3.15
15	Disrupt order	3.21	Disrupt order	3.32	Disrupt order	3.39	Enforce norms	3.46
16	Expose injustices	3.26	Put others in place	3.34	Put others in place	3.41	Disrupt order	3.49
17	Put others in place	3.43	Expose injustices	3.36	Create solidarity	3.44	Create solidarity	3.49
18	Create solidarity	3.51	Create solidarity	3.43	Expose injustices	3.61	Expose injustices	3.66
19	Express hostility	3.77	Express hostility	3.89	Express hostility	3.93	Express hostility	3.80

item 'to be creative with language' was ranked higher by Mexican-Americans than by Anglo-Americans (3 versus 7, respectively). Similarly, in the Culture condition, the use of humor 'to manage one's anxieties or fears' was ranked higher by Anglo-Americans than it was by Mexican-Americans (9 versus 14, respectively). By contrast, using humor 'to be affectionate' was ranked higher by Mexican-Americans than it was by Anglo-Americans (6 versus 11, respectively).

On certain items the groups gave different rankings across conditions. For example, although the use of humor 'to tease' was ranked third highest by Anglo-Americans in Self and Culture conditions and by Mexican-Americans in the Culture condition, it was given a rank of 6 by Mexican-Americans in the Self condition. Similarly, Anglo-Americans ranked humor 'to manage one's anxieties or fears' as ninth in the Culture condition but 13th in the Self condition.

Analyses of humor use per item.   Separate analyses of variance were performed per item to statistically compare mean humor use ratings as a function of Group, Gender, and Condition. Although all effects that were significant at the $p < 0.05$ level or beyond are reported here, given the large number of analyses performed and the increased likelihood, therefore, of a Type I error, only the effects that were significant at the more stringent confidence levels should be considered reliable.

For the majority of the items, participants in both groups tended to show similar ratings for Self and Culture. A main effect of Condition was only obtained for one item: 'to reduce tension or conflict in a situation' ($p < 0.006$), indicating a higher use for Self than for Culture (2.31 versus 2.75). For the item, 'to show romantic interest in someone' a Condition by Gender effect was found ($p < 0.002$), which indicated that in the Culture condition males gave higher use ratings than females (2.76 versus 3.16, respectively, t(86) = 2.01, $p = 0.05$). In addition, women rated their own use of this item higher than that for their culture (2.60 versus 3.16, respectively, t(50) = -3.68, $p = 0.001$).

For the item, 'to let others know one's likes/dislikes', a Condition by Group by Gender effect emerged ($p < 0.04$). Further analysis of the interaction revealed a tendency for a higher rating for Culture than for Self by Mexican-American women (2.79 versus 3.12, respectively, $p < 0.06$).

An effect of Group was significant or near significant for nearly half of the items. Group emerged as a main effect for 'to be affectionate' ($p < 0.002$), indicating a higher use by Mexican-Americans than Anglo-Americans (2.45 versus 3.01, respectively). A near significant main effect of Group occurred for the item 'to be a good sport' ($p < 0.057$), indicating a higher use by Mexican-Americans than Anglo-Americans (2.50 versus 2.87, respectively). A near significant effect of Group also emerged for the item 'to show romantic interest' ($p < 0.064$), indicating a higher use by Mexican-Americans than by Anglo-Americans (2.71 versus 3.02, respectively).

Group interacted with Gender on three items: 'to share funny personal experiences' ($p < 0.05$), 'to be playful' ($p < 0.027$), and 'to express hostility or aggression' ($p < 0.028$). Humor used to share funny personal experiences was used more by Mexican-American men than Anglo-American men (1.66 versus 1.89, respectively, $t(35) = 2.16$, $p = 0.04$). Anglo-American women showed higher use for sharing funny experiences than Mexican-American women (1.59 versus 1.83, respectively, $t(45) = 2.06$, $p = 0.04$). Humor used to be playful was rated higher by Mexican-American men than by Anglo-American men (1.46 versus 2.10, respectively, $t(35) = 2.48$, $p = 0.02$) and by Mexican-American men than Mexican-American women (1.46 versus 2.15, respectively, $t(45) = 2.56$, $p = 0.01$). Humor used to express hostility showed a crossover interaction, with Anglo-American men rating it higher than Anglo-American women (3.54 versus 4.04, respectively), but with Mexican-American women rating it higher than Mexican-American men (3.56 versus 4.11, respectively).

Analysis of humor use by dimension. A four-way analysis of variance of mean humor ratings was performed as a function of Condition (self versus culture), Humor Dimension (individual, interpersonal versus societal), Group and Gender. A main effect of Humor Dimension was found, $F(2, 168) = 41.19$, $p < 0.0001$, indicating that humor directed at the individual level (2.46) was rated higher in use than humor directed at the interpersonal level (2.72) which, in turn, was rated higher than humor directed at the societal level (3.08).

Analysis of humor use by humor affect. A four-way analysis of variance was performed as a function of Humor Affect Type (Affiliative versus Non-Affiliative), Group, Gender, and Condition. The analysis yielded a main effect of Humor Type ($F(1, 84) = 62.33$, $p < 0.0001$) and a Type by Group by Gender interaction ($F(1, 84) = 5.13$, $p < 0.026$). Breakdown of the interaction revealed that, for Affiliative humor, there was a Group by Gender effect indicating higher humor use rating by Mexican-American men than women ($t(45) = 2.48$, $p = 0.018$) and by Mexican-American men than Anglo-American men ($t(35) = 2.53$, $p = 0.016$). Non-Affiliative humor showed no group or gender effects (see Figure 6.1).

Discussion

The survey responses on relative frequency of humor use by self and by typical members of one's culture revealed a complex pattern, with some uses of humor being ranked comparably across groups or conditions and others showing differences. The data on relative ranking of frequency of humor revealed that Mexican-Americans and Anglo-Americans

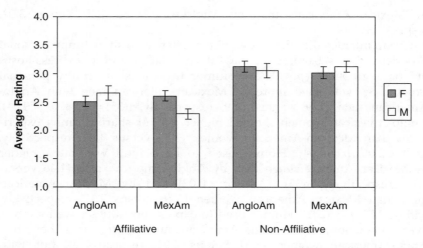

Figure 6.1 Mean rating of frequency of humor use by group, gender, and humor type (affiliative versus non-affiliative)

concurred in giving positively valenced humor uses ('to share funny personal experiences' and 'to be playful') the highest ranking for Self and Culture conditions alike, and negatively valenced uses ('to express hostility or aggression') the lowest ranking across conditions. Further, both groups gave similar high rankings to other uses of humor to manage emotions, that is, 'to reduce tension or conflict in a situation' and 'to increase liking by others'. Societal uses of humor (e.g. 'to create solidarity' or 'to expose injustices and right social wrongs') were given low frequency ratings overall.

Some intriguing group differences were also suggested by the ranking data, with Mexican-Americans giving higher Self rankings than Anglo-Americans on the use of humor 'to be creative with language' but lower Self rankings to the teasing function of humor. Anglo-Americans' rankings of the use of humor 'to be self-mocking' were in turn higher than those of Mexican-Americans. This pattern of convergence and divergence in perceptions of humor as emotion management was also apparent in the statistical analyses performed on the data as a function of condition, item valence, item dimension, and gender.

Where differences occurred across conditions, they tended to be in the direction of higher Self than Culture uses of humor to reduce tension, and (among women) to show romantic interest. For using humor to show one's likes and dislikes, Culture use was rated higher than Self by Mexican-American women. For humor items involving interpersonal or societal dimensions, responses tended to be similar across groups.

Group differences were more apparent for items at the individual level: Mexican-Americans (particularly men), relative to Anglo-Americans, were more likely to use humor to be playful, affectionate, a good sport, and to share funny personal experiences. These differences were confirmed by a significant Group by Gender by Affect Type effect interaction, which indicated a higher frequency rating for affiliative humor by Mexican-American men as compared to that by Mexican-American women or Anglo-American men.

To sum up, the survey data on perceptions of humor use by self and typical members of one's culture suggest an interesting pattern of group and gender differences in the functional significance of humor to manage emotions in everyday interaction, with Mexican-Americans' (and particularly, Mexican-American men's) use of humor being more playful and affectionate relative to that of Anglo-Americans. These group differences in self-reported frequency of humor use will need to be supplemented by observational data on humor practices of Mexican-Americans versus Anglo-Americans in actual conversational settings to get a fuller understanding of the precise workings of humor in diverse settings, for example, in same-sex versus mixed-sex, and same cultural group versus mixed group settings.

Study 2: Humor beliefs and practices of Mexican-Americans as a function of cultural orientation

This study was part of a larger project aimed at exploring bilinguals' humor practices and beliefs about humor in relation to their language experience and cultural identification (see Vaid, 2003; Vaid *et al.*, 2003). It was hypothesized that bilinguals who reported keeping their two cultures distinct would show more differentiation across languages in their humor use as compared to those who perceived their two cultures as being more integrated. In addition, the study explored humor practices as a function of the respondents' generational status by comparing respondents whose parents were from Mexico to those whose parents were born in the United States.

Method

Participants. Participants were 80 Spanish- and English-speaking college students enrolled in a psychology course at Texas A&M International University in the border community of Laredo, in south Texas. They ranged in age from 18 to 22 years.

The participants were subdivided into two groups based on their responses on two items in Part I of the survey. One of these was cultural self-identification. This item asked participants to select one of six statements that best described their cultural identity. The majority ($n = 68$) chose the statement that they considered their two cultures to be integrated and were designated as Integrated, whereas the remainder ($n = 12$) selected the statement that their two cultures were separated, and were designated as Separated. The second item on which participants were subdivided was on the basis of their response to the item about their parents' country of origin. Respondents were considered to be of Mexican origin or US origin, depending on how they filled out this item. There were 20 participants with US origin parents and 56 with Mexican origin parents; four respondents did not complete this item. Designation of parents as 'US origin' does not preclude Mexican ethnicity of the parents; it mainly concerns where the parents were raised. Respondents with Mexican origin parents represented 74% of the Integrated respondents and 70% of the Separated respondents.

Description of the survey instrument. The survey instrument, developed by the author, contained four parts. Part I contained questions about demographic variables, language proficiency, language acquisition background and cultural identification. Part II required participants to estimate their relative language preference for a variety of interactional contexts. The contexts related to humor included expressing amusement, teasing, expressing sarcasm or hostility, telling or hearing jokes, and recounting funny personal experiences (see the appendix to this chapter for the exact contents of Parts I and II of the survey instrument).

Part III consisted of 10 statements about humor on which respondents had to state their degree of agreement using a five-point Likert scale, where 1 = strongly agree and 5 = strongly disagree. Many of the statements concerned the stability or fluidity of participants' humor use and their perception of their sense of humor in each language. Part IV contained a set of items designed to measure humor styles per language. The results of Part IV are omitted in the present report due to space considerations (but see Vaid *et al.*, 2003).

Results
Part 1: Language proficiency, cultural involvement, and code-switching frequency. Responses were analyzed separately by the two grouping variables used. Statistical comparisons using *t*-tests yielded no significant differences between Integrated and Separated groups in their self-ratings of English or Spanish language comprehension (1.16 versus 1.15 on a five-point scale where 1 = very proficient), or in their estimated frequency of code-switching (which was fairly high), degree of cultural involvement (also fairly high), experience of discrimination, or self-consciousness about accent. Parental origin affected respondents' ratings on the following measures: English comprehension (respondents with US origin parents gave significantly higher English comprehension ratings than those with Mexican origin parents, $p < 0.01$); Spanish comprehension (higher ratings by participants with Mexican origin parents $p < 0.0001$);

self-consciousness about English accent (higher among respondents with Mexican origin parents, $p < 0.003$); discrimination by members of another cultural group (higher among respondents with US origin parents, $p < 0.06$); and code-switching frequency (higher among respondents with Mexican origin parents, $p < 0.09$).

On self-designation of ethnic identity, 51.7% of the Integrated respondents selected the term 'Hispanic', whereas 48.3% chose 'Mexican-American' or 'Mexican'. Of the Separated respondents, 67% chose the term 'Hispanic' and 33% chose either 'Mexican-American' or 'Mexican'.

Part 2: Language preference for humor and non-humor activities. Responses in this section were analyzed in terms of the percent of Integrated and Separated subjects who showed a single language preference (i.e. reported using either mostly or only English or Spanish) versus a dual language preference (i.e. reported using both languages equally).

A greater percentage of Integrated than Separated respondents reported a dual language preference for praying, teasing someone, expressing sarcasm or hostility, and recounting funny personal experiences. A significant group difference emerged on the item 'to express sarcasm or hostility'. On this item, 56% of Integrated respondents versus 8% of Separated respondents reported using both languages equally ($p < 0.02$). By contrast, 67% of Separated respondents versus 35% of Integrated respondents showed a preference for English in expressing sarcasm or hostility.

An analysis of single versus dual language use by parent origin revealed a greater preference for the use of English among respondents with US origin parents versus Mexican origin parents for such items as thinking to oneself (80% versus 42%), mental arithmetic (95% versus 66%), singing (53% versus 22%), and recounting funny personal experiences (70% versus 34%). There was no significant effect of parent origin on language preference for speaking with the family, friends, expressing romantic feelings, cursing, grieving, expressing amusement, teasing, telling or hearing jokes, or expressing sarcasm or hostility.

Part 3: Humor beliefs and attitudes. Table 6.3 summarizes participants' mean agreement with statements about humor. As a reminder, a rating of 1 indicated strong agreement, whereas 5 indicated strong disagreement with the statement. In addition to mean ratings, responses were analyzed in terms of the percentage of participants per group who showed agreement. For this measure, ratings of 1 or 2 were collapsed and considered as 'agreement' and ratings of 4 and 5 were collapsed and considered as 'disagreement', with ratings of 3 indicating 'neutral' responses. Both measures were examined as a function of participants' cultural identity and parent origin.

Table 6.3 Percent agreement and mean ratings on humor statements in Study 2 by Cultural Identity and Parent Origin (1 = strongly agree, 5 = strongly disagree)

Statement	Integrated	Separated	US	Mexican
When speaking in English I come across to others as having a different sense of humor than what I actually see myself as having	19% 3.43	8% 3.25	15% 3.85	23% 3.21
When speaking in Spanish I come across to others as having a different sense of humor than what I actually see myself as having	22% 3.31	8% 3.25	30% 3.35	21% 3.25
I find that my sense of humor changes depending on the language in which I am interacting	35% 3.16	25% 3.58	15% 3.55	41% 31.6
I think English-speaking and Spanish-speaking groups find humor in the same kinds of social situations	47% 2.81	33% 3.0	50% 2.70	48% 2.77
I find that my sense of when it is socially appropriate or not appropriate to use humor changes depending on the language I am using	49% 2.54	42% 2.58	50% 2.65	50% 2.48
I switch back and forth between my languages or impersonate accents to create humourous effect	50% 2.72	33% 3.08	52% 2.85	50% 2.66
Knowing two languages and belonging to two cultures has expanded what I find funny – I find humor in more things compared to those who know only one language/culture	68% 2.07	67% 2.33	55% 2.30	73% 2.04
I find the style of humor in most Spanish sitcoms is very different from the style of humor in most English-language sitcoms	69% 2.19	67% 2.17	55% 2.35	73% 2.18
I think English-speaking and Spanish-speaking groups use humor for the same reasons (e.g. to tease, to reassure, to cope, to enforce norms, etc.)	71% 2.01	67% 2.67	75% 2.00	71% 2.02
I find humor to be a revealing indicator of a person's values, beliefs, and desires	54% 2.36	67% 2.17	45% 2.65	60% 2.22

In the analysis based on the mean ratings on the five-point scale, none of the 10 items elicited significant group differences related to cultural identity or parent origin. However, two items approached statistical significance. One of these was the item: 'I think English-speaking and Spanish-speaking groups use humor for the same reasons'. Integrated respondents ($n = 68$) tended to show more agreement with this statement than did Separated respondents ($n = 12$); the mean rating scores were 2.01 and 2.67, respectively, $t(78) = 1.667$, $p < 0.09$. The other item on which group differences approached significance was: 'When speaking in English I come across to others as having a different sense of humor than what I actually see myself as having'. For this item, respondents with Mexican origin parents ($n = 56$) showed greater agreement than those with US origin parents ($n = 20$); the mean ratings were 3.21 versus 3.85, respectively, $t(74) = -1.949$, $p < 0.055$.

In the analysis based on the percentage of participants who agreed or disagreed with each statement, no significant group differences were evident. A majority of respondents (67.5%) agreed with the statement that knowing two languages and belonging to two cultures has expanded what they find funny. A majority also agreed with the statement that English- and Spanish-speaking groups use humor for the same reasons (69%), and that the style of humor is very different in Spanish and in English-language sitcoms (68%). In the latter case, respondents whose parents were of Mexican origin were more likely to agree with the statement than were respondents with US origin parents (73% versus 55%, respectively).

Only half of the respondents per parent origin group agreed with the statement that their sense of when it is socially appropriate to use humor shifts with the language they are using. Similarly, about half of the respondents in each group agreed with the statement that they switch back and forth between languages or impersonate accents to create humorous effect. When subdivided by cultural identification, 50% of the Integrated group and only 33% of the Separated group agreed with the statement.

Only a third of the Integrated and a fourth of the Separated respondents agreed with the statement that their sense of humor changes depending on the language in which they are interacting. Among respondents classified by parent origin, however, 41% of participants with Mexican parent origin agreed with the statement, whereas only 15% of the participants with US parent origin agreed with it.

Differences between Integrated and Separated respondents emerged in percent agreement on the statements: 'when speaking in English/Spanish I come across as having a different sense of humor than what I actually see myself as having'. Although agreement with these statements was around 20% for the Integrated group, it was only 8% for the Separated group. For

Mexican parent origin respondents, agreement was also around 20% for these statements; however, for US origin respondents, agreement was 30% when the language was Spanish and 15% when the language was English.

Discussion

The findings from this survey point to certain domains in which there may be differences among bilinguals in the preferred language used for specific kinds of humor and in their perceptions of how their humor differs by language. In general, no differences between culturally integrated versus separated bilinguals were found in the preferred language for expressing amusement, recounting funny personal experiences, teasing, or telling or hearing jokes. The only instance where a group difference in language use emerged pertained to expressing sarcasm or hostility – the findings from this survey indicated higher dual language use among Integrated than Separated respondents; the latter preferred English for expressing sarcasm or hostility. The theoretical significance of this finding must await further inquiry.

In general, on several items, Integrated respondents reported using both languages equally to a greater degree than Separated respondents; however, there was too much variability for significant differences to emerge. Further work with a larger sample size may be needed to determine if this trend is supported. Respondents with US origin parents showed an English language preference for recounting funny personal experiences, but no language preference emerged for expressing amusement, telling or hearing jokes, or teasing. In sum, the results from Part II of the survey suggest that, whereas there is some differentiation in language used for emotional expression through humor, the use of a larger sample would substantiate the patterns observed.

With regard to bilinguals' attitudes and beliefs regarding their humor practices as a function of language used, the findings from Part III of the survey offered modest support for the hypothesis that cultural identification affects perception to the degree to which humor varies by language. In general, however, few significant differences emerged on this section of the survey as a function of respondents' cultural identification or parent origin. Most respondents agreed with the statement that their biliguality has expanded what they find funny. Most also agreed that the style of humor portrayed in the English-speaking and Spanish-speaking sitcoms differs. However, they also agreed with the statements that English- and Spanish-speaking groups use humor for the same reasons and in the same social situations.

Whereas, in general, the respondents did not agree with the statement that their humor changes as a function of which language they are using, those who considered their two cultures to be integrated and those with

Mexican origin parents were more likely to agree with this statement than respondents with US origin parents or those who perceived their cultures as being separate. Furthermore, to the statement about a humor persona shift by language (i.e. when speaking a particular language, do others perceive the respondents as manifesting a different sense of humor than the humor persona the respondents believe themselves to possess), there was greater agreement by Integrated than Separated respondents. Further, US parent origin respondents were more likely to agree to being regarded by others as showing a different humor persona when speaking in Spanish than when speaking in English, and the reverse was the case for respondents with the parents of Mexican origin.

Taken together, the results from the two surveys reported here, though preliminary, point to interesting differences in perceptions of humor use, practices, and styles as a function of cultural group identification. The findings suggest that one's cultural identification influences one's perceptions of one's own humor, the humor of one's cultural group, and the degree to which one's humor varies or does not vary depending on the language one is using and the nature of the interactions in each language. Interesting differences were also found in ways in which humor was reported to be used in the presentation of self and in the expression or perception of emotions. However, replication with a larger sample, as well as studies of actual interactions, are needed before any definitive conclusion can be arrived at.

Humor and Bilingualism: Closing Thoughts and Directions for Further Research

Limiting the target of study to one language at a time has meant that researchers have ignored the fact that most people live in or alongside more than one language and commonly engage in the switching of codes, cultures, and perspectives (Sommer, 2004). The present survey data suggest that one cannot generalize about the ways in which humor is used for emotion management based solely on a consideration of speakers of a single language or of members of a majority culture. Members of a minority culture may use humor somewhat differently than members of a majority culture. Furthermore, ways in which bilinguals relate to their two cultures appear to affect their perception of humor uses and their reported language preference for recounting funny personal experiences and expressing sarcasm or hostility, and their beliefs about how others view their sense of humor when they are speaking in one language compared with another.

A limitation of the present research is that it is based solely on participants' own perceptions of humor uses and practices. Further research on bilingualism and humor use should build on these survey findings by expanding the scope of the questions asked and by supplementing the survey approach with comparative ethnographic accounts of humor performance in bilinguals in single-language and mixed-language interactional contexts with a variety of interlocutors. Elicitation data, such as provided by a discourse completion task, may offer another rich source of evidence about humor use among bilinguals and can be particularly informative to assess the circumstances in which humor, as compared to some other mode of response, is the preferred response mode (e.g. in response to embarrassment, anger, or anxiety).

Further research on bilingualism and humor should explore how cultural beliefs and values can shape the form that humor may take or whether humor is used at all. One can imagine that the impetus to joke about certain things in a particular language community may be heightened if those things are considered, for whatever reason, more taboo among members of that community. Given that what is considered taboo or inappropriate may well differ across cultures, one may find that whereas one may joke a lot about some things in a particular speech community it may be completely unnecessary to joke about those same things in another community. Thus, bilinguals belonging to the two communities may use humor quite differently when operating in one or the other cultural mode.

Furthermore, bilinguals may find it easier to joke about some things in one of their languages, perhaps because there is less emotional baggage associated with that topic when one talks about it in that language. Conversely, poking fun at the linguistic and cultural habits of speakers who are native or non-native users of one of their languages may be a way that bilinguals can bond with members of their speech or cultural community. Exploring what is the target of humor by bilinguals in different interactional contexts should provide us with important insights into the attitudes, values, and ambivalences of those who inhabit more than one cultural space.

Finally, it would be interesting to examine from a cognitive perspective how the category of humor itself undergoes change as a function of the emergence of a dual cultural identity following a process of conceptual socialization, or gradual restructuring of a first language and culture-dominated conceptual base with increasing second language and cultural exposure and mastery (Kecskes, 2003; Pavlenko, 2002; Schrauf & Rubin, 2003). One could imagine that in the process of acquiring a second culture one may no longer find funny what one once found funny. The dual cultural identity may make the earlier, monocultural perspective seem unduly narrow and based on ignorance. Alternatively, a dual cultural perspective may lead one to find unexpected humor in contexts where one previously did not and may expand the kinds of humor one can produce or appreciate. The development of a dual cultural identity may even foster a readiness to perceive humor. Just as early mastery of two linguistic systems is known to confer increased flexibility, creativity, and agility, might one expect that it may also confer a keen sensitivity to ambiguity, intertextuality, and irony, elements that underlie the perception and expression of humor?

Acknowledgements

The studies described here were carried out with the able assistance of Hyun Choi, Francisco Martinez, and Hsin Chin Chen. I am indebted to Roberto Heredia of TAMIU, Laredo, for providing access to his students for the second study. Nancy Bell, Giovanna Del Negro, Willibald Ruch, Robert Schrauf, and Tom Ward provided useful references and insights that helped shape my thinking. Aneta Pavlenko's editorial comments were invaluable.

Correspondence concerning this chapter may be directed to Dr. Jyotsna Vaid, Department of Psychology, Texas A&M University, College Station, TX 77843-4235; e-mail: jxv@psyc.tamu.edu.

References

Adelsward, V. and Oberg, B. (1998) The function of laughter and joking in negotiation activities. *Humor* 11(4), 411–29.
Al-Khatib, M. (1999) Joke-telling in Jordanian society: A sociolinguistic perspective. *Humor* 12(3), 261–88.
Apte, M. (1985) *Humor and Laughter: An Anthropological Approach*. Ithaca: Cornell University Press.
Attardo, S. (1994) *Linguistic Theories of Humor*. Berlin: Mouton de Gruyter.
Bell, N. (2002) *Using and understanding humor in a second language: A case study*. Unpublished doctoral dissertation, Graduate School of Education, University of Pennsylvania.
Chafe, W. (2003) Laughing while talking. In D. Tannen and J. Alatis (eds) *Linguistics, Language, and the Real World: Discourse and Beyond. Georgetown University Roundtable on Languages and Linguistics 2001* (pp. 36–49). Washington, DC: Georgetown University Press.
Chiaro, D. (1992) *The Language of Jokes: Analyzing Verbal Play*. New York: Routledge.
Chirico, M. (2002) Laughter and ethnicity in John Leguizamo's one-man worlds. *Latin American Theatre Review* 36(1), 29–50.
Cohen, A. (2001) From L1 to L12: The confessions of a sometimes frustrated multiliterate. In D. Belcher and U. Connor (eds) *Reflections on Multiliterate Lives* (pp. 79–95). Clevedon: Multilingual Matters.
Cook, G. (2001) Less work and more play: Towards a ludicrous linguistics. In R. Napoli, L. Plezzi and A. King (eds) *Fuzzy Boundaries: Reflections on Modern Languages and the Humanities* (pp. 141–56). London: The Center for Information on Language and Teaching.
Crawford, M. (2003) Gender and humor in social context. *Journal of Pragmatics* 35(9), 1413–30.
Cromdal, J. and Aronsson, K. (2000) Footing in bilingual play. *Journal of Sociolinguistics* 4, 435–57.

Davies, C. (2003) How English-learners joke with native speakers: An interactional sociolinguistic perspective on humor as collaborative discourse across cultures. *Journal of Pragmatics* 35, 1361–85.

Del Negro, G. (2004) *Transcultural Performance and the Stand Up Comedy of Shazia Mirza*. Paper presented at the Eighth Congress of the Societé Internationale d'Ethnologie et de Folklore (SIEF), Marseille, April 2004.

Douglas, M. (1968) The social control of cognition: Some factors in joke perception. *Man* 3, 361–76.

Francis, L. (1999) A laughing matter? The uses of humor in medical interactions. *Motivation and Emotion* 23(1), 155–74.

Gilbert, J. (2004) *Performing Marginality: Humor, Gender and Cultural Critique*. Detroit: Wayne State University Press.

Graham, E., Papa, M. and Brooks, G. (1992) Functions of humor in conversation: Conceptualization and measurement. *Western Journal of Communication* 56, 161–83.

Hall, E. (1959) *The Silent Language*. Garden City, NY: Doubleday.

Haugen, E. (1986) Bilinguals have more fun! *Journal of English Linguistics* 19(1), 106–20.

Hay, J. (2000) Functions of humor in the conversations of men and women. *Journal of Pragmatics* 32, 709–42.

Holmes, J. and Hay, J. (1997) Humor as an ethnic boundary marker in New Zealand interaction. *Journal of Intercultural Studies* 18(2), 127–51.

Kachru, B. (1985) The bilingual's creativity. *Annual Review of Applied Linguistics* 6, 20–33.

Kecskes, I. (2003) *Situation-Bound Utterances in L1 and L2*. New York: Mouton de Gruyter.

Koestler, A. (1964) *The Act of Creation*. New York: MacMillan.

LaFromboise, T., Coleman, H. and Gerton, J. (1993) Psychological impact of biculturalism: Evidence and theory. *Psychological Bulletin* 114(3), 395–412.

Laurian, A. (1992) Possible/impossible translation of jokes. *Humor* 5(1/2), 111–27.

Leeds, Ch. (1992) Bilingual Anglo-French humor: An analysis of the potential for humor based on the interlocking of the two languages. *Humor* 5(1/2), 129–48.

Limon, J. (1977) *Agringado* joking in Texas Mexican society. *New Scholar* 6, 33–50.

Martineau, W. (1972) A model of social functions of humor. In H. Goldstein and P. McGhee (eds) *The Psychology of Humor* (pp. 101–25). New York: Academic Press.

Mulkay, M. (1988) *On Humor*. New York: Basil Blackwell.

Murphy, C. (2004) Poking fun, in good faith: Muslim comics laugh in the face of intolerance. *The Washington Post*, 25 April 2004, p. C01.

Nehrlich, B. and Clarke, D. (2001) Ambiguities we live by: Towards a pragmatics of polysemy. *Journal of Pragmatics* 33, 1–20.

Nilsen, D. (1981) Bilingual and bidialectical language play. *Rocky Mountain Review of Language and Literature* 35(2), 128–37.

Nilsen, D. (1989) Better than the original: Humorous translations that succeed. *Meta* 34(1), 112–24.

Norrick, N. (1986) A frame theoretical analysis of verbal humor: Bisociation as schema conflict. *Semiotica* 60, 225–45.

Paredes, A. (1968). Folk medicine and the intercultural jest. In J. Helm (ed.) *Spanish Speaking People in the United States: Proceedings of the 1968 Annual Spring Meeting of the American Ethnological Society* (pp. 104–19). Seattle: University of Washington Press.

Pavlenko, A. (2002) Bilingualism and emotions. *Multilingua* 21, 45–78.

Price, D. (2000) Mixed laughter. In P. Spickard and W. Jeffrey Burroughs (eds) *We are a People: Narrative and Multiplicity in Constructing Ethnic Identity* (pp. 171–91). Philadelphia: Temple University Press.

Prodromou, L. (2003) Idiomaticity and the non-native speaker. *English Today* 19(2), 42–48.

Reyna, J. and Herrera-Sobek, M. (1998) Jokelore, cultural differences, and linguistic dexterity: The construction of the Mexican immigrant in Chicano humor. In D. Maciel and M. Herrera-Sobek (eds) *Culture Across Borders: Mexican Immigration and Popular Culture* (pp. 203–26). Tucson: University of Arizona Press.

Scherzer, J. (2002) *Speech Play and Verbal Art*. Austin: University of Texas Press.

Schrauf, R. (2002) Comparing cultures within-subjects: A cognitive account of acculturation as a framework for cross-cultural study. *Anthropological Theory* 2, 98–115.

Schrauf, R. and Rubin, D. (2003) On the bilingual's two sets of memories. In R. Fivush and C. Haden (eds) *Autobiographical Memory and the Construction of A Narrative Self: Developmental and Cultural Perspectives* (pp. 121–45). Mahwah, NJ: Lawrence Erlbaum.

Siegel, J. (1995) How to get a laugh in Fijian: Code-switching and humor. *Language in Society* 24, 95–110.

Sommer, D. (2004) *Bilingual Aesthetics: A New Sentimental Education*. Durham, NC: Duke University Press.

Stefanowitsch, A. (2002) Nice to *miet* you: Bilingual puns and the status of English in Germany. *Intercultural Communication Studies*, 11, 67–84.

Thomas, M. (2001) *Folk Psychologies Across Cultures*. Thousand Oaks, CA: Sage.

Vaid, J. (1999) The evolution of humor: Do those who laugh last? In D. Rosen and M. Luebbert (eds) *Evolution of the Psyche* (pp. 123–38). Westport, CT: Praeger.

Vaid, J. (2000) New approaches to conceptual representations in bilingual memory: The case for studying humor interpretation. *Bilingualism: Language and Cognition* 3(1), 28–30.

Vaid, J. (2003) *Joking Across Languages: Towards a Theory of Humor Interpretation in Bilinguals*. Paper presented at Panel on Bilingualism and Emotions, Fourth International Symposium on Bilingualism (ISB4), University of Arizona, April 2003.

Vaid, J. (2004) *Playing with Language and Through Language: Bilingual Humor as Artful Transgression*. Forum Lecture, annual meeting of the International Association of World Englishes, Syracuse University, July 2004.

Vaid, J., Chen, H., Choi, H. and Martinez, F. (2003) *Cultural Identity Affects Joking Across Languages: Survey Data from Spanish–English Speakers in Laredo, Texas*. Poster, Southwest Cognition Conference, Texas A&M University, October 2004.

Vaid, J., Choi, H., Martinez, F. and Chen, H. (2004) *Perceptions of Humor Uses for Self vs. Culture Across Four Groups*. Poster, American Psychological Society, Chicago, May 2004.

Vivero, V. and Jenkins, S. (1999) Existential hazards of the multicultural individual: Defining and understanding 'cultural homelessness'. *Cultural Diversity and Ethnic Minority Psychology* 5(1), 6–26.

Zenner, W. (1970) Joking and ethnic stereotyping. *Anthropological Quarterly* 43, 93–113.

Zentella, A. (2003) 'Jose, can you see?' Latin@ responses to racist discourse. In D. Sommer (ed.) *Bilingual Games: Some Literary Investigations* (pp. 51–66). NY: Palgrave MacMillan.

Appendix: Vaid Bilingual Language, Culture, and Humor Survey

Part I

Today's date

Participant's ID

Participant's gender

Participant's age

Participant's country of birth

Participant's upbringing (city)

Years in the US

Length of time spent outside the US

Parents' country of origin

(1) Please list the languages you speak, and indicate for each when you acquired them (around what age) and where (at home, at school, etc.)

LANGUAGE   WHEN ACQUIRED   WHERE ACQUIRED

(2) Please rate how proficient you are in each language: 1 = very proficient, 5 = not at all proficient

Language   Speaking   Comprehension   Reading   Writing

(3) Please circle the term or terms that you would use to best describe your ethnic identity:

Mexican   Chicano/a   Mexican-American   Spanish

Cuban-American   Latin American   Hispanic   Anglo-American

Euro-American   American   Asian-American

African-American   Other (specify)

(4) Please select the statement which best describes your cultural identity:

(a) I keep my two cultures separate and compartmentalized and am comfortable in each

(b) I keep my two cultures separate and compartmentalized and am uncomfortable and conflicted about them

(c) My two cultures are integrated and I am comfortable with them

(d) My two cultures are integrated but I am uncomfortable and conflicted about them

(e) My cultural identity is a hybrid and I identify with neither culture totally

(f) I am basically monocultural in my values and beliefs (specify dominant cultural affiliation:_____)

(5) Using the scale: 1 = Not at all, 2 = Very little, 3 = A little, 4 = A lot, 5 = Very much, please indicate how much you enjoy:

listening to music in Spanish

watching TV programs or movies in Spanish

eating food from your culture of origin

traveling and visiting in countries that speak your other language

listening to music in English

watching TV programs or movies in English

eating American food

traveling and visiting in the US

(6) Using the above 5-point scale, please indicate how much you

are self-conscious about your accent in Spanish

are self-conscious about your accent in English

feel culturally isolated

are perceived as being too 'American'

are perceived as being too 'ethnic'

have experienced discrimination by members of another cultural group

(7) When speaking with others who know both of your languages, how often do you switch between your two languages?

(1) almost always

(2) fairly often

(3) not often

(4) almost never

(8) Using the following scale, please indicate in which language you prefer to do each of the activities listed below:

1 = Spanish only

2 = Mostly Spanish

3 = Spanish and English equally

4 = Mostly English

5 = English only

ACTIVITY

Think to yourself

Express romantic feelings

Curse/express frustration

Express grief/sadness

Pray

Do mental arithmetic (add, multiply)

Tease someone playfully

Express sarcasm or hostility

Tell/hear jokes

Recount funny personal experiences

Sing

Speak to your friends

Speak to your family

Chapter 7

Translating Guilt: An Endeavor of Shame in the Mediterranean?

ALEXIA PANAYIOTOU

If one should seek to name each particular one (of the emotions) of which the human heart is at seat, it is plain that the limit to their number would lie in the introspective vocabulary of the seeker, each race of men having found names for some shade of feeling which other races have left undiscriminated.

William James, 1890/1955: 299

—You don't believe in shame?
—I believe in happiness!

Mr Todd, in *Victor, Victoria*, 1982

I purposely decided to not feel guilty.

George, English interview, p.17

Introduction

What James wrote in *The Principles of Psychology* (1890) is by now a widely documented argument in the literature on the social construction of emotions (Armon-Jones, 1986; Averill, 1980; Harré, 1986; Pavlenko, 2002a,b; Wierzbicka, 1992, 1999; Winegar, 1995). This literature seems to highlight the proposition that emotions that seem key in some cultures may be linguistically non-existent in others (Doi, 1962, 1990; Lutz, 1987, 1988; Wierzbicka, 1998). Similarly, it supports the idea that certain emotion terms may have translation equivalents, but these equivalents are inadequate given the varying importance and meaning they carry in different cultural contexts. One such example is 'guilt', an emotion term that, although translatable in many languages, varies in cultural significance, ranging from pivotal in so-called 'guilt cultures' to marginal in so-called 'shame cultures' (Stocker & Hegeman, 1996; Wallbott & Scherer, 1995). In fact, even translatability of 'guilt' is contested by some researchers. Wierzbicka (1999), for instance, argues that the English 'guilt' has no equivalent in French, German, Russian, or Polish, all of which have words that correspond to 'guilt' only in the sense of 'fault'.

This study, which uses a constructionist framework, focuses on guilt and shame and explores the construction of these terms in a bilingual–bicultural setting, the target languages and cultures being American English and Cypriot Greek. Specifically, it explores the verbal construction of the Greek *ntropi* (linguistically translated as 'shame') and the English 'guilt' (translated in Greek as *enohi*). The study employs bilingual informants to access the representations of these emotions (for a similar approach, see also Dewaele & Pavlenko, 2002; Pavlenko, 2002b) and asks how bilinguals make sense of *ntropi* and 'guilt'. The chapter then argues that, although the terms have linguistic equivalents in Greek and English, these are inexact because the meanings of these translations differ in the cultures examined.

Guilt and Shame Across Cultures: Literature Review

The main question addressed in this chapter is whether translation equivalents of emotion terms are also cultural equivalents. Previous work in both anthropology and psychology has shown that even some taken-for-granted English emotion terms, such as 'love' (Averill, 1985; Derné, 1994) and 'anger' (Averill, 1982) may lack adequate linguistic equivalents and that the manifestation and understanding of these terms is culture-specific and socially constituted. This study joins the discussion of the inadequacy of translation equivalents by examining two emotion terms, 'guilt' and *ntropi*, and advocates the use of bilingual informants as a way to circumvent some of the problems raised in the previous studies. I begin the literature review by citing some of the anthropological and psychological studies on shame and guilt in order to highlight, at least partly, the dominant understanding of these terms and to raise some questions about the cultural construction of this understanding.

The English terms 'shame' and 'guilt' are often treated as belonging to the same emotional category in the literature on emotions, perhaps because they are seen as simultaneously moral and social emotions – moral because they involve the judgement of ourselves or others and social because they always occur in an interpersonal context. A popular distinction between the two terms is based on internal and external sanctions. In *Cultural Determinants in Experiencing Shame and Guilt*, Wallbott and Scherer (1995) note that whereas 'shame cultures' regulate the behavior of their members via external sanctions, 'guilt cultures' have internalized sanctions. In other words, shame cultures regulate conduct via compliance and external pressure on the individual, and guilt cultures do the same via internalization. This distinction of cultures has been heavily criticized, but Wallbott and Scherer (1995) focus less on these critiques and more on using cultural dimensions to differentiate between these terms. Their results on one dimension, individualism versus collectivism, show that shame is a rather acute, short-lived emotional experience in collectivistic cultures (shorter duration, less immorality involved, fewer negative influences on self-esteem and on relationships, more laughing/smiling and higher felt temperature) compared to individualistic cultures. For guilt, on the other hand, differences seem less pronounced. In fact, the researchers do not refer to 'guilt cultures' but to 'guilt–shame' cultures, in which shame experiences have features very similar to guilt experiences. Shame in these cultures turns to guilt or has a large number of guilt components. The countries fitting this profile in their sample are Sweden, Norway, Finland, New Zealand, and the United States. Notably, the dominant populations in these countries are white, Anglo-Saxon/Nordic, and committed to the protestant ethic (Weber, 1904). Countries that tend to be collectivistic, high in power distance,[1] and high in uncertainty avoidance,[2] include Mexico, India, Venezuela, Brazil, France, Chile, Spain, Portugal, and Greece – in other words, countries that do not share the protestant ethic. Here 'shame seems to be an emotion in its own right' (Wallbott & Scherer, 1995: 482). What these authors are claiming then is that guilt and shame may be found on a continuum, even within the same culture. I will return to this point when I note the similarities in the Greek *ntropi* and the English 'guilt'.

It should be noted here that the above cultural categorization, which is often cited in both anthropological and psychological literature, is not without value judgements. As Scheff (1990) writes, in modern societies it is almost taken for granted that shame is a rare emotion among adults, prevalent only among small children. This belief is reflected in the division between shame and guilt cultures, he says, with traditional societies relying on shame for social control and modern societies on guilt. In this view, shame is seen as a regressive or childish emotion, whereas guilt is assumed to be the adult emotion of self-control. In fact, shame, guilt, and embarrassment all help maintain the social order and the underpinning social relations. Shame is considered a primary social emotion because it is linked to intense and automatic bodily signs that communicate the state of one's bonds to others: shame is simply the sign of a severed bond. If shame is generated through constant self-monitoring then it is an important social emotion in terms of understanding what others think of one's behavior. It is also important because non-conformity in these cultures is punished by feelings of shame, providing an explanation of how social control operates. In fact, shame, according to Scheff (1990), becomes so well managed by most people that it becomes barely visible.

Wollheim (1999) refers to guilt and shame as 'moral emotions', but makes sure to note the differences between the two. First, he says, in the case of shame, we feel criticized for the kind of person we have become; in the case of guilt, we feel criticized for what we have done. Second, in the case of shame, criticism invokes an ideal to which we have failed to live up; in the case of guilt, the criticism involves a set of injunctions we have transgressed. Third, in the case of shame, the criticism is based less and in the case of guilt more on identifiable harm or damage that we have caused, albeit not intentionally. Fourth, in the case of shame, the criticism can be met and turned by changing how we are; in guilt, we must compensate for what we have done. Fifth, if both emotions call for a response on the part of others, what shame calls for is that others should forget what we have become, and what guilt calls for is that others should forgive what we have done. Finally, in the case of shame the criticism is experienced as being conveyed to us by a look – we feel the *eyes* of disapproval upon us. In guilt, however, the criticism is experienced as conveyed in words – we hear the *voice* of disapproval (Wollheim, 1999: 155–156).

Another differentiation argument is advanced by Tangney who notes that 'the clinical, social and developmental literatures have often not made a clear distinction between shame and guilt' (1995: 115). Both, she says, are 'private emotional experiences intimately related to the self . . . and derive from a sense that our behavior or some aspect of ourselves is at odds with our moral standards' (1995: 114). In comparing these terms, she notes the following features shared by shame and guilt: both can be considered 'moral' emotions (see also Wollheim, 1999); both are self-conscious, self-referential emotions; both involve internal attributions; both are typically experienced in interpersonal contexts; and the negative events that give rise to the two emotions are highly similar, often involving moral failures (Tangney, 1995: 116). On the other hand, the two also differ in some fundamental points: whereas the focus of evaluation for shame is the self ('*I* did that horrible thing'), in guilt the focus is the behavior ('I did that horrible *thing*'). Also, she says, whereas in shame one is concerned with the evaluation of others regarding the self, in guilt, one is concerned with one's effect on others. Finally, in shame, the self feels 'shrinking, small, worthless', whereas in guilt the self may feel 'tension, remorse and regret' (Tangney, 1995: 116). To summarize, it seems that both emotions are considered social emotions, in the sense of occurring in interpersonal relations (see also Barrett, 1995; Lindsay-Hartz *et al.*, 1995), both are associated with particular appreciations regarding self and other (Barrett, 1995: 25) and both are influenced by socialization (see also Wallbott & Scherer, 1995).

Admittedly, the distinctions noted above may be problematic in a social constructionist framework given the rather essentialist presupposition of a neat division between shame and guilt cultures. The point I wish to raise, however, is not the division amongst cultures, but the problems raised in trying to cross linguistic and cultural boundaries with terms that are so bound in their English emotionology (Stearns & Stearns, 1988). It is in this crossing that I believe the use of bilinguals is particularly valuable. Bilinguals, as people who cross physical, linguistic, and cultural boundaries, may offer an optimal population for a cross-linguistic and cross-cultural comparison of emotion terms because they subjectively experience two languages and two cultures.

Theoretical Framework

The social constructionist approach suggests that any coherent and complete theory of emotion should include a strong linguistic and cultural element, a position supported by the rich literature on the social construction of emotions (Kitayama *et al.*, 1995; Pavlenko, 2002a,b; Rosaldo, 1980; Shaver *et al.*, 1992; Wierzbicka, 1994). Language in this study is assumed to be at the core of psychological constructs and the focus is on the use of 'vocabularies through which emotions are described and catalogued in particular cultures' (Harré & Gillett, 1994: 160). Without negating the bodily component of emotions, I argue in this paper that emotions are 'language dependent' (Searle, 1995: 62) because the raw or bodily experience of an emotion must be filtered through a cultural meaning making system (Parrott & Harré, 1996: 2), that is, language, before it can be defined as an emotion. Language, in other words, is assumed to both 'actively construct and reconstruct' emotions (Pavlenko, 2002a: 209). I will focus, therefore, on guilt, shame, *enohi*, and *ntropi* as they are constituted in context (Josephs, 1995).

This approach differs from other theories of emotions that discuss emotions as physiological reactions to environmental stimuli (Ekman, 1980, 1992), cognitive schemas (Averill, 1996), rational choices (Solomon, 1980), or even states of belief (Thalberg, 1984). A major contrast is found between the theorists who are concerned with the raw experience of emotions (e.g. Winegar, 1995) and those who are concerned with their cultural underpinnings (e.g. Rosaldo, 1980). My research follows the approach that raw experience must be filtered through a cultural meaning making system (Parrott & Harré, 1996: 2) before it is defined as an emotion. This also entails the view that there is an evaluative component at the core of emotions that is largely influenced by the culture in which we live.

I, therefore, define *emotions* as a subcategory of feelings (Levy, 1984) that help organize thoughts, behavior and meaning systems (Lutz, 1987). They are 'biologically generated elements which must be enriched by meanings before becoming emotional experiences' (Parrott & Harré, 1996: 2). Simultaneously, I acknowledge that even the word 'emotion' is an English classificatory term that has been borrowed from 'folk English' into the language of scholarly literature, where, according to Wierzbicka, 'it is now used in a variety of non-defined ways colored by the folk concept and where it has contributed to a culturally shaped view of "human psychology"' (1999: 23). Greek, on the other hand, does not differentiate between 'feeling' and 'emotion'. Whereas a distinction is made between sensations such as hunger, pain, and thirst (*esthima*) and feelings/emotions such as guilt and shame (*synesthima*), there is no specific word for emotion. The latter word, made up of the preposition 'syn' and the word 'esthima' (sensation) literally translates as 'to feel with'. Although the etymology noted for the word in Bambiniotis' *Dictionary of the Modern Greek Language* (1998) does not mention this proposition, I believe that the literal meaning is indicative of what Wierzbicka (1999: 35) notes as the ethnopsychology of certain languages; it is, in other words, indicative of the view that feelings/emotions are relational, as opposed to the individualistic or disconnected view of emotions assumed in the dominant paradigm in American psychology. *Synesthimata* are psychological events that occur between people, in connection to people, and in relation to other people; they are not solitary experiences as sometimes implied by the Jamesian tradition. At the same time, the American and Greek emotionologies may not be as dramatically different as emotionologies of a European and an Asian culture.

The whole premise of my study is that every language contains its own 'naïve picture' of the world including its own emotionology[3] (Stearns & Stearns, 1988). As Wierzbicka argues, by relying, uncritically, on ordinary English words we unwittingly fall prey to the 'naïve picture' that is reflected in them (1999: 35). Whereas this is precisely what I tried to establish in my study by showing that even the emotion terms we take for granted, like shame and guilt, are culturally constructed, in writing up my findings I ran into the very problem that I am trying to counteract – that is, I was forced to present bilingual findings in a monolingual form. While I have knowingly tried to circumvent some of these issues by providing thick descriptions of the emotion terms given (Geertz, 1973), inevitably some may be 'lost in translation' (Hoffman, 1989).

In any case, it is only by studying words that we can go beyond words. As Sapir warned, 'the philosopher needs to understand language if only to protect himself against his own language habits' (Sapir, 1929/1949: 165). Because language inevitably stands between us and the emotions we wish to study, by refusing to pay attention to it, some researchers fall prey to their own 'language habits' (Wierzbicka, 1999: 29). I attempt to counteract these traps by being explicit about my methods and definitions.

Research Design

Objective

The present study attempts to answer the following research question: What are the similarities and differences in the cultural meanings of the four emotion terms, guilt/*enohi* and *ntropi*/shame? These terms will be examined in interviews with ten bicultural bilinguals and in responses elicited from these bilinguals through Greek and English versions of the same story.

Participants

As pointed out earlier, bicultural bilinguals constitute an optimal population for cross-linguistic and cross-cultural studies of emotion terms, because they subjectively experience two languages and two cultures. The cross-cultural comparison exists then within the individual, who is simultaneously the vehicle of two cultures – it is not a comparison to another group or a comparison between two individuals as is usually the case for other cross-cultural studies (e.g. Hoffman *et al.*, 1986; Kitayama *et al.*, 1995).

In the present study, the participant pool consisted of five English–Greek bilinguals and five Greek–English bilinguals, two men and eight women, middle to upper class, between the ages of 25 and 50, living in Boston, Massachusetts, and Nicosia, Cyprus, at the time of the interview.[4] Because bilinguals are informants who allow us to hold individual variables constant, the interviewees in this study acted simultaneously as informants and as native anthropologists. The selection of participants then was guided not by the demographic characteristics, but by the participants' ability and willingness to talk about emotions in the cultural contexts and languages in question. I used only ten participants because this is a number that allowed me to conduct an in-depth qualitative analysis.

Table 7.1 gives a brief description of the participants. At the same time, as a sociolinguistic study, this paper gives less importance to the individual psychological profiles of the respondents than to the language they use to describe emotions. As already noted, my primary selection criterion was whether respondents were bilingual and bicultural. Other participant characteristics – such as gender, age of second language acquisition (Grosjean, 1982), years in the mother and adopted country,

Table 7.1 Description of participants[a]

Leonidas	Leonidas is a 30-year-old Greek Cypriot who spent the first few years of his life in the United States and then went back for his university studies at age 20. As a child, he spoke English with his family, even upon returning to Cyprus, but stopped doing so a few years after entering elementary school because he did not want to be 'different'. He completed his undergraduate and graduate studies in the United States and then worked for a well-known consulting firm for several years. Currently, his home is in Cyprus where he works as a consultant. He is married to a Greek Cypriot.
George	George is a Greek Cypriot who attended English-speaking schools all his life. He is an engineer who studied and then worked in the United States, for nearly ten years. Recently married to a Greek Cypriot, he had just returned to Cyprus when I interviewed him.
Nefeli	Nefeli is a Greek–Cypriot artist living in the United States. She learned English at the age of five when she moved with her family to the United States for a few years. She spoke English with her siblings and parents until she graduated from high school. She is married to a Greek Cypriot and is the mother of a young bilingual girl.
Lydia	Lydia is a Greek–Cypriot architect in her late thirties. She learned English in the United States at the age of 11 when her family moved to the Midwest for a few years. She returned to the United States again as a college student and stayed there until her late twenties. She is married to a Greek Cypriot and has two young children.
Christina	Christina is a Greek Cypriot in her late thirties who had learned English in Cyprus at a young age. She had lived in New York for ten years as an adolescent and young adult. She says that she feels a New Yorker at heart and had it not been for family circumstances she would have lived there 'for ever and ever'. Christina runs her own company and is married to a Greek Cypriot who only recently learned English. She has a young son to whom she speaks only in English.
Sofia	Sofia's first language is Spanish. She learned English as a child when her family immigrated to the United States and had lived in the United States until marrying her Greek–Cypriot husband. She speaks several languages and had lived all over the world. She has been living in Cyprus for the last seven years with her husband and two children. Sofia holds a degree in the social sciences and is in her early forties.

(continued)

Table 7.1 *Continued*

Lila	Lila is a multilingual. Her first languages were Arabic and German, but all of her education was in English, even while attending a Cypriot high school for three years. She has lived all over the world and moved to the United States when she was an adolescent. There she met her husband, but after living in the United States for seven years, the family moved back to Cyprus. She has been living in Cyprus for the last 13 years. Lila is a businesswoman and a lecturer at a private college. She is in her early forties and has two trilingual children.
Julia	Julia is a multilingual American in her late forties. She has lived in Cyprus for the last three years. She is a language teacher who learned Greek in her early twenties when she met her first husband, a Greek. Before going to Cyprus she had lived in Greece for ten years and then in various countries around the world.
Camille	Camille is an American in her late thirties who has been living in Cyprus for the last four years. She is married to a Greek and before coming to Cyprus she had lived all over the world. Camille is a researcher with an advanced degree in the humanities. She has a toddler whom she is raising as a bilingual Greek–English speaker.
Jackie	Jackie is an American who has been living in Cyprus for the last 12 years after she married her Greek–Cypriot husband. She holds a Bachelor's in Social Sciences from a US university and runs her own business. She has three bilingual children.

[a]All names have been changed to ensure confidentiality and anonymity.

and frequency of travel between the two cultures – are only included as part of my participant description.

Finally, it is worth mentioning that some of the participants were either multicultural or multilingual, with two American informants not having English as their mother tongue but Spanish and Arabic. Whereas these characteristics may add another layer of complexity to my subject description, this complexity was not problematic in my data collection because my primary objective was to understand how these participants talk about their emotions in the two languages and cultures in which they were immersed and fluent. The fact that the American speakers form a less homogeneous group than the Greek–Cypriot informants may be simply indicative of the diversity of the United States versus the relative homogeneity of Cyprus; thus, it was not seen as a source of concern for the validity of my conclusions.

Recruitment and screening

My primary recruitment method was *snowballing*, that is, using one contact to recruit another contact, who in turn put me in touch with someone else (Valentine, 1997). In terms of screening interested volunteers, I conducted a brief screening interview in which I spoke briefly about my work and interest in bilingual and bicultural experiences and explored (1) whether the volunteer defined him/herself as bilingual and bicultural; (2) whether he or she was comfortable in both languages (this was done by asking questions in both Greek and English); and (3) whether he or she was bicultural (this was accomplished by looking at his or her cultural sensitivities and references, such as acknowledgement of status differences in Cyprus, food associations, and so on). I also required that (1) people had lived in both countries for at least three years,[5] (2) they continue to speak both Greek and English, and (3) they continue to travel between the two cultural settings.

Data collection

Two methods were used in this study: (1) semi-structured interviews in both languages; and (2) scenarios that elicit emotional responses (a more detailed description of these methods can be found in Panayiotou, 2004a,b).

Interviews

I conducted two semi-structured interviews with each participant, one in English and the other in Greek. Participants were allowed to codeswitch freely, as this is probably the most comfortable language mode for bilinguals (Zentella, 1997). The first participant interview (conducted after the screening interview), was designed to 'lay the terrain' by inquiring about participants' emotional experiences in the two languages/ cultures. This interview lasted between one and one-and-a-half hours for each person. The interview asked questions on the interviewees' experiences of being bilingual and bicultural, the 'move' from one country to another, their childhood experiences, what they missed from either country/culture, difficulties they faced in their family relationships or in raising their children, other difficulties and/or funny stories they wanted to share, as well as how they saw their identity (Greek? American? Cypriot?) and their definition of 'home'.

The second interview, conducted in the language not chosen in the first interview, focused on the cultural untranslatability of emotions; this interview also lasted between one and one-and-a-half hours. This interview could be considered a follow-up to the second one, asking for clarifications or going into more depth on some issues raised. It focused on the emotional experiences of the interviewees. In this context, it raised specifically issues of untranslatability and asked the participants to offer their own definitions for terms that they had already identified as 'difficult to translate' or of emotion terms for which they code-switched.

Scenarios

The scenario presented to the bilingual speakers involved, in its two cultural versions, Andy, an American, and Andreas, a Cypriot, who live, respectively, in the United States and Cyprus.[6] I asked the participants to assume that Andy/Andreas is a person close to them, as the participant's definition of 'closeness' may also indicate a relevant cultural value that is related to his or her emotional reaction. The scenarios (in English and in Greek) appear below. The first reading of the scenario was in American English and the participants were asked to describe their emotional reaction to the story. About a month later, the participants were told the same story in Standard Modern Greek (SMG) (with some changes to make it culturally realistic, as shown below) and questioned again about their emotional reaction. A subsequent brief interview inquired about any possible differences in the two accounts. It is worth mentioning here that, while text was read to the participants in SMG, as would be culturally appropriate given that Cypriot Greek is rarely used in writing, the participants were explicitly told that they could use Cypriot Greek in their responses. In addition, I spoke in the dialect throughout the interview, thus encouraging them to respond in this way.[7]

The English story is as follows:

Andy, a person close to you, is a 30-year-old Harvard graduate. He has an MBA (Master's in Business Administration). He is an accomplished, successful and driven young man who is currently working as a business analyst for a large multinational corporation in Boston. He says that he is very ambitious and that his ultimate goal is to manage his own company. He works late hours and, at the sacrifice of his friendships and family obligations, including his elderly divorced mother and his girlfriend, he has devoted all of his time and energy to his work. He says that this is absolutely necessary if he is going to become successful.

To give a culturally appropriate account in Greek, the main character, Andreas, was an honors graduate from the Athens School of Engineering (*Ethniko Metsoveio Polytechneio*):[8]

Ο Αντρέας, ένα στενό σου άτομο, είναι 30 χρονών και απόφοιτος του Πολυτεχνείου Αθηνών στη μηχανική. Μετά τις μεταπτυχιακές του σπουδές στο Λονδίνο, επέστρεψε στην Κύπρο και τώρα εργάζεται για μια μεγάλη πολεοδομική εταιρία στον ιδιωτικό τομέα στη Λευκωσία. Είναι ήδη πετυχημένος στον τομέα του και έχει σίγουρα καλές προοπτικές για την ηλικία του. Εργάζεται σκληρά και συχνά ξενυκτά στη δουλειά του, με αποτέλεσμα να μη βλέπει πολύ τη χήρα μητέρα του, τους παιδικούς του φίλους ή την αρραβωνιαστικιά του. Λέει ότι αυτό πρέπει να κάνει αν πρόκειται να πετύχει στον τομέα του και να ξεκινήσει τη δική του δουλειά.

Andreas, a person close to you, is a 30-year-old engineering graduate of the Athens School of Engineering. After completing his graduate studies in London, he returned to Cyprus and now works for a large construction company in the private sector in Nicosia. He is successful for his age and has many prospects. He works hard and often stays at his job until late at night, so he does not spend enough time with his elderly widowed mother, his childhood friends or his fiancée. He says that this is absolutely necessary if he is going to become successful and start his own company.

The two questions after each story were:

(a)	What would you say to Andy/Andreas if he were a person close to you?
(b)	How do you feel about Andy/Andreas? [9]

Transcription and translation of the interviews
The transcription of the interviews and responses was an essential part of the data collection because the words chosen by the interviewees were the focus of the study. When a respondent changed languages I noted the change in bold. Furthermore, I wanted to establish the overall emotional experience and state of the respondents and so I transcribed every pause, every 'um' and word spoken by the bilinguals. I should also note that the transcription in Greek was very difficult because my respondents spoke primarily in the Cypriot–Greek dialect, which, although similar to formal Greek, is not a written language. I kept the dialect form in my transcripts to maintain the authenticity of the people's voices.

The difficulties arising from transposing an oral text to a written one were compounded by the difficulties of translating a narrative from one language to another and from one cultural context to another. As Duranti (1997) says:

This activity involves more than going from one language to another. It implies a long series of interpretations and decisions that are rarely made apparent in the final product ... (Translation) implies an understanding not only of the immediate context but also of more general assumptions, such as people's worldview, including the ways of relating the use of language with social action ... (Duranti, 1997: 154).

Translation in a study such as this one becomes 'intimately linked to ethnography' (Duranti, 1997: 154), because my choices reflect the larger sociopolitical context to which both I and my interviewees belong as bicultural bilinguals. Yet it is not an entirely subjective enterprise – to validate the accuracy of the transcription, translation, and analysis, both transcriptions and translations were read by the participants themselves and by two bilingual bicultural colleagues.

Data Analysis

Miles and Huberman (1984) note that data analysis contains three linked subprocesses: data reduction, data display, and conclusion drawing. This general approach was followed in this study as well (see also Huberman & Miles, 1998: 181).

The data collected from the interviews require a discourse analysis technique. The primary concern guiding my analysis was listening closely to the people's choice of words and the way they talked about emotions. The steps I followed in the analysis are:

(1) *Making the data manageable.* After reading and listening to each of the 20 interviews several times, I divided the data collected into two sections so that the analysis would be more manageable (Crang, 1997; Maxwell, 1996). These sections were: (1) the description of the overall experience of living in two cultures and two languages, which often included the story of how the respondents became bilinguals and the conflicts, privileges, or problems that arose from this situation; and (2) the way the respondents talked about the emotions in question. I then isolated all references to emotion terms, either explicit or implicit (when talking about an emotional experience related to being bicultural, for example), into an abridged interview or a 'profile' (Casey, 1998) which I called 'Interview A'.

(2) *Identifying emotion words and phrases.* Using the newly formed profile or Interview A for all respondents, I listened to the ways that my interviewees talked about specific emotions. In each of the abridged interviews I made a note of all references to emotions and teased out single words or phrases. For example, when one of the respondents identified 'frustration' as an untranslatable emotion, I marked this in blue. When she answered my question on how she sees 'shame' in English and *ntropi* in Greek, I underlined her responses in red (this coding method is discussed by Crang, 1997).

(3) *Categorizing the emotion terms in a coding chart.* After going through
     the same process with each of the profiles, I constructed a coding
     system that highlighted the distinctions important in the study
     (as proposed by Crang, 1997; Huberman & Miles, 1998; Maxwell,
     1996).
(4) *Conducting a cross-case analysis.* In order to examine how bilinguals
     talk about the identified untranslatable emotions, I continued my
     cross-case analysis by looking for specific quotes that indicated
     how the respondents spoke about the various emotion terms out-
     lined in my coding chart (Merriam, 1988; Patton, 1990). For
     example, I looked for all quotes that referred to 'guilt' and grouped
     all responses sequentially under the heading 'guilt'. Following the
     process recommended by Crang (1997: 186), I cut up a copy of the
     materials and put the coded sections into piles, so that each
     emotion term formed a pile. Agar (1986) has called this the 'long
     couch or short hall approach', where stacks and piles of materials
     accumulate (cited in Crang, 1997: 186). Sorting the material into
     chunks of text gave me the opportunity to sift through the material
     and to analyze similarities and differences in the uses and discus-
     sions of the emotion terms in question.

Results

Guilt/*enohi*

'Guilt', translated as *enohi* in Greek, is an emotion to which my respondents had diverse reactions. Julia said that 'Americans use "guilty" a lot,
especially Catholics, I am the oldest of six children so I use the word
"guilty" a lot' (English interview, p. 14), while other respondents said
things like 'I purposely decided to *not* feel guilty' (George, English interview, p. 17) or '[Guilt] is not really something I use' (Leonidas, English
interview, p. 19). Some Greek–English bilinguals noted however that
after learning the word in English and using it in contexts such as 'I
feel guilty for eating too much cake', they unconsciously transferred
the word to their Greek vocabulary, at which point they got many
stares 'and then eventually stopped doing that' (Lydia, English interview, p. 21). Nefeli also noted that the Greek *eho typsis* (I feel remorseful)
may be more culturally equivalent to guilt than *enohi*. Julia agreed with
this statement:

> [Guilt and shame are] on a continuum, I think, a lot more serious than
> being inconsiderate ... if you know you've been inconsiderate then
> maybe you feel a little bit ashamed of yourself ... then you could say
> **ntrepome gi'afto pou ekana** [I am ashamed of what I did] ... how
> would you say it? I am deeply ashamed of what I have done ... (pause)

I don't know ... I remember that was hard ... also I feel guilty for what I did ... I know I always used to translate I feel guilty with eho typsis [I feel remorseful] but **typsis** was ... maybe because it's close to tipsy for me **typsis** was a very playful word! I always felt that it was more a playful thing ... even when Greeks were saying it ... **Eho typsis giati den se pira tilefono** [literally: I am remorseful/it is on my conscience that I didn't call you] ... it was something insignificant ... it sounds light .... (English interview, p. 14)

The only thing I remember Greeks saying when they had something bad is **esthanome para poly ashima gi' afto pou ekana** [I feel very bad for what I did] ... but I can't think of anything else that people were saying so yeah you are reminding me that those were the things that were a problem for me ... (English interview, p. 15)

What Julia is pointing to here is very interesting because it shows that the best translation for 'feeling guilty' is either *I feel bad* (thus the Bambiniotis, 1998, definition of 'an unpleasant feeling') or *I am ashamed*. In this sense, it should be highlighted that 'feeling guilty' is perhaps different from the noun 'guilt' and the contextualization of the term prompts a different response for the bilinguals. Below I will return to the idea that feeling guilty and *ntrepome* may be similar.

An interesting aspect of *enohi* or *eho typsis* (I feel remorseful) was the connection that some participants made with the concept of *ypohreosi*, a sense of obligation and duty that they describe as arising only within the Greek Cypriot cultural context. Although this sense of duty would not be seen as an emotion in the Anglo tradition, based on the descriptions below it would fulfill the criteria for the definition of emotion given earlier. Furthermore, it seems that not fulfilling this obligation is an instance (perhaps even the most important instance) in which feelings of *enohi* would arise.

Julia described the term as an integral part of Greek society:

Ah, I know another word that's difficult to translate ... **ypohreosi** ... there's a social sense of **eho ypohreosis** [I have obligations/duties/things to make up for] ... and really I don't mean it in the sense of a responsibility a man has to his family because there we can use responsibility but the idea that you have obligations ... because you've been to someone's house and you have to pay them back, Greeks can be maniacal about that, they feel very uncomfortable if you've done something for them ... it could even lead to animosity ... it's a constant social battle ... I remember the anxiety with which people would tell me about **ypohreosis** ... **prepi na vgalo tis ypohreosis mou** [to pay back, to return the favor] ... I mean this is where people really feel bad if they do not .... (English interview, p. 13)

George also addressed this issue:

> It was really difficult to get used to being here [Cyprus] ... even though I *am* from here, but after thirteen years in America, I think I forgot what it is like to live here ... these concepts like people becoming paranoid with 'ah we have to go to his wedding because his father came to your sister's', 'but you don't even *know* the guy,' 'yeah, but we know his father and he came all the way from tatatata ... and he gave twenty pounds and what would they say ta ta ta ... ' I can't stand that I can't stand that, this paranoia, it is a paranoia it's an illness this whole thing with paying back the *ypohreosi* [obligation], *imaste ypohreomenoi* [we are indebted to people, we owe them] and because someone gave you twenty pounds you have to give thirty because what would they say ... and it's usually for stupid things that you feel *ypohremenos* [indebted] ... *enohes* [guilt] ... I just don't understand ... (Greek interview, p. 17)

It is interesting, I think, that both Julia, an American, and George, a Cypriot, use the words 'maniacal' and 'paranoia' to describe the condition of feeling *ypohreomenos/i/*indebted. Julia said that this emotion could lead to 'feelings of animosity' and is definitely connected to discomfort and anxiety, while George sees it as 'an illness'. Another interesting issue here is Julia's explanation of the social underpinnings of the emotion, something George seems unaware of when he says 'I just don't understand':

> ... because if you've done something it has something to do maybe with you being in a superior level because of that so ... almost the person who does who is reciprocal brings himself to the same level again, it's a constant social battle ... (English interview, p. 13)

Julia believes that this emotion is intertwined with a 'social battle' of gaining, losing, then regaining a superior status in society by being able to offer something to others, 'treating' others, doing favors or helping others. In this context, *ypohreosi* is tied to social and psychological anxiety, both resulting from this anxiety and resulting in this anxiety or, as the interviewees are noting, in feelings of *enohi* when one is unable to do so. While Harré (1986) says that European cultures make a strong connection between guilt and responsibility, the idea of *ypohreosi* is different, because it has less to do with fulfilling one's obligations to a community from an empowered position (responsibility) and more to do with gaining status in a (psychologically) disadvantaged position. In a society like Cyprus where status is more clearly and more strictly defined than in the United States, in terms of concrete hierarchical structures of age, gender, family background, social class, profession and education, a 'social battle' makes sense in ways that it does not in the United States, which, at least on a surface level, is more egalitarian.

Other interviewees also noted that the Greek language structure itself imposes a certain social hierarchy (see also Ochs, 1990) and that even this linguistic indexing feeds into the creation of a less egalitarian system, ridden with expectations, obligations and rules of conduct, and hence more feelings of *ntropi* for failing to meet those rules. Actually, when Camille called a few weeks after the interview to thank me for the flowers I had sent her (as a token of appreciation for her time), she said she felt ashamed (*ntrepome*) it had taken her so long to get back to me, especially given how *indebted* she was to me for listening to her story (the indebtedness was, of course, completely on my part!). To substantiate my argument that 'guilt' and *ntropi* are conceptually related, I now turn to the discussion of *ntropi* and 'shame'.

Ntropi/shame

All ten respondents pointed out that *ntropi* is a complex term, which shares some elements with the English words 'shame', 'embarrassment', and 'shyness'. In fact, it seems that shame, embarrassment, and discomfort, as well as the notion of 'being dishonored', are all lumped into '*ntropi*' in Greek. One could, for example, feel *ntropi* in the following instances:

- You are embarrassed to disrobe in front of another person (*ntrepome*)
- You are uncomfortable at a party where you do not know many people (*ntrepome*)
- You are uncomfortable about asking a favor from somebody (*ntrepome*)
- You are ashamed about your family's bad reputation in the community (*ntrepome*)
- You embarrassed your family by getting bad grades in school or by making a fool of yourself in public (*ntrepome*)

Parents will also often tell their young children '*ntropi!*' when they are doing something unacceptable in public (e.g. screaming) or when they have violated social norms (e.g. asked a host for more dessert). In general, '*ntropi*' is a very powerful and frequently used emotion word in the Greek language. As Sofia pointed out, it is a very powerful concept yet also part of everyday life:

> Um I'll tell you what I mean, in in Cyprus I think it's a very it's a very powerful concept. Mmh. Like you'll hear the mother talking **ntropi, ntropi** . . . that what, that's what my husband did to my son, he made him cry you know when we were visiting these friends the other day. And then in English though it's shame is just so, so overwhelming. I mean it's such a big deal that you would rarely use 'shame' I think in

English. Whereas in Cyprus I think it's just part of everyday life, every-thing is **ntropi** ... (English interview, p. 6)

Sofia also pointed out that she does not like using the term because she cannot really see its purpose, especially in disciplining children, which is the norm in Cyprus:

Now well I wouldn't use 'shame' for anything like this you know, like if my child takes too much or whatever, I would tell him like, you know in regard to food, he is greedy, so I say to him 'you're greedy' you know that's not nice, but I would never tell him, 'Oh shame on you', that you're you know, that you're eating too much .... And I don't use it in Greek with them and, yeah you see, and like I cannot because it's not accomplishing anything. I would tell him 'Oh you're greedy', because for me 'greedy' is you know, the concept that he's taken too much of something. Yeah, you're greedy with your with your posses-sions or your food or whatever. Yeah. So shame now to me shame has to do with a much more serious action, sort of shame like um, well actually I would I would say two different things. One is shame, like oh what a pity that something has not happened, 'oh what a pity that you didn't pass your exam', for example. Or I would say 'Oh shame that um that you've done something wrong', you know which is sort of he is of guilty of something. In that way I use it. Yeah. And then I would differentiate between shame and embarrassment. Yeah, you know, don't embarrass me, let's say if I say 'don't embarrass me' by by by not eating nicely in front of people or making a mess of your you know in front of people, you know what I mean, I would use 'don't embarrass me' but I would never say **ntropi**, you know, I wouldn't say 'oh shame on you' because shame is more powerful form of method, shame is either the negative that you've done something bad or something didn't happen to you what a shame, what a pity that you know this didn't happen ... (English interview, p. 7)

Although Sofia sees shame as 'serious' and different from *ntropi*, she stres-ses that she does not use *ntropi* either with her children. Julia agrees:

Alexia: You think 'shame' is stronger than **ntropi** then?

Julia: Oh definitely, although **ntropi** if you call that to someone you know then it is like shame but this deep feeling of shame ... no, both of those concepts are more or less absent in Greek ... Don't they feel ashamed though? They feel ashamed in the sense of **ntrepome** if they have done something wrong but not in the *deep* sense of shame or they express it in different ways ... in relation to the community at large and not something that is so interior ... We internalize it in American culture ... shame and guilt are internalized ... very deep and it would be logical that a Cypriot would not have that because they don't have, they don't have a responsibility for what's outside them, they are very individualist, you know ... no one is going to feel very deep shame if they've thrown something on the pavement but we've learned to that we have this responsibility to the world outside us and to other people and if we do wrong it's a matter of shame ... (English interview, p. 14)

Julia is again making some fascinating comments: first, she says that both shame and guilt are deeply internalized in American culture and that both are stronger emotions than *ntropi*, which is consistent with what the other respondents are saying. Secondly, she says that shame and guilt are related to a sense of responsibility for what is outside a person, a connection to the rest of the world (this connection is also emphasized in the literature; see Frijda & Mesquita, 1995; Griffiths, 1997; Scheff, 1990). Thirdly, she argues that this connection is absent in the Greek context because Cypriot culture is individualistic.

Other respondents have also noted that 'shame' is really powerful, like 'I cheated on my partner' (Leonidas, Greek interview, p. 7) or something that 'defines social borders' (Lydia, Greek interview, p. 26) but *ntropi* is something that they either connect to children (Lydia, Greek interview, p. 26) or to embarrassment and discomfort (Nefeli, Greek interview, p. 27). In addition, when Nefeli was asked where she would locate *ntropi*, she said 'in the cheeks'. Darwin (1872) did note, in fact, that blushing is both unique and universal to humans.

It seems then from the discussion that there is a difference in the cultural understanding of terms that are assumed to be linguistically equivalent: *shame* and *ntropi* do not appear to be culturally equivalent and neither are *guilt* and *enohi*. It seems, in fact, that *guilt* and *ntropi* are more equivalent in a cultural sense than the direct linguistic translations of these terms.

Let us now look at the responses to the story about Andy/Andreas summarized in Table 7.2 (there are only nine responses, because Julia participated in the interviews only). In the table, Greek responses are given in English translation in italics, with the exception of the Greek emotion terms that were discussed earlier and appear in transliterated form. Code-switching into the other language is marked in bold.

The responses in Table 7.2 show that the participants had different reactions to the two versions of the story, expressing greater overall concern for Andreas and either indifference or disapproval for Andy (for a detailed discussion, see Panayiotou, 2004b). What is of particular interest for this chapter is the use of *guilty* in two instances in the first scenario, the lack of its use in the second one, and the use of *ntropi* in one case in response to the Greek story. The three instances clearly do not offer

Table 7.2 Responses to Andy/Andreas story

	Emotion words/phrases given by participants when the story was read in English	Emotion words/phrases given by participants when the story was read in Greek
Leonidas	He's just doing what everyone does at that age; he's just following the rules; I feel **indifferent** to this.	He's just immature; I would probably warn him about the future, to be careful; he just shouldn't overdo it; I guess I am **concerned.**
George	**Frustrated; disapproval** because his **priorities** are wrong. I don't feel much **sympathy** for him, he is not excused in my eyes ... If I were him I would feel **guilty.**	I can sympathize with him even though I don't agree with his thinking process. I feel some admiration but some sadness as well if he feels he has no other hoice. It feels that he has a need to do this.
Lydia	I feel sorry for him; that sounds like [a mutual acquaintance] so I think he sounds pathetic, I could never live this way; he is missing out on life. I would be <u>guilty</u> if I did this.	Mana mou re [Greek expression of sympathy] ... What is his financial situation though? Is he doing it for his mom you mean?... Stenahoroume [I feel sad] ...
Christina	He's trying to get ahead; he's doing whatever it takes in the society we live in; good for him to be able to work so hard.	He's just doing what everyone in the private sector is doing here; he's young, let him work while he can — that's what I do; I just feel sorry for his mom
Nefeli	I don't really know anyone like that except for doctors here [the United States] but if this is what he wants, let him be! I don't really feel anything about him.	Will his engagement survive? If he were a friend I would tell him to be careful, this is a trap and people are not aware of this sometimes ...
Lila	I feel sorry for him but maybe he is just doing what he has to do as a thirty-year-old male. No, he would not be a friend.	**I pity him. Isn't this the same story pretty much as last time? If he were my son I would feel that I failed as a mother,** I would feel <u>ntropi</u> ...
Jackie	I don't feel anything in particular about him; that's just **the American work ethic,** what everyone does.	I don't know about him but I feel stenahoria for his mom ...

(continued)

Table 7.2 *Continued*

	Emotion words/phrases given by participants when the story was read in English	Emotion words/phrases given by participants when the story was read in Greek
Camille	I am so not in touch with people like him, on purpose … because I knew too many like him, so I guess I feel resentful for people like that. I distance myself from these go-getter types.	**I feel sad because I feel that it's this American mentality that is transferring all over the world; maybe worried too because of that. Does his mom live with him though?**
Sofia	I feel sad and frustrated that he has to prove himself this way because that's what he is trying to do I think.	*His woman will find someone else! What is he doing all that for, that is what I would ask him.*

sufficient data for any definite conclusions, but they do offer a preliminary support to the argument that where 'guilt' is used and perhaps even experienced in English, *ntropi* may be used in Greek. This small example is also in accordance with the interview findings that indicated that respondents would use the verb *ntrepome* in the contexts where they would use 'I feel guilty' in English.

It should also be noted here that during a subsequent interview inquiring about the scenario, Nefeli code-switched to 'I feel guilty' during her Greek interview when discussing her own absence from her family in Cyprus. Although phrased as a question to herself, Nefeli switched into English, possibly because there is no exact cultural equivalent of the term in Greek; *enohi* would sound too serious and *typsis* too temporal.

Other interviewees also noted the connection between 'guilt' and *ntropi* because, as they said, what evoked the English guilt is the same as that which evokes the Greek *ntropi*. Both Julia and Lydia noted, for example, that, having forgotten to call a friend or having eaten too much cake, they would say that they felt 'guilty' in English but in Greek they would say they felt 'bad' (*ashima*) or that they were ashamed (*ntrepome*).

Conclusion

This chapter explored the verbal construction of English 'guilt' (translated in Greek as *enohi*) and the Greek *ntropi* (translated as 'shame') by employing bilingual informants and asking how bilinguals make sense of these terms and their translations in Greek and English. The data show that although these terms have linguistic equivalents in Greek and English, the meanings of these translations differ in the cultures examined. Based on these results, I argue that the translation equivalents of these terms are not cultural equivalents. It is even possible to go a step further and claim that in some instances a more accurate cultural equivalent of 'guilt' is not *enohi* but *ntropi*. These findings seem consistent with previous work on the cultural construction of emotions and highlight the proposition that some terms are unique to certain languages and cultures.

What bilinguals are saying then is that there may be two emotional universes from which they are borrowing emotion terms but that these universes are interconnected and guided by one unified 'experiencer' of the terms. The descriptions noted above are displayed in the very poignant image that one of my participants gave. When asked about his experiences, George said that bilingualism gives him the chance to 'fine-tune (his) emotions'. 'When you are a bilingual/bicultural person, I think that you can move the needle of your emotions a little bit to the left or a little bit to the right until you land on the most precise description of what you are trying to say' (English interview, p. 12). He added that 'maybe monolingual people have the same needle but it's the ability to *move* this needle yourself that makes one a bilingual person' (English interview, p. 12).

The question remains, however, what can bilinguals tell us about the experience of shame and guilt if they are individuals who cross borders and simultaneously experience a guilt culture and a shame culture? Maybe what the findings here show is that an understanding of the subtleties of these terms makes one reluctant to use them. Nearly all participants commented, for example, that guilt and shame are not emotions they experience or they are emotions that they purposely chose not to experience as they see them as destructive. This rejection of particular emotions offers an interesting direction for future inquiry.

I will end this discussion by quoting Foucault, who said once that 'in any given effort to capture the order of things in language, we condemn a certain part of that order to obscurity' (White, 1978: 239 as cited in Mageo, 1995: 291). This chapter sought to raise some questions in regard to the verbal construction of emotions in bilingual/bicultural settings and to address the question of translation equivalents for certain emotion terms. Whereas more work is clearly needed in this area, this study will hopefully incite some further interest in the possibility that shame in the Mediterranean is guilt-full.

Acknowledgements

The author wishes to thank the editor, Aneta Pavlenko, and the anonymous reviewers for their valuable insights and thought-provoking questions raised during the preparation of this chapter.

Notes

1. Power distance is the extent to which the less powerful members of institutions and organizations accept that power is distributed unequally. For a further discussion of these categorizations, see Hofstede (1997).
2. Uncertainty avoidance is the extent to which people feel threatened by ambiguous situations and have created beliefs and institutions that try to avoid these. See also Hofstede (1997).
3. According to Stearns and Stearns (1988: 30), *emotionology* refers to ways in which people in a particular culture identify, classify, and recognize emotions. To study emotionology, one must try to discover the rules of use of the local vocabulary of emotion words. According to Harré and Gillett (1994), such a theory will rarely be explicit but is immanent in the ways that words are used in describing and commenting on how emotions are displayed and felt.
4. I chose to focus on Greek/English bilingual/bicultural adults who live in the Cypriot and American cultural contexts, specifically because these are the languages and cultures in which I am most 'fluent'. As argued elsewhere (Panayiotou, 2004a), linguistic and cultural fluency are crucial for a thorough analysis of emotion terms and for explanation of the results (see also Denzin and Lincoln, 1998; Maxwell, 1996). Because the Cypriot culture is distinct from the Greek culture – despite the many similarities and shared history – and the Greek–Cypriot dialect is different from Standard Modern Greek (SMG), for the purposes of the study, I recruited Greek–English bilinguals who were Greek Cypriots (and thus knowledgeable of both SMG and the Cypriot dialect) and English–Greek bilinguals who were fluent in both SMG and the Cypriot dialect and had Cyprus as their home base for at least three years.
5. Birdsong (1992), for example, reported that adult second language learners who achieve native-like competence in this second language have it by about the end of three years in the target language context.
6. Similar work with Chinese/English bilinguals was conducted by Hoffman and her colleagues (1986). In this study, Hoffman *et al.* found that bilingual speakers may develop different impressions of a person depending on which language they were using when forming an impression.
7. For a discussion of the differences between SMG and the Cypriot dialect, see Hadjioannou (1996).
8. The story was made culturally relevant using the help of a focus group.
9. Tannen (1986) used a similar method with Greek Americans when she asked them to talk about a film they saw (further details about this film in Chafe, 1980).

References

Armon-Jones, C. (1986) The thesis of constructionism. In R. Harré (ed.) *The Social Construction of Emotions* (pp. 32–56). Oxford, UK: Basil Blackwell.

Averill, J. (1980) A constructionist view of emotion. In R. Plutchik and H. Kellerman (eds) *Emotion: Theory, Research and Experience* (pp. 305–39). New York, NY: Academic Press.

Averill, J. (1982) *Anger and Aggression: An Essay on Emotion.* New York, NY: Springer.

Averill, J. (1985) The social construction of emotion with special reference to love. In K. Gergen and K. Davis (eds) *The Social Construction of the Person* (pp. 173–95). New York, NY: Springer-Verlag.

Averill, J. (1996) Intellectual emotions. In R. Harré and G. Parrott (eds) *The Emotions: Social, Cultural and Biological Dimensions* (pp. 24–39). London, UK: Sage.

Bambiniotis, G. (1998) *Lexico tis Neas Ellinikis Glossas* [Dictionary of the Modern Greek Language]. Athens, Greece: Kentro Lexikologias.

Barrett, K. (1995) A functionalist approach to shame and guilt. In J. Tangney and K. Fischer (eds) *Self-Conscious Emotions: The Psychology of Shame, Guilt, Embarrassment and Pride* (pp. 25–64). New York, NY: Guildford.

Birdsong, D. (1992) Ultimate attainment in second language acquisition. *Language* 68, 706–55.

Casey, M. (1998) *Lectures in Developmental Qualitative Data Analysis*. Cambridge, MA: Harvard Graduate School of Education.

Chafe, W. (1980) *The Pear Stories: Cognitive, Cultural and Linguistic Aspects of Narrative Production*. Norwood, NJ: Ablex Publishing Corporation.

Crang, M. (1997) Analyzing qualitative materials. In R. Flowerdew and D. Martin (eds) *Methods in Human Geography* (pp. 183–196). Essex, UK: Addison Wesley Longman.

Darwin, Ch. (1872) *The Expression of the Emotions in Man and Animals*. London: John Murray.

Denzin, N. and Lincoln, Y. (1998) Introduction: Entering the field of qualitative research. In N. Denzin and Y. Lincoln (eds) *Collecting and Interpreting Qualitative Materials* (pp. 1–35). Thousand Oaks, CA: Sage.

Derné, S. (1994) Structural realities, persistent dilemmas, and the construction of emotional paradigms: Love in three cultures. *Social Perspectives on Emotion* 2, 281–308.

Dewaele, J.M. and Pavlenko, A. (2002) Emotion vocabulary in interlanguage. *Language Learning* 52(2), 263–322.

Doi, T. (1962/1981) *The Anatomy of Dependence*. Tokyo, Japan: Kodansha International.

Doi, T. (1990) The cultural assumptions of psychoanalysis. In J. Stigler, R. Shweder, and G. Herdt (eds) *Cultural Psychology: Essays on Comparative Human Development* (pp. 446–54). Cambridge, UK: Cambridge University Press.

Duranti, A. (1997) *Linguistic Anthropology*. Cambridge, UK: Cambridge University Press.

Ekman, P. (1980) Biological and cultural contributions to body and facial movement in the expression of emotions. In A. Rorty (ed.) *Explaining Emotions* (pp. 73–103). Berkeley, CA: University of California Press.

Ekman, P. (1992) An argument for basic emotions. *Cognition and Emotion* 6, 169–200.

Frijda, N. and Mesquita, B. (1995) The social roles and functions of emotions. In S. Kitayama and H. Markus (eds) *Emotion and Culture: Empirical Studies of Mutual Influence* (pp. 51–89). Washington, DC: American Psychological Association.

Geertz, C. (1973) *The Interpretation of Cultures*. New York, NY: Basic Books.

Griffiths, P. (1997) *What Emotions Really Are*. Chicago, IL: The University of Chicago Press.

Grosjean, F. (1982) *Life with Two Languages: An Introduction to Bilingualism*. Cambridge, MA: Harvard University Press.

Hadjioannou, K. (1996) *Etymologiko Lexiko tis Omiloumenis Kypriakis Dialektou* [Definitive Dictionary of the Spoken Cypriot Dialect]. Nicosia, Cyprus: Ekdosis Tamasos Ltd.

Harré, R. (1986) An outline of the social constructionist viewpoint. In R. Harré (ed.) *The Social Construction of Emotions* (pp. 2–14). Oxford, UK: Basil Blackwell.

Harré, R. and Gillett, G. (1994) *The Discursive Mind*. London, UK: Sage.
Hoffman, E. (1989) *Lost in Translation: A Life in a New Language*. New York, NY: Penguin Books.
Hoffman, C., Lau, I. and Johnson, D. (1986) The linguistic relativity of person cognition: An English–Chinese comparison. *Journal of Personality and Social Psychology* 51, 1097–105.
Hofstede, G. (1997) *Cultures and Organizations: Software of the Mind*. New York, NY: McGraw-Hill.
Huberman, A. and Miles, M. (1998) Data management and analysis methods. In N. Denzin and Y. Lincoln (eds) *Collecting and Interpreting Qualitative Materials* (pp. 179–211). Thousand Oaks, CA: Sage.
James, W. (1890/1955) *The Principles of Psychology* (Vol. 2). New York: Dover Publications.
Josephs, I. (1995) The problem of emotions from the perspective of psychological semantics. *Culture and Psychology* 1, 279–88.
Kitayama, S., Markus, H. and Matsumoto, H. (1995) Culture, self and emotion: A cultural perspective to 'self-conscious' emotions. In J. Tangney and K. Fischer (eds) *Self-Conscious Emotions: The Psychology of Shame, Guilt, Embarrassment and Pride* (pp. 439–64). New York, NY: Guilford.
Levy, R. (1984) Emotion, knowing, and culture. In R. Shweder and R. LeVine (eds) *Culture Theory: Essays on Mind, Self and Emotion* (pp. 214–37). Cambridge, UK: Cambridge University Press.
Lindsay-Hartz, J., De Rivera, J. and Mascolo, M. (1995) Differentiating guilt and shame and their effects on motivation. In J. Tangney and K. Fischer (eds) *Self-Conscious Emotions: The Psychology of Shame, Guilt, Embarrassment and Pride* (pp. 274–301). New York, NY: Guilford.
Lutz, C. (1987) Goals, events, and understanding in Ifaluk emotion theory. In D. Holland and N. Quinn (eds) *Cultural Models in Language and Thought* (pp. 290–312). Cambridge, UK: Cambridge University Press.
Lutz, C. (1988) *Unnatural Emotions: Everyday Sentiments on a Micronesian Atoll and Their Challenge to Western Theory*. Chicago, IL: University of Chicago Press.
Mageo, J. (1995) The reconfiguring self. *American Anthropologist* 97(2), 282–96.
Maxwell, J. (1996) *Qualitative Research Design: An Interactive Approach*. Applied Social Research Series, (41). Thousand Oaks, CA: Sage Publications.
Merriam, S. (1988) *Case Study Research in Education: A Qualitative approach*. San Francisco, CA: Jossey-Bass.
Miles, M. and Huberman, A. (1984) *Qualitative Data Analysis: A Sourcebook of New Methods*. Newbury Park, CA: Sage.
Ochs, E. (1990) Indexicality and socialization. In J. Stigler, R. Shweder and G. Herdt (eds) *Cultural Psychology: Essays on Comparative Human Development* (pp. 287–309). Cambridge, UK: Cambridge University Press.
Panayiotou, A. (2004a) Bilingual emotions: The untranslatable self. *Estudios de Sociolinguistica* 5(1), 1–19.
Panayiotou, A. (2004b) Switching codes, switching code: Emotional responses of bilinguals in English and Greek. *Journal of Multilingual and Multicultural Development* 25(2–3), 124–39.
Parrott, W. G. and Harré, R. (1996) Introduction: Some complexities in the study of emotions. In R. Harré and G. Parrott (eds) *The Emotions: Social, Cultural and Biological Dimensions* (pp. 1–20). London, UK: Sage.
Patton, M. (1990) *Qualitative Evaluation and Research Methods* (2nd edn). Newbury Park, CA: Sage.

Pavlenko, A. (2002a) Emotions and the body in Russian and English. *Pragmatics and Cognition* 10(1–2), 207–41.

Pavlenko, A. (2002b) Bilingualism and emotions. *Multilingua* 21(1), 45–78.

Rosaldo, M. (1980) *Knowledge and Passion: Ilongot Notions of Self and Social Life*. Cambridge, UK: Cambridge University Press.

Sapir, E. (1929/1945) The status of linguistics as a science. In D. Mandelbaum (ed.) *Selected Writings of Edward Sapir in Language, Culture, and Personality* (pp. 160–66). Berkeley, CA: University of California Press.

Scheff, T. (1990) *Microsociology: Discourse, Emotion, and Social Structure*. Chicago, IL: The University of Chicago Press.

Searle, J. (1995) *The Construction of Social Reality*. London, UK: Penguin.

Shaver, P., Wu, S. and Schwartz, J. (1992) Cross-cultural similarities and differences in emotion and its representation. In M. Clark (ed.) *Review of Personality and Social Psychology, 13 Emotion* (pp. 175–212). Newbury Park, CA: Sage.

Solomon, R. (1980) Emotions and choice. In A. Rorty (ed.) *Explaining Emotions* (pp. 251–83). Berkeley, CA: University of California Press.

Stearns, C. and Stearns, P. (1988) *Emotion and Social Change*. New York: Holmes and Meier.

Stocker, M. and Hegeman, E. (1996) *Valuing Emotions*. Cambridge, UK: Cambridge University Press.

Tangney, J. (1995) Shame and guilt in interpersonal relationships. In J. Tangney and K. Fischer (eds) *Self-Conscious Emotions: The Psychology of Shame, Guilt, Embarrassment and Pride* (pp. 114–43). New York, NY: Guilford.

Tannen, D. (1986) Introducing constructed dialogue in Greek and American conversational and literary narrative. In F. Coulmas (ed.) *Direct and Indirect Speech* (pp. 56–83). New York, NY: Mouton de Gruyter.

Thalberg, I. (1984) From *Emotion and Thought*. In C. Calhoun and R. Solomon (eds) *What is an Emotion?* (pp. 291–305). New York, NY: Oxford University Press.

Valentine, G. (1997) 'Tell me about...': Using interviews as a research. In R. Flowerdew and D. Martin (eds) *Methods in Human Geography* (pp. 110–26). Essex, UK: Addison Wesley Longman.

Wallbott, H. and Scherer, K. (1995) Cultural determinants in experiencing shame and guilt. In J. Tangney and K. Fischer (eds) *Self-Conscious Emotions: The Psychology of Shame, Guilt, Embarrassment and Pride* (pp. 465–88). New York, NY: Guilford.

Weber, M. (1904/2002) *The Protestant Ethic and the Spirit of Capitalism* (3rd edn). New York, NY: Roxbury Publishing.

White, H. (1978) *Tropics of Discourse: Essays in Cultural Criticism*. Baltimore, MD: Johns Hopkins University Press.

Wierzbicka, A. (1992) *Semantics, Culture and Cognition: Universal Human Concepts in Culture-Specific Configurations*. New York, NY: Oxford University Press.

Wierzbicka, A. (1994) Emotion, language, and cultural scripts. In S. Kitayama and H. Markus (eds) *Emotion and Culture: Empirical Studies of Mutual Influence* (pp. 133–96). Washington, DC: American Psychological Association.

Wierzbicka, A. (1998) Angst. *Culture and Psychology* 4(2), 161–88.

Wierzbicka, A. (1999) *Emotions Across Languages and Cultures: Diversity and Universals*. Cambridge, UK: Cambridge University Press.

Winegar, L. (1995) Moving toward culture-inclusive theories of emotion. *Culture and Psychology* 1, 269–77.

Wollheim, R. (1999) *On the Emotions*. New Haven, CT: Yale University Press.

Zentella, A.C. (1997) *Growing Up Bilingual*. Malden, MA: Blackwell Publishers.

Chapter 8

Envy and Jealousy in Russian and English: Labeling and Conceptualization of Emotions by Monolinguals and Bilinguals[1]

OLGA STEPANOVA SACHS and JOHN D. COLEY

Introduction

It is a frustrating experience familiar to many bilinguals – something that is easily said in one language requires an awkward and lengthy explanation in another. This problem is particularly pervasive when it comes to talking about abstract concepts or intangible things, such as emotions. There are many known cases of emotion terms that exist in one language but do not exist in others. For example, *Schadenfreude* in German means pleasure derived from another's displeasure (Russell, 1991). This term does not exist in English, except as a lexical borrowing, although by imagining a romantic rival suffering a tragic accident, we can easily understand the concept behind it. Nevertheless, the really interesting question is whether this linguistic difference causes German and English speakers to categorize emotions differently. Russell (1991) suggested that there is a particularly strong relationship between linguistic labeling and categorization of emotions. One reason for this is the fact that much of the evidence for categorization of emotions involves words – something researchers have to resort to in the absence of Munsell chips for emotions.

More generally, Russell proposed that labeling an emotion may have an effect on subsequent cognitive processes, such as encoding, responding to, and remembering emotions. Cross-linguistic variability of emotion terms may lead to the possibility that people who speak different languages have different conceptual representations of emotions. For example, speakers of different languages may disagree on what emotions seem more similar to them or on the degree of overlap between various members in the domain of emotion terms. Alternatively, it could be that underlying conceptual structure of emotions is fairly universal, and that differences in how language maps onto this conceptual structure have no impact on the structure itself. A study by Romney, Moore and Rusch (1997) showed that a combination of the two alternatives is possible as well. While they found a number of significant and interesting differences in the Japanese and English semantic structures of emotion terms, they concluded that these differences represented a very small proportion of the overall effect and argued that English and Japanese share a single model of the semantic structure of emotion terms.

The question whether cross-linguistic variability of emotion terms is a reflection of the differences in the conceptual structure of emotions will be addressed in this paper. We will focus on the habitual use of words *jealous* and *envious* by American English speakers, and words *revnuet* (s/he is being jealous) and *zaviduet* (s/he is being envious) by Russian speakers (we used adjectives in English and verbs in Russian to reflect language-specific patterns of emotion encoding). Members of each pair refer to two distinct emotions identified by social psychologists – the emotion of jealousy and the emotion of envy (Parrott & Smith, 1993; Salovey & Rodin, 1986). The emotion of jealousy is usually described as a situation where a person fears losing an important relationship with another person to a rival. The emotion of envy is defined as a situation where a person lacks another's superior quality, achievement, opportunity, or possession and either desires it or wishes that the other lacked it (Parrott & Smith, 1993). These definitions are very similar to the definitions provided for these words in English and Russian dictionaries.

At first glance the situation looks simple: there are two emotion terms in each language, and two emotions that these words refer to. One would expect that these words would map on to emotions the same way in both languages. However, any Russian–English bilingual will agree that the reality of how these words are used by Russian and English speakers is far from being that simple. In Russian there is a one-to-one mapping of emotion terms to emotions described in the literature: the word *revnuet* is used to refer to the emotion of jealousy; the word *zaviduet* is used to refer to the emotion of envy. In English, on the other hand, the word *jealous* is applied to both jealousy and envy (see Figure 8.1).

American English speakers habitually refer to different kinds of situations using the word *jealous*; for example:

You have a nice car. I'm so **jealous**!
Don't flirt with that man. Your boyfriend is already **jealous**.

In contrast, Russian speakers use the formal equivalent of jealous, *revnuet*, to refer only to what Americans often call romantic jealousy. If the two

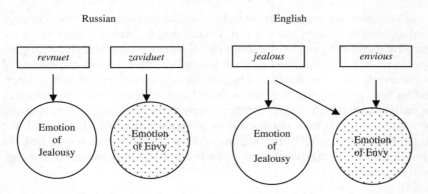

Figure 8.1 Mapping of the words ZAVIDUET/REVNUET and ENVIOUS/ JEALOUS to the emotions of jealousy and envy in Russian and English

sentences above were to be said in Russian, two different words would have to be used to describe the emotions elicited by someone's car and the emotional state of a man whose girlfriend is flirting with someone else; for example:

*U tebia khoroshaia mashina. Ya tak tebe **zaviduiu**!*
[You have a nice car. I am so envious!]
*Ne zaigryvai s tem muzhchinoi. Tvoi paren' uzhe **revnuet**.*
[Don't flirt with that man. Your boyfriend is already jealous.]

We are interested in whether this discrepancy in the way that labels map onto categories of emotions is a reflection of how speakers of English and Russian conceptualize situations that evoke envy or jealousy. To answer this question we must first show a systematic linguistic difference in the way Russian and English speakers use words *jealous/envious* and *revnuet/zaviduet* to refer to the emotions of jealousy and envy. This step will be taken in Experiment 1. The second step is to see whether there is a corresponding conceptual difference in the way Russian and English speakers categorize envy and jealousy situations. This will be done in Experiment 2. The important difference between the two experiments is that the first experiment is designed to investigate how these emotions are labeled in the two languages. Therefore, it involves words *jealous/envious* and *revnuet/zaviduet*. The second experiment, on the other hand, is designed to look into conceptual representations of envy and jealousy and examine how situations that usually make one experience these emotions are categorized by Russian and English speakers. To limit any linguistic interference, actual words *jealous/envious* and *revnuet/zaviduet* were not used in the second experiment.

In addition, we are interested in the mechanism by which such conceptual differences, if any, come about. We attempt to pinpoint these mechanisms by examining not only monolingual Russian and American English speakers, but also Russian–English bilinguals, that is, native speakers of Russian who are also fluent in English. Bilinguals are a particularly interesting test case because they allow us to begin to tease apart the influence of native language, language being spoken at the time, and mere exposure to a language that may parse emotional space differently. In general, we hope that examining bilinguals as well as monolinguals will help to shed light on the mechanisms by which language may influence conceptual structure.

Experiment 1

Method

Participants

Three groups of subjects were involved in Experiment 1: 22 monolingual speakers of Russian (MR), 22 monolingual speakers of American English (ME), and 22 Russian–English bilinguals. Bilinguals were randomly assigned to either Russian or English testing conditions. Overall, 11 bilinguals were tested in Russian (BR) and 11 were tested in English (BE). The age of MR ranged from 19 to 37 years (M = 24.9), ME ranged from 18 to 28 (M = 21.4), and bilinguals ranged from 19 to 28 (M = 23.3).

The MR subjects were recruited in one of the Moscow public libraries. They were rewarded for participation in the study with Northeastern University T-shirts. ME subjects were undergraduates at Northeastern University fulfilling their Introductory Psychology research participation requirement. Bilinguals were recruited in Moscow and in Boston. Bilinguals from Moscow ($n = 18$) were either English majors in local universities, or worked at a workplace where English was the dominant language, or had spent a considerable amount of time in the United States. Bilinguals from Boston ($n = 4$) grew up speaking Russian and learned English in their teens when their families moved to the United States. Although it is possible that bilinguals recruited in Moscow were different from bilinguals recruited in Boston, there was no difference in their self-assessed knowledge of English or in the number of years they have been speaking English. Also, as seen in Table 8.1, there were no significant differences between bilinguals tested in English and bilinguals tested in Russian.

Materials

Each subject was presented with five stories describing prototypical envy- or jealousy-arousing situations (two jealousy stories and three

Table 8.1 Russian–English bilinguals: second language (L2) proficiency and age of acquisition

	Bilinguals tested in Russian	*Bilinguals tested in English*
L2 speaking	5.73	6.27
L2 listening/comprehension	5.91	6.18
L2 reading	6.30	6.5
L2 writing	5.09	5.91
Years speaking English	13.82	12.55
Age	23.5	23.1

envy stories). No boundary envy–jealousy scenarios were used in this experiment because of the lack of clear theoretical predictions for such cases. A typical envy story would describe a situation where one of the two friends gets something that the other one wants very much – a job or a role in a play, while both of them are equally qualified for it. A typical jealousy story would describe a couple involved in a romantic relationship where one of the partners suspects the other one's unfaithfulness. Full stories in English are provided in Appendix A to this chapter.

The stories had been pretested to ensure that they indeed describe prototypical envy and jealousy situations. Twenty-five English speakers were asked to assign them to one of three categories.

(1) Stories that are consistent with the emotion that has the following definition: a person lacks another's superior quality, opportunity, or possession and either desires it or wishes that the other lacked it. This is one of the standard definitions of envy in social psychology literature that we adopted for the task (Parrott & Smith, 1993).
(2) Stories that are consistent with the emotion that has the following definition: a person fears losing an important relationship with another person to a rival. This is one of the standard definitions of jealousy (Parrott & Smith, 1993).
(3) Stories that are not consistent with any of the emotions defined above.

The actual words *jealousy* and *envy* were never mentioned either in the stories or in the instructions given to the subjects. Results of this pretesting showed that the stories were consistent with the definitions; every subject assigned the stories to the expected category, and no stories were assigned to the third category.

All stories were translated into Russian and then subjected to back-translation into English by another translator who was not familiar with the experiment. The final English translation was virtually identical to the original English copy. The Russian version of the materials is provided in Appendix B.

Procedure

Participants were tested individually in a quiet room. Instructions to MR and ME were given in Russian or English, respectively. Bilinguals were randomly assigned to either Russian or English condition. Depending on what condition they were assigned to, they were given instructions in either Russian or English. The experiment was conducted by a Russian native speaker who was also fluent in English.

After reading each story, participants were presented with 10 words denoting various emotions (happy, jealous, upset, satisfied, glad, proud, surprised, envious, sad, content), envy and jealousy among them, and asked to rate the appropriateness of each of those words for the description of the emotion one of the protagonists was likely to feel in the situation described in the story. Filler terms were used to avoid making the purpose of the experiment too obvious; responses to these terms are not further analyzed. The ratings in this paper and pencil task were to be done on a 1 to 7 scale, with 1 meaning 'not appropriate' and 7 'very appropriate'.

Results

Envy stories

The data were analyzed by calculating the mean appropriateness rating for words *jealous/revnuet* and *envious/zaviduet* across all three envy stories and comparing them for each group of subjects (see Figure 8.2). As expected, Russian speakers made a sharp distinction between the appropriateness of *zaviduet* and *revnuet* to describe the emotion of characters in envy stories. They rated *zaviduet* as much more appropriate than *revnuet* ($M_{zav} = 5.30$ and $M_{rev} = 2.62$, $t(65) = 8.41$, $p < 0.001$). English speakers, on the other hand, rated *envious* and *jealous* as being equally appropriate for describing emotions of the main characters in envy stories ($M_{env} = 6.02$ and $M_{jel} = 5.97$, $t(65) = 0.40$, $p = 0.371$). Bilinguals tested in Russian showed results similar to Russian monolinguals, rating *zaviduet* higher than *revnuet* ($M_{zav} = 5.52$ and $M_{rev} = 4.21$, $t(32) = 3.73$, $p = 0.009$). Bilinguals tested in English showed no such distinction ($M_{env} = 4.64$ and $M_{jel} = 4.42$, $t(32) = 0.93$, $p = 0.141$).

An additional analysis was done to compare difference scores between ratings of *zaviduet* and *revnuet* for each group of subjects tested in Russian and *envious* and *jealous* for subjects tested in English. The difference score

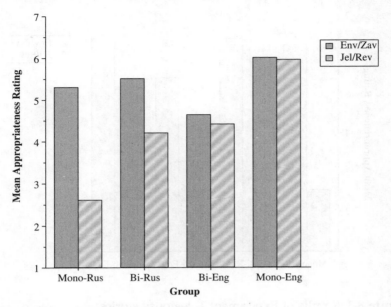

Figure 8.2 Results of Experiment 1: Envy stories

for each subject was obtained by subtracting the mean *revnuet/jealous* rating (across all envy stories) from the mean *zaviduet/envious* rating (across all envy stories). A high difference score would mean a high degree of differentiation between the two emotion terms; a low score indicates little differentiation. The results of a single factor ANOVA showed that the difference scores were significantly higher for Russian monolinguals than for any other subject group, $F(3, 62) = 14.76$, $p < 0.001$. Paired comparisons (Fisher's PLSD tests) also showed that bilinguals tested in Russian had higher difference scores than English monolinguals ($p = 0.02$) and bilinguals tested in English (this difference was marginal, $p = 0.08$). English speakers did not differ from bilinguals tested in English ($p = 0.75$).

Jealousy stories

The data were analyzed by calculating the mean appropriateness rating for words *jealous/revnuet* and *envious/zaviduet* across the two jealousy stories and comparing them for each group of subjects (see Figure 8.3). All groups of subjects rated *jealous* higher than *envious* when they had to describe the emotion of characters in jealousy stories. Russian speakers rated *revnuet* much higher than *zaviduet* ($M_{rev} = 6.23$ and $M_{zav} = 2.55$, $t(43) = 12.37$, $p < 0.001$) and English speakers rated

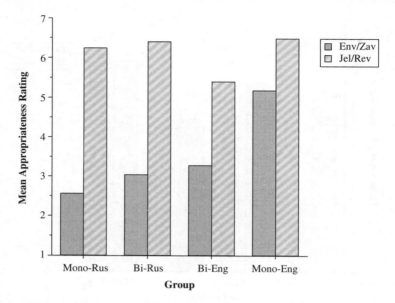

Figure 8.3 Results of Experiment 1: Jealousy stories

jealous higher than *envious* ($M_{jel} = 6.48$ and $M_{env} = 5.18$, $t(43) = 6.04$, $p < 0.001$). Bilinguals tested in Russian rated *revnuet* higher than *zaviduet* ($M_{rev} = 6.41$ and $M_{zav} = 3.05$, $t(21) = 8.46$, $p < 0.001$) and bilinguals tested in English rated *jealous* higher than *envious* ($M_{jel} = 5.41$ and $M_{env} = 3.27$, $t(21) = 4.49$, $p = 0.004$).

However, the results of a single factor ANOVA show that the difference between the ratings of *jealous/revnuet* and *envious/zaviduet* was greater for Russian speakers than for English speakers and bilinguals tested in English $F(3, 62) = 10.38$, $p < 0.001$. Fisher's PLSD paired comparisons showed that bilinguals tested in Russian also had higher difference scores than English speakers ($p < 0.001$) and marginally higher than bilinguals tested in English ($p = 0.06$). Russian speakers did not differ from bilinguals tested in Russian ($p = 0.57$) and English speakers did not differ from bilinguals tested in English ($p = 0.14$).

Discussion

The results of Experiment 1 show a clear linguistic difference between subject groups. Monolingual Russian speakers applied words *zaviduet* and *revnuet* differently to envy and jealousy stories. They gave *zaviduet* much higher appropriateness ratings than *revnuet* for envy stories and they did the opposite on jealousy stories – *revnuet* was rated much higher than *zaviduet*. In contrast, monolingual English speakers viewed the words *envious* and *jealous* as being equally appropriate for describing the emotions of characters in envy stories. Monolingual English speakers did rate *jealous* as more appropriate than *envious* for jealousy stories, but the differentiation was still less pronounced than for monolingual Russian speakers.

For bilinguals, testing language determined responses. Bilinguals tested in Russian responded like Russian monolinguals, whereas bilinguals tested in English responded like English monolinguals, despite the fact that both groups of bilinguals had Russian as their native language and were similar in their self-rated English proficiency. Bilinguals speaking English seemed to blur the distinction between envy- and jealously-invoking situations in a way that bilinguals speaking Russian did not. However, bilinguals tested in Russian did not respond exactly like monolingual Russian speakers; for envy stories, the difference between the ratings of *revnuet* and *zaviduet* was greater for Russian speakers than for bilinguals tested in Russian. So while they clearly differed from English monolinguals and bilinguals tested in English, these two groups also differed from each other, with bilinguals 'moving' in the direction of English monolinguals. This raises the possibility that the overlapping conceptual representation of the two emotions in English has affected bilinguals by making jealousy and envy seem more similar to each other than they normally would to native Russian speakers. Apparently, it also affected the way they use words *revnuet* and *zaviduet* in Russian. Bilinguals tested in English, on the other hand, did not differ from English monolinguals in the difference score analyses, either on jealousy or on envy stories. Therefore, in addition to the previously identified comparisons (Russian monolinguals versus English monolinguals, bilinguals tested in Russian versus bilinguals tested in English), we might also expect conceptual differences between Russian monolinguals and bilinguals tested in Russian.

Overall, results of Experiment 1 provide clear evidence for linguistic differences in how emotion terms map onto emotion-laden situations in English and Russian, and allow us to build a schematic representation of how the Russian words *zaviduet* and *revnuet* and the English words *envious* and *jealous* apply to emotions (see Figure 8.4). We can conclude that these terms overlap only marginally in Russian but strongly in English. The next step will be to see if these differences in labeling envy and jealousy situations will translate into differences in how these emotions are represented on the conceptual level. Therefore, in the next experiment we will ask whether Russian and English speakers differ in how they classify situations that would make one either jealous or envious.

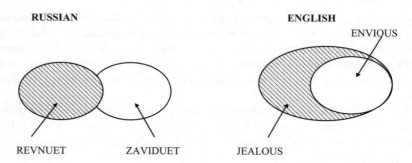

Figure 8.4 Schematic representation of the relationship between the domains in the world to which the Russian words ZAVIDUET and REVNUET and the English words ENVIOUS and JEALOUS apply

Experiment 2

Experiment 1 provided evidence that monolingual speakers of Russian show a strong preference for using *zaviduet* to describe situations involving envy and *revnuet* to describe situations involving jealousy. Monolingual speakers of English show a preference, albeit a weaker one, to use *jealous* to describe jealousy situations, but use *jealous* and *envious* interchangeably to describe envy situations. In Experiment 2 we used a triad sorting and a free sorting task to examine possible conceptual differences in how Russian and English speakers categorize jealousy and envy situations. Considering monolinguals only, based on the results of Experiment 1 we could make a prediction that English speakers may fail to differentiate situations designed to invoke jealousy versus envy, or may do so much less reliably than Russian speakers. We may also predict that although both groups are able to differentiate the situations, jealousy and envy situations might seem more similar to English speakers than to Russian speakers. Both of these outcomes would mean that conceptual representations of the emotions envy and jealousy may be different for speakers of Russian and English. Finally, a lack of conceptual differences would indicate a common underlying representation of emotional terms regardless of linguistic differences in labeling situations evoking envy and jealousy.

Conceptual differences between monolingual speakers of English and Russian – if found – could be elucidated by bilingual responses in several ways. First, all native Russian speakers may perform similarly – regardless of testing language – and differently from the native English speakers. This would suggest that one's native language establishes some conceptual constraints that later language learning does not change. Secondly, monolingual Russian speakers and bilinguals tested in

Russian might perform similarly, and look distinct from bilinguals tested in English and native English speakers, suggesting the presence of relatively flexible emotion categories, and indicating that the language spoken may render certain distinctions or similarities salient online. Finally, all speakers of English (i.e. monolingual speakers of English and both bilingual groups) might pattern similarly, and differ from the monolingual Russian speakers. This would suggest that learning English had some effect on how bilinguals' emotions concepts are organized.

Method

Participants

These were the same as in Experiment 1.

Materials

Twenty-seven one-sentence-long situations were developed for this experiment using some of the materials designed by the social psychology research on the emotions of jealousy and envy (Salovey & Rodin, 1986). The situations were of three kinds: jealousy-evoking (e.g. 'Your boyfriend dances with someone else at a dance'), envy-evoking (e.g. 'Your boyfriend buys something you want but cannot afford'), and controls that evoked generally negative feelings (e.g. 'Your boyfriend lost your dog'). For a complete list of all situations in English see Appendix C. All situations involved a boyfriend or a girlfriend to avoid the possibility that subjects use the differences in the kind of person involved to guide their reasoning in the tasks.

As in Experiment 1, these situations were pre-tested by asking 25 English speakers to assign them to one of the three categories: (1) a category that contained a standard definition of envy; (2) a category that contained a standard definition of jealousy; (3) a category for situations that were not consistent with any of the definitions. Again, the actual words *jealous* or *envious* were not mentioned either in definitions or instructions given to subjects. All envy, control, and five out of nine jealousy situations were unanimously assigned to the expected category. The remaining four jealousy situations were assigned to the expected category by the majority of the participants (all $\chi^2(2) > 18.47$, $p < 0.001$).

All situations were translated into Russian and back-translated into English. The final English translation was virtually identical to the original copy. The Russian version of the situations is provided in Appendix D. Each situation was written on a small (8 cm × 3 cm) card.

Procedure

Task 1: Triads. Subjects were presented with 12 triads of the following types: Type JJE, 2 jealousy and 1 envy situation; Type EEJ, 2 envy and

1 jealousy situation; Type JJB, 2 jealousy and 1 control situation; Type EEB, 2 envy and 1 control situation; Type EJB, 1 envy, 1 jealousy, and 1 control situation. There were three triads of type JJE and EEJ, and two triads of types JJB, EEB, and EJB. Three different sets of triads were created, each set made up of different combinations of the same situations. All subjects were randomly assigned to one of the three sets. The order of presentation of triads in a set was randomized as well. Participants were presented with each triad and asked to 'pick any 2 situations that go together'. After the completion of the task subjects were asked to provide an explanation for each of their selections.

Task 2: Free sort. Subjects were given all 27 cards with situations, asked to read them carefully and to 'sort them into as many groups as they liked according to the kind of emotion they would be likely to experience in such situations'. After the sorting had been completed, subjects were asked to explain what emotion united the situations in each group that they had formed.

Because the same group of subjects was used in Experiment 1 and both tasks of Experiment 2, the order of presentation of all three tasks was completely counterbalanced across subjects to avoid systematic effects of tasks on each other. Subjects' responses and sorts were recorded by the experimenter on a data sheet.

Results and discussion

Triad sorting task

Subjects' sortings were analyzed by calculating the proportion of times they selected two envy situations in EEJ and EEB triads, two jealousy situations in JJE and JJB triads, and the envy and jealousy situations in EJB triads (see Table 8.2).

Table 8.2 Results of triad sorting task showing the percentage of times different groups of subjects separated jealousy and envy situations from each other and from control 'bad' situations

	JJE Triad	*EEJ Triad*	*JJB Triad*	*EEB Triad*	*EJB Triad*
MR	88%	74%	75%	77%	21%
BR	64%	73%	73%	68%	59%
BE	79%	70%	82%	82%	50%
ME	91%	74%	91%	84%	52%
Mean	80%	73%	80%	78%	46%

Triads where jealousy and envy situations were pitted against each other or against controls were sorted in a very similar way by all subjects. Separate ANOVAs run for each type of triad showed no difference between subject groups. On average, subjects in all groups separated envy and jealousy situations from each other and from control situations 78% of the time. This pattern shows clear differentiation of jealousy and envy situations. Already at this point we have evidence against the 'strong' prediction regarding conceptual representation of emotion terms in Russian and English. All groups of subjects reliably distinguished between envy and jealousy situations.

The only triad where the difference between subject groups was found was the EJB triad where all three kinds of situations were combined – envy, jealousy, and controls. Monolingual Russian speakers were less likely to pick envy and jealousy situations from this triad than any other group of subjects (F(3, 62) = 4.26, $p < 0.01$). They did it only 21% of the time. In fact, the most common response that monolingual Russian speakers gave when presented with an EJB triad was that all situations looked very different to them and they could not pick any two that go together. They gave this response about 50% of the time. In contrast, bilinguals tested in Russian, bilinguals tested in English, and English monolinguals picked envy and jealousy situations from the EJB triad 59%, 50%, and 52% of the time, respectively (these groups did not differ reliably from each other).

Overall, we can conclude from the triad sorting task that all groups of subjects were able to distinguish between envy and jealousy situations, and did so to similar degrees. This shows remarkable convergence, and suggests that linguistic differences documented in Experiment 1 do not lead English speakers to conflate envy and jealousy situations.

However, monolingual English speakers and bilinguals were more likely than monolingual Russian speakers to group envy and jealousy situations together. This finding corresponds to the linguistic difference found in Experiment 1 – that English speakers use the word *jealous* to refer to both envy and jealousy situations and Russian speakers do not. Perceiving greater similarity among envy and jealousy situations may be a cognitive consequence of that linguistic difference. Interestingly, bilinguals – regardless of whether they were tested in English or Russian – responded very much like English speakers on the EJB triads. Most strikingly, Russian–English bilinguals tested in Russian performed differently from Russian monolinguals. The only factor that can explain this difference is exposure to English – both groups were native Russian speakers tested in Russian. It may be that bilinguals' familiarity with the English way of labeling the emotions of jealousy and envy highlighted the similarity between them, thus altering bilinguals' conceptual representation of these emotions.

Free sorting task

Three kinds of analysis were performed on the data collected in the free sorting task. The first analysis was designed to examine overall agreement between subject groups in how they sorted envy, jealousy, and control situations. A procedure well-suited to address this question is the Cultural Consensus Model (Romney *et al.*, 1986). To perform this analysis, we scored each participant on each possible pair of situations (there were a total of 81 possible pairs). Each pair was coded as 1 if the situations were sorted into the same group and 0 if they were not. The resulting matrix consisted of subjects (the horizontal axis) × pairs of situations (the vertical axis). It was subjected to the principal component factor analysis. Using this procedure, consensus is indicated if:

(1)   The first factor eigenvalue is much greater than subsequent eigenvalues;
(2)   The first factor accounts for much more variance than the following factors;
(3)   All subjects load positively on the first factor.

All these criteria were met by the results of the analysis:

(1)   The first eigenvalue was 22.41, which is greater than subsequent eigenvalues 3.28, 2.68, 2.05;
(2)   The first factor accounted for 34% of the variance with subsequent factors accounting only for 5%, 2.68%, and 2.05%;
(3)   All subjects loaded positively on the first factor.

There was no difference between subject groups in the amount of agreement with the first factor, $F(3, 62) = 1.327$, $p = 0.274$. We can conclude from this analysis that a strong consensus exists among all participant groups in how they sorted envy, jealousy, and control situations.

The second analysis was an attempt to follow up the findings of the triad sorting task, suggesting that English speakers and bilinguals perceived envy and jealousy situations as more similar than Russian bilinguals. If so, those exposed to English might be more likely to form groups in the free-sorting task that mix envy and jealousy situations than Russian monolinguals. The groups formed by each subject were analyzed by calculating a proportion of mixed jealousy/envy groups out of all groups formed by each subject. Any group that had one or more situations of each kind was considered a mixed jealousy/envy group. Overall, the number of such groups was low. On average, 19% of all groups formed by Russian monolinguals, 18% by English monolinguals, 15% by bilinguals tested in Russian, and 22% by bilinguals tested in English were mixed. There was no difference between the groups $(F(3, 62) = 0.294, p = 0.83)$. In spite of the linguistic difference seen in

Experiment 1, groups did not differ in the frequency of combining envy and jealousy situations in a free-sorting task.

In the third analysis we looked at the groups formed by subjects with two specific questions in mind:

(1) Do Russian and English speakers differ in how many separate envy and jealousy groups they formed in their sorting?
(2) Do Russian and English speakers differ in how they assigned labels to groups they had formed?

To examine this, groups formed by each subject were coded in the following way: the group was labeled 'Envy group' if more than half the situations in it were envy situations; the group was labeled 'Jealousy group' if more than half the situations in it were jealousy situations. Groups made of control situations and groups made of only one situation were excluded from the analysis. Of interest is the number of each kind of group, and the way in which the group was labeled. The results of this coding procedure are presented in Table 8.3 along with the number of groups that were called jealousy and/or envy.

Two results of this analysis are of note. First, in line with the consensus analysis reported above, subject groups did not differ on the number of envy and jealousy groups formed (see Table 8.3). This was confirmed by a 2 (Situation Group: Envy, Jealousy) × 4 (Participant Group)

Table 8.3 Groups and their labels in a free sorting task

	Called 'jealousy'	Called 'envy'	Called 'jealousy and envy'
English monolinguals			
36 'jealousy groups'	11 (31%)	0	1 (3%)
28 'envy groups'	10 (36%)	4 (14%)	2 (6%)
Russian monolinguals			
32 'jealousy groups'	17 (53%)	0	0
25 'envy groups'	0	7 (28%)	0
Bilinguals tested in English			
20 'jealousy groups'	7 (35%)	0	0
12 'envy groups'	0	1 (8%)	0
Bilinguals tested in Russian			
18 'jealousy groups'	9 (50%)	0	0
14 'envy groups'	0	8 (57%)	0

Chi-square analysis ($\chi^2(3) = 0.93$, $p = 0.82$). Secondly, despite the strong agreement in how situations were sorted into groups, there were striking differences in how these groups were labeled (see Table 8.3). English speakers assigned the term *jealousy* to jealousy groups 31% of the time, but also used the term to describe envy groups 36% of the time. This fits with the results from Experiment 1, suggesting that English monolinguals apply *jealous* to both jealousy and envy situations. Moreover, English monolinguals applied both *envy* and *jealousy* to a single group on three occasions. In striking contrast, native Russian speakers, whether mono- or bilingual, never described an envy group using the terms *jealous/revnuet*, nor did members of these groups ever use both words for a single group. Even bilinguals who were tested in English labeled the groups in a way that was consistent with their native language, and not the language in which they were tested. This is slightly at odds with the results from Experiment 1, in which bilinguals tested in English responded very similarly to English speakers.

In sum, the results of Experiment 2 provide little evidence for crosslinguistic differences in conceptualization of envy and jealousy. Few conceptual differences emerged; participants were remarkably similar in their patterns of grouping situations both in triads and in a free-sorting task. This outcome is very similar to the one reported by Romney *et al.* (1997), who found that 66% of the total semantic structure of Japanese and English emotion terms came from a common model shared by both English and Japanese speakers. Only 6% of that structure was due to Japanese and English culture-specific models. Despite the overwhelming conceptual universality that emerged from the 'global picture' in our study, there was, however, evidence for a very specific effect of language on conceptual structure. Participants who had learned English either as a first or second language saw envy and jealousy situations as more similar than participants who had never learned English. Finally, justifications for free-sort grouping clearly distinguished native English speakers from native Russian speakers. Thus, in contrast to Experiment 1, performance on the conceptual tasks in Experiment 2 reveals an influence of exposure to English, and also an influence of being a native speaker of Russian, but little effect of language being spoken at the moment.

General Discussion

The goal of this study was to investigate the possibility of cross-linguistic differences in conceptual representation of emotion terms, and to test bilinguals as well as monolinguals to help pinpoint the source of any differences. We sought first to document systematic differences in ways in which Russian and English speakers map the terms *revnuet/zaviduet* and *jealous/envious* onto situations designed to evoke emotions of envy or jealousy. Experiment 1 revealed a clear linguistic difference. Russian monolinguals preferentially applied *revnuet* to jealousy situations and *zaviduet* to envy situations. In contrast, English monolinguals were equally likely to apply *jealous* or *envious* to envy stories, although they applied *jealous* preferentially to jealousy situations. In sum, Russian monolinguals mapped their terms onto emotions in a mutually exclusive way, whereas English speakers used their terms interchangeably, at least for envy stories.

In Experiment 2 we looked for non-linguistic conceptual correlates of this linguistic difference, predicting that Russian speakers should make clearer conceptual distinctions between envy and jealousy situations than English speakers. Two general findings emerged. First, we were largely unable to find conceptual differences corresponding to the linguistic differences from Experiment 1. When asked to perform a free-sorting of situations designed to elicit emotions of envy, jealousy, or simply negative emotions, we found a remarkable consensus in responses. Not only was there a clear consensus statistically, but contrary to predictions based on performance on the linguistic task, English speakers were no more likely than Russian speakers to group envy and jealousy situations together. Likewise, on the triad oddity task, no differences were observed in the tendency to differentiate envy situations from jealousy situations. Thus, the bulk of evidence suggests few conceptual differences despite clear linguistic differences.

We did, however, obtain one finding pointing toward differences on the conceptual level of representation. In mixed triads, English monolinguals and both bilingual groups were more likely to group envy and jealousy situations together than were Russian monolinguals. This effect illustrates the value of testing bilinguals as well as monolinguals. Had we tested only monolinguals, the interpretation of this effect would necessarily remain ambiguous; the linguistic difference might have caused the conceptual difference, but it is equally plausible that a cognitive difference, due to any of a myriad of cultural factors, might have caused the linguistic difference. However, examining responses from bilinguals allows us to begin to answer questions about causal direction. Regardless of the native language or the language being spoken at the moment, all and only fluent speakers of English perceived envy and jealousy situations as similar in the triad task. This suggests that the process of becoming fluent in English may have had the conceptual consequence of highlighting similarities between envy and jealousy that might not otherwise be salient.

While the finding just discussed suggests only a small influence of language on conceptual structure, a number of other results suggest the influence of one language on the use of another. These results necessarily focus on the bilingual populations. First, consider performance on

Experiment 1. For the most part, bilinguals performed in a way that was consistent with the language in which they were tested. Bilinguals tested in Russian made the Russian distinction in labeling jealousy and envy stories, whereas bilinguals tested in English made no distinction for envy stories, just like native English speakers. However, analysis of difference scores revealed greater differentiation between *revnuet* and *zaviduet* in envy stories for Russian monolinguals than for bilinguals tested in Russian. Thus, bilinguals tested in their native language are affected by the knowledge of their second language: Advanced knowledge of English may have influenced their use of *revnuet* and *zaviduet*. Otherwise, performance in Experiment 1 was completely consistent with the language being spoken.

In contrast, Experiment 2 reveals evidence for the effects of native language on how participants labeled the groups they formed. Specifically, despite forming comparable proportions of envy, jealousy, and mixed groups, English monolinguals were equally likely to label envy groups and jealousy groups with the term *jealousy*, but Russian monolinguals and both groups of bilinguals never used the word *revnost'* or *jealousy* to label envy groups. In this respect, all native speakers of Russian were similar, and contrasted with native speakers of English. For bilinguals tested in English, this seems to contrast with their willingness to apply the term *jealous* to envy stories in Experiment 1.

These results allow us to begin to paint a picture of the interaction between semantic and conceptual levels of representation in the domain of emotion terms. First, we found few conceptual differences between speakers of English and Russian; how one categorizes emotional situations appears to be largely independent of how emotional terms map onto those situations in one's language. However, becoming fluent in a language that shows a different mapping of labels onto emotions seems to have both the conceptual effect of increasing the perceived similarity between emotions, and the linguistic effect of influencing how labels are mapped onto situations in one's native language. Moreover, by examining bilingual as well as monolingual speakers, we were able to transcend correlations between language and thought and begin to understand more complex underlying relations. In sum, we have shown that despite clear linguistic differences in how emotion terms map onto situations, speakers of English and Russian for the most part share an underlying conceptual organization of those situations, but also that language can have local effects on that organization.

On a more general level, besides highlighting the benefits of using bilinguals for cross-linguistic research, our results suggest that a lot can be learned from examining specific cases where languages differ in how words map onto concepts. Identifying such cases and using them for investigating the relationship between linguistic and conceptual representations of emotions, as well as other domains of experience, offers exciting opportunities for further research.

Acknowledgements

We would like to thank members of the Categorization and Reasoning Lab and Fei Xu for helpful comments and discussions of this research; Anna Britaeva, Marina Vaks, and Jim Akula for their help in data collection; and Natasha Zabeida for translating experimental materials. We also thank the staff of the American Center, Moscow, for their assistance and all Russian speakers and bilinguals who participated in this study.

Note

1. A different version of this paper appeared previously in the *Journal of Cognition and Culture* (2002), 2(4), 235–62.

References

Parrott, W. and Smith, R. (1993) Distinguishing the experiences of envy and jealousy. *Journal of Personality and Social Psychology* 64(6), 906–20.

Romney, A., Moore, C. and Rusch, C. (1997) Cultural universals: Measuring the semantic structure of emotion terms in English and Japanese. *The National Academy of Sciences of the USA* 94, 5489–94.

Romney, A., Weller, S. and Batchelder, W. (1986) Culture as consensus: A theory of culture and informant accuracy. *American Anthropologist* 88, 313–38.

Russell, J.A. (1991) Culture and the categorization of emotions. *Psychological Bulletin* 110(3), 426–50.

Salovey, P. and Rodin, J. (1986) The differentiation of social-comparison jealousy and romantic jealousy. *Journal of Personality and Social Psychology* 50(6), 1100–12.

Appendix A

Jealousy stories

Anthony and Julia have known each other since they first met in 8th grade. Now they are grownups and their friendship has developed into a romantic relationship. Anthony appreciates the mutual trust in their relationship, but the events of the last week made him doubt Julia's faithfulness. A few days ago when he called her late at night, a male voice he has never heard before answered the phone, and yesterday Anthony saw Julia at a café engaged in a conversation with an attractive man.

Marina and Andrew have been friends ever since they first met in 10th grade. Many years have passed and their friendship developed into a romantic relationship. Marina is very committed to Andrew, but she's beginning to doubt whether he feels the same way. She was unpleasantly surprised a few days ago when she saw Andrew not only dancing but also flirting with one of her friends at a party, and yesterday Andrew mentioned that he is going away for a weekend to visit his former girlfriend.

Envy stories

Boris and Natasha are a married couple. They are very happy together and want to have a big family with a lot of kids. However, they found out that they'll never be able to have their own children. The only option they have is adoption that is a long and complicated process. Last weekend they went to visit their friends whom they've known since they were college students. These friends of Boris and Natasha's just had their second baby who is incredibly beautiful and looks a lot like her parents.

Paul and Max are friends. They are college seniors and they both dream of working for the same company – IBM. Having done equally well on their interviews, they were both offered three-month internships. After their internship was over Paul and Max applied for the same job at IBM. However, despite them both being equally well qualified, Max got the job and Paul did not.

Anna and Maria are friends. It's their last year of training in a theater/acting college and they both dream of playing Ophelia in their favorite play 'Hamlet'. Unexpectedly, they get a chance to audition for this role in a theater. Anna and Maria's instructors think that both women are very talented and are equally fit to play this role. However, after the audition the role was offered to Maria, and not Anna.

Appendix B

Антон и Юлия знают друг друга с 8-ого класса, где они и познакомились. Сейчас они взрослые и их дружба переросла в романтические отношения. Антон ценит взаимное доверие, установившееся в их отношениях, но события последней недели заставили его усомниться в верности Юлии. Несколько дней назад, когда Антон позвонил ей домой поздно вечером, ему ответил незнакомый мужской голос, а вчера он случайно увидел Юлию в кафе, сидящую за столиком с привлекательным мужчиной и увлеченную разговором с ним.

Марина и Андрей были друзьями с тех пор, как они познакомились в 10-ом классе. Прошло много лет и их дружба переросла в романтические отношения. Марина очень привязана к Андрею, но она начала сомневаться в том, что Андрей испытывает сходные чувства. Несколько дней назад она была неприятно удивлена, увидев как Андрей не только танцевал, но и заигрывал с одной из ее подруг на вечеринке у друзей, а вчера Андрей упомянул, что уезжает на выходные навестить свою бывшую девушку.

Борис и Наталия женаты. Они очень счастливы и хотят иметь большую семью и много детей. Однако они узнали, что никогда не смогут иметь своих собственных детей. Их единственный выход – усыновление – долгий и сложный процесс. На прошлые выходные они ездили в гости к друзьям, которых они знают со студенческих времен. У этих друзей только что родился второй ребенок – невероятно красивая девочка, очень похожая на ее родителей.

Павел и Максим – друзья. Они учатся на последнем курсе и оба мечтают работать на одну компанию – IBM. После того, как они одинаково успешно прошли собеседование, им обоим предложили трехмесячную практику в этой компании. По окончании практики оба Павел и Максим подали документы на одну и ту же открывшуюся вакансию в IBM. Однако, несмотря на то, что они были одинаково квалифицированы, работу получил Максим, а не Павел.

Анна и Мария – подруги. Они учатся на последнем курсе театрального училища и обе мечтают сыграть Офелию в их любимой пьесе "Гамлет". Неожиданно у них появляется возможность участвовать в прослушивании на эту роль в театре. Преподаватели Анны и Марии считают, что обе девушки очень талантливы и одинаково подходят на эту роль. Однако, после прослушивания роль предложили только Марии, а не Анне.

Appendix C

Envy situations

Your boyfriend has a better job than you.
Your boyfriend is more attractive than you.
Your boyfriend appears to have everything.
Your boyfriend buys something you wanted but could not afford.
Your boyfriend is more intelligent than you.
Your boyfriend is more talented than you.
You have to work while your boyfriend is out partying.
Your boyfriend gets a job that you want.
Your boyfriend has a more impressive resume than yours.

Jealousy situations

You phone your boyfriend and a voice you haven't heard before answers.
Your steady date has lunch with an attractive opposite sex person.
Your date dances with someone else at a dance.

Someone is flirting with your date.
Your boyfriend wants to see other people.
Your boyfriend visits the person he used to go out with.
You find out your lover is having an affair.
Your boyfriend goes on a long trip without you.
Your boyfriend breaks up with you.

Control situations

Somebody is gossiping about your boyfriend.
Your boyfriend lost in a competition.
You are late for a date with your boyfriend.
A party you were going to with your boyfriend was cancelled.
Your computer crashed and you lost all of your boyfriend's documents.
Your boyfriend lost your dog.
Your boyfriend got a really bad haircut.
Your boyfriend is very sick.
Your boyfriend crashed your car.

Appendix D

У вашего парня работа лучше, чем у вас.
Ваш парень более привлекательный, чем вы.
Кажется, что у вашего парня есть абсолютно все.
Ваш парень покупает то, что вы хотите, но не можете себе
     позволить.
Ваш парень умнее, чем вы.
Ваш парень талантливее, чем вы.
Вам приходится работать в то время, как ваш парень веселится на
     вечеринке.
Ваш парень получает работу, которую хотите вы.
У вашего парня более впечатляющее резюме, чем у вас.

Вы звоните своему парню и вам отвечает незнакомый голос.
Ваш парень обедает с привлекательным представителем
     противоположного пола.
Ваш парень танцует не с вами на дискотеке.
Кто-то заигрывает с вашим парнем.
Ваш парень желает встречаться с другими девушками.
Ваш парень идет в гости к девушке, с которой он встречался раньше.
Вы узнаете, что у вашего парня роман с кем-то другим.
Ваш парень уезжает надолго без вас.
Ваш парень бросает вас.

Кто-то сплетничает о вашем парне.
Ваш парень проиграл на соревновании.

Вы опаздываете на свидание с вашим парнем.

Вечеринка, на которую вы собирались с вашим парнем, отменена.

Ваш компьютер сломался и вы потеряли документы вашего парня.

Ваш парень потерял вашу собаку.

Вашего парня очень плохо подстригли.

Ваш парень очень болен.

Ваш парень разбил вашу машину.

Chapter 9

Cognitive Approaches to the Study of Emotion-Laden and Emotion Words in Monolingual and Bilingual Memory

JEANETTE ALTARRIBA

Introduction

Cognitive theorists interested in language representation and processing have capitalized on several techniques aimed at understanding the structure and function of human memory. These techniques involving word representation have included ratings, recall, recognition paradigms, and priming techniques. Recently, all of these techniques have been applied to the study of emotion words (e.g. joy, happy, sad) and emotion-laden words (e.g. kiss, death) in both monolingual and bilingual speakers (see e.g. Altarriba, 2003; Altarriba & Bauer, 2004; Altarriba & Canary, 2004; Altarriba *et al.*, 1999). The purpose of this chapter is to review novel applications of cognitive methodologies to the study of the representation of words expressing emotion in both English monolingual and Spanish–English bilingual speakers. This work offers new directions for the study of mental processes involved in the encoding, storage, and retrieval of this particular class of words and important modifications for psycholinguistic and memory models that have been proposed to explain language processing in general.

The study of the representation and expression of emotion is critical to further the understanding of the mental processes that lead to good health and well-being (see e.g. Altarriba & Morier, 2004; Goleman, 1995). The idea that emotions are often labeled with words such as 'happy', 'sad', 'scared', and the like, indicates that psycholinguistic properties operate as a vehicle through which the feelings that are elicited by emotions are expressed, categorized, stored, and catalogued. Even though the use of words to label emotions is as old as language itself, it is only recently that this mode of expression has been investigated within a cognitive framework. The field of cognitive psychology had its inception with

Tolman's (1948) 'Cognitive maps in rats and men' and Chomsky's (1957) *Syntactic Structures*. It was not until much later, however, that the investigation of emotion word memory would occur with the use of experimental techniques that tap the automatic processing of emotion-based knowledge in humans. The primary aims of this chapter are to introduce readers to the cognitive methodology that has been used for several decades to investigate lexical representations and to discuss recent developments in the study of emotion words from a cognitive perspective.

In terms of bilingualism and emotion, the study of emotions, especially as expressed through the use of words, has been a highly neglected area of investigation – at least from an empirical standpoint. In many ways, this void in the literature is similar to that in the monolingual literature from a cognitive, experimental perspective. Most of the research can be found either within studies of individual differences in clinical populations (i.e. individuals with phobias or those with alexythimia) or in social explorations of attitudes and the automatic evaluation of stimuli (e.g. Chen & Bargh, 1999; Goleman, 1995). Overall, there is a dearth of research focusing on the words that either label emotion (e.g. love, joy) or are related to emotion in some way (e.g. death, coffin). Given that these words form part of one's lexicon (or lexicons, in the case of a bilingual), it seems important to ask the questions of how these words are acquired, how they are stored in memory, and how they are later retrieved or possibly forgotten. Moreover, knowing how these words are represented in memory can inform basic models of word representation and lexical access, helping to generate testable research hypotheses. Given that, anecdotally, individuals seem to recall personal events that are more emotional in nature more readily than those that are not (see e.g. Christianson & Lindholm, 1998), it would seem that emotion as a construct is closely tied to the formation of memories – some of which are richly coded and durable. It would therefore seem important to investigate the characteristics of these word types and delimit the factors that contribute to their durability in human memory.

The current chapter will address three basic questions:

(1) How are emotion-related words characterized in monolingual and bilingual memory?
(2) What is the organizational format for the representation of these words in memory?
(3) How are these representations influenced by valence and arousal components?

Each of these issues will be explored following a cognitive science approach detailing data regarding emotion word processing and representation, first from a monolingual perspective and then from a bilingual perspective, within each section. These questions range from more general to more specific and represent a program of current and future research that maximizes the basic tools and paradigms that the cognitive psychologist would use to approach the field of *emotion word memory*.

Characteristics of Emotion Words

The monolingual case

One approach that has been used to understand the representational nature of the mental lexicon (one's mental 'dictionary' of words) is to try to uncover the features that characterize different types of words. Researchers have typically examined words on a continuum that ranges from concrete to abstract ('table'–'liberty'; e.g. Bleasdale, 1987; Schwanenflugel *et al.*, 1988). So-called *concreteness effects* indicate that concrete words are often better recalled, more easily recognized, and easier to imagine and to contextualize than abstract words. It is presumed that this advantage for concrete words emerges from the duality of their coding – they have both a verbal and a pictorial referent (Paivio, 1971, 1986). That is, concrete words possess several featural advantages that lead to better memorability than abstract words. Having the added advantage of an image indicates more routes by which the concrete word can be stored and retrieved, as an image can provide a cue for the processing of these words.

In addition to their pictureable quality, concrete words might also benefit from the ease with which a context might be retrieved that is highly associated to these words. The notion of *context availability* dictates that concrete words might show enhanced memory because these words lead more easily to specific contexts or circumstances in which they can appear or have been experienced (Kieras, 1978; Schwanenflugel *et al.*, 1992; Schwanenflugel *et al.*, 1988). It might be easier, for example, to think of a context for the word 'computer', but more difficult to think of a context for the word 'mastery'. Thus, concrete words might elicit a greater number of contexts in which they occur and they might therefore activate various related concepts in memory. When a context in which a word may fit is encountered, that context might serve as a retrieval cue to assist in remembering that particular word. Tasks that involve the recall of words from memory, or the recognition of previously presented words on a list, might benefit from the idea that these words can be easily cued depending upon the context that surrounds these words in that specific test situation.

In summary, it appears that the idea that concrete words are multiply represented by both verbal labels and images, and that they might easily be cued by retrieval contexts, indicates that they may often outperform abstract words on a variety of memory tasks. Where do emotion words come in? According to Altarriba and Bauer (2004), words whose meanings are affective and have pleasantness and unpleasantness, as well as arousal, components are classified as *emotion words*. Although researchers may vary on how to define them, most researchers would agree that emotion words carry some level of arousal (i.e. low, moderate, or high), as well as valence (i.e. positive, negative, or neutral; see Altarriba & Bauer, 2004, for further references regarding the definitions of these word types).

Throughout the discussions of the representation of concrete and abstract words in research involving monolingual speakers, investigators have examined these words in terms of their meaningfulness (Paivio *et al.*, 1968), their emotionality and pronounceability (Rubin & Friendly, 1986), and their pleasantness and familiarity (Toglia & Battig, 1978). However, none of these or similar works has compared concrete, abstract, and emotion words within the same study. In many cases, an examination of the abstract words that have been used indicates that emotion words are included within the abstract category as a single group of items. In order to create a framework from which to investigate emotion words and how they are represented in isolation as well as across a variety of contexts, it is important to understand and delimit the *mental properties* that characterize them.

Using the above concern as a starting point, Altarriba *et al.* (1999) set out to uncover the characteristics that differentiate concrete, abstract, and emotion words from each other. A specific aim was to understand how abstract words are represented distinctly from emotion words in terms of their concreteness, imageability, and context availability. In their first experiment, Altarriba *et al.* examined word ratings for concrete, abstract, and emotion words in English on three specific word dimensions: concreteness, imageability, and context availability.

Altarriba *et al.* (1999) created a list of 326 English words. Of these, 155 were abstract words, 100 were concrete words, and 71 were emotion words. Concrete words denoted actual objects, whereas abstract words included terms that did not refer to objects and did not contain a material basis. Also, the list of abstract words did not contain any emotion-related terms. Finally, emotion words were those that had previously been defined as having an affective meaning and containing various degrees of arousal and pleasantness. In addition, they represented both negative and positive valence. The authors noted that these words had been selected from pre-established norms for these word types – norms such as 'The Dictionary of Affect in Language' by Whissell (1989) and others (see Altarriba *et al.*, 1999, for a complete listing). All three sets of words were randomized and typed into a single list. Each of the 78 English-speaking monolingual participants rated all of the words on a single dimension, using a seven-point scale (Figure 9.1). High values indicated that the words were viewed as more concrete, easier to imagine, or

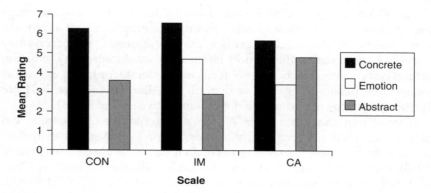

Figure 9.1 Mean ratings for emotion, concrete, and abstract words on the dimensions of concreteness (CON), imageability (IM), and context availability (CA) (seven-point scale: 1 = low; 7 = high). Adapted from Altarriba *et al.* (1999)

easier to fit into a context. Each of the rating scales that was devised for each of the three dimensions included specific instructions and examples to guide the rating of the words. The use of rating tasks in this field of study is quite common. Ratings are accepted as an indication of the relative amount of a given dimension or component that a word possesses when it is first brought to mind. Raters are typically asked to respond quickly with the first response that comes to mind. Although some have argued that ratings may be biased on a variety of dimensions due to their somewhat subjective nature, researchers have adopted this type of task in the basic field of word representation.

The results of this rating task can be viewed in Figure 9.1. In general, the findings indicated that each of the three word types were rated differently within each of the three scale types (all p-values <0.05). That is, all three word groups were distinguishable on all of the attributes that were under investigation. Specifically, emotion words were rated as being less concrete and lower in context availability than either abstract or concrete words. However, emotion words were rated as more imageable than abstract words. It is possible that because emotions are often tied to facial expressions or facial representations, these instances actually provided images that aided in the rating process for these words on an imageability scale. Additionally, emotion words may be more imageable because they relate to typical situations or scripts in which the emotions themselves are experienced. It was also found that emotion word ratings on the concreteness scale were highly correlated to ratings for these same words on the context availability scale. Emotion words that

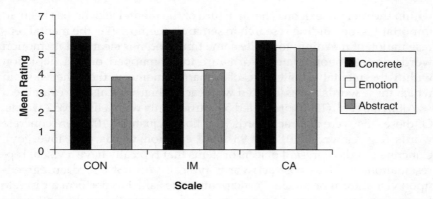

Figure 9.2 Mean ratings for concrete, emotion, and abstract words as a function of rating scale (CON = concreteness; IM = imageability; CA = context availability; seven-point scale: 1 = low; 7 = high). Adapted from Altarriba (2003)

rate highly on concreteness also rate highly on context availability – a result that had previously only been reported for concrete words (Schwanenflugel *et al.*, 1988). Cronbach's alpha was used as a measure of internal consistency for the ratings produced in the Altarriba *et al.* (1999) study, and the values for this measure were quite high for all word types on each of the scales of interest.

These results indicated that abstract, concrete, and emotion words possess significantly different degrees of the three word characteristics examined here (i.e. concreteness, imageability, and context availability) and therefore should likely be treated as *separate* word types. Of specific importance was the finding that emotion words were found to be represented by distinct characteristics as compared to both concrete and abstract words. These findings also indicate that various cognitive effects involving abstract words might have been masked or attenuated by the inclusion of emotion words within stimulus lists. Clearly, these classes of words behave differently in tasks that are touted to reflect differences in the mental representation of these words. The existence of these word type differences should be kept in mind when both designing and analyzing studies that involve the combinations of different word classes.

In a second experiment, Altarriba *et al.* (1999) investigated the nature of word associations that are made to concrete, abstract, and emotion words. The use of word associations and norms based on word associations is important to the field of psychology as a whole (Hunt & Ellis, 2004). The idea that one word elicits another specific word as a response has been taken to imply that these two words are stored close together within the mental lexicon. The structure of the mental lexicon has been an important issue guiding research in semantic memory (i.e. the mental representation of meaning) for quite some time, and it is clear that if emotion words and emotion-related words are to be mapped onto a depiction within the mental architecture of semantic memory, then the ways in which these words are associated with each other must also be examined.

Altarriba *et al.* (1999) presented 55 participants with a list of 352 words. Of these, 154 were abstract words (e.g. liberty, justice), 100 were concrete words (e.g. clown, ball), and 98 were emotion words (e.g. love, joy). Concrete words represent objects or items that typically have a visual representation, whereas abstract words typically do not afford an agreed-upon visual form or image. Participants were asked to perform a discrete association task in which they were asked to write down the first word that came to mind when they thought of a given target word. Specifically, the instructions read: '. . . please write down the FIRST word that comes to mind that is MEANINGFULLY related to the presented word'. In this type of task, individuals write down a single word. Other types of association tasks, namely, those that are continuous, may call for participants to write down as many words as they can think of. However, this latter procedure often produces a 'chaining effect', wherein participants write down associates to the previously written word rather than to the original target word. To avoid this type of response, the current authors sought only the most 'automatic' of responses – the first one that came to mind.

The results were interesting and provocative. Emotion words produced the greatest number of different associates, followed by abstract words, and then concrete words. It appears that emotion words are linked to many more distinct concepts than either of the other two word types. Emotion words produced an average of 23 different associates, followed by 21 for abstract words, and 17 for concrete words. (If we conditionalized the number of associates as a function of number of words rated, we would also find that proportionally, emotion words produced a larger proportion of different associates as compared to the other two word types.) According to work by Anderson (1974), this finding would indicate that it may be more difficult to retrieve a specific emotion word from memory when cued or prompted with a related word, as each emotion word is associated to a variety of different words. As a single cue is activated in memory, that activation spreads across the various paths that connect that cue to related emotion words, making it difficult to access any single associated word. Therefore, these results would indicate that the retrieval of any one specific emotion word in memory, as a response to a word cue, might be more difficult than retrieving a specific concrete word given a related word cue. Reaction time studies related to the mental architecture of emotions in bilingual speakers confirm this possibility and are reviewed, in turn, below.

The bilingual case

How are emotion words represented within the bilingual lexicon? The aforementioned work indicated that monolingual English speakers differentiate between concrete, emotion, and abstract words within their mental lexicons. This specification occurs on the basis of components such as concreteness, imageability, and context availability. While English was the only language known to participants, a question that can be raised is how the findings reported above relate to the representation of these same word types for multilingual speakers – specifically, Spanish–English bilinguals. Altarriba (2003) used the above approach to examine the status of Spanish emotion word memory in Spanish–English bilinguals. This work was also motivated by the observation that emotion words, unlike say, concrete words, might be represented in a unique language-specific mode within a given language.

Take, for example, the Spanish word *cariño*. This word can be described as a cross between 'liking' and 'affection', with a dash of a familial or relational quality. For example, one might use this word in a context such as '*Le tengo cariño a mis estudiantes*'. Loosely translated, this sentence expresses a kind of 'liking' for my students, yet it is not the same as liking a particular color, for example, or a particular type of car. At the same time, the sentence does not denote 'love' for my students either. Rather, I have some affection for them that stems from a kind of liking that is not related to 'love' in the way 'affection' may be in English. Most Spanish speakers would agree that this word has no single translation equivalent in English that would capture its connotative and denotative features (Heredia & Altarriba, 2001). Only a subgroup of features that would define these words overlaps across languages, whereas each of these words carries its own unique features that are derived in part from the language itself and in part from the culture (Kitayama & Markus, 1994). Could similar emotion words in Spanish behave differently than their supposed counterparts in English in terms of their concreteness, imageability, and context availability? Altarriba (2003) set out to determine how emotion, concrete, and abstract words were represented in the native language of a bilingual population.

Theoretically, researchers have suggested that emotion words might be more deeply coded in the native or dominant language than in a second language (Altarriba, 2000; Altarriba & Santiago-Rivera, 1994; Bond & Lai, 1986; Gonzalez-Reigosa, 1976; Santiago-Rivera & Altarriba, 2002). Emotion words are often reported as having a broader range of emotional qualities and eliciting a more diverse set of associates when accessed and retrieved in the native language. It has been argued that this finding arises due to the fact that emotion words, when first learned, are learned in the native language and are attached to a variety of contexts and situations.

These varied contexts appear to create stronger, more durable mental traces for these words in memory, as compared to the acquisition of their counterparts in a second or even third language. Thus, encountering a word in a second language may not activate as many different situations or contexts or indeed feelings of emotion as activating its presumed associates in a different language. Concrete words (e.g. chair), on the other hand, may be linked to far fewer situations or contexts and to much less intensity in terms of the activation of accompanying physiological reactions.

Altarriba (2003) gathered ratings of Spanish words representing emotion, concrete, and abstract word types from a group of fluent Spanish–English bilinguals. In the same vein as in Altarriba *et al.* (1999), 63 participants were presented with a list of 98 concrete words, 61 emotion words, and 156 abstract words. The scales used by Altarriba *et al.* (1999) were translated into Spanish, and each participant rated all 315 words on a single scale. Again, higher ratings on the concreteness, imageability, and context availability scales indicated the presence of a higher level of each of these three attributes in memory. Instructions were presented in Spanish by experimenters who were Spanish–English bilinguals. These bilingual participants rated themselves highly on their ability to read and comprehend written English and written Spanish and, in general, they appeared to be balanced in their ability to comprehend spoken English and spoken Spanish. These attributes were measured through the use of a Language History Questionnaire administered to each participant upon completion of the study as well as by actual interviews conducted by the experimenter.

The mean ratings produced by participants in this investigation are presented in Figure 9.2. All three scales produced ratings that were significantly different from each other within each of the word types. That is, as in the monolingual case reported by Altarriba *et al.* (1999), these word types in Spanish possessed different degrees of concreteness, imageability, and context availability. Specifically, while emotion words had low mean ratings on the concreteness scale (M = 3.3), these same words produced relatively high scores on the context availability scale (M = 5.3). In fact, unlike the previous English data, the current data revealed that context availability scores were identical for both emotion and abstract words. In other words, the context availability for emotion words in Spanish rose to the level of their abstract competitors. Likewise, imageability ratings were almost identical for emotion and abstract Spanish words. In all other respects, the data for the three word types replicated those reported by Altarriba *et al.* (1999) for English words. For emotion words in Spanish, therefore, it seems that an increased ability to think of a context for emotion words also indicates an increased ability to provide an image that represents those words.

Quite possibly, then, Spanish words that label emotions carry with them a higher level of context availability, indicating that they are associated to a greater number of contexts that can be more easily accessed than those of their English counterparts, as reported by Altarriba *et al.* (1999). These results imply that, at least for emotion words, there may be ways in which the Spanish language as the native language contributes to specific effects that are moderated by contextual influences during acquisition.

Summary

Taken together, the results of Altarriba *et al.* (1999) and those of Altarriba (2003) indicate that words that label emotion are distinguishable from abstract and concrete words as evidenced by word ratings and word association tasks. The results reported in English were later replicated by Altarriba and Bauer (2004; Experiment 2), further emphasizing the separateness of the three word classes under investigation. Their characteristics in Spanish differ from those in English as well, specifically in terms of context availability and imagery. These findings indicate that emotion words in general might contain components that are language specific and that language or 'language tags' (Altarriba & Soltano, 1996) might be coded in memory along with other attributes when encoding emotion word information. Of course, future research should explore these effects across a multitude of languages – both alphabetic and non-alphabetic – and should likely include all language conditions for a given set of participants. For example, in Altarriba's (2003) work, participants responded to words that appeared in Spanish. Presenting words in both languages to participants in a counterbalanced manner would likely provide a more powerful measure of the relative differences across languages for various word types.

Work such as that described in the current chapter has many implications for situations in which bilingual speakers are asked to consult their memories for emotional events. That is, when individuals are interviewed in a variety of settings in a non-dominant language, and the nature of the interview is particularly emotional, it might be beneficial to also conduct the interview in the native language in order to elicit a broader range of related information (see e.g. Schrauf, 2000). The current work, therefore, has implications for the study of autobiographical memory in bilingual speakers and for the investigation of methods of retrieval of emotion-related information from memory. Further, in settings that involve the disclosure of personal, emotional events by bilingual speakers such as in the cases of mental health settings, for example, it would likewise be beneficial to use a bilingual mode of communication and to map out a strategic use of languages so as to maximize the nature and accuracy of reporting by the client (see e.g. Altarriba & Santiago-Rivera, 1994; Altarriba & Morier, 2004).

The Mental Architecture of the Emotion Word Lexicon

As mentioned earlier, one of the goals of research on emotion word representation is to uncover the structure and function of the emotion word lexicon. Cognitive researchers interested in the mental representation of semantic memory have devised a series of models from which predictions can be made and tested regarding the functioning of semantic networks in memory (see e.g. Collins & Loftus, 1975; Collins & Quillian, 1969). A model suggested by Collins and Loftus (1975), spreading activation, is one of the more widely accepted models in the study of semantic memory (Hunt & Ellis, 2004). In this model, words are connected to each other within the mental lexicon based on semantic relatedness. These interconnections occur through pathways of activation that emanate across conceptual nodes in memory. The idea is that words and the concepts they represent are stored in memory as an interconnected framework of nodes much like a neural network. These nodes are organized based on semantic association, and the model proposes that words that share a high degree of semantic overlap are stored more closely together in memory than words that are semantically distinct. Thus, the words 'cat' and 'dog' would be stored more closely to each other in an individual's semantic network than the words 'cat' and 'chalk', for example. Activation of one of the nodes, the source node, leads to the activation of all related nodes in a radial pattern. However, as the activation spreads farther and farther from the source node, it dampens, making it difficult for activation to reach nodes that are distant in the network. While this model has been broadly applied, and has been accrued to as an explanation for many cognitive phenomena, it has been applied in a very limited fashion with regard to emotion word representation. A recent study conducted by Altarriba and Bauer (2004; Experiment 3) set out to provide a first demonstration of word priming effects for emotion words that would further test the claims of the spreading activation model of semantic memory.

An effect that typically occurs when pairs of words are presented in close temporal proximity to each other for response is called *semantic priming*. Priming paradigms in general have a long history in the cognitive literature (see e.g. McNamara & Holbrook, 2003, for a review) and a more modest history in the bilingual literature (see e.g. Meyer & Ruddy, 1974). The basic paradigm works as follows. Suppose an individual is shown a word centered on a computer screen (e.g. cat) and is asked to read that word. Shortly thereafter, a second word appears on the computer screen (e.g. dog). The target word replaces the prime. The participant is then instructed to make a response to the second word, or target, and that response is typically timed. The response might include an instruction to name the word aloud or to make a lexical decision regarding the word – that is, to decide whether or not the word is a real word in a given language.

Facilitation in responding to the target word is assumed to reflect the degree of semantic overlap or semantic relatedness between the two words – the prime and the target. In other words, the typical finding is that 'cat' primes or facilitates responses to 'dog', whereas 'lamp' does not. The former pair is referred to as the related condition and the latter pair as the unrelated condition. The unrelated condition is considered the control condition with which to compute the magnitude of the semantic priming effect. To compute a semantic priming effect, one would take the reaction time (RT, typically measured in milliseconds) to 'dog' when preceded by 'lamp', and subtract from it the reaction time to 'dog' when preceded by 'cat'. This computation (i.e. unrelated mean RT − related mean RT) is a measure of the semantic priming effect. A positive value resulting from this computation would be termed 'facilitation' and a negative value would be termed 'inhibition'. Clearly, spreading activation would predict facilitation in responding to related pairs as compared to unrelated pairs based on the semantic relatedness of the former.

Priming paradigms have also been used to examine cross-language relationships. For example, imagine that a prime word like 'cat' is followed by a target word such as *perro* (the Spanish word for dog). Researchers have asked whether or not the activation of the word 'cat' would facilitate making a lexical decision to the word *perro* in, say, a Spanish–English bilingual. Presumably, if one word primes another word across languages, then these words are perhaps connected via a conceptual link, or an underlying associative pathway (see e.g. Altarriba, 1992, for a discussion of priming effects across languages). The evidence that exists to date across languages has indicated the possible existence of cross-language connections such as these, mainly from a dominant to a non-dominant language.

The evidence in the opposite direction is not as clear. A recent review of all of the priming literature to date in the cross-language domain conducted by Altarriba and Basnight-Brown (in press) indicates that many methodological issues make it difficult to conclude whether or not there is evidence of cross-language priming of the kind described here. Nevertheless, the few papers that have reported significant findings and that have followed the more stringent procedures indicate that words from one's dominant language can prime or activate related words in one's second language, and that this effect occurs automatically. However, for the present discussion, these studies do not shed light on the emotion word issues as those studies did not systematically examine wordtype or word class.

Altarriba and Bauer (2004; Experiment 3) pioneered the use of semantic priming paradigms to investigate the representation of emotion words in semantic memory. In their study, they sought to investigate the degree to which emotion words primed other emotion words and whether or not they also primed related abstract words. Their work stemmed from research on concrete and abstract words performed earlier by Bleasdale (1987). Bleasdale constructed sets of prime-target word pairs that were either matched or mismatched on the basis of concreteness. The four primary conditions within his study were concrete–concrete, abstract–abstract, concrete–abstract, and abstract–concrete. The two former pairs were referred to as homogenous pairs, whereas the latter pairs were termed heterogeneous pairs. In addition, while word type differed, all four conditions were matched on the basis of association strength. That is, it was determined that the degree to which primes elicited their respective targets in each of the conditions was equivalent across conditions. This parameter is important in investigations of semantic priming in memory, as it is thought that degree of association moderates the magnitude of the effect. Bleasdale was interested in whether or not these different prime-target pairs would produce facilitation in priming while association strength was held constant.

In Experiment 4 (Bleasdale, 1987), participants were asked to perform lexical decisions to word targets that were preceded by word primes in one of the four conditions mentioned above. Participants were to respond as quickly and as accurately as possible. Bleasdale also used a very short presentation rate for primes and followed the primes by visual masks in order to reduce the possibility of strategic processing and its possible influences on the priming effect. Priming effects are taken to reflect the automaticity of semantic access, if the proper conditions are observed in order to minimize guessing and elaborative processes on the part of participants. The results indicated that words primed each other only within homogenous conditions and not in either of the two heterogeneous conditions. Bleasdale reasoned that, given that the pairs were matched in terms of association strength and other related features, the priming effects were moderated by the use of similar lexical processes when processing primes and targets of the same word type. That is, when encountering a concrete word, certain characteristics are activated in memory and can then carry over to the recognition of a target word if it happens to be of the same type. Even though words were just as associated within the heterogeneous word pairs, the processing involved in accessing the primes did not seem to aid processing of targets of a different type. Therefore, Bleasdale concluded that there are functionally distinct lexical processes involved in the retrieval of concrete and abstract words.

Building on this work, Altarriba and Bauer (2004; Experiment 3) reasoned that the above 'test' of the specificity of the mental lexicon with regard to wordtype might be useful in the distinction between abstract and emotion word representations. They constructed word pairs in the following four conditions: abstract–abstract, emotion–emotion, emotion–abstract, and abstract–emotion. All of this work was conducted in English with 80 English-speaking monolingual participants. Again, all four conditions were matched in terms of association strength as gathered from published norms (Altarriba *et al.*, 1999). Each participant was presented with a total of 10 pairs of each kind along with a set of 40 word–non-word pairs, in random order. Non-word targets are used in tests of lexical decision so that some proportion of the time, participants respond 'non-word' when making a lexical decision. Non-words are often constructed by changing a single letter within a real word; however, they retain their pronounceability (e.g. 'blot' becomes 'blit'). Typically, participants are asked to press one of two keys on a computer keyboard or one of two buttons on a button box – one representing 'word' responses and the other, 'non-word' responses. Responses to the target words are timed. The presentation of the prime was constrained as in Bleasdale (1987) and appeared for 125 milliseconds (ms) followed by a visual mask (e.g. #####) prior to the presentation of the word target. Again, the idea is to promote responses that reflect automatic processing rather than more strategic or conscious processing.

The results of Altarriba and Bauer (2004; Experiment 3) indicated that both of the homogeneous word pairs produced a positive semantic priming effect. That is, in each case, responses were facilitated for prime-target pairs that were related as compared to unrelated in both the abstract–abstract (e.g. easy–hard) and emotion–emotion conditions (e.g. happy–sad). Responses were also facilitated for prime-target pairs in the abstract–emotion condition (e.g. soft–sensitive). However, an interesting finding emerged with regard to emotion–abstract pairs (e.g. rage–violence). Even though these items were just as associated to each other as primes and targets in the other three conditions, this latter condition did not show facilitation as compared to unrelated controls. According to Bleasdale (1987), these findings would suggest that, as is the case with concrete and abstract words, abstract and emotion words are also processed using different types of lexical representations. Hence, these findings would indicate, yet again, that abstract words and emotion words are separable word types that should not be combined in studies of word representation.

The above findings were explained in various ways by the authors (Altarriba & Bauer, 2004). It is possible that processing abstract words activates processes that are suitable for the processing of subsequently presented emotion words. However, the reverse is not true. When emotion words are encountered first, the processing that is involved, the activation of other related emotion words, and so on, do not easily lead to facilitation of subsequent abstract words, even when those words have been shown to be highly associated to their emotion-word primes. Anderson (1974), in his now famous 'fan effect', noted that words that have many varied associations share their activation across these associates when initially activated. The more 'paths' that are present, the more diffuse the priming to any one path – that is, to any one associated item. In the case of emotion words, given that it has already been established that they possess many more distinct associates as compared to abstract words, it is more difficult to find priming to any specific abstract word target when preceded by a given emotion word prime. However, the converse holds as well. That is, having abstract words that possess few associates, and following those words with specific, related emotion words should produce significant priming, because activation is shared by far fewer associates within the semantic network. Again, these findings underscore the fact that the mental lexicon that encompasses emotion words is much broader and much more varied than the one that encompasses abstract words. Therefore, the evidence seems to suggest that both of these word classes should be viewed as distinct and discriminable word types.

To sum up, the current section was aimed towards uncovering the mental structure or architecture in which emotion words are represented within a single language. The priming paradigm was invoked, because it has been used successfully in the past to uncover the ways in which concepts are interconnected and mentally represented within a semantic network. Specifically, the ability for one word to prime or to otherwise facilitate responding to a subsequently presented related target has been taken as an indication of the ways in which primes and targets are organized in human memory. Altarriba and Bauer (2004; Experiment 3) demonstrated that when participants operate under conditions that promote automatic lexical processing, emotion words and abstract words prime associated words of the same type. However, emotion words do not prime or facilitate the processing of related abstract words. These results are consistent with the predictions of the spreading activation model of semantic memory and indicate that concepts that represent emotions are characteristically distinct from those that represent abstract ideas.

Specifying the Dimensions of Emotion Words: Valence and Arousal

Affective priming

Thus far, the literature has explored the characteristics that differentiate emotion words (Altarriba, 2003; Altarriba *et al.*, 1999) from other types of words and the ways in which different types of processing influence the ability of emotion words to prime or be primed by other, non-emotion words (Altarriba & Bauer, 2004; Experiment 3). These latter results indicate that emotion words may possess many more associates and be linked to a variety of different concepts, more so than is the case for either concrete or abstract words. Although it has been shown that emotion words possess some degree of imageability and context availability, there are other dimensions that characterize emotion words that have received virtually no attention in the cognitive literature on bilingualism. These components include valence and arousal. Altarriba and Canary (2004) set out to examine the influence of these dimensions on the processing of emotion-laden words in English by English monolingual speakers and Spanish–English bilingual speakers.

Emotion words denote feelings or emotional states and can be characterized by values on the dimensions of valence and arousal (see e.g. Compton *et al.*, 2003). Russell (1978: 1166) has noted: 'Beyond these two dimensions, the structure of emotion terms became more difficult to interpret clearly, to validate empirically, or to replicate convincingly . . .'. Likewise, words that are considered emotion-laden also conjure feelings and emotional states (e.g. coffin, kiss). Whissell (1989) describes words that have emotional connotations along the dimensions of arousal or 'Activation' and pleasantness or 'Evaluation'. *Arousal* has been defined as the negative probability of falling asleep (Corcoran, 1965, 1981) or as an invigorating response to stimulation (Duffy, 1957, 1972). *Valence* is the term applied to the dimension that qualifies words as being either positive or negative (Ferré, 2003). Researchers have shown that words that are positive or negative in terms of their valence are more memorable than words that have been rated as neutral.

How are the dimensions of valence and arousal represented in the mental lexicon for monolingual and bilingual speakers? Altarriba and Canary (2004) examined this question in a series of two experiments. Their aims were to gather further evidence regarding the structure of semantic memory for emotion-related words and to understand the ways in which the above dimensions moderate behavior in a word priming task. Is it the case that arousal, for example, is yet another way in which words are organized in a semantic network, over and above mere semantic relatedness? Is arousal automatically activated? These are just some of the questions that Altarriba and Canary sought to answer through the use of a word priming paradigm.

The area of *affective priming* has received some attention in the literature pertaining to social cognition. As in semantic priming described above, affective priming is applied in situations where researchers are interested in knowing the extent to which word primes facilitate responses to word targets. However, in the current case, the primes and targets are related in terms of their emotional qualities. Researchers have reported that primes and targets that match in valence (i.e. positive–positive, negative–negative) tend to prime each other more than words that differ in terms of these dimensions (Fazio *et al.*, 1986; Spruyt *et al.*, 2002). This effect has been shown with words and with real-life color pictures (see e.g. Hermans *et al.*, 1994; Spruyt *et al.*, 2002).

In a typical study, individuals are asked to read or study a prime word or picture and then make some type of judgement for a related or unrelated picture or word. In many of the published works, the decision that participants must make regarding the target is an evaluative one: 'good' or 'bad', 'pleasant' or 'unpleasant', 'emotion' or 'neutral'. Hermans *et al.* (1994) claimed that this type of task could engender the use of conscious, strategic processes and, therefore, the results are merely a function of post-lexical or elaborative processing. When Hermans *et al.* eliminated this possibility by asking participants to name the target aloud (i.e. a pronunciation task), the valence congruency effect still materialized. In other words, even under conditions that are believed to demonstrate automatic or 'pure' processing, the effect of valence still emerged. To explain this effect, Masson (1995) argues that the activation of an emotion-laden prime word tends to activate a number of related words or concepts that are semantically related, but also are affectively congruent. Words like 'happy' and 'joyful' tend to activate related words such as 'glee' and 'cheerful'. Taken together, the above findings suggest that one might be able to demonstrate word–word priming for emotion-laden words, and that a task that minimizes strategic processing by requiring a judgement that does not directly point to the emotional content of words should be applied.

Although the evidence cited above indicates that some emotional qualities tend to moderate priming effects across words and pictures, a constant feature of the published literature has been the confound between valence and arousal. The perceived arousal of the prime and target stimuli used in these studies has been free to vary, while valence has often been controlled across prime-target pairs. In addition, word length and word frequency – parameters that could influence the outcome of word priming paradigms – have often been left free to vary as well. Researchers who investigate the mental lexicon via the use of priming paradigms are typically concerned with the control of characteristics of words that could influence judgements made on those words. Among these are issues such as word frequency, word length, association strength, valence, arousal, as well as several others. The idea is that words should be well controlled except for the dimension or dimensions of interest in order to provide for a clear interpretation of the data and generalizability of the results.

Altarriba and Canary (2004) sought to investigate the issue of the representation of emotion-laden words by better controlling some of the above features. In addition, as the bulk of the research to date has been conducted with monolinguals and within a single language, Altarriba and Canary wanted to examine the processing of arousal in a bilingual population as well. In their first experiment, 30 English-speaking monolinguals were presented with a list of 45 emotion-laden words, 45 concrete words, and 45 abstract words, in random order. Their task was to rate these words on seven-point scales on the dimensions of valence (positive/negative) and arousal (neutral, low, and high). Although the focus was on the emotion-laden words, concrete and abstract words were included so that participants would not be biased to respond in a prescribed manner based solely on the characteristics of the emotion-related items.

Based on the above rating task, words were placed within the following three groups: positive (4.66 or above), neutral (3.65 to 4.65, inclusive), and negative (3.64 or below). Likewise, words could also be grouped in the same way, with the same ranges above, for the arousal dimension (i.e. high, moderate, and neutral, with the same values as above, respectively). Virtually no emotion-laden words were rated as 'low' on the arousal dimension. Thus, Altarriba and Canary (2004; Experiment 1) established a set of word norms specifically for emotion-laden words that would allow the selection of these words as experimental stimuli maintaining the proper control over specific word characteristics. These norms were then used to construct the prime-target pairs that were used in Experiment 2 to investigate affective priming for English stimuli, in English monolingual and Spanish–English bilingual speakers.

Monolingual findings

Altarriba and Canary (2004; Experiment 2) constructed sets of prime-target word pairs based on the norms for emotion-laden words that they had collected within Experiment 1. These prime-target pairs were of three types: high arousal (e.g. prisoner–jail), moderate arousal (e.g. criminal–jail), and unrelated (e.g. guitar–jail). Note that across these three words types, the target remained the same, and the primes were matched in word frequency, word length, and valence on average, across conditions. The only factor of interest that varied across the three pairs was level of perceived arousal. Further, both arousal conditions (i.e. high and moderate) were matched on the basis of association strength. Thus, primes were equally associated to their targets, across these two conditions.

Forty-five English-speaking monolingual participants took part in this study. They were screened with regard to proficiency in a second language, and none reported to have any degree of fluency or proficiency in a second language. Participants engaged in a lexical decision task where the prime (i.e. prisoner) was presented centered on a computer screen for 200 ms and was then replaced by a target word (i.e. jail) for response. Individuals were asked to judge whether or not the word was a real word in English and to do so as quickly and as accurately as possible. This procedure is typical for the priming paradigm in general and is similar to that used by Altarriba and Bauer (2004; Experiment 3), as noted earlier. Participants viewed an equal number of primes and targets (i.e. five) of each of the three main conditions. In addition, an equal number of word–non-word pairs were constructed and randomly intermixed with the word–word pairs. Again, this is the standard procedure used when lexical decision tasks are applied.

The data for this group can be viewed in Figure 9.3. This table contains the mean reaction times in the related and unrelated conditions across the three levels of arousal for the monolingual participants. Note that subtracting mean RTs for related conditions from unrelated conditions yields an affective priming effect of +63 ms in the high arousal condition and +62 ms in the moderate condition. Both findings were statistically significant ($p < 0.05$). Primes in both arousal conditions facilitated responses to related targets, as compared to the unrelated condition (i.e. the control). These findings indicate that arousal can moderate a priming effect and that arousal components are automatically processed and accessed when emotion-related concepts are accessed from memory. (Note that while the word pairs related in terms of arousal were also somewhat semantically related, measures of semantic association for these pairs, as per established norms, were quite low, and typically not in the range that would produce semantic priming devoid of the

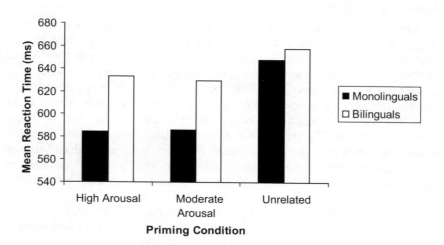

Figure 9.3 Mean reaction times (RT in milliseconds) for monolingual and bilingual participants as a function of level of arousal (From Altarriba & Canary, 2004; Experiment 2)

arousal components; see Altarriba & Canary, 2004, for further clarification on this point.) These findings are supported by theories of spreading activation (e.g. Collins & Loftus, 1975) as described earlier and indicate that semantic networks that contain emotion-related words organize those words based on valence as well as arousal. More importantly, these results demonstrate the *automatic* nature of the activation of these two dimensions.

Bilingual findings

Forty-five Spanish–English bilingual participants also took part in the above study. They too were shown the pairs of items described above, in English, and participated in a lexical decision task. These bilingual speakers rated themselves quite highly on their ability to comprehend spoken English and spoken Spanish. However, they rated themselves slightly higher in their ability to comprehend written English as compared to written Spanish. Clearly, this tends to occur as these participants attend courses taught in English in an English-speaking university, and they report using English a significantly greater proportion of time than Spanish.

The bilingual participants also demonstrated significant priming effects in the high and moderate arousal conditions (see Figure 9.3). In the high condition, a +25 ms effect emerged, whereas in the moderate condition, the effect was +29 ms. Both effects were significant ($p < 0.05$). Thus, when operating in a dominant language, one that is not the native language, facilitation effects also occur with emotion-laden stimuli – effects moderated mainly by arousal. Moreover, the effects across the two language groups were interesting in that in both cases the unrelated conditions produced similar mean reaction times. That is, the baselines for both groups were not significantly different from each other. Therefore, one can conclude that for the bilinguals, the effect of arousal is moderated by the knowledge of a second language. Facilitation was less pronounced overall, within the two main conditions of interest, for the bilingual participants as compared to the monolingual participants.

These data indicate that perhaps bilingual speakers access related information not only in the target language, but also in the other language that is known to them. This knowledge, then, affects processing in the target language, in a highly implicit manner. That is, Spanish–English bilinguals may process emotion-laden words in English differently than non-emotional words. Pure association strength was likely not the main reason that priming emerged equally in both arousal conditions, for both monolingual and bilingual participants, as the values for association strength were relatively low as compared to other demonstrations of priming (see e.g. McCarthy, 1973; Palermo & Ullrich, 1968).

Summary

In conclusion, the work of Altarriba and Canary (2004) indicates that arousal is automatically activated in the access of emotion-laden words. Also, facilitation is less pronounced for the bilingual speakers, even though baselines for the two groups were relatively the same. Thus, processing information in one's second language seems to be influenced by information in one's native language. This is particularly true given that emotion-related words are often first encoded in the native language, and that processing English emotion words may have activated features of their Spanish counterparts in memory, resulting in longer reaction times. Further research is necessary to uncover the roles that dominant versus subordinate languages play in influencing reactions and indeed behavior in general when processing emotion-related words.

Conclusions

Several final conclusions may be drawn based on the work reviewed within the current paper. First, words that label emotions form a distinct word class in memory (Altarriba, 2003; Altarriba & Bauer, 2004; Altarriba *et al.*, 1999). Second, these words may not be represented in the same way across a bilingual's two lexicons (Altarriba, 2003; Altarriba & Bauer, 2004). Third, arousal components are activated in a subordinate though native language when processing emotion-related words in the dominant language (Altarriba & Canary, 2004). Finally, cognitive approaches allow for the identification of the mental architecture that stores these word types.

With regard to the three main questions posed at the outset of the current chapter, the following main formulations might be drawn. First, with regard to the characterization of emotion words in monolingual and bilingual memory, the current Figure 9.1 and Figure 9.2 point to several conclusions. These words clearly differ in terms of their concreteness, imageability, and context availability as compared to concrete and abstract words. In English, emotion words are viewed as less concrete and lower in context availability than abstract words. However, they are seen as more imageable than abstract words. In Spanish, emotion words are just as imageable as abstract words and are equal in context availability to those words, as well. Thus, some language-specific effects emerge with regard to the three word characteristics that were under investigation. Emotion words are also seen to produce a broader range of different associations as compared to concrete words and to abstract words. Second, it appears that emotion-related words are also represented in memory by their semantic relatedness with an additional set of parameters, namely, valence and arousal. A theory that is based on a model of spreading activation (based on semantic network theory) appears adequate as a description of how emotion-related words are organized in memory. Thus, those that share a similar valence tend to prime each other, indicating their proximity to each other in memory, and those that are related via perceived arousal are also stored in close proximity as arousal tends to automatically facilitate the access and retrieval of these words.

Although researchers have investigated the structure and function of emotion words in memory, there still needs to be more work done on the definition of emotion word labels, particularly as compared to emotion-laden terms (Ortony *et al.*, 1987). Future research should focus on the distinction between different classes of emotion-related words and the features that might define and distinguish them from each other. What attributes fully define these classes of emotion words? Could it be the case that some languages are simply 'more emotional' than other languages? There is an important need in this field to compare and contrast a variety of languages – ones with differing etymologies and grammatical nuances (e.g. Spanish and French as compared to German or Arabic). Perhaps it is not simply a case of one language having more emotion-related words and phrases than another; rather, there can be a qualitative difference across languages that favors a particular type of expression. Might this issue be best examined by investigating emotion word representation in multilingual speakers or polyglots, particularly those with knowledge of languages that do not share etymologies?

Perhaps these are questions that can also be addressed using a variety of physiological measures such as heart rate, skin conductance, or evoked related brain potentials. Could we possibly map out a series of physiological responses that mediate the expression of emotion in different contexts? Future work should also closely examine age and context of acquisition as mediating variables in the mental representation of emotion. Perhaps the factors age and word type interact such that emotion words are encoded in a particular way earlier in life that codes them more deeply as compared to concrete words. Put another way, perhaps the acquisition of a concrete word is not necessarily affected by age of learning, as might be the case with a highly arousing positive or negative emotion word.

There is also a need for greater specificity of models that would explain the variety of data that relate to words, pictures, and psychophysical responses in a more inclusive manner. By developing theoretical models that can encompass a broad variety of data, empirical work devoted to the study of the emotion lexicon can proceed based on clear theoretical predictions. Finally, as some would argue that categories of emotion are formed on the basis of experiences that are derived over time and through interaction with one's environment (see e.g. Shaver *et al.*, 1987), the processing of emotion words within naturalistic settings and across a variety of environments – linguistic and cultural – should be pursued in order to produce results that can be generalized across a broad set of populations. For example, the work of Pavlenko (2002) and others has used films or video depictions of individuals acting out varying scripts related to emotional events. Stimuli of this type provide a more realistic situation in which to explore the pragmatic nuances of language use – that is, emotion in real-world contexts. To the extent that laboratory findings can be found to generalize to these types of contexts, applied theorists can develop ways of characterizing emotion scripts and schemata and fold them into methods of training individuals on how to quickly interpret and act upon individuals' expressions of emotion. Thus, this work has a broader implication – that of improving both verbal and non-verbal cross-cultural communication.

Acknowledgments

Portions of this work were presented at the annual meeting of the American Association for Applied Linguistics, Portland, Oregon. Thanks to Dana M. Basnight-Brown, Jennifer L. Gianico, Dorota Majcher-Tinney and Tina M. Sutton (Canary) for their comments on an earlier draft of this chapter. Correspondence concerning this paper may be sent to Jeanette Altarriba, Ph.D., Department of Psychology, Social Science 369, University at Albany, State University of New York, Albany, New York, 12222. Electronic mail may be sent to ja087@albany.edu (third character is a zero).

References

Altarriba, J. (1992) The representation of translation equivalents in bilingual memory. In R. Harris (ed.) *Cognitive Processing in Bilinguals* (pp. 157–74). Amsterdam: Elsevier.

Altarriba, J. (2000) Language processing and memory retrieval in Spanish–English bilinguals. *Spanish Applied Linguistics* 4, 215–45.

Altarriba, J. (2003) Does *cariño* equal 'liking'? A theoretical approach to conceptual nonequivalence between languages. *International Journal of Bilingualism* 7, 305–22.

Altarriba, J. and Basnight-Brown, D. M. (in press). Methodological considerations in performing semantic and translation priming experiments across languages. *Behavior Research Methods, Instruments, and Computers.*

Altarriba, J. and Bauer, L. (2004) The distinctiveness of emotion concepts: A comparison between emotion, abstract, and concrete words. *American Journal of Psychology* 117, 389–410.

Altarriba, J., Bauer, L. and Benvenuto, C. (1999) Concreteness, context-availability, and imageability ratings and word associations for abstract, concrete, and emotion words. *Behavior Research Methods, Instruments, and Computers* 31, 578–602.

Altarriba, J. and Canary, T. (2004) Affective priming: The automatic activation of arousal. *Journal of Multilingual and Multicultural Development* 25(2/3), 248–65.

Altarriba, J. and Morier, R. (2004) Bilingualism: Language, emotion, and mental health. In T. Bhatia and W. Ritchie (eds) *The Handbook of Bilingualism* (pp. 250–80). Oxford, UK: Blackwell.

Altarriba, J. and Santiago-Rivera, A. (1994) Current perspectives on using linguistic and cultural factors in counseling the Hispanic client. *Professional Psychology: Research and Practice* 25, 388–97.

Altarriba, J. and Soltano, E. (1996) Repetition blindness and bilingual memory: Token individuation for translation equivalents. *Memory & Cognition* 24, 700–11.

Anderson, J. (1974) Retrieval of prepositional information from long-term memory. *Cognitive Psychology* 6, 451–74.

Bleasdale, F. (1987) Concreteness-dependent associative priming: Separate lexical organization for concrete and abstract words. *Journal of Experimental Psychology: Learning, Memory, and Cognition* 13, 582–94.

Bond, M. and Lai, T. (1986) Embarrassment and code-switching into a second language. *Journal of Social Psychology* 126, 179–86.

Chen, M. and Bargh, J. (1999) Consequences of automatic evaluation: Immediate behavioral predispositions to approach or avoid the stimulus. *Personality and Social Psychology Bulletin* 25, 215–24.

Chomsky, N. (1957) *Syntactic Structures*. The Hague, Netherlands: Mouton.

Christianson, S. and Lindholm, T. (1998) The fate of traumatic memories in childhood and adulthood. *Development and Psychopathology* 10, 761–80.

Collins, A. and Loftus, E. (1975) A spreading-activation theory of semantic processing. *Psychological Review* 82, 407–28.

Collins, A. and Quillian, M. (1969) Retrieval time from semantic memory. *Journal of Verbal Learning and Verbal Behavior* 8, 240–47.

Compton, R., Banish, M., Mohanty, A., Milham, M., Herrington, J., Miller, G., Scalf, P., Webb, A. and Heller, W. (2003) Paying attention to emotion: An fMRI investigation of cognitive and emotional Stroop tasks. *Cognitive, Affective, and Behavioral Neuroscience* 3, 81–96.

Corcoran, D. (1965) Personality and the inverted-U relation. *British Journal of Psychology* 56, 267–73.

Corcoran, D. (1981) Introversion–extraversion, stress and arousal. In M. Eysenck (ed.) *A Model for Personality* (pp. 111–27). Berlin: Springer-Verlag.

Duffy, E. (1957) The psychological significance of the concept of 'arousal' or 'activation'. *Psychological Review* 64, 265–75.

Duffy, E. (1972) Activation. In N. Greenfield and R. Sternbach (eds) *Handbook of Psychophysiology* (pp. 577–622). New York: Holt, Reinhart, and Winston.

Fazio, R., Sanbonmatsu, D., Powell, M. and Kardes, F. (1986) On the automatic activation of attitudes. *Journal of Personality and Social Psychology* 50, 229–38.

Ferré, P. (2003) Effects of level of processing on memory for affectively valenced words. *Cognition and Emotion* 17, 859–80.

Goleman, D. (1995) *Emotional Intelligence*. New York: Bantam.

Gonzalez-Reigosa, F. (1976) The anxiety-arousing effect of taboo words in bilinguals. In C. Spielberger and R. Diaz-Guerrero (eds) *Cross-Cultural Anxiety* (pp. 89–105). Washington, DC: Hemisphere.

Heredia, R. and Altarriba, J. (2001) Bilingual language mixing: Why do bilinguals code-switch? *Current Directions in Psychological Science* 10, 164–68.

Hermans, D., De Houwer, J. and Eelen, P. (1994) The affective priming effect: Automatic activation of evaluative information in memory. *Cognition and Emotion* 8, 515–33.

Hunt, R. and Ellis, H. (2004) *Fundamentals of Cognitive Psychology* (7th edn). Boston, MA: McGraw-Hill.

Kieras, D. (1978) Beyond pictures and words: Alternative information processing models for imagery effects in verbal memory. *Psychological Bulletin* 85, 532–54.

Kitayama, S. and Markus, H. (eds) (1994) *Emotion and Culture: Empirical Studies of Mutual Influence.* Washington, DC: American Psychological Association.

Masson, M. (1995) A distributed memory model of semantic priming. *Journal of Experimental Psychology: Learning, Memory, and Cognition* 21, 3–23.

McCarthy, S. (1973) Verbal discrimination learning as a function of associative strength between noun pair members. *Journal of Experimental Psychology* 97, 270–71.

McNamara, T. and Holbrook, J. (2003) Semantic memory and priming. In A. Healy and R. Proctor (eds) *Handbook of Psychology: Experimental Psychology* (Vol. 4) (pp. 447–74). New York, NY: John Wiley & Sons.

Meyer, D. and Ruddy, M. (1974) *Bilingual Word Recognition: Organization and Retrieval of Alternative Lexical Codes.* Paper presented at the meeting of the Eastern Psychological Association, Philadelphia, PA, April 1974.

Ortony, A., Clore, G. and Foss, M. (1987) The referential structure of the affective lexicon. *Cognitive Science* 11, 341–64.

Paivio, A. (1971) *Imagery and Verbal Processes.* New York: Holt, Rinehart & Winston.

Paivio, A. (1986) *Mental Representations: A Dual Coding Approach.* New York: Oxford University Press.

Paivio, A., Yuille, J. and Madigan, S. (1968) Concreteness, imagery, and meaningfulness values for 925 nouns. *Journal of Experimental Psychology Monographs* 76, 1–25.

Palermo, D. and Ullrich, J. (1968) Verbal discrimination learning as a function of associative strength between the word-pair members. *Journal of Verbal Learning and Verbal Behavior* 7, 945–52.

Pavlenko, A. (2002) Bilingualism and emotions. *Multilingua* 21, 45–78.

Rubin, D. and Friendly, M. (1986) Predicting which words get recalled: Measures of free recall, availability, goodness, emotionality, and pronounceability for 925 nouns. *Memory & Cognition* 14, 79–94.

Russell, J. (1978) Evidence of convergent validity on the dimensions of affect. *Journal of Personality and Social Psychology* 36, 1152–68.

Santiago-Rivera, A. and Altarriba, J. (2002) The role of language in therapy with the Spanish–English bilingual client. *Professional Psychology: Research and Practice* 33, 30–38.

Schrauf, R. (2000) Bilingual autobiographical memory: Experimental studies and clinical cases. *Culture & Psychology* 6, 387–417.

Schwanenflugel, P., Akin, C. and Luh, W. (1992) Context availability and the recall of abstract and concrete words. *Memory & Cognition* 20, 96–104.

Schwanenflugel, P., Harnishfeger, K. and Stowe, R. (1988) Context availability and lexical decisions for abstract and concrete words. *Journal of Memory and Language* 27, 499–520.

Shaver, P., Schwartz, J., Kirson, D. and O'Connor, C. (1987). Emotion knowledge: Further exploration of a prototype approach. *Journal of Personality and Social Psychology* 52, 1061–86.

Spruyt, A., Hermans, D., Houwer, J. and Eelen, P. (2002) On the nature of the affective priming effect: Affective priming of naming responses. *Social Cognition* 20, 227–56.

Toglia, M. and Battig, W. (1978) *Handbook of Semantic Word Norms.* Hillsdale, NJ: Lawrence Erlbaum.

Tolman, E. (1948) Cognitive maps in rats and men. *Psychological Review* 55, 189–208.

Whissell, C. (1989) The dictionary of affect in language. In R. Plutchik and H. Kellerman (eds) *Emotion: Theory, Research, and Experience* (Vol. 4) (pp. 113–31). New York: Academic Press.

Chapter 10

When is a First Language More Emotional? Psychophysiological Evidence from Bilingual Speakers

CATHERINE L. HARRIS, JEAN BERKO GLEASON and
AYŞE AYÇIÇEĞI

Introduction

This chapter will review recent studies measuring physiological aspects of bilinguals' emotional response to stimuli presented in speakers' first and second language. We also introduce a new theory, 'the emotional contexts of learning theory', developed to account for findings from existing studies of bilingualism and emotion. We then evaluate the data consistent with this theory, the new predictions it makes, and the overall prospects for integrating psychophysiological research with cross-linguistic and cross-cultural research.

The connections between emotion and cognition have been increasingly studied over the past decade (e.g. Damasio, 1994, 1999; LeDoux, 1996, 2002; Panksepp, 1998). Less attention has been paid to the emotional correlates of language. One arena in which emotional concomitants of language are keenly felt is in bilingual speakers' sense that there is greater emotional arousal associated with their first language compared to their second language. Intuitions like these have been documented in the writings of bilingual authors (Pavlenko, 1998), testimonials of patients undergoing psychotherapy (Altarriba & Santiago-Rivera, 1994; Santiago-Rivera & Altarriba, 2002; Schrauf, 2000), and in laboratory studies (Anooshian & Hertel, 1994; Ayçiçeği & Harris, 2004; Bond & Lai, 1986; Marian & Neisser, 2000; Schrauf & Rubin, 1998). However, investigation of personal emotional experiences, such as which language feels more emotional, has traditionally been assumed to lie outside the scope of scientific research.

The cognitive sciences have avoided studying emotion and subjective experience for several reasons: (1) the origins of the cognitive revolution emphasized the computational metaphor (Gardner, 1985); (2) until the late 20th century, logic and reasoning were still regarded as the essence of human cognition; and (3) early cognitive scientists wanted to uncover the universals of human thought, with subjective experience seen as an idiosyncratic and distracting overlay on these universals. Such abstract and cerebral constructs were also key parts of the revolution within linguistics inspired by Chomsky (1965), as illustrated by the well-known concepts of language universals, the language acquisition device, the autonomy of syntax hypothesis, and the competence/performance distinction.

The priority of these conceptual orientations is reduced among contemporary students of language and cognition (Gazzaniga, 1999). Current research emphasizes understanding neural mechanisms, not abstract computational architecture (e.g. O'Reilly & Munakata, 2000). Pattern recognition and evolutionarily derived motivations are assumed to underlie the greater part of human thought and action. Because cognitive science has been broadened to include both animal behavior and the evolutionary roots of human thought and behavior, emotion is now regarded as essential to human cognition. Breakthrough books of the 1990s include Damasio's (1994) treatise on the crucial role of emotion in decision making, and Panksepp's (1998) textbook on affective neuroscience. Philosophers have joined forces with experimental psychologists to theorize about why conscious experience has the subjective qualities that it has (e.g. O'Regan & Noe, 2001). The embodiment movement has emphasized how cognitive processing draws on bodily movements (Barsalou, 2003). Contemporary linguistic theorists have argued that semantics and even some aspects of grammar draw on speakers' experience of the physical world (Lakoff & Johnson, 1999).

This 'emotion revolution' has occurred most strongly for cognition; it has made few inroads into psycholinguistics and even fewer into bilingualism. Cognitive scientists have pursued a monolingual agenda, meaning that when the emotion–language connection is studied, monolingual speakers are the typical research participants (a noteworthy exception being Schumann's 1997 work on the motivational basis for second language acquisition). One reason researchers are cautious about studying bilingual speakers is that language-learning histories are highly variable across bilinguals. The myriad factors at play in second language acquisition (SLA) include age of acquisition, naturalistic versus classroom learning, and the personal meaning that learning a language has for an individual. Variables such as these and the subjective nature of emotional experience can be seen as obstacles to scientific research on the perceived emotionality of a first versus a second language.

The view that subjective experience is too inconsistent to yield identifiable causal factors has become outdated, however. Subjective experience

– the felt quality of a specific experience – can be highly similar across individuals. This is true of two key sensory experiences that have been intensely studied by scientists: taste and pain. Indeed, the starting point for the current research is an aspect of emotional responsiveness that is fairly uniform: bilingual speakers commonly report experiencing greater emotional intensity when using swearwords or taboo words in their first (or dominant) language compared to their second language (L2) (Dewaele, 2004).

We also argue against the claim that accounting for individuals' emotional experience would involve too many factors. Contemporary science frequently deals with phenomena with multiple causes, and multifactorial data sets are common. Multiple regression can be used to study many predictors at once. Furthermore, it is useful to identify the relative strength of causal agents, to learn which are close to being universal, and which are subject to individual variation.

Emotional experience need not be viewed as inherently subjective and unquantifiable. The current paper documents how subjective accounts of emotional experience can be fruitfully studied in the laboratory using psychophysiological techniques. One can investigate the general factors associated with language that hold true across most individuals (e.g. early age of acquisition, naturalistic learning context), and also examine factors likely to vary across individuals, to determine why a specific language comes to be experienced as highly emotional.

Assessing Emotional Intensity by Measuring Autonomic Arousal

Our perspective on emotion and language is unique in that our key laboratory technique does not depend on self-report. In our studies we have used skin conductance, which is a well-known psychophysiological measure. Skin conductance amplitudes are, for instance, a component of the polygraph or lie-detector test. In research dating to the mid-20th century, researchers used the term galvanic skin response, or GSR, for this measure, but the preferred contemporary term is electrodermal recording (Boucsein, 1992).

The autonomic nervous system responds to signs of threat by preparing systems of the body to take action (e.g. the fight-or-flight response; Hugdahl, 1995). Part of the overall physical response to danger is sweating of the palms and fingertips, signals that can be quantified by measuring the transient increase in the skin's electrical conductivity. A transient increase that can be time-locked to a specific stimulus is called a *skin conductance response* (SCR). These occur within 1 to 1.5 seconds following presentation of the stimulus, and may last for 2 to 6 seconds.

The phasic amplitude of the SCR is most sensitive to threatening stimuli, but may also index relevance of a stimulus. Thus, even a photograph of the face of an acquaintance, when embedded in a stream of unfamiliar faces, will elicit heightened responsiveness (Channouf & Rouibah, 1997; Tranel *et al.*, 1985). Language studies have shown that reading or hearing taboo words elicits a stronger SCR than reading or hearing neutral words (Bingham, 1943; Gray *et al.*, 1982; Manning & Melchiori, 1974; Mathews & MacLeod, 1985; Mathews *et al.*, 1989). Among monolinguals, emotionally laden words, such as 'cancer' and 'kill', elicit stronger responses than neutral words (Dinn & Harris, 2000). Taboo words in particular are known to activate the amygdala and other brain structures, which mediate the arousal that accompanies detection of threat (LaBar & Phelps, 1998).

Single words (or at most phrases) have been the main type of language studied using the electrodermal technique. The focus of these studies has generally been not so much language itself, but personality and psychiatric variables indexed by language (Barry, 1980; Dinn & Harris, 2000; Grings & Zeiner, 1965; Mathews *et al.*, 1989; Stelmack *et al.*, 1983a,b). Skin conductance has only recently been used to test hypotheses about the interconnections between emotional arousal and the language system. Bowers and Pleydell-Pearce (2005) investigated the emotional consequences of using swearwords versus euphemisms. It is commonly accepted that one function of euphemisms is to protect speakers from undesired emotional arousal (Brown & Levinson, 1987). Intuitively, words such as 'death' and 'kill' convey more emotion compared to euphemisms such as 'passed away' and 'collateral damage'. An obvious way to explain the reduced emotion of euphemisms is to propose that direct associations develop between word forms and emotions. However, this contradicts standard models of the lexicon according to which word forms activate abstract, amodal semantic representations (e.g. Levelt, 1989). These abstract conceptual structures then activate relevant meaning structures. In these models, phrases and words with emotional connotations generate emotional arousal indirectly, via these conceptual structures, and language forms themselves do not have direct connections with emotional connotations.

This standard view is plausible and explains a great deal of psycholinguistic research, as reviewed by Levelt (1989). However, it does not explain euphemisms well, because euphemisms are understood to mean the same thing as their emotionally laden counterparts. To make headway in this debate, Bowers and Pleydell-Pearce (2005) measured emotional arousal via skin conductance. Euphemisms for taboo words (e.g. the term 'f-word') elicited weaker SCRs than the taboo words themselves. Bowers and Pleydell-Pearce noted: 'The suggestion that the sounds (and spellings) of words are associated with emotional responses amounts to the same thing as associating a tone or visual signal with a stimulus that evokes an emotional response' (2005: 5). These authors situated their findings in the context of debates about linguistic relativity – the form of language influences cognitive processing, because word forms can directly activate emotion.

In the next section, we describe our own prior work investigating electrodermal differences elicited by bilinguals' first and second language. In our studies of bilingual individuals, we have focused on sequential bilinguals, with English as the second language. Many of our participants were first immersed in English when they moved to North America to attend university or take jobs as adults. They frequently had formal English instruction in their country of origin, and identified English as their less proficient language. A second category of sequential bilinguals included in our studies immigrated to North America in childhood with their parents. In general, the earlier their age of arrival in an English-speaking community, the more proficient they judged their English to be; this is consistent with other studies of how age of arrival influences proficiency (Birdsong & Molis, 2001; Johnson & Newport, 1989; Moyer, 1999). A third category included in our work consists of bilinguals born in the United States to immigrant parents. They acquired their first language from family members, and their second language (English) from a mixture of peers, family, and school settings at ages 4 to 6.

Given our focus on these bilingual acquisition patterns, it is important to add one note about terminology. Many theorists consider a first language to be the language acquired before adulthood, that is the speakers' primary or dominant language. In our approach, the term *first language* (or L1) refers to the chronologically first acquired language, even if it is not the language the individual currently knows best or uses most frequently. We will separately note whether participants view their first language to be their most proficient language.

Lacking in the electrodermal literature are systematic manipulations of the variables of interest to psycholinguists. Researchers have not designed experiments to test, for instance, whether SCRs are greater to single words than to words in context, to low-frequency versus high-frequency words, or to the first occurrence of a word or a phrase compared to a later occurrence. Indeed, current state-of-the-art reviews of electrodermal research, such as the chapter by Dawson *et al.* (2000) and the book by Boucsein (1992), do not have sections or index items on language.

Electrodermal Recording of Bilingual Speakers with Late Acquisition of English

In our first study (Harris *et al.*, 2003), native speakers of Turkish ($n = 32$) currently residing in the United States, heard and read a variety of word types in L1 Turkish and L2 English. Participants responded to items by rating them for pleasantness, while skin conductance activity was monitored via fingertip electrodes. Items included taboo words (curse words, body parts, and sexual terms), reprimands ('Don't do that!'), aversive words (cancer, kill, death), positive words (bride, joy, kind), and neutral words (column, table). The reprimands were of the type that parents use in admonishing children, such as 'Shame on you!' and 'Go to your room!' The aversive, positive, and neutral words were single words (generally nouns and adjectives) selected to have comparable print frequency and familiarity, using Toglia and Battig's (1978) norms. The taboo items and reprimands included phrases, and were selected to be emotionally evocative (see discussion of stimulus selection processes and differences between Turkish and English stimuli in Harris *et al.*, 2003).

A continuum of responsiveness was found. The strongest skin conductance responses were elicited by taboo words, followed by reprimands, negative words, positive words, and neutral words. Unexpectedly, among these L1 speakers of Turkish, responsiveness to L2 English taboo words was also very high, showing that taboo words in either language activate emotionally-arousing conceptual structures. The strongest difference between a first and second language was for childhood reprimands. The difference between a first and second language for the reprimands suggests that the childhood learning context, including fear or anxiety associated with parental reprimands, contributed to an enduring language-specific response.

Heightened responsiveness to reprimands in the first language but not in the second language is consistent with prior theory and empirical work. Bloom and Beckwith (1989) noted that language is acquired during the same years of life (early childhood) as the development of emotional regulation systems. It is known that bilingual speakers can categorize autobiographical memories as occurring in their first or their second language (Schrauf & Rubin, 1998; see also Schrauf & Durazo-Arvizu, this volume). This suggests that at least the conversational aspects of memories are stored in a specific language. Memories of being reprimanded, including the words in the reprimand itself, may thus be stored with their emotional contexts.

Skin conductance responses also varied depending on auditory versus visual presentation, but only for Turkish stimuli. That is, for Turkish, words presented auditorially elicited stronger responses than those presented as visual stimuli. There were no modality differences for English, with both visual and auditory stimuli eliciting the same strength of response as visual stimuli in Turkish. The difference in modality effects for English and Turkish could reflect distinct learning environments. As the first language, auditory Turkish words were learned before visual words, whereas many English spoken words may have been learned at the same time as, or even after, their print counterparts.

This work demonstrates that electrodermal monitoring is a robust and reliable method for investigating differences in emotional reactivity to a first and second language. However, the study raises many questions. What are the mechanisms underlying the greater emotionality of the first language? How do age of acquisition and language proficiency influence autonomic reactivity? Would the pattern of results be different if the second language were acquired in childhood? Our second study addressed this last question.

Emotional Responsiveness when a Second Language is Acquired in Early Childhood

The most obvious question generated from the study of Turks who learned English as a foreign language is whether a first language is always more arousing than a second. Would the language that was acquired first continue to be more arousing, even if in adulthood it became the speaker's less proficient and less dominant language?

To investigate this question, bilinguals who were early learners of English and bilinguals who became proficient in English somewhat later in life were recruited (Harris, 2004). The early learners were typically children of immigrants. Children of immigrants to the United States frequently acquire their parents' language in the home, and acquire English when they enter school around age 5 (Homel *et al.*, 1987; Köpke, 2003). They usually identify English as their strongest, most proficient language, because of immersion in U.S. culture and 12 (or more) years of education in English-speaking schools.

All 52 Spanish–English bilinguals enrolled in this study were Boston University students, and highly proficient in English. The students were divided into two groups based on age of acquisition. The early learners ($n = 31$) were born in the United States or immigrated by age 7. The late learners ($n = 21$) arrived in the United States at age 12 or older. Note that they had generally been first exposed to English during middle childhood (age 8–12) while residing in a Latin American country. For those who arrived in the United States at 18 to attend college, age of acquisition was frequently in middle childhood while attending a bilingual school.

The early learners who had been born in the United States regarded themselves as native English speakers, and judged English to be their better, more proficient language. Three who arrived in the United States at age 6 or 7 regarded themselves as balanced bilingual speakers, rating themselves as having native-speaker or near-native-speaker abilities in both languages. The late learners regarded Spanish as their strongest language and rated themselves as having less than native-speaker abilities in English.

We did not ask participants to evaluate language dominance and proficiency separately. Language dominance refers to which language is generally most accessible in day-to-day life (Bahrick *et al.*, 1994; Marian & Kaushanskaya, 2004). It is the language that is most highly activated, and can be the default language for speaking and thinking. For immigrants with many years of immersion in their second language, the second language can come to be the most dominant language, even if it remains the less proficient language, as measured by tests of grammar and vocabulary. We asked participants to declare their stronger language and to rate their proficiency on a seven-point scale. In all cases, participants nominated their most proficient language to be their stronger language. We thus set aside the question of dominance, but note that for our late learners, Spanish was probably not just their most proficient language, but also their dominant language, as the length of residence in the United States was an average of only 2.4 years.

Stimulus materials resembled the study of Turkish–English bilinguals, with the addition of two categories of phrases: insults ('You suck!') and endearments ('I love you!'). Insults were included to expand the repertoire of negatively valenced expressions. Endearments were added to determine if skin conductance can be used to measure responsiveness to positively valenced language stimuli. A full description of the method employed appears in Harris (2004). The analysis in the current paper includes an additional 16 participants whose data were recently collected and added to the prior results.[1]

Skin conductance amplitudes were converted to z-scores, with outliers (defined as data points ± 2.5 standard deviations from the mean) truncated to the values of $+2.5$ or -2.5. For ease of graphing and interpretation, in the current paper, z-scores were transformed in the following way: 2.5 was added to each score and the result was multiplied by 100, yielding a data set ranging from 0 to 500, with a mean of 250.

Figures 10.1 and 10.2 present SCRs for the late and early learners, respectively. Error bars are the standard error of the mean for each condition. These indicate variability that could be due to sampling error. When words in the emotional categories were compared to neutral words, both early and late learners had stronger SCRs to emotional stimuli than to neutral words.

For the late learners (Figure 10.1), childhood reprimands presented in the L1 elicited stronger skin conductance responses than reprimands in the L2. None of the other categories elicited different SCRs for L1 compared with L2. Interestingly, the reprimands were also the category that showed the largest difference between L1 and L2 in our earlier study of Turkish–English bilinguals. These data are thus consistent

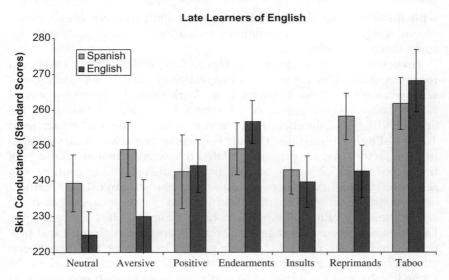

Figure 10.1 Skin conductance responses elicited by different stimulus categories for Spanish–English bilinguals who acquired English either via formal instruction in Latin America (after age 8) or when they arrived in North America (after age 12)

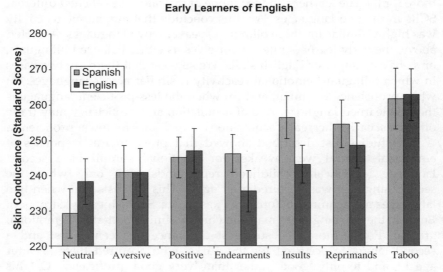

Figure 10.2 Skin conductance responses elicited by different stimulus categories for Spanish–English bilinguals who were born in the United States or immigrated by age 7

with findings from the Turkish study and with the hypothesis that a second language is less emotionally evocative than a first, at least for some kinds of words.

However, overall, as shown in Figure 10.1, differences in emotional reactivity evoked by L1 and L2 were relatively small. These differences were weaker than those obtained in the Turkish study. There are several reasons why weaker effects of L1 versus L2 would be found for the Spanish–English bilingual speakers compared to the study that used Turkish–English bilinguals. The late learners in these two studies differed in three factors that are plausibly related to electrodermal arousal: age of first exposure to L2, age of arrival in an English-speaking country, and self-rated proficiency in L2 as an adult. The Spanish–English late learners began learning English in middle-childhood (between ages 8 and 12) while attending bilingual schools in Latin America. They arrived in the United States between the ages of 12 and 18, and had high self-rated proficiency in English (very good to near-native). In contrast, the Turks began classroom English instruction later (at age 12 or older), arrived in the United States at a mean age of 24 and rated their English proficiency as only good to very good.[2] Any of these differences could explain why the Spanish late learners had only modest differences in electrodermal responsiveness between their two languages.

Turning to the early learners of English, what is striking in Figure 10.2 is that responses are even more similar between the two languages than those for the late learners. Indeed, none of the categories elicited different SCRs in the two languages. We thus conclude that autonomic reactivity was highly similar for these bilingual speakers' two languages. As noted above, the early learners rated themselves as either balanced bilinguals, or as having superior English skills. We suggest that there are two cases in which bilinguals' emotional reactivity is similar across languages: (a) when proficiency is similar, and (b) when the less-proficient language is the first learned language. Age of acquisition and proficiency may trade off against each other; early acquisition compensates for lower proficiency.

The studies just described showed that physiological responses of emotional arousal were weaker for emotional stimuli in a second language (specifically, childhood reprimands), but only when the second language was acquired after age 7. This suggests that when two languages are acquired before age 7, as in our Spanish early learners of English, the two languages may elicit highly similar patterns of emotional arousal. Furthermore, the strongest difference between a first and a second language occurred for the Turks, who acquired their L2 after age 12, and to only 'good' rather than 'very good' proficiency. On this basis, one might predict a general decline in the emotional force of language as age of acquisition increases and proficiency decreases, similar to the self-report findings of Dewaele (2004). Whether proficiency or age of acquisition is more important for emotional responsiveness remains to be studied.

Ratings of Emotional Intensity as a Check on Language Differences

Note, however, that if items in one language were intrinsically more emotional than the corresponding items in the other language, this could influence skin conductance amplitudes and compromise our ability to attribute electrodermal differences to a language's status as a first versus a second language. We thus review here two types of ratings obtained on the stimuli used in the Spanish–English bilingual study.

Participants' task during electrodermal recording was to rate words for pleasantness on a 1–7 scale. Words in Spanish and English were rated very similarly, for both the early and late learners of English. However, participants were likely consulting their semantic knowledge of words' meaning when they did this rating. Indeed, the ratings for the positive, negative, and neutral words were very close to the pleasantness ratings obtained by Toglia and Battig (1978). This occurred both for the English items (the same ones rated by Toglia & Battig, 1978), and for their Spanish translations, supporting the validity of the translations. The reprimands and taboo items also received similar pleasantness ratings (see discussion in Harris, 2004).

Spanish and English items may have differed in their perceived emotional intensity, even though they were judged to be similar in pleasantness. For example, the Spanish reprimands included items such as 'Sabes que me lo vas a pagar' (literally, 'You know, you're going to pay for this'). Perhaps this was more emotional than its corresponding English items (in this case, 'Now you're in trouble'):

To examine whether the items were similar in emotional intensity, we obtained ratings from American college students ($n = 44$) and Spanish speakers residing in Columbia ($n = 12$). The English speakers were students, age 18–22, who responded to a paper-and-pencil questionnaire. The following instructions were used: For each word or phrase, imagine a situation in which this item was used, and rate the emotional intensity of that situation on a 1-to-7 scale, with 7 indicating highly emotional, and 1 indicating non-emotional. Give a medium score of 3 or 4 for an item of moderate emotionality.

The Columbian participants were recruited by word of mouth and e-mail by a research assistant who traveled to Bogota while this study was being conducted. Because university students in Columbia frequently have good English ability, we did not try to obtain exclusively monolingual Spanish speakers. The participants ranged in age from 24 to

41 years and rated themselves as having either good or very good English skills. However, they had not lived in an English-speaking country and considered Spanish to be their primary language.

Columbian and American respondents rated the items similarly, as shown in Figure 10.3. *t*-Tests conducted on the English and Spanish ratings for each category revealed no significant differences. Across all items, emotional intensity ratings for the Spanish and English items correlated at $r = 0.73$, a strong correlation. The rating study thus indicates that the Spanish and English items were similar in their emotional intensity. This similarity allows us to be more confident that similarities and differences in electrodermal responsiveness between Spanish and English items presented to the bilingual participants reflect differences in the languages' status as a first or a second language.

Ideally, rating studies should be conducted before stimuli are chosen, and stimuli should be matched on a number of dimensions, including familiarity, frequency of use, and word length. Our laboratory has begun collecting normative data on emotional phrases in a number of languages. One such rating study revealed unexpected differences in emotional intensity. When we normed the stimuli used in the Turkish–English bilingual study described above (Harris *et al.*, 2003), students at Istanbul University rated the Turkish stimuli. Their emotional intensity ratings were higher than those of American monolingual speakers rating the English items, but only for some categories. The two groups

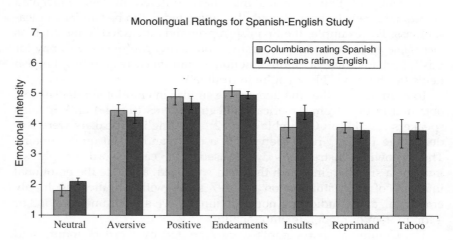

Figure 10.3 Emotional intensity ratings of the stimuli used in the Spanish–English bilingual study by monolingual English speakers in Boston and Spanish speakers in Bogota, Columbia (error bars represent one standard error of the mean)

evaluated the neutral and taboo items similarly, but Turks gave higher intensity ratings to both positive and aversive items, and to childhood reprimands, than did Americans. For example, on the seven-point scale, Turks gave mean ratings of 5.7, 5.4, and 5.3 to 'grave', 'war', and 'disease', respectively, while Americans rated these as 3.8, 3.6, and 4.2.

Could we attribute these differences to shortcomings in stimulus selection? That is, could it be that we selected emotionally pallid terms when selecting English terms, and emotionally colorful terms when selecting Turkish items? We do not feel this interpretation is tenable. We chose basic-level terms in both languages, not arcane or literary terms. Instead, differences in emotionality ratings could reflect differences in cultural connotations, differences in how participants approached the rating task, or cultural differences in the frequency of use of emotion-laden expressions (Fridlund, 1997; Goddard, 2002; Matsumoto, 2001). One could argue that words like 'war' and 'disease' might have more immediacy for members of Turkish culture, and that American college students are more removed from war than are members of some other cultures. This could be why Turkish college students rated emotion words as having greater intensity than did American students.

Cross-cultural researchers have long warned of the problems of stimulus equivalence when comparing ratings across cultures, and have suggested some remedies and guidelines (Poortinga, 1989). Bilingualism research faces the same pitfalls. We advocate obtaining ratings on multiple dimensions of the stimuli, and trying different response formats. For example, use of a five-point scale rather than the seven-point scale could prompt the Americans to use the high end of the emotionality intensity scale, meaning that Americans and Turks would end up rating words similarly (see Hui & Triandis, 1989, for discussion of how cultural differences can appear or disappear depending on response format). We return to the problem of stimulus equivalence in the conclusion of this paper, advocating the use of multiple testing settings, different cultures, and the balanced bilingual design.

In the next section we integrate the findings of our skin conductance studies with the literature on emotional arousal and bilingualism, and propose our own theoretical framework for explaining these results and generating predictions.

When is the First Language More Emotional?

Interviews, surveys, studies of autobiographical memory, and a few laboratory experiments have produced a consensus that bilingual speakers experience reduced emotionality when speaking their second language (Altarriba & Santiago-Rivera, 1994; Anooshian & Hertel, 1994; Bond & Lai, 1986; Dewaele, 2004; Dewaele & Pavlenko, 2002;

Gonzalez-Reigosa, 1976; Marian & Neisser, 2000; Pavlenko, 1998, 2002, 2004; Schrauf, 2000; Schrauf & Rubin, 1998). Dewaele (2004) asked bilingual and multilingual speakers to rate the emotionality of swearwords in their various languages. Swearwords in the native language were rated as the most forceful. Perceived forcefulness declined with age of acquisition and the languages' rank-order of acquisition. Naturalistic learning contexts also led to more perceived emotional force than formal instruction.

Differences in emotionality have been documented by analyzing narratives and autobiographical memories. Immigrants' childhood memories were shown to be more emotionally charged when described in their native language (Koven, 2001; Schrauf & Rubin, 1998, 2000). Accurate recall of autobiographical memories depends on the language in which recall takes place. If language of recall matches the language in which the specific episode was originally encoded, recall is enhanced (Marian & Neisser, 2000; Schrauf & Rubin, 1998, 2000). Marian and Neisser (2000) demonstrated that Russian–English bilinguals produced higher levels of recall for specific life events if interviews were conducted in the language in which the experiences originally took place, an effect termed 'language-dependent memory'. In this view, language appears to be tied to memory traces and these traces carry 'language tags'.

So far, the research on emotion and bilingualism has been relatively atheoretical: scholars have needed to explore and document effects. The empirical findings are now substantial enough for us to consider two broad questions. What language learning factors promote the experience of emotional forcefulness, and what mechanism underlies emotionality effects in bilingualism?

Questions about 'mechanism' are facilitated by adopting a psycholinguistic perspective. For example, Johnson and Newport (1989) adopted a psycholinguistic perspective in their study of Korean and Chinese L1 learners of English as a second language. These researchers found that grammatical knowledge of English was strongly influenced by age of immigration to the United States, but minimally influenced by learning and biographical factors such as motivation and duration of time speaking the second language. To explain this pattern of results, Johnson and Newport (1989) posited a maturational mechanism, such as a set of genes for easily acquiring language that would be most strongly expressed in early childhood. A maturational mechanism, they argued, would not be influenced by language history variables or additional factors such as L1 and L2 similarity.

Birdsong and Molis (2001) also adopted a psycholinguistic perspective but came to different conclusions. In a sample of Spanish–English bilingual speakers, these authors found that motivation and frequency of L2 use did correlate with higher scores on L2 grammaticality judgement tests. Bialystok and Miller (1999) noted that similarity between the L1 and L2 also influenced degree of L2 attainment. Birdsong and Molis (2001) thus argued that the contexts of learning and use are important in addition to a maturational mechanism (see also Hakuta *et al.*, 2003; Marinova-Todd *et al.*, 2000; Moyer, 1999).

Our approach in this paper will be similar, in that we will consider the influence of three categories of mechanisms – brain maturation, links to autobiographical memory, and context-depending learning – on bilingual emotionality. As with other speculations about brain maturation (e.g. Johnson & Newport, 1989), the specific brain mechanism that would cause the first language to be experienced as more emotional than subsequent languages remains to be determined. One could posit that words and phrases that are acquired early will have strong connections to the amygdala (LaBar & Phelps, 1998), because early language develops at the same time as emotional regulation systems (Bloom & Beckwith, 1989). Later learned language may have a more purely cortical representation, lacking connections to subcortical areas (Lieberman, 2000). A prediction of this view is that early age of acquisition will generally be a potent predictor of heightened emotional reactivity, allowing some exceptions in the case of some (unknown) level of L1 attrition.

A second approach is to posit that the memorial basis for emotion is autobiographical (Conway & Haque, 1999). There is evidence that autobiographical events are mentally represented along with words and phrases from the language in which they occurred (Marian & Neisser, 2000; Schrauf, 2000; Schrauf & Rubin, 1998, 2000; Schrauf & Durazo-Arvizu, this volume). Bilinguals may perceive a first language to be emotionally evocative because words and phrases in the first language are linked to emotionally relevant personal memories. An implication of the autobiographical approach is that second language learners will experience greater emotionality over time as words and phrases in their L2 lexicon are linked to emotional memories.

A similar approach has been proposed by Altarriba (2003), but the emotional context need not be an autobiographical memory. Simply, emotion words in the first language have typically been experienced in a larger diversity of contexts than have emotion words in a second language. The context in which emotion words appear creates multiple traces in memory for these words and strengthens their semantic representation. Words in a second language have been practiced less and applied in fewer contexts. The result is that encountering L2 emotion words activates fewer associations than would the same word in the first language.

This notion of L2 words having fewer conceptual associations than L1 words is at the heart of the revised hierarchical model of Kroll and Stewart

(1994). This model is thus also a useful framework for understanding emotionality effects. Kroll and Stewart (1994) proposed that words in L1 are directly linked to conceptual representations (the conceptual store), but that L2 words are initially learned via translations to L1 words. Early in second language learning, L2 words have only weak links to the conceptual store. As proficiency in L2 increases, the links between L2 words and the conceptual store are strengthened. The conceptual store is the repository of meaning and thus includes the emotional and visceral connotations of words and phrases. Stronger connections to the conceptual store for L1 than for L2 means that stimuli in L1 will elicit a stronger emotional reaction. An implication is that as proficiency in L2 increases, the subjective impression of emotionality for L2 will increase.

Our own approach is to articulate a context-of-learning theory. Learning contexts influence proficiency (Ervin-Tripp, 1981; Grosjean, 1982) and thus must play a role in emotionality, regardless of whether or not brain maturation is also operative. The common ingredient behind the autobiographical and lexical linkage approaches is that greater exposure to L2 increases the links to long-term emotional memory associations, following the logic of Kroll and colleagues discussed above (Kroll & Stewart, 1994; Kroll & Sunderman, 2003). The main way we add to Altarriba's approach is to propose a mechanism that could involve the language-learning factors known to influence bilingual emotionality. From Dewaele's (2004) Internet survey, we know that age of acquisition of a language, naturalistic learning context, and proficiency correlated with judgements of the emotional force of swearwords. Our electrodermal studies have demonstrated that age of acquisition influenced emotional experience, but mainly for later learners, who happened also to be more proficient in their L1. When the L2 was the more proficient language, electrodermal responses did not differ for L1 and L2, suggesting that proficiency and age of acquisition may trade off against each other. These findings are compatible with the idea that age of acquisition is not itself a causal factor in bilingual emotionality. It may simply be highly associated with language learning factors, which are themselves causal (as we explain further below). The actual causal factor is the emotional context in which language is learned and used.

We propose that language comes to have a distinctive emotional feel by virtue of being learned, or habitually used, in a distinctive emotional context. We will refer to this as the 'emotional contexts of learning' theory. How or why does learning or using a language in emotional contexts provide it with a subjective feeling of emotional force? Simply because human experiences are generally learned and stored in a context-dependent manner. As psychologists have observed and theorized for a century, human learning is associative (Anderson & Bower, 1973; Thorndike, 1927). Scientists continue to employ the mechanism of associative learning to explain context-dependent representations, as proposed by cognitive scientists working in the connectionist framework (Rumelhart & McClelland, 1986). Associative learning causes language forms to be mentally stored with their contexts of use. Distributed representations (also called 'superpositional' representations; Harris, 1994) assume that memories are composites of many individual experiences.

With context-dependent learning, distributional analysis sorts out, via exposure to many examples, which aspects of the overall meaning most frequently co-occur with specific words. This type of distributional learning has been illustrated for learning of grammatical categories and joint blending of semantics and grammatical knowledge (e.g. Rumelhart & McClelland, 1986; Elman *et al.*, 1996). Connectionist models illustrate pattern completion; activation of already learned patterns as well as learning can proceed even if the input is only partial. Connectionist networks have been used to illustrate learning of cognitive and perceptual prototypes and have been frequently used to model aspects of language learning and use. Indeed, they are recognized as one of the types of models that are particularly useful for understanding second language acquisition (Ellis, 2002).

Our 'emotional contexts of learning' theory is not merely stating the obvious. The view that language is stored with its contexts of occurrence is contrary to decades of linguistic theorizing. Most language learning theorists assume that non-linguistic correlates are stripped away during learning, allowing the abstraction of linguistic meaning and context-independent grammatical rules (Chomsky, 1965; Jackendoff, 1997; Pinker, 1984, 1994).

The emphasis on abstraction became the dominant view in 20th-century linguistics, and was exemplified by Chomsky's (1965) claims about the autonomy of syntax and by the enthusiasm for the concept of modularity in language in the following 40 years (Fodor, 1983; Frazier, 1999; Pinker, 1994). Some linguists have always questioned this view, and during the past few decades a particularly strong and coherent alternative has formed under the name of Cognitive Linguistics (Lakoff, 1987; Langacker, 1987; Talmy, 2000; Taylor, 2003). The emotional contexts of learning theory thus find a natural home under the umbrella of cognitive linguistics.

Evaluating the Emotional Contexts of Learning Theory

Our theory accounts for the basic observation that bilinguals usually report their first language to be their most emotional language. A first language is universally learned in a highly emotional context, the context of attachment to caregivers. In contrast, second languages vary in the emotionality of their context. They can be acquired in the emotional context of attachment to caregivers and peers, or may be acquired in formal settings such as school or work, settings with fewer intense personal attachments (Schumann, 1997). Early age of acquisition thus functions as a proxy for a more emotional context of learning.

Our theory accommodates the finding that languages learned in naturalistic contexts are experienced as more emotional than those acquired in formal schooling contexts (Dewaele, 2004). Naturalistic learning contexts are more social than classroom contexts. They can also provide the social motivation that facilitates second language learning (Ervin-Tripp, 1981; Schumann, 1997). Explaining the association between proficiency and perceived emotionality is more difficult. Emotional contexts of learning may contribute to proficiency because emotional contexts are likely to be interpersonal and thus more motivating for learners. But the causal arrow may go in the other direction; having high proficiency in an L2 may facilitate one's access to emotional contexts, because it facilitates one's access to native speakers of that language and to interpersonal contexts. So, our view is that proficiency does not itself cause a language to be experienced as emotional, but high proficiency is frequently a marker of having had exposure to emotional contexts of learning.

Our framework is broad, but nevertheless makes predictions contrasting with those made by three simpler approaches:

(1) The chronologically first-acquired language is always (or at least usually) more emotional, regardless of other aspects of participants' learning history.
(2) Age of acquisition determines emotionality, meaning a second language learned early will be more emotional than a second language learned late.
(3) The more proficient language is generally more emotional, meaning a second language will be more emotional than a first if it is learned to greater proficiency.

Before beginning this research, we were open to the prospect that hypothesis (1) might be the proper generalization. This could occur if early-acquired language becomes neurally connected to other regions of the brain that are undergoing rapid development, such as the emotional regulation centers of the brain. Findings in our study of Spanish–English bilinguals (Harris, 2004) were not consistent with hypothesis (1). Overall, emotionality was similar for Spanish–English bilinguals when both Spanish and English were acquired before age 7. These findings are not consistent with the proficiency hypothesis (3), because most of the early learners rated English as their more proficient language, yet their electrodermal responsiveness did not differ to stimuli in English and Spanish. Of course, strong conclusions cannot be drawn from failure to find statistically significant differences, and thus future work is necessary to confirm or qualify these results. We are still interested in hypothesis (1), and indeed the truth may be that maturation has a causal role in addition to emotional contexts of learning. However, following Occam's razor, the simplest explanation should be preferred as long as data are consistent with it.

Because we think it unlikely that age and proficiency are themselves causal factors, our theory makes the prediction that it should be possible for a language to be perceived as highly emotional, even if it is acquired in adulthood and to lower than native-speaker levels of proficiency. However, the context of learning and use must be highly emotional, approximating the immersion in emotional interpersonal interactions that occurs in childhood. An example of where this might occur is when immigrants acquire a second language in the country while married to a native speaker and raising children, as described by Pavlenko (2004). Supporting anecdotes are easy to find. One of our colleagues, a native German speaker, resides in North America, where she teaches at a university and lives with her American husband and children. She reports that when on the telephone to her parents in Germany, speaking German feels like 'wearing mittens'. In our study of Turkish–English bilingual speakers, one participant showed stronger SCRs to English words than Turkish. As she was the only participant who displayed this pattern, we returned to the notes from our debriefing interview. We learned that the participant had immigrated to the United States in her 20s, married an American, had two children, and expressed no nostalgia for Turkey. In fact, she had expressed surprise when informed of our hypothesis and rejected the notion that her mother tongue would be the language that felt more emotional.

We are making the strong claim that, although age of acquisition is frequently correlated with measures of emotional force, the real causal factors are the language contexts that typically co-occur with early learning. Yet it is likely that in statistical studies that use multiple regression to consider multiple factors, age of acquisition may turn out to be strongest predictor of emotional force. We will illustrate how this is not necessarily evidence of causation by returning to the findings of Johnson and Newport (1989) and Birdsong and Molis (2001).

Birdsong and Molis (2001) found that learning factors were correlated with native-like grammaticality judgements in adulthood, but age of acquisition remained the strongest factor. Indeed, several learning factors dropped to non-significance when partial correlations were included in multiple regression. For this reason, Birdsong and Molis (2001) accepted Johnson and Newport's (1989) claims that biological maturation has causal force. This conclusion can be disputed. Maturational aspects of age may have no causal force, but the biological age of L2 exposure/acquisition is likely overwhelmingly and regularly correlated with social, motivational, and learning factors. In contrast, social factors such as context of learning (peers/family versus school), amount of L2 use, and perceived importance of learning the L2 (Schumann, 1997) are subjected to considerable variation across L2 learners. As Grosjean (1982) has long noted, differing ages of acquisition imply differences in the learning context. Many L2 learners will learn in the classroom and have little contact with native speakers. Other late learners may acquire L2 outside the classroom but still lack the emotional connections contributed by speaking with friends and family. Consider that these helpful learning factors probably have only a small- to moderate-sized correlation of 0.15 to 0.45 with ultimate proficiency or grammatical attainment, as reported in Birdsong and Molis (2001). Across L2 learners, what remains consistent is the reliable correlation that biological age has with this large set of factors. Thus, in multiple regression, age of acquisition may emerge as the single strongest predictor.

Using this logic, age of acquisition may have the highest correlation with emotional responsiveness, yet not itself be a causal factor. Proficiency can also be understood as the type of variable that may correlate with emotionality but not cause it. Causal interpretations of proficiency and age of acquisition would be undermined if languages learned late in life were experienced as highly emotional even when learned to less than native-speaker proficiency. The causal force of early age of learning would be supported if languages learned early elicited strong emotional reactions even when learned to low proficiency.

Conclusions and Directions for Future Research

Can psychophysiological methods be used to measure differences in emotions experienced by bilingual speakers? We measured skin conductance responses to emotional phrases and neutral words presented in speakers' first and second languages for bilingual speakers who spoke Turkish or Spanish as their first language. The strongest language effects were found in the Turkish study, where childhood reprimands elicited stronger skin conductance responses in L1 Turkish than in L2 English (Harris *et al.*, 2003). This study raised the question of whether emotionality effects would be stronger in a first language even if the first language was the weaker language. To answer this question, two groups of Spanish–English bilinguals were compared: the adult offspring of Latin American immigrants, for whom English was considered L2 but was the dominant language, and those who moved from Latin America to the United States in their teen years (Harris, 2004). Only the latter group had heightened emotionality to reprimands in Spanish, thus replicating the finding of the Turkish study. The early learners of English had similar patterns of electrodermal responding in their two languages.

This indicates that when two languages are learned in childhood, they elicit similar physiological reactions.

To explain why a first language was not more emotional than a second language which was acquired in childhood, we proposed a mechanism independent of age, the emotional contexts of learning hypothesis: language is experienced as emotional when it is acquired and used in an emotional context. We noted the similarity between this view and that of others (Altarriba, 2003; Marian & Neisser, 2000; Schrauf, 2000; Schrauf & Rubin, 1998, 2000), and discussed novel aspects of our proposal.

If language acquired and used in emotional contexts comes to be experienced as emotional, then one prediction is that emotion words acquired in early childhood will elicit stronger SCRs than emotion words acquired in middle childhood. Our reasoning here is that childhood provides an emotional context of learning because emotional regulation systems are developing. Such a finding would contribute to the ongoing debate about whether the age at which words are acquired influences their mental representation (Ghyselinck *et al.*, 2004; Gilhooly & Logie, 1980).

We have not examined cases where a second language is acquired late, but comes to be the dominant language. This can happen when one immigrates and marries a native speaker of the L2, and raises children whose dominant language is the L2 (see cases discussed by Pavlenko, 2004). Our prediction is that in this case at least some emotional phrases presented in the L2 will elicit skin conductance amplitudes that are similar to those elicited by the first language.

Our data suggest that age of acquisition is an important correlate of emotional reactivity. What remains unknown is whether a maturational mechanism underlies this correlation, or if early acquisition simply correlates with emotional contexts of learning. If a maturational mechanism is at work, then language learned early should elicit greater physiological responses beyond what would be predicted via proficiency. This could occur if early acquired language is stored with early developing emotional regulation systems. Independently of questions about causal mechanisms, it would be useful to quantify how proficiency and age of acquisition quantitatively trade off against each other.

As noted earlier, our current research has the drawback that the set of stimuli (e.g. the reprimands) chosen for one language could have been inherently more arousing than analogous items selected for the other language. Thus, differences between a first and second language could be attributed to differences in items rather than status of the language as being acquired early or late. Even after matching items according to monolingual ratings of emotionality, such matching can be imperfect (e.g. individuals from different cultures may respond to rating scales differently). One solution is to use a balanced bilingual design (as in, for example, Anooshian & Hertel, 1994). This is a design in which the same language functions as the first language for one group of speakers and the second language for a different group. We are currently pursuing this option by studying English–Turkish bilinguals residing in Istanbul. Their physiological responses will be compared to Turkish–English bilinguals residing in Boston. Thus, in both studies, speakers are immersed in the language of their L2. Participants in the two locations can also be matched for their language-learning history, that is, have comparable age of acquisition, proficiency, and length of residence.

The balanced bilingual design minimizes problems of stimulus equivalence, but does not eliminate cultural effects. Cultures are known to differ in the social acceptability of employing emotion-laden expressions (Fridlund, 1997; Goddard, 2002; Matsumoto, 2001). For example, Turks may have greater responsiveness to childhood reprimands than do North Americans, because an authoritarian parenting style is more common in Turkey than in North America (Kagitcibasi, 1992). This authoritarian style may engender more fear or anxiety in children who are being reprimanded than might occur in a more laissez-faire environment, and we propose that a representation of the heightened emotion is stored along with the phrases themselves. As noted earlier, SCRs are particularly sensitive to feelings of threat, and it is in just those anxiety-provoking childhood reprimands where we find the greatest responses in our Turkish participants.

Our response to this issue is not to give up on this research as inherently indeterminate, but to study multiple languages and cultures. Consistent patterns that hold across many languages can be attributed to universal psychological mechanisms, whereas inconsistent patterns will indicate cultural or language-specific findings. Cultural and language-specific findings can then be linked to anthropological and sociolinguistic research, whereas cross-culturally consistent patterns will inform theories about the nature of universal cognitive and physiological processes.

Acknowledgements

Dialma Miranda assisted with translation, selection, and recording of Spanish stimuli. Karen Meersohn, Neela Swaminathan, and Nisha Mehta assisted with recruitment and administered the electrodermal protocol. Karen Meersohn collected the Spanish emotional intensity ratings in Columbia. Bruce Mehler of Neurodyne Medical Corporation offered technical advice on interpreting the skin conductance data. Wayne Dinn provided comments on an earlier version of this paper.

Notes

1. The overall pattern of results has not changed with the addition of more participants. The additional data points allowed us to explore a slightly different graphing of the data. In Harris (2004), the positive, negative, and neutral single words were grouped into a common category, called single words. Having more participants reduces within-category variance, making it feasible to plot these categories separately.
2. Note that length of stay in the United States was slightly higher for the Turks, with a mean of 4 years, compared to a mean of 2.4 years for the Spanish–English late learners. One would expect greater length of immersion in one's second language to correlate with greater emotional reactivity. If the Turks had only 2.4 years of immersion, they might have shown even less emotional reactivity in English.

References

Altarriba, J. (2003) Does cariño equal 'liking'? A theoretical approach to conceptual nonequivalence between languages. *International Journal of Bilingualism* 7, 305–22.

Altarriba, J. and Santiago-Rivera, A. (1994) Current perspectives on using linguistic and cultural factors in counseling the Hispanic client. *Professional Psychology: Research and Practice* 25, 388–97.

Anderson, J.R. and Bower, G. (1973) *Human Associative Memory*. Washington, DC: Winston and Sons.

Anooshian, J. and Hertel, T. (1994) Emotionality in free recall: Language specificity in bilingual memory. *Cognition and Emotion* 8, 503–14.

Ayçiçegi, A. and Harris, C. (2004) Bilinguals' recall and recognition of emotion words. *Cognition and Emotion* 18, 977–87.

Bahrick, H., Hall, L. and Goggin, J. (1994) Fifty years of language maintenance and language dominance in bilingual Hispanic immigrants. *Journal of Experimental Psychology: General* 123, 264–83.

Barry, R. (1980) Electrodermal responses to emotive and non-emotive words as a function of personality differences in affect level. *Biological Psychology* 11, 161–68.

Barsalou, L. (2003) Situated simulation in the human conceptual system. *Language and Cognitive Processes* 18, 513–62.

Bialystok, E. and Miller, B. (1999) The problem of age in second language acquisition: Influences from language, task, and structure. *Bilingualism: Language and Cognition* 2, 127–45.

Bingham, W. (1943) A study of the relations which the galvanic skin response and sensory reference bear to judgments of the meaningfulness and importance of 72 words. *Journal of Psychology* 16, 21–34.

Birdsong, D. and Molis, M. (2001) On the evidence for maturational constraints in second language acquisition. *Journal of Memory and Language* 44, 235–49.

Bloom, L. and Beckwith, R. (1989) Talking with feeling: Integrating affective and linguistic expression in early language development. *Cognition and Emotion* 3, 315–42.

Bond, M. and Lai, T. (1986) Embarrassment and code-switching into a second language. *Journal of Social Psychology* 126, 179–86.

Boucsein, W. (1992) *Electrodermal Activity*. New York: Plenum.

Bowers, J. and Pleydell-Pearce, K. (2005) Verbal conditioning, euphemisms and linguistic relativity. Manuscript under review. Available from Jeffrey Bowers, University of Bristol, U.K.

Brown, P. and Levinson, S. (1987) *Politeness: Some Universals in Language Usage.* Cambridge: Cambridge University Press.

Channouf, A. and Rouibah, A. (1997) Suboptimal familiar faces exposure and electrodermal reactions. *Anuario de Psicologia* 74, 85–97.

Chomsky, N. (1965) *Aspects of the Theory of Syntax.* Cambridge, MA: MIT Press.

Conway, M. and Haque, S. (1999) Overshadowing the reminiscence bump: Memories of a struggle for independence. *Journal of Adult Development* 6, 35–44.

Damasio, A. (1994) *Descartes' Error: Emotion, Reason, and the Human Brain.* New York: Putnam.

Damasio, A. (1999) *The Feeling of What Happens: Body and Emotion in the Making of Consciousness.* New York: Harcourt Brace.

Dawson, M., Schell, A. and Filion, D. (2000) The electrodermal system. In J. Cacioppo and L. Tassinary (eds) *Handbook of Psychophysiology* (2nd edn) (pp. 200–23). Cambridge: Cambridge University Press.

Dewaele, J-M. (2004) The emotional force of swearwords and taboo words in the speech of multilinguals. *Journal of Multilingual and Multicultural Development* 25, 204–22.

Dewaele, J-M. and Pavlenko, A. (2002) Emotion vocabulary in interlanguage. *Language Learning* 52, 263–322.

Dinn, W. and Harris, C. (2000) Neurocognitive function in antisocial personality disorder. *Psychiatry Research* 97, 173–90.

Ellis, N. (2002) Constructions, chunking, and connectionism: The emergence of second language structure. In C. Doughty and M. Long (eds) *The Handbook of Second Language Acquisition* (pp. 33–68). Oxford: Blackwell.

Elman, J., Bates, E., Johnson M., Karmiloff-Smith, A., Parisi, D. and Plunkett, K. (1996) *Rethinking Innateness: A Connectionist Perspective on Development.* Cambridge, MA: MIT Press.

Ervin-Tripp, S. (1981) Social process in first and second language learning. In H. Winitz (ed.) *Native Language and Foreign Language Acquisition* (pp. 33–47). New York: New York Academy of Science.

Fodor, J. (1983) *The Modularity of Mind.* Cambridge, MA: MIT Press.

Frazier, L. (1999) Modularity and language. In R. Wilson and F. Keil (eds) *The MIT Encyclopedia of the Cognitive Sciences* (pp. 558–60). Cambridge, MA: MIT Press.

Fridlund, A. (1997) The new ethology of human facial expressions. In J. Russell and J. Fernandez-Dols (eds) *The Psychology of Facial Expression* (pp. 103–29). New York: Cambridge University Press.

Gardner, H. (1985) *The Mind's New Science: A History of the Cognitive Revolution.* New York: Basic Books.

Gazzaniga, M. (1999) *The New Cognitive Neurosciences* (2nd edn). Cambridge, MA: MIT Press.

Ghyselinck, M., Lewis, M. and Brysbaert, M. (2004) Age of acquisition and the cumulative-frequency hypothesis: A review of the literature and a new multi-task investigation. *Acta Psychologica* 115, 43–67.

Gilhooly, K. and Logie, R. (1980) Methods and designs: Age-of-acquisition, imagery, concreteness, familiarity and ambiguity measures for 1944 words. *Behavior Research Methods and Instrumentation* 12, 395–427.

Goddard, C. (2002) Explicating emotions across cultures: A semantic approach. In S. Fussel (ed.) *The Verbal Communication of Emotions: Interdisciplinary Perspectives* (pp. 19–54). Mahwah, NJ: Lawrence Erlbaum.

Gonzalez-Reigosa, F. (1976) The anxiety arousing effect of taboo words in bilinguals. In C. Spielberger and R. Diaz-Guerrero (eds) *Cross-Cultural Anxiety* (pp. 89–105). Washington, DC: Hemisphere.

Gray, S., Hughes, H. and Schneider, L. (1982) Physiological responsivity to a socially stressful situation: The effect of level of moral development. *Psychological Record* 32, 29–34.

Grings, W. and Zeiner, A. (1965) Autonomic responses to words modified by sensitizing and conditioning experiences. *Journal of Psychosomatic Research* 8, 373–78.

Grosjean, F. (1982) *Life with Two Languages*. Cambridge, MA: Harvard University Press.

Hakuta, K., Bialystok, B. and Wiley, E. (2003) Critical evidence: A test of the critical-period hypothesis for second-language acquisition. *Psychological Science* 14, 31–38.

Harris, C. (1994) Coarse coding and the lexicon. In C. Fuchs and B. Victorri (eds) *Continuity in Linguistic Semantics* (pp. 205–29). Amsterdam: John Benjamins.

Harris, C. (2004) Bilingual speakers in the lab: Psychophysiological measures of emotional reactivity. *Journal of Multilingual and Multicultural Development* 25, 223–47.

Harris, C., Ayçiçegi, A. and Gleason, J. (2003) Taboo words and reprimands elicit greater autonomic reactivity in a first than in a second language. *Applied Psycholinguistics* 4, 561–78.

Homel, P., Palij, M. and Aaronson, D. (eds) (1987) *Childhood Bilingualism: Aspects of Linguistic, Cognitive, and Social Development*. Hillsdale, NJ: Lawrence Erlbaum.

Hugdahl, K. (1995) *Psychophysiology: The Mind-Body Perspective*. Cambridge, MA: Harvard University Press.

Hui, C. and Triandis, H. (1989) Effects of culture and response format on extreme response styles. *Journal of Cross-Cultural Psychology* 20, 296–309.

Jackendoff, R. (1997) *The Architecture of the Language Faculty*. Cambridge, MA: MIT Press.

Johnson J. and Newport, E. (1989) Critical period effects in second language learning: The influence of maturational state on the acquisition or English as a second language. *Cognitive Psychology* 21, 60–99.

Kagitcibasi, C. (1992) Research on parenting and child development in cross-cultural perspective. In M. Rosenzweig (ed.) *International Psychological Science* (pp. 137–60). Washington, DC: APA Publications.

Köpke, B. (2003) Neurolinguistic aspects of attrition. *Journal of Neurolinguistics* 17, 3–30.

Koven, M. (2001) Comparing bilinguals' quoted performances of self and others in tellings of the same experience in two languages. *Language in Society* 30, 513–58.

Kroll, J. and Stewart, E. (1994) Category interference in translation and picture naming: Evidence for asymmetric connections between bilingual memory representations. *Journal of Memory and Language* 33, 149–74.

Kroll, J. and Sunderman, G. (2003) Cognitive processes in second language acquisition: The development of lexical and conceptual representations. In C. Doughty and M. Long (eds) *Handbook of Second Language Acquisition* (pp. 104–29). Cambridge, MA: Blackwell Publishers.

LaBar, K. and Phelps, E. (1998) Arousal-mediated memory consolidation: Role of the medial temporal lobe in humans. *Psychological Science* 9, 490–93.

Lakoff, G. (1987) *Women, Fire, and Dangerous Things: What Categories Reveal About the Mind*. Chicago: Chicago University Press.

Lakoff, G. and Johnson, M. (1999) *Philosophy in the Flesh*. New York: Basic Books.

Langacker, R. (1987) *Foundations of Cognitive Grammar, Vol. I: Theoretical Prerequisites*. Stanford, CA: Stanford University Press.

LeDoux, J. (1996) *The Emotional Brain.* New York: Simon and Schuster.

LeDoux J. (2002) *Synaptic Self.* New York: Viking.

Levelt, W. (1989) *Speaking: From Intention to Articulation.* Cambridge, MA: MIT Press.

Lieberman, P. (2000) *Human Language and Our Reptilian Brain: The Subcortical Bases of Speech, Syntax, and Thought.* Cambridge, MA: Harvard University Press.

Manning, S. and Melchiori, M. (1974) Words that upset urban college students: Measures with GSRs and rating scales. *Journal of Social Psychology* 94, 305–306.

Marian, V. and Kaushanskaya, M. (2004). Self-construal and emotion in bicultural bilinguals. *Journal of Memory and Language* 51, 190–201.

Marian, V. and Neisser, U. (2000) Language-dependent recall of autobiographical memories. *Journal of Experimental Psychology: General* 129, 361–68.

Marinova-Todd, S., Marshall, B. and Snow, C. (2000) Three misconceptions about age and L2 learning. *TESOL Quarterly* 34, 9–34.

Mathews, A. and MacLeod, C. (1985) Discrimination of threat cues without awareness in anxiety states. *Journal of Abnormal Psychology* 95, 131–38.

Mathews, A., Richards, A. and Eysenck, M. (1989) Interpretation of homophones related to threat in anxiety states. *Journal of Abnormal Psychology* 98, 31–34.

Matsumoto, D. (2001) Culture and emotion. In D. Matsumoto (ed.) *The Handbook of Culture and Psychology* (pp. 171–94). New York: Oxford University Press.

Moyer, A. (1999) Ultimate attainment in L2 phonology. *Studies in Second Language Acquisition* 21, 81–108.

O'Regan, K. and Noe, A. (2001) A sensorimotor account of vision and visual consciousness. *Behavioral and Brain Sciences* 24, 939–73.

O'Reilly, R. and Munakata, Y. (2000) *Computational Explorations in Cognitive Neuroscience.* Cambridge, MA: MIT Press.

Panksepp, J. (1998) *Affective Neuroscience: The Foundations of Human and Animal Emotions.* New York: Oxford University Press.

Pavlenko A. (1998) Second language learning by adults: Testimonies of bilingual writers. *Issues in Applied Linguistics* 9, 3–19.

Pavlenko, A. (2002) Bilingualism and emotions. *Multilingua* 21, 45–78.

Pavlenko. A. (2004) 'Stop Doing That, *Ia Komu Skazala*!': Language choice and emotions in parent–child communication. *Journal of Multilingual and Multicultural Development* 25, 179–203.

Pinker, S. (1984) *Language Learnability and Language Development.* Cambridge, MA: Harvard University Press.

Pinker, S. (1994) *The Language Instinct.* New York: Harper Collins.

Poortinga, Y. (1989) Equivalence of cross-cultural data: An overview of basic issues. *International Journal of Psychology* 24, 737–56.

Rumelhart, D. and McClelland, J. (1986) *Parallel Distributed Processing: Explorations in the Microstructure of Cognition* (Vol. 1). Cambridge, MA: MIT Press.

Santiago-Rivera, A. and Altarriba, J. (2002) The role of language in therapy with the Spanish–English bilingual client. *Professional Psychology: Research and Practice* 33, 30–38.

Schrauf, R. (2000) Bilingual autobiographical memory: Experimental studies and clinical cases. *Culture and Psychology* 6, 387–417.

Schrauf, R. and Rubin, D. (1998) Bilingual autobiographical memory in older adult immigrants: A test of cognitive explanations of the reminiscence bump and the linguistic encoding of memories. *Journal of Memory and Language* 39, 437–57.

Schrauf, R. and Rubin, D. (2000) Internal languages of retrieval: The bilingual encoding of memories for the personal past. *Memory and Cognition* 28, 616–23.

Schumann, J. (1997) *The Neurobiology of Affect in Language.* Malden, MA: Blackwell.

Stelmack, R., Plouffe, L. and Falkenberg, W. (1983a) Extraversion, sensation seeking and electrodermal response: Probing a paradox. *Personality and Individual Differences* 4, 607–14.

Stelmack, R., Plouffe, L. and Winogron, W. (1983b) Recognition memory and the orienting response: An analysis of the encoding of pictures and words. *Biological Psychology* 16, 49–63.

Talmy, L. (2000) *Toward a Cognitive Semantics, Volume 1: Conceptual Structuring Systems.* Cambridge, MA: MIT Press.

Taylor, J. (2003) *Cognitive Grammar.* New York: Oxford University Press.

Thorndike, E. (1927) The law of effect. *American Journal of Psychology* 39, 212–22.

Toglia, M. and Battig, W. (1978) *Handbook of Semantic Word Norms.* Hillsdale, NJ: Lawrence Erlbaum.

Tranel, D., Fowles, D. and Damasio, A. (1985) Electrodermal discrimination of familiar and unfamiliar faces: A methodology. *Psychophysiology* 22, 403–408.

Chapter 11

Bilingual Autobiographical Memory and Emotion: Theory and Methods

ROBERT W. SCHRAUF and RAMON DURAZO-ARVIZU

Introduction

Does remembering an event in another language affect the feel of that memory? Would the immigrant's memories of childhood in another country feel less poignant when recalled in a second language? Do the sojourners' tales of life 'over-there' seem less emotionally powerful when translated for the folks at home? Certainly, some clinical reports suggest that the emotional power of a memory can be held at bay by talking about it in another language (Schrauf, 2000). Is emotion lost in translation? Experimental work on emotion in bilingual autobiographical memory is fairly recent, and in what follows, we address three broad questions: What is autobiographical memory? Where is the emotion in autobiographical memory? Where is the language in autobiographical memory? Over the course of the chapter, we offer a view that dissects a memory into (a) some details that are rather vividly re-experienced at recall and (b) some details that are supplied by other sources in memory. We suggest that both emotion and language are present in memories in both these ways. The sections on emotion and language include summaries and critiques of current research procedures and suggestions for improvements. In a final section, we present the findings from two recent studies of emotion in bilingual autobiographical memory (Marian & Kaushanskaya, 2004; Schrauf & Rubin, 2004) and advocate the use of more advanced statistical methods for the analysis of autobiographical memory data.

What is Autobiographical Memory?

I was in a hurry and really uptight about going dancing with Jessica because I was SO in love with her and I was late and just grabbing shoes and finally at the first slow dance while I was holding her

I looked down and realized that I had put on TWO DIFFERENT TENNIS SHOES, and I was SO embarrassed. (constructed example)

The retrieval of an autobiographical memory may be either spontaneous or effortful. Spontaneous memories, called 'unbidden' memories, are usually triggered by associations made to environmental stimuli (Bernsten, 1996, 1998). Effortful retrieval describes remembering in response to a request or memory cue. Effortful remembering moves through memory in an iterative, cyclic process (Conway, 1996; Reiser *et al.*, 1985, 1986). In a first step, information in the cue and information in the retrieval environment are combined to make up the search criteria or task model. Let us say that I am a member of a group of freshman college students, who at the icebreaker at new student orientation is asked to relate a funny story about myself. This situation comprises the retrieval environment (which is as much a social as it is a mental environment). As an explicit cue, I ask myself, 'When have I made a fool of myself?' This becomes the search criterion, and it is mentally held in working memory and used to search through my mental hierarchy of events in my life (Conway, 1996), organised into *lifetime periods* (e.g. high school, years in the Peace Corps, and so on), *generic events* (e.g. summer camps as a kid, going out to dinner with Sonia), and *specific memories*. I search my memory for a time when I made a fool of myself, and my best guess is that I did lots of socially inept things when I was in junior high school (lifetime period). Then, I think of whether I ever made a fool of myself in class, or in the gym, and so on (generic events). As information becomes available, it is evaluated against the search criteria, retained if pertinent, and re-entered into the next search cycle. No classroom experiences come to mind, but I land on my first, fumbling dates as a likely category for making a fool of myself.

Research on retrieval at the level of the specific event (Anderson & Conway, 1993) suggests that the first memory feature to be retrieved seems to be a distinctive detail that serves to characterize the memory (e.g. 'looking at my feet and realizing that I had put on two different tennis shoes'), along with some contextual detail (e.g. 'at the junior high dance with Jessica'). This is followed by the recall of the details in a temporal, forward chronological pattern (e.g. 'I was in a hurry and really uptight about going dancing with Jessica because I was SO in love with her and I was late and just grabbing shoes and finally at the first slow dance while I was holding her I looked down and realized that I had put on TWO DIFFERENT TENNIS SHOES, and I was SO embarrassed').

Not all of the information in a memory is directly remembered. Rather, certain elements seem to be vividly recalled, whereas other elements must be supplied from scripts or schemata. Wheeler *et al.* (1997) distinguish episodic memory (memory for events) from semantic memory (memory for facts) by noting that episodic memory is marked by a sense of reliving or, more lyrically, mental time travel. Tulving (1985) has coined the term *autonoetic consciousness* for this quality of re-experiencing and *noetic consciousness* for what we simply seem to know without a sense of reliving or 'being-there' again.

What is interesting here, however, is that autobiographical memories generally contain both kinds of remembered information: semantic and episodic (Table 11.1). We propose a model of autobiographical recall based on these distinctions:

(1) Some recalled details are 're-experienced'. In the example above, I may have a very vivid memory of one particular detail: looking down and seeing two different tennis shoes on my feet. This comes to consciousness with a 'quality of re-experiencing'.
(2) Some details are simply known (without a sense of reliving) or they are inferred. At least two types of such information are involved in a memory.
   (a) Information from higher levels in the structure of autobiographical memory (e.g. lifetime periods) is semantic in character. In the example, I do not actually experience junior high again; I just know it as a place and time of my life. Similarly, facts about oneself (e.g. 'I'm a bad dancer') are semantic and not episodic (Robinson & Swanson, 1990).
   (b) Some details and/or bits of information are inferred from script- and schema-based memory (Schank, 1982; Schrauf, 1997). So, for example, I am sure the dance took place on a Friday night, not because I remember it, but because almost all dances took place on Friday nights. It is an inference from other material in memory.

Table 11.1 Kinds of information in a reconstructed retrieval of a personal event (memory)

Type of memory process	*Type of information in memory*		*Degree of 'sense of reliving' accompanying recall*
Autonoetic consciousness or episodic remembering	Event-specific knowledge		Re-experienced details (remembered)
Noetic consciousness or semantic remembering	Personal themes/life periods	Schema- and script-based knowledge	Inferred details (known)

Finally, all memories, including unbidden or spontaneous ones, are triggered by some association and by some personal, and often social, motive. Explicit memory especially is goal-driven and uniquely self-relevant (Conway & Pleydell-Pearce, 2000), both at the moment of encoding (we encode into memory those events that have some personal relevance to us) and at retrieval (we recall from memory those events that have some relevance to our present concerns). This implies that events may be remembered as more consistent with the current self than they actually are (Ross, M., 1989; Ross, B., 1991). Lastly, memory serves different developmental needs across the lifespan, such as problem-solving in early and middle adulthood, or intimacy maintenance in old age (Webster, 1995).

In the next two sections of this chapter, on emotion and language, respectively, these specifications on how autobiographical information is stored and accessed will be used to talk about remembered emotion and remembered language – sometimes recalled and re-experienced episodically and sometimes simply known or inferred as semantic knowledge. In this model, emotion and language are part of the content of memories (although, as we suggest later on, language may play a much larger role and act as the 'integrator' of sensory and conceptual information in autobiographical retrieval).

What is an autobiographical memory? It is a mental reconstruction of a past event made by an individual for some current purpose (Brewer, 1996). Thus, to remember is not to reproduce a faithful copy of a pristine original, but rather to reconstruct a mental representation of an event out of variously available and selectively chosen details. In a strict sense, all of the information concerning a remembered event comes from memory, but some of the information will be accompanied by a sense of reliving (a re-experiencing), while other information will be inferred and not possess this 're-experienced' quality. These sources of information in the mental representation of personal events provide a structure for locating both emotion and language in autobiographical memory.

Where is the Emotion in Autobiographical Memory?

Empirical and theoretical considerations

In this chapter we assume a cognitive theory of emotions applied in cross-cultural work by a number of researchers (Mesquita & Frijda, 1992; Ortony et al., 1988; Scherer, 1984; Scherer & Wallbott, 1994; Shweder, 1991). In this framework, emotions are elicited by antecedent events in the sociocultural environment, which are culturally coded as a particular kind of event (insult, bereavement, success in a competition, and so on). The individual makes an appraisal of the event in terms of his or her well-being and goals (hence, this is often called 'appraisal theory'), and this is accompanied by some physiological reaction and emotion behavior (Scherer, 1999). Damasio (1994) suggests that these emotional reactions depend primarily on representations in the medial prefrontal cortex resulting from repeated linkings of events and their affective import. Cross-cultural similarities and differences in emotion are due (in part) to cross-cultural similarities and differences in how cultures categorize and code antecedent events and how individuals are enculturated to react to them (Mesquita & Frijda, 1992). In terms of the emotion lexicon, this results in a few pancultural emotion terms with high concordance across cultures, and numerous terms that are culture-specific (Schrauf & Sanchez, 2004).

These are also the elements that are retained in memory for emotion: the event, how the individual understood the event, and his or her reaction to it. Not all of these components are subsequently retained in memory for emotion. For instance, physiological reactions (increased heartbeat, shortness of breath – the actual *feeling*) may not be well remembered in memory. Strongman and Kemp (1991) asked undergraduates to recall emotional events of different types. Content analyses of the memories showed that participants recalled objective details but little in the way of behavioral or physiological response. Thus, in one sense, it is questionable whether the emotion associated with an event is actually replayed at the moment of recall, or whether it is the cognitive recall of details and reconstruction of the event that trigger an emotional response similar to the one felt at the time of the event (Ross, 1991).

In our description of autobiographical memory in the previous section, we noted that, in remembering any one event, some details are episodically recalled and more or less vividly re-experienced, whereas other details are semantically recalled and simply known (or inferred) to have been part of the event (Table 11.1). Applied to emotion, this suggests that some emotional detail in memory is remembered (i.e. re-experienced), while other emotional detail in memory is simply known. Returning once more to the constructed memory at the beginning of this chapter, it is entirely possible that the feelings of being 'uptight about going dancing with Jessica' and being 'SO in love' with Jessica are both remembered now in the sense of being 'known' (but not now re-experienced), whereas the feeling of being 'SO embarrassed' may still cause an interior cringing – and hence be re-experienced.

More formally, we would say that, at the moment of encoding, emotional information is laid down as part of the memory of that event. Then, at the moment of retrieval, this information may be episodically recalled with more or less intensity. At one end of the intensity spectrum might be especially vivid memories that are recalled with considerable intensity. When commemorating striking public events, these are called 'flashbulb memories' (e.g. the Kennedy assassination, Brown & Kulik, 1977; the Challenger Disaster, Neisser & Harsch, 1992; or 9/11, Talarico *et al.*, 2003), but of course memories for personal events can have the same kind of vivid emotional intensity (Rubin & Kozin, 1984). At the other end of the intensity spectrum might be details recalled and re-experienced but only mildly so. However, it is also true at the moment of retrieval that a good deal of 'remembered' emotion is semantically recalled, and not actually re-experienced. In experimental protocols, this is especially evident when people report many, and sometimes contradictory, feelings about a single event, usually by taking perspectives on the event from different levels of the memory hierarchy. Emotion can also be inferred from script- or schema-based elements. For example, after first moving to Chicago, I (the first author) remember getting lost one night while driving from North Side to South Side and feeling quite panicky that I would not find my way back home. Finally, I found a major road and got home quickly. I recall the panic quite explicitly, but I can only infer the sense of relief that I must have felt at finding the main road. That is, I do not actually recall feeling relieved; rather I infer it from the typical 'getting lost' schema that ends with 'finally finding one's way back'.

Similarly, as the research on emotion and states of the current self shows, the emotion felt at the time of an event may well be remembered differently depending on changes in current self, attitudes, and beliefs. This may involve an unconscious altering of the memory (Bluck & Li, 2001; Levine, 1997; Levine *et al.*, 2001; Walker *et al.*, 2003) or it may involve some conscious re-framing (Beike & Landoll, 2000). For instance, applicants for admission to medical school may be asked to write an essay about important figures from their lives who shaped their interest in medicine. Given such a charge, individuals may well remember fonder feelings toward certain past mentors than they felt in the actual past.

Where is the emotion in autobiographical memory? Considerations about 'supplied' emotion are not meant to suggest in any way that some feelings are validly remembered while others are not. This is not a question of genuine versus 'fake' feeling. Some feelings may have been strikingly intense at the time of an event but rarely ever remembered with much intensity afterwards. Rather the difference is in the status of information in memory: some details are remembered (re-experienced), some are simply known (Tulving, 1985). The distinction between the 're-experienced felt' and the 'simply known felt' serves to highlight that remembered emotion is precisely that: *remembered* emotion. The range of emotions that a person felt at the time of an event may come back in memory, and they may not. The strength, or intensity, of a remembered emotion may replay itself when the event is remembered, or it may not.

Finding emotion in memory: Methodological considerations

How do we go about probing remembered emotion? Research on the phenomenological experience of emotion has concentrated on two dimensions of emotion: valence and intensity (Feldman, 1995; Feldman-Barret, 1998). *Valence* refers to the pleasantness versus unpleasantness of an emotion. *Intensity* usually refers to the amount of arousal associated with a particular emotion. Any emotion may be characterized along these two dimensions. Anger, for instance, is an unpleasant emotion with high intensity. Disappointment would be an unpleasant emotion with lower intensity. Similarly, romantic love is pleasant, with high intensity. Contentment is a pleasant emotion with rather low intensity. A variety of cross-cultural studies suggest that these two basic dimensions may be pancultural in emotion experience (Herrmann & Raybeck, 1981; Romney *et al.*, 1997; Russell, 1991). This work suggests that valence contrasts are fairly stable. Hate, anger, and sadness, for example, are unpleasant; joy and love are pleasant. Research on intensity, on the other hand, shows that it is an individual differences variable (Larsen & Diener, 1987; Schimmack & Diener, 1997). Some individuals experience emotion (both positive and negative) more intensely than others – their highs are higher and their lows are lower.

In studies of autobiographical memory, information on valence and intensity comes from self-reports or from post-hoc coding of memory transcripts (Table 11.2). In self-report, the participant is questioned about the valence and intensity of emotion at the moment of retrieval (Larsen *et al.*, 2002; Schrauf & Rubin, 1998, 2000). In post-hoc coding, the participant narrates his or her memory, either out loud or in written form, after which the researcher transcribes and codes the memory narrative for valence and intensity (Marian & Kaushanskaya, 2004; Schrauf & Rubin, 2001).

Self-report

When asking about valence and intensity at the moment of retrieval, researchers can phrase questions to direct the participant's attention to the experience of retrieval or to the experience of encoding (or both). Participants are then asked to rate the pleasantness/unpleasantness of an experience on a Likert scale. Alternatively, because the relative valence of common emotions is fairly well-defined, as well as cross-culturally similar, investigators could simply ask participants to name the emotions associated with a memory, and then assign valence ratings from rankings of emotion terms on the pleasant/unpleasant dimension from the literature (e.g. for Spain, Vietnam, Hong Kong, Haiti, Greece, and the United States; Herrmann & Raybeck, 1981). This seems a defensible procedure, because the relative ranking of the valence of different kinds of emotion does not differ across individuals.

Table 11.2 Methods of gathering information about emotion in autobiographical memories

Type of observation	Identifying emotion type	Characterizing valence	Characterizing intensity
Asked at the moment of recalling a memory	• Ask what emotions accompany the event (free-recall) • Check off emotions from a list (recognition)	• Ask for ratings of (un) pleasantness • Code emotions named, e.g. using rankings from previous cross-cultural research	• Ask for ratings of intensity on a Likert scale
'Coded post-hoc' – coding transcripts of memories	• Code transcripts via a concordance of emotion words plus circumlocutions	• Code transcripts via a scheme, e.g. using rankings from previous cross-cultural research	• Code transcripts for intensity via some scheme developed from the whole corpus

Ratings of emotional intensity, however, do differ considerably from event to event within participants and from person to person across participants. Questions about intensity usually involve a rating on a Likert scale, and participants' attention may be directed to either the experience of retrieval or encoding or both. An example of a question focusing on retrieval is: 'I can feel now what I felt then...' (1 = not at all, 3 = vaguely, 5 = distinctly, 7 = as clearly as if it were happening right now). Note that this question actually asks about emotional reinstatement (i.e. how intensely the emotion felt at the moment of encoding is felt at the moment of retrieval). This seems true to common experience in that a very emotional experience may be recalled without much emotional accompaniment. Indeed, Walker and colleagues (2003) argue that, over time, negative emotions are recalled with less intensity – a phenomenon they call the 'fading affect bias'. On the other hand, the participant's attention can be directed toward the experience of encoding. Participants can be asked to rate the intensity of the emotion at the time of the event itself.

Post-hoc coding of transcripts

Coding transcribed narratives involves the intermediate steps of transcribing taped memories, developing a coding scheme, and coding the transcripts. Developing a coding scheme that catches different kinds of emotion and that is sensitive to valence and intensity is an intricate process. For example, identifying which emotions were felt is more complex than looking for emotion words, because people often use circumlocutions to describe their feelings (e.g. 'I was boiling' instead of 'I was furious'). Wilma Bucci suggests that 'emotional experience may be captured most effectively by the verbal system by describing specific images and episodes, as poets know . . .' (1995: 103–104). To find such circumlocutions requires developing a codebook of emotional expressions to accompany actual emotion words.

Coding for intensity requires interpreting just how strongly an emotion is felt from verbal intensifiers (e.g. very, so, really, absolutely, crazy with ____ , wild with ____ , and so on). Deriving intensity ratings from verbal descriptions is problematic because coded intensity may then reflect the participants' verbal abilities instead of their actual emotional experience. For example, two participants who react with similar intensity to the same event may differ in their emotional expressivity; one has a florid emotion vocabulary, the other employs few emotion words. Post-hoc coding may overestimate the reactions of the first and underestimate the reactions of the second. One could argue that in explicitly bilingual research this point is moot, because each person serves as his or her own control, but then (as we will argue below) the focus subtly shifts from an examination of emotion to an examination of types of persons and individual differences in expressivity.

In the case of bilinguals, a second problem with post-hoc coding of emotion is that the step from retrieval to report-in-words involves employing the narrative conventions of spoken language. This introduces a cross-linguistic confound. Considerable research now shows that languages differ in how their particular morphological, lexical, and syntactic conventions shape the expression of detail in narrative (Berman & Slobin, 1994; Slobin, 1996). By implication, some information may well be retrieved from memory but not be narratively expressed, because the language spoken (or written) does not provide for the obligatory expression of those details (Clark, 2003). Further, languages seem to differ in how many emotion words actually exist in their lexicons and/or in the working emotion vocabularies of individual speakers. As an example of the former, research suggests that English has some 577 emotion words (Storm & Storm, 1987), whereas Tagalog has around 256 (Church et al., 1996). As an example of the latter, the working emotion vocabulary of a particular group can be established by having participants free-list as many emotion words as they can in a determined amount of time (Schrauf & Sanchez, 2004).

Above, we have discussed the organization and functioning of autobiographical memory and the retrieval of remembered emotion as part of that personal recollection. We have also discussed methods of querying emotion in autobiographical recall, emphasizing self-reported emotion at the moment of recall and the post-hoc coding of memory transcripts.

We suggest that remembering an event is a dynamic mental process – a mental reconstruction – that combines some details that are vividly re-experienced in the moment of recall and other details that are simply known or inferred. The emotional content of memories is subject to the same recollective dynamic – some emotions are re-experienced at recall, some are simply known or inferred. The same model applies to language, although bilingualism makes the case all the more interesting. We turn to this material in the following section.

Where is the Language in Autobiographical Memory?

Empirical and theoretical considerations

Over a series of studies of older bilingual immigrants, research has shown that language plays a crucial role in bilinguals' recall of personal memories. Studies of Spanish–English immigrants in the United States (Schrauf & Rubin, 1998, 2000, 2004) show consistent results. Participants in these studies were immigrants, 50 years old and above, who emigrated from the country of origin to the country of adoption in late adolescence through middle adulthood. All were highly educated and had conducted their professional lives in the second language. Protocols were as follows: they received word cues to which they associated memories on one day in one language and on another day in the other language. They were asked to indicate 'in which language(s) each memory came to them' (e.g. none, Spanish, English, both). Similar results were found across three studies; the majority of Spanish memories commemorate events prior to immigration when only Spanish was spoken, while English memories were for events after immigration.

In Denmark, older Poles who had been forced for political reasons to emigrate from Poland to Denmark in 1969–1971 participated in a similar protocol (Larsen et al., 2002). Two groups were recruited: Early Immigrators were approximately 24 years old at the time of immigration, Later Immigrators were 34. Predictably, Early Immigrators' memories in Polish drop off after their immigration to Denmark, while Later Immigrators' Polish memories span an additional ten years in accord with their later immigration. Memories seem to be tagged by the language of encoding in some durable way, and this language is effective at retrieval. Using cuing procedures in work with young adult Russian–English bilinguals, Marian and Neisser (2000) also found that cues and sessions in Russian generated more Russian memories than English memories.

The cognitive literature presents two similar explanations for this phenomenon: encoding specificity and state-dependent learning. Encoding specificity suggests that 'recollection of an event, or certain aspects of it, occurs if and only if, properties of the trace of the event are sufficiently similar to the properties of the retrieval situation' (Tulving, 1983: 223). Applied to bilingual recollection: the language of the cue matches some linguistic element in the autobiographical memory trace. A more global version of encoding specificity is state-dependent learning (Weingartner, 1978). Here the language spoken at the time of the event, whether the event was explicitly conversational or not, is considered a cognitive state that conditions the information processing that took place at the time of the event. In either case, the underlying supposition is that memories are tagged by language.

As discussed in the first two sections of this chapter, the mental representation of an autobiographical memory is a reconstruction of an event out of various sources of remembered information. That is, some memory detail and information will be re-experienced at recall (retrieved episodically), whereas other details will be known or inferred (Table 11.1). Just as with emotion, the presence of 'language' or 'linguistic elements' in an autobiographical memory correspond to these distinctions. In what follows, we argue that there are three sources of language content in autobiographical memories: explicit content, inner speech, and propositional thought. Some language is explicitly remembered and re-experienced. This is language as *explicit content* of memory (e.g. I can hear the person speaking the words). Some language is part of a memory because I remember my thinking in language at the time of the event or when I remember it. This is *inner speech*. Finally, there is the possibility that language itself structures remembering. This is a more radical claim about *propositional thought*.

Explicit content

Some of the language in memory may well be directly re-experienced. To wit, language may be explicitly represented as part of the content of a remembered event. A remembered conversation, phrases from a public speech, recorded messages on answering machines, words of advice from one's mentor are all examples of explicit language content in a memory, as are words from a newspaper article or a street sign.

Inner speech

Language elements (e.g. morphosyntactic items, lexical items) may also be added to explicitly encoded information. In an experiment in which Spanish–English bilinguals were asked to think aloud from the moment they saw the memory cue word through the narration of a relevant autobiographical memory, Schrauf (2003) found that participants mentioned various ways in which linguistic elements mentally triggered further associations in memory. This happened at the level of morphemes, as in the following example of an individual responding to the cue word *solito* (alone):

I guess ... I don't know, first I started thinking about the 'ito' – it makes me think of my little nephews and stuff, just because that's something they'd say... but the memory that comes to mind is actually me, and um, when I was younger, camping out ...

And it happened at the level of words and phrases, as with this participant responding to the cue word 'doubt':

... it reminds me of ... a phrase in Spanish ... 'sin duda' ... and, I don't know, like an event ... it reminds me of my mom, and she would ask me, she would try to verify what I'm trying to say ...

In both cases, participants talk about mental words (or word forms) that influence the act of retrieval.

An association model of memory suggests that as information is retrieved it serves to activate related information (Collins & Loftus, 1975). Thus, we might expect that language elements would act as cues for additional details during retrieval. A parallel is found in psycholinguistic models of memory-based text processing (Keenan & Jennings, 1995; Kintsch, 1988; McKoon & Ratcliff, 1992a,b; Ratcliff & McKoon, 1994). Here, the words, concepts, and propositions of texts trigger information in long-term memory, and this information is, in turn, coordinated into coherent interpretations during text comprehension. Thus, beyond simply representing specific pieces of information as contents of memory, language plays a much more active role in the process of reconstructive retrieval of memories (Schrauf *et al.*, 2003).

This is not to imply that autobiographical memories are produced in full-blown sentences, as if memory took place in neat little paragraphs. Rather, the suggestion here is that many autobiographical memories are accompanied by inner speech (Vygotsky, 1962) – some snippets, some phrases, some full-blown sentences. This inner speech involves auditory imagery (Reisberg, 1992), whereby the mind accesses the phonological forms of morphemes and lexemes (i.e. they are mentally heard and mentally spoken). The protocol analysis described above suggests how this might work (Schrauf, 2003). Far from the production of complete sentences, inner speech is intermittent. It is also 'syntactically crushed' in that, for example, 'the subject of a thought is almost always known to the speaker and so is seldom stated' (Korba, 1990: 1044). Further, it is semantically elaborate: words are polyvalent and have multiple references. The suggestion here is that, at points in memory retrieval in which information from various sources in memory is integrated in the production of a mental representation of a previously experienced event, inner speech can often play a key role.

Propositional thought

A more radical argument can be mounted that the integration of information in an autobiographical memory, from a variety of sources in the mind/brain, is actually facilitated by natural language below awareness. These notions are grounded in the work of Peter Carruthers (1998, 2002), who suggests that natural language provides the medium of non-domain-specific, propositionally based inferential thought. The critical difference from inner speech is that such propositional thought does not involve auditory imagery. That is, language is not mentally heard or spoken. As an example, Carruthers points to a cognitive task – problem solving – in which information must be integrated from a variety of domain-specific information processors, and he suggests that the central processor employs natural language syntax from the peripheral language module to integrate the information. Natural language could play a similar role in the formation of autobiographical memories in which various kinds of information from different brain centers (visual, linguistic, emotional, and so on) must be integrated into a coherent narrative whole. Obviously, this is a hypothetical account of the role of language in autobiographical memory, and subject to experimental investigation, but bilinguals might offer ideal research participants because natural language for them would be variable. More to the point, the awareness at some level that language is involved in remembering might explain how bilingual participants judge that certain memories came to them in one language rather than another. Either of the bilingual's languages might provide the organizational syntax that organizes the details of a remembered event (Schrauf, 2002).

Where is the language in memory? Language is found in many memories as explicit content of those memories. Conversations, advice, speeches, even self-talk at time of the event, are all examples of remembered language. However, many memories also include inner speech generated during the time of retrieval itself. Arguably, whenever reasoning accompanies a memory (e.g. 'Why was I running away?' 'What made me think she was Italian?') or the search for additional details is triggered (e.g. 'What was the name of that restaurant?' 'How did that whole thing get resolved?'), then pieces of language come into consciousness as part of retrieval. Finally, at a more controversial level, it may be that any memory processed by a mind that already regularly functions as a language processor will be tagged by a particular language (Carruthers, 1998). That is, it is possible that the bilingual mind encodes and retrieves memories in either or both languages at this deep, propositional level and that this processing leaves its linguistic mark on particular memories (Schrauf, 2002).

Finding language in memory: Methodological considerations

Determining whether and how language affects retrieval in bilingual memory involves determining the language of remembering at two moments: encoding and retrieval.

Language of encoding

In the best of worlds we would manipulate the language of encoding by having bilingual individuals participate in constructed events that somehow involved one or the other language and then having them recall those events at a later date. However, given the temporal dynamics of human consolidation of long-term memories, we would have to wait several years from 'study' to 'test'. This seems impractical. In research to date, then, two proxy methods have been used.

On the one hand, Schrauf and colleagues (Larsen *et al.*, 2002; Schrauf & Rubin, 1998, 2000, 2004) recruited consecutive bilinguals (immigrants) who were monolingual in one language for many years and who then learned a second language as a result of immigration. Thus, events encoded into memory prior to immigration (while participants were monolingual in their L1) are L1 memories while memories encoded after immigration and the acquisition of L2 could be either L1 or L2 or mixtures of both. This approach takes advantage of an experiment conducted by nature (or history); some monolingual/monocultural minds become bilingual/bicultural minds via immigration. During a monolingual period, any language effect on an encoded memory can only come from the one language. Then, during a bilingual period, any memory could be affected by bilingual encoding. Thus, some memories are unquestionably monolingual at encoding (e.g. pre-immigration events), while all others are potentially bilingual at encoding (e.g. post-immigration events).

On the other hand, participants can also be directly asked about the language of encoding. For each memory, Schrauf and Rubin (2000) asked participants two questions: (1) 'In the memory, I can hear myself or other people talking...' and (2) 'In the memory I can see written words on a sign, in a note, in a newspaper, etc....' Both questions were answered on Likert scales (1 = not at all, 3 = vaguely, 5 = distinctly, 7 = as clearly as if it were happening right now). To determine the language spoken at the time of the memory, they asked: 'I usually spoke Spanish, English, or both with the person in the memory (even if they were not talking in the memory itself)'. Similarly, Marian and Neisser (2000) asked participants to indicate for each memory what language(s) they themselves (the participants) spoke, what language(s) were spoken to them, or what language(s) they were surrounded by in the memory. This approach has the advantage of allowing the researcher to eliminate 'noisy' memories in which more than one language was associated with the memory at the time of encoding and to distinguish 'pure' L1 memories from 'pure' L2 memories.

Both approaches make attempts to query what exactly is linguistic in the encoding of a memory. The Schrauf and Rubin (2000) study includes heard speech and the presence of written words. The Marian and Neisser (2000) procedure asks about heard and spoken speech and the language spoken in general in the memory. As indicated above, however, inner speech may also play an important role in rendering memories linguistic.

Neither approach is sensitive to recoding effects. That is, the researcher cannot be sure that a memory that was in fact originally encoded in one or the other language has not been recoded (as a result of intervening recall) in the other language. For example, a Puerto Rican adult who came to the mainland United States at the start of junior high school may have a clear memory of being scolded (in Spanish) by his first grade teacher in Puerto Rico. However, he may have told this story so many times to friends in English that the memory has been recoded into English – in which case it is not really a 'Spanish' memory. Both of these issues (the range of linguistic features in a memory and recoding effects) can, however, be dealt with at retrieval, and this will be discussed in what follows.

Language at retrieval

Language effects at retrieval may be either manipulated, assessed, or both. Language is manipulated when participants are asked to recall memories while in specific language conditions (all instructions, memory cues, and conversation in the experimental session are in either L1 or L2). All of the studies mentioned heretofore have manipulated language of retrieval in this way. The Marian and Neisser (2000) study then analyzed memories matched on language of encoding and language of retrieval versus those that were unmatched.

Language effects at retrieval can also be directly assessed – albeit through self-reports. This has been the practice of Schrauf and colleagues. On the logic that what makes a memory linguistic can range from verbatim memory for conversation to snippets of inner speech, and given that recoding memories at subsequent retrievals can involve 'translating' them, Schrauf and Rubin (2003) have reasoned that it is better to ask participants in what language a memory seems to come to them. Thus, in an attempt to get as close as possible to the retrieval experience, Schrauf and Rubin asked participants, for each memory: (1) what language it came in (if any), and (2) 'There were words in the memory ...' (1 = no language element whatsoever, 4 = vague words, phrases or fragments, 7 = very clear words).

Although the strength of this approach is its immediacy (the participant is asked about language at the very moment of encoding), its weakness is that it relies on participants' intuitions about their experience. In fact, it is possible that participants do not consult the experience of retrieval to decide if a memory came to them in a particular language but rather make inferences based on other information. Gulgoz, Schrauf, and Rubin (2001) attempted to parse these intuitions.

Participants in this experiment were 20 simultaneous, Ladino–Turkish bilinguals from the Jewish community in Istanbul, Turkey, who ranged in age from 39 to 88 years (M = 56.5, SD = 12.9). All were born of bilingual Turkish–Ladino parents in Istanbul, and all reported acquiring both languages by four years of age. Eight individuals reported Ladino as their native language, and 12 reported Turkish as their native language. The same protocol was used as in previous work. Participants recalled 15 memories to Turkish cue words in one session and 15 memories to Ladino cue words in another session. Cue words were carefully chosen so that their phonetic form would not trigger recall of the translation equivalent in the other language. In addition to reporting their age at the time of the event and in what language the memory came to them, participants were also asked about the context of the memory, including: the language usually spoken with others in the memory, the setting of the event and language associated with that setting, and frequency of rehearsal of the event.

These variables were entered as predictors in a stepwise logistic regression with *memories identified as having come in Ladino* and *memories identified as having come in Turkish* as dependent variables. That is, assuming that individuals were making language judgements based on contextual information, the authors tested for what that contextual information might be. Four predictors emerged from the resulting significant model (Nagelkerke $R^2 = 0.695$; $\chi^2(6) = 217.72$, $p < 0.001$). These were the language of the session, increasing the chances that the memory would be recalled in the same language as that of the session (Wald $(1) = 8.43$, $p < 0.005$), the language used with the actors of the event, also increasing the chances that the memory would be recalled in the same language as that spoken by the actors (Wald $(3) = 88.10$, $p < 0.001$), the age at which the participant experienced the event (older age predicted Turkish memories; Wald $(1) = 12.02$, $p < 0.005$), and finally the frequency of rehearsal, such that more rehearsed events tended to be recalled in Ladino (Wald $(1) = 4.64$, $p < 0.05$). Each of these pieces of information could act as triggers for an inference about the 'language in which the memory came to me'. Only further research, with more sensitive measures, can resolve the issue of whether participants actually experience language in their retrievals or simply infer it. Given the theoretical model advanced in the course of this chapter, future efforts might focus on attending to the kinds of linguistic information contained in retrieval: explicit content, inner speech, and propositional thought.

Depending on the research question, then, the language(s) accompanying an autobiographical memory may be manipulated or reported either at time of encoding or time of retrieval (Table 11.3).

Findings and a Critique: Using Multilevel Modeling

Given that the data have been collected in the ways described above, the researcher will want to test for particular relationships. Typically, such analyses involve *simple* and *multiple regression*, in which one (or more) variables are used to predict an outcome variable. For example, what predicts that some memories are very emotional? The importance of the event? The vividness of recall? Another frequent method is *analysis of variance* (ANOVA), in which groups are compared with respect to some variable. For example, are first language memories more emotional than second language memories? Do bilinguals recall childhood memories with more emotional intensity in the first compared to the second language, and so on? These are common techniques found throughout the literature. However, these methods have come in for some criticism.

Recent research on statistical techniques suggests that newer methods of *multilevel modeling* may be more appropriate for autobiographical memory research than the traditional regression and ANOVA models. Standard treatments of multilevel modeling, also called random

Table 11.3 Methods of gathering information about the language of autobiographical memories

Memory stage or process	Manipulation of L1 vs. L2 as context of event or condition of remembering	Self-report of L1 vs. L2 in memory
Encoding (language at the time of the event)	• Use consecutive bilingual participants (immigrants): pre-immigration *monolingual* (L1) events vs. post-immigration, *bilingual* (L1 + L2) events	• Enquire about language spoken/heard by ego or people in the event • Enquire about words seen or read (e.g. signs, newspapers) in the event
Retrieval (language at the time of remembering the event)	• Block retrieval sessions by L1 vs. L2 • Manipulate language of cues (L1 vs. L2)	• Enquire whether memory comes in no language, L1, L2, or both • Enquire whether remembering involves no language, vague words and phrases, very clear words and phrases

coefficient models and hierarchical linear models, can be found in Kreft and de Leeuw (1998) and Snijders and Bosker (1999). In a seminal paper, Wright (1998) introduced multilevel modeling to research on autobiographical memory. Of various examples that he employed, his illustration of analyses of the relation between the importance and emotion in autobiographical memory is most pertinent here. He outlined three approaches to these data in which the importance of memories was the predictor variable and the emotion of memories was the response variable. Following Wright's example, let us assume that 30 participants recall 30 memories. Participants rate each memory for its importance and for their emotional reaction to the event. We predict a relationship between importance and emotion – the more important the memory, the more emotional the reaction.

In a first approach, an investigator could treat the individual memories as a unit of analysis and run a simple regression. Thus, there are 30 memories and 30 participants, so there are 900 memories. Each memory has both an importance rating and an emotion rating associated with it. In a simple regression, the 900 importance ratings are used to predict the 900 emotion ratings. This is problematic, however, because individual memories are not independent observations (in a statistical sense), but are clustered within participants. All of Joe's memories, for example, are dependent on one another by virtue of being generated by Joe. Pooling them indiscriminately with Susie's and Jim's and Jane's memories ignores this fact.

In a second approach, an investigator might treat the person (participant) as the unit of analysis by taking the mean importance rating of all the memories of each participant and the mean emotion rating of all the memories of each participant and then running a regression on these participant means. Thus, Joe has a mean importance rating (obtained by averaging all of the importance rating for all of his memories) and a mean emotion rating (obtained by averaging all of the emotion ratings for all of his memories), Susie has a mean importance rating and a mean emotion rating, and so on. With 30 participants, there will be 30 participant means for importance and 30 participant means for emotion. Again, in a simple regression, the 30 participant importance means are used to predict the 30 participant emotion means. The problem here is that the analysis now concerns persons (participants), not memories, and much information is lost by averaging out the variability in importance and emotion ratings of the memories. After all, we set out to find out about the effect of importance on emotion in memories, not in persons.

The third approach, multilevel modeling, overcomes these problems by treating the data as clustered from the start. Thus, in the multilevel model of the effect of importance on emotion, the ratings of importance and emotion are allowed to vary within participants (first level) and participants are allowed to vary among themselves (second level). At the (first) level of the memories, within each participant, the mean emotion rating and the variance of ratings around that mean are both represented, so that each participant has his or her own regression coefficient expressing the relation between importance and emotion. In the example used above, we would compute a regression between importance ratings and emotion ratings just on Joe's memories, and then another regression just on Susie's memories, and so on. In addition, participants are allowed to vary. That is, the mean of participant means and variation around that group mean are also represented. Again, in the example, Joe's average would be different from Susie's, and so on. Stated otherwise, each participant has its own intercept, and the mean of these intercepts has a certain variance associated with it.

In two recent studies on bilingual autobiographical memory, both the first and second approaches have been used. In the following paragraphs, these will be reviewed and critiqued in light of the foregoing, after which a re-analysis in terms of multilevel modeling will be offered.

Marian and Kaushanskaya (2004) recruited Russian–English bicultural bilinguals who had migrated to the United States at a mean age of 14 years (SD = 3.4) and whose mean age at time of study was 21 years (SD = 2.6). Participants were presented with 16 cue words in Russian and in English and asked to describe the first event from their life that came to mind. All memories were transcribed and coded by Russian–English bilinguals for valence and intensity. The valence scale ranged from 1 (narratives that expressed completely negative affect) to 7 (narratives that expressed completely positive affect). Intensity was rated from 1 (no emotion) to 6 (extremely high emotion). Details about how these codings were applied to the texts were not provided. To determine language at encoding, participants were asked what language they used at the time of the event. Language of retrieval was manipulated, of course, by the languages of cues and session. Memories were then grouped into two encoding–retrieval conditions for each participant: matches (Russian encoding–Russian retrieval, English encoding–English retrieval) and mismatches (Russian encoding–English retrieval, English encoding–Russian retrieval).

To test for the effects of language on intensity, mean intensity ratings were taken for each participant, and these were entered into a 2 (language of encoding) × 2 (language of retrieval) ANCOVA, in which narrative length was entered as a covariate. Results show that those memories in which language of encoding matches language of retrieval (e.g. Russian encoding–Russian retrieval) are rated as more emotionally intense than when language is not matched (e.g. Russian encoding–English retrieval). Note, however, that by using each participant's mean intensity ratings as the unit of analysis, the analysis actually draws conclusions about individual differences between persons and not memories.

To examine the effect of language on valence, the authors integrated another concept of interest into the analysis. Because they were interested in collectivism versus individualism, they coded each memory for whether the actors in the memory were the self (ego) or others, and constructed a three-way ANOVA with language of encoding, language of retrieval, and main agent as independent variables and valence ratings as dependent variables. The authors used the individual memory (and not participant means) as the unit of analysis (because entering participant means would have made the design too complex). Results showed a main effect of agent and a main effect of encoding, but no main effect of retrieval. In sum, when the agent was others, memories were more positive, and in general, memories encoded in Russian were less positive than English memories or mixed language memories. Note, however, that by using individual memories as the unit of analysis, the study treats memories as if they were independent, whereas they are in fact dependent on the individuals within whom they are clustered.

Schrauf and Rubin (2004) studied older, Spanish–English speaking, Puerto Rican bilinguals whose mean age at the time of the study was 69.35 (SD = 6.90), and who had emigrated from the island to the mainland between the ages of 15 and 38 years. In the experimental protocol, participants retrieved memories across blocked Spanish sessions (2) and English sessions (2) to words and pictures, and then made judgements about certain phenomenological properties of those memories. Concerning language, participants were asked to judge whether the memory came to them in no language, Spanish, English, or both Spanish and English. Concerning emotion, participants were asked to name the emotion(s) they felt at the time of the memory (and were provided a list of emotions to trigger their memories). In addition, they were asked to rate the intensity of the reinstatement of those feelings at the time of retrieval: 'I can feel now what I felt then . . .' (1 = nothing, 3 = vaguely, 5 = distinctly, 7 = as clearly as if it were happening right now).

The question posed here was simply, does the language of retrieval affect the intensity of emotional reinstatement? The data were analyzed by repeated measures on person means. Each person contributed three scores to the analysis: the means of his or her emotion ratings for Spanish, English, and Mixed Spanish–English memories. The single factor analysis of variance with three levels (Spanish, English, and Mixed memories) showed a significant difference between these means. Post-hoc comparison of means suggested that ratings of emotional reinstatement for English memories (M = 5.99, SD = 1.49) and mixed language memories (M = 5.88, SD = 1.26) were higher than ratings for Spanish memories (M = 5.38, SD = 5.38). The authors speculated that the novel cultural and linguistic framing of these English and mixed language memories may have rendered them more emotionally salient than first language memories. Note, however, that by averaging intensity ratings per participant and then entering these into the ANOVA, this procedure has ignored each participant's variation around his or her mean score. This information is lost. For example, how would it affect the analysis if all participants had very large variations around their English means but small variations around their Spanish means? Again, the focus has shifted from memories to persons. In one sense, the finding should read: 'Individuals who rated as high in emotional reinstatement for their English memories and mixed language memories also rated as low in emotional reinstatement for their Spanish memories'. This is certainly informative, but the question originally posed was about memories, not individuals.

Both studies employ repeated measures designs, and these are certainly powerful techniques, because each participant serves as his or her own control. Nevertheless, by treating participants as the unit of analysis, the statistical procedure has subtly shifted the question from the emotional intensity of memories to the emotional intensity of participants. This suggests that the study of emotion in bilingual autobiographical memory is ripe for multilevel modeling. To illustrate these applications, the following paragraphs articulate a re-analysis of some of the findings in Schrauf and Rubin (2004). The two levels of analysis are the person (participant) level and the memory level. Memories are nested within participants. The model is as follows:

$$\text{Intensity}_{ij} = \beta 0_{ij}\text{cons} + 0.237(0.081)\text{english}_{ij} + 0.253(0.061)\text{mixed}_{ij}$$

$$\beta 0_{ij} = -0.140(0.091) + u_{0j} + e_{0ij}$$

$$[u_{0j}] \sim N(0, \Omega_u) : \Omega_u = [0.229(0.063)]$$

$$[e_{0ij}] \sim N(0, \Omega_e) : \Omega_e = [0.802(0.028)]$$

$$-2 * \text{loglikelihood (IGLS)} = 4575.917$$

Intensity is the dependent variable, and scores have been standardized. Predictors are the languages at retrieval: Spanish, English, and Mixed-Spanish-and-English (with English and Mixed memories used as dichotomous variables to represent all three language conditions). The subscripts i and j indicate that emotion ratings are left to vary at both levels: the memory level (i) and the person level (j). (Note that variation at the memory level is information lost in the traditional model in which person means alone are analyzed, and deviations around those means are ignored.) Variation at the person and memory levels is represented by the letters u and e, where u represents the person level residuals, and e represents memory level residuals. Numbers in parentheses are standard errors.

There is, of course, a large difference in variability at the person level (0.229) versus the memory level (0.802), and this makes perfect sense in that people commonly have both highly emotional recalls as well as recalls with no emotion whatsoever. The variance at the person level is also significant ($u_{oj} = 0.229$, SE $= 0.063$; z $= 3.64$), and this suggests that accounting for differences between persons is important. Stated otherwise, the assumption of independence is not valid. $\beta 0_{ij}$ represents the mean intercept, in this case, ratings of emotional reinstatement for Spanish memories (which serves as the reference category), and its value is -0.140. English memories are rated 0.237 of a standard deviation higher than Spanish memories (z $= 2.92$). Mixed memories are rated 0.253 of a standard deviation higher than Spanish memories, and the difference is significant (z $= 4.15$).

Findings are the same as the repeated measures ANOVA. The research question motivating the study was: does the language of retrieval affect the intensity of emotional reinstatement? The answer is yes. The fit of the null model of no affect is $\chi^2 = 4605.14$, whereas the model with three language conditions is $\chi^2 = 4575.91$. This difference (29.23) with three degrees of freedom is significant at well below $p < 0.001$. What is the language effect? English memories and English–Spanish mixed memories are rated as significantly more intense than Spanish memories. (Possible explanations for this result are explored in Schrauf & Rubin, 2004.) English memories were also found to be more vivid than Spanish memories, and the authors suggest that the Anglo cultural framing of these memories might make them more mentally salient in general than first language memories.

Whereas this re-analysis yields the same result as the traditional repeated measures, single factor ANOVA, this may not always be true. More importantly, multilevel modeling provides a more sensitive test of the hypotheses advanced in most research on bilingual autobiographical modeling. Where data are clearly clustered, as here memories are clustered within individuals, it is important to attend to this structure. Particularly in the case of autobiographical memory where repeated measures designs commonly focus on person means with the resultant loss of information at the lowest (memory) level, this new technique allows us to include information about both, while simultaneously avoiding both the atomistic and ecological fallacies. As Wright (1998) argues, it is by far the more appropriate analytic technique for studies of this sort.

In these latter sections of the chapter, we have more explicitly discussed bilingualism and emotion in autobiographical memory as well as statistical methods for analyzing such data. The literature suggests a consistent finding that language has an effect on memory retrieval, with memories preferentially retrieved in the language in which they were encoded. We suggest that memories may be linguistically tagged in memory in at least three ways: either as content (e.g. memory for conversation), as inner speech (e.g. words and phrases with inner auditory imagery that emerge as one thinks about a memory), or as propositional thought (e.g. natural language syntax mediates the integration of information in memory). Memories in the bilingual's mind may be tagged as L1 or L2 memories by any of these methods. In this last section, we explored the advantages of using multilevel modeling as more appropriate than traditional methods for the clustered nature of autobiographical memory data (memories nested within persons).

Conclusion

In the beginning of this chapter we asked: Does remembering an event in another language affect the 'feel' of that memory? Would the immigrant's memories of childhood in another country feel less poignant when recalled in a second language? Do the sojourners' tales of life 'over-there' seem less emotionally powerful when translated for the folks at home?

Results of recent experimental work suggest that, in fact, when immigrants recall first language memories from childhood in a second language, some emotional intensity is lost (Schrauf & Rubin, 2004). Further, when the language of encoding and the language of retrieval are matched, remembered emotion is recalled with more intensity (Marian & Kaushanskaya, 2004). These initial findings (along with others we have reviewed) are consistent with anecdotal evidence, bilinguals' intuitions, and the observations made by psychotherapists. Much work, however, remains to be done, and we have taken the liberty of offering theoretical and methodological suggestions for where the field might go.

Via review of the extant empirical literature on the structure and functioning of autobiographical memory, we propose that as an individual memory comes into consciousness, some details (perhaps central ones) emerge into consciousness with a vivid sense of being 're-experienced', while other details (and framing) are provided by memory but lack this sense of reliving. On this basis, we have suggested that both the 'feel' of a memory and the language of a memory are in part re-experienced and in part inferred. In the case of emotion, this accounts for the complexity of remembered emotion, which is multiple and often contradictory.

It also accounts for how individual memories, which in the end are online reconstructions each time they are recalled, can be so variably 'felt', in terms of both valence and intensity, from retrieval occasion to retrieval occasion. We have also used this particular view of memory to suggest what is linguistic about autobiographical memories. To wit, we suggest that some memories commemorate language events (e.g. conversations), some memories involve inner speech at the time of retrieval, and (perhaps) all memories involve natural language as the 'glue' for the different types of information that make them up. These articulations are important for determining in what sense the bilingual's autobiographical memories are different according to language.

We have argued that when a bilingual recalls a particular memory, he or she engages (albeit below awareness) in the mental reconstruction of some event that was originally encoded into memory in a particular place and time – in a determined sociocultural and linguistic environment. The emotional tone of the experience and perhaps some explicitly remembered words or phrases from the event are encoded as well, necessarily in an L1 or L2 or mixed language context. In the moment of recalling the memory, these various bits of information are reintegrated into the whole narratively structured memory again, and some of them are vividly re-experienced, while others are almost or merely conceptual in status (much of this depends on the sociocultural and linguistic context of retrieval). The linguistic content and/or content of the original event will have left its mark as well. Memories are tagged by language, and at recall this too will be more or less vividly experienced. We believe that this model provides the necessary clues for how and where to look for emotion and language in bilingual memory so that we can fruitfully answer the questions that we want to ask (e.g. Are first language memories more emotional than second language memories? Are the immigrant's childhood memories recalled with more emotional intensity in the first versus the second language?).

Methodologically, the chapter has reviewed the techniques currently used in research on emotion and bilingual autobiographical memory, and on the basis of these we have made suggestions for improving our instruments. Finally, we have argued that the nature of autobiographical memories, nested as they are within individual minds, requires a statistical technique more sensitive to this structure. Multilevel modeling is an advance over traditional regression and analysis of variance, and we argue that its adoption will do greater justice to the data. In the larger context of studies of bilingualism and emotion in cognitive psychology, autobiographical memory offers a unique site to investigate the complicated and multidimensional relation between language, memory, and emotion. We hope that these reflections will serve to refine our science and advance our knowledge of bilingualism.

Acknowledgements

This research was supported by grants from the National Institute on Aging (R01 AG16430 and R03 AG19957).

References

Anderson, S. and Conway, M. (1993) Investigating the structure of autobiographical memory. *Journal of Experimental Psychology: Learning and Memory* 19(5), 1178–96.

Beike, D. and Landoll, S. (2000) Striving for a consistent life story: Cognitive reactions to autobiographical memories. *Social Cognition* 18(3), 292–318.

Berman, R. and Slobin, D. (1994) *Relating Events in Narrative: A Crosslinguistic Developmental Study*. Hillsdale, NJ: Lawrence Erlbaum.

Bernsten, D. (1996) Involuntary autobiographical memories. *Applied Cognitive Psychology* 10, 435–54.

Bernsten, D. (1998) Voluntary and involuntary access to autobiographical memory. *Memory* 6(2), 113–41.

Bluck, S. and Li, K.Z.H. (2001) Predicting memory completeness and accuracy: Emotion and exposure in repeated autobiographical recall. *Applied Cognitive Psychology* 15, 145–58.

Brewer, W. (1996) What is recollective memory? In D. Rubin (ed.) *Remembering Our Past: Studies in Autobiographical Memory* (pp. 19–66). Cambridge: Cambridge University Press.

Brown, R. and Kulik, J. (1977) Flashbulb memories. *Cognition* 5, 73–99.

Bucci, W. (1995) The power of narrative: A multiple code account. In J.W. Pennebaker (ed.) *Emotion, Disclosure, and Health* (pp. 93–122). Washington, DC: American Psychological Association.

Carruthers, P. (1998) Thinking in language? Evolution and a modularist possibility. In P. Carruthers and J. Boucher (eds) *Language and Thought: Interdisciplinary Perspectives* (pp. 94–114). Cambridge, UK: Cambridge University Press.

Carruthers, P. (2002) The cognitive functions of language. *Behavioral and Brain Sciences* 25(6), 657–726.

Church, A., Katigbak, M. and Reyes, J. (1996) Toward a taxonomy of trait adjectives in Filipino: Comparing personality lexicons across cultures. *European Journal of Personality* 10, 3–24.

Clark, E. (2003) Languages and representations. In D. Gentner and S. Goldin-Meadow (eds) *Language in Mind: Advances in the Study of Language and Thought* (pp. 17–24). Cambridge, MA: MIT Press/Bradford.

Collins, A. and Loftus, E. (1975) A spreading activation theory of semantic processing. *Psychological Review* 82, 407–28.

Conway, M. (1996) Autobiographical knowledge and autobiographical memories. In D. Rubin (ed.) *Remembering Our Past: Studies in Autobiographical Memory* (pp. 67–93). Cambridge: Cambridge University Press.

Conway, M. and Pleydell-Pearce, C. (2000) The construction of autobiographical memories in the self-memory system. *Psychological Review* 107, 261–88.

Damasio, A. (1994) *Descartes' Error: Emotion, Reason and the Human Brain*. New York: Putnam.

Feldman, L. (1995) Valence focus and arousal focus: Individual differences in the structure of affective experience. *Journal of Personality and Social Psychology* 69(1), 153–66.

Feldman-Barret, L. (1998) Discrete emotions or dimensions? The role of valence focus and arousal focus. *Cognition and Emotion* 12(4), 579–99.

Gulgoz, S., Schrauf, R. and Rubin, D. (2001) Language effect in bilingual autobiographical memory. Unpublished manuscript.

Herrmann, D. and Raybeck, D. (1981) Similarities and differences in meaning in six cultures. *Journal of Cross-Cultural Psychology* 12(2), 194–206.

Keenan, J. and Jennings, T. (1995) Priming of inference concepts in the construction-integration model. In C.A. Weaver, S. Mannes and C.R. Fletcher (eds) *Discourse Comprehension: Essays in Honor of Walter Kintsch* (pp. 233–44). Hillsdale, NJ: Lawrence Erlbaum.

Kintsch, W. (1988) The role of knowledge in discourse comprehension: A construction-integration model. *Psychological Review* 95, 163–82.

Kreft, I. and de Leeuw, J. (1998) *Introducing Multilevel Modeling*. Thousand Oaks, CA: Sage.

Korba, R.J. (1990) The rate of inner speech. *Perceptual and Motor Skills* 71, 1043–52.

Larsen, R. and Diener, E. (1987) Affect intensity as an individual difference characteristic: A review. *Journal of Research in Personality* 21, 1–39.

Larsen, S., Schrauf, R., Fromholt, P. and Rubin, D. (2002). Inner speech and bilingual autobiographical memory: A Polish–Danish cross-cultural study. *Memory* 10(1), 45–54.

Levine, L. (1997) Reconstructing memory for emotions. *Journal of Experimental Psychology: General* 126(2), 165–77.

Levine, L., Prohaska, V., Burgess, S., Rice, J. and Laulhere, T. (2001) Remembering past emotions: The role of current appraisals. *Cognition and Emotion* 15(4), 393–417.

Marian, V. and Kaushanskaya, M. (2004) Self-construal and emotion in bicultural bilinguals. *Journal of Memory and Language* 51(2), 190–201.

Marian, V. and Neisser, U. (2000) Language-dependent recall of autobiographical memories. *Journal of Experimental Psychology: General* 129(3), 361–68.

McKoon, G. and Ratcliff, R. (1992a) Inference during reading. *Psychological Review* 99, 440–66.

McKoon, G. and Ratcliff, R. (1992b) Spreading activation versus compound cue accounts of priming: Mediated priming revisited. *Journal of Experimental Psychology: Learning, Memory, and Cognition* 18, 1155–72.

Mesquita, B. and Frijda, N. (1992) Cultural variations in emotions: A review. *Psychological Bulletin* 112(2), 179–204.

Neisser, U. and Harsch, N. (1992) Phantom flashbulbs: False recollections of hearing the news about Challenger. In E. Winograd and U. Neisser (eds) *Affect and Accuracy in Recall: Studies of 'Flashbulb' Memories* (Vol. 4) (pp. 9–31). New York: Cambridge University Press.

Ortony, A., Clore, G. and Collins, A. (1988) *The Cognitive Structure of Emotions*. Cambridge, UK: Cambridge University Press.

Ratcliff, R. and McKoon, G. (1994) Retrieving information from memory: Spreading activation theories versus compound cue theories. *Psychological Review* 101, 177–84.

Reisberg, D. (ed.) (1992) *Auditory Imagery*. Mahwah, NJ: Lawrence Erlbaum.

Reiser, B., Black, J. and Abelson, R. (1985) Knowledge structures in the organization and retrieval of autobiographical memories. *Cognitive Psychology* 17, 89–137.

Reiser, B., Black, J. and Kalamarides, P. (1986) Strategic memory search processes. In D. Rubin (ed.) *Autobiographical Memory* (pp. 100–22). Cambridge, UK: Cambridge University Press.

Robinson, J. and Swanson, K. (1990) Autobiographical memory: The next phase. *Applied Cognitive Psychology* 4, 321–35.

Romney, A., Moore, C. and Rusch, C. (1997) Cultural universals: Measuring the semantic structure of emotion terms in English and Japanese. *Proceedings of the National Academy of Sciences* 94, 5489–94.

Ross, B. (1991) *Remembering the Personal Past.* New York: Oxford University Press.

Ross, M. (1989) Relation of implicit theories to the construction of personal histories. *Psychological Review* 96, 341–57.

Rubin, D. and Kozin, M. (1984) Vivid memories. *Cognition* 16, 81–95.

Russell, J. (1991) Culture and the categorization of emotions. *Psychological Bulletin* 110(3), 426–50.

Schank, R. (1982) *Dynamic Memory: A Theory of Reminding and Learning in Computers and People.* Cambridge, UK: Cambridge University Press.

Scherer, K. (1984) Emotion as a multicomponent process: A model and some cross-cultural data. In P. Shaver and L. Wheeler (eds) *Review of Personality and Social Psychology: Emotions, Relationships, and Health* (Vol. 5) (pp. 37–63). Beverly Hills, CA: Sage.

Scherer, K. (1999) Appraisal theory. In T. Dalgleish and M. Power (eds) *Handbook of Cognition and Emotion* (pp. 637–63). New York: John Wiley.

Scherer, K. and Wallbott, H. (1994) Evidence for universality and cultural variation of differential emotion response patterning. *Journal of Personality and Social Psychology* 66(2) 310–28.

Schimmack, U. and Diener, E. (1997) Affect intensity: Separating intensity and frequency in repeatedly measured affect. *Journal of Personality and Social Psychology* 73(6), 1313–29.

Schrauf, R. (1997) ¡Costalero quiero ser! Autobiographical memory and the oral life story of a Holy Week Brother in Southern Spain. *Ethos* 25(4), 428–53.

Schrauf, R. (2000) Bilingual autobiographical memory: Experimental studies and clinical cases. *Culture and Psychology* 6(4), 387–417.

Schrauf, R. (2002) Bilingual inner speech as the medium of cross-modular retrieval in autobiographical memory. *Behavioral and Brain Sciences* 25, 698–99.

Schrauf, R. (2003) A protocol analysis of retrieval in autobiographical memory. *International Journal of Bilingualism* 7(3), 235–56.

Schrauf, R., Pavlenko, A. and Dewaele, J.-M. (2003) Bilingual episodic memory: An introduction. *International Journal of Bilingualism* 7(3), 221–33.

Schrauf, R. and Rubin, D. (1998) Bilingual autobiographical memory in older adult immigrants: A test of cognitive explanations of the reminiscence bump and the linguistic encoding of memories. *Journal of Memory and Language* 39(3), 437–57.

Schrauf, R. and Rubin, D. (2000) Internal languages of retrieval: The bilingual encoding of memories for the personal past. *Memory and Cognition* 28(4), 616–23.

Schrauf, R. and Rubin, D. (2001) Effects of voluntary immigration on the distribution of autobiographical memories over the lifespan. *Applied Cognitive Psychology* 15, 75–88.

Schrauf, R. and Rubin, D. (2003) On the bilingual's two sets of memories. In R. Fivush and C. Haden (eds) *Autobiographical Memory and the Construction of a Narrative Self: Developmental and Cultural Perspectives* (pp. 121–45). Mahwah, NJ: Lawrence Erlbaum.

Schrauf, R. and Rubin, D. (2004) The 'language' and 'feel' of bilingual memory: Mnemonic traces. *Estudios de Sociolinguistica* 5(1), 21–39.

Schrauf, R. and Sanchez, J. (2004) The preponderance of negative emotion words in the emotion lexicon: A cross-generational and cross-linguistic study. *Journal of Multilingual and Multicultural Development* 25(2–3), 266–84.

Shweder, R. (1991) *Thinking Through Cultures: Expeditions in Cultural Psychology.* Cambridge, MA: Harvard University Press.

Slobin, D. (1996) From 'thought and language' to 'thinking for speaking'. In J. Gumperz and S. Levinson (eds) *Rethinking Linguistic Relativity* (pp. 70–96). New York: Cambridge University Press.

Snijders, T. and Bosker, R. (1999) *Multilevel Analysis: An Introduction to Basic and Advanced Multilevel Modeling.* Thousand Oaks, CA: Sage.

Storm, C. and Storm, T. (1987) A taxonomic study of the vocabulary of emotions. *Journal of Personality and Social Psychology* 53, 805–16.

Strongman, K. and Kemp, S. (1991) Autobiographical memory for emotion. *Bulletin of the Psychonomic Society* 29, 195–98.

Talarico, J., LaBar, K. and Rubin, D. (2003) Confidence, not consistency, characterizes flashbulb memories. *Psychological Science* 14(5), 455–61.

Tulving, E. (1983) *Elements of Episodic Memory.* Oxford: Clarendon Press.

Tulving, E. (1985) Memory and consciousness. *Canadian Psychology* 26, 1–12.

Vygotsky, L. (1962) *Thought and Language.* Cambridge, MA: MIT Press.

Walker, W., Skowronski, J. and Thompson, C. (2003) Life is pleasant – and memory helps to keep it that way! *Review of General Psychology* 7(2), 203–10.

Webster, J. (1995) Adult age differences in reminiscence functions. In B. Haight and J. Webster (eds) *The Art and Science of Reminiscing: Theory, Research, Methods, and Applications* (pp. 89–102). Washington, DC: Taylor and Francis.

Weingartner, H. (1978) Human state-dependent learning. In B. Ho, D. Richards and D. Chute (eds) *Drug Discrimination and State-Dependent Learning* (pp. 361–82). New York: Academic Press.

Wheeler, M., Stuss, D. and Tulving, E. (1997) Toward a theory of episodic memory: The frontal lobes and autonoetic consciousness. *Psychological Bulletin* 121(3), 331–54.

Wright, D. (1998) Modelling clustered data in autobiographical memory research: The multilevel approach. *Applied Cognitive Psychology* 12, 339–57.

Afterword

ANETA PAVLENKO

Now, where to from here? Below, I will offer a brief overview of questions that have been asked to date in the study of multilingualism and emotions, of theories that have been advanced, of data types that have been collected, and of analytical approaches applied to these data. This overview will help me to identify the gaps in the present inquiry and to sketch promising directions for future work.

Let us begin with the questions. In the traditional study of 'affective factors', the key question has been: what affective factors influence acquisition and use of a second language? The inquiry into multilingualism and emotions has significantly expanded the range of questions that are asked about the relationship between the two. These questions can be subdivided into three groups: some are centrally concerned with bi- and multilinguals' emotional experiences, others with emotional expression in multilingual contexts, and yet others with representation of emotion words, concepts, and autobiographic memories in bi- and multilingual minds.

The first group of questions considers bi- and multilinguals' *emotional experience*: What emotional worlds are created by different languages for their speakers, and, more specifically, what role do forms of emotional expression play in this experience (Besemeres)? Are some emotion concepts experienced in culturally unique ways, as argued by Panayiotou (2004) with regard to physical correlates of *stenahoria* (discomfort/sadness/suffocation)? And if this is the case, does second language socialization reroute 'the trajectory of feeling' (Hoffman, 1989: 269) and engender new forms of emotional experience (Besemeres)? How do different types of bi- and multilinguals perceive and experience the emotionality of their languages (Harris, Gleason & Ayçiçeği; Pavlenko)? How do these perceptions affect their experiences of self in their respective languages (Pavlenko)? What discourses of bi- and multilingualism and ideologies of emotion affect people's self-perceptions, emotional experiences, and linguistic trajectories (Besemeres; Pavlenko; Piller & Takahashi)? What constitutes desire for another language and how are speakers socialized into this desire (Piller & Takahashi; see also Pérez Firmat, 2003; Piller, 2002, in press)? Does language desire affect their emotional experiences, romantic and sexual choices, and linguistic trajectories (Piller & Takahashi; see also Kinginger, 2004a; Pérez Firmat, 2003; Piller, 2002)? How do negative experiences with and in a language impact speakers' willingness to use the language and the level of language attrition (Pavlenko, 2005; Schmid, 2002)?

The second group of questions addresses *emotional expression*: What affective repertoires are offered by different languages to their speakers and how are they appropriated creatively by bi- and multilinguals (Besemeres; Koven; Panayiotou; Vaid)? How are bi- and multilingual speakers' performances of self perceived by their interlocutors (Koven; Pavlenko)? How does perceived emotionality affect language choice for emotional expression in speaking (Dewaele) and in writing (Kellman, 2000; Kinginger, 2004b; Pavlenko, 2005)? What other factors, including self-identification and proficiency, might affect language choice for emotional expression (Dewaele; Vaid)? How do bi- and multilingual speakers and writers discuss their emotional experiences and perform affect, in particular in cases when emotion concepts and affective repertoires offered by their respective languages do not fully match (Besemeres; Koven; Panayiotou)? How do they use various speech acts, and in particular humor, for emotion management (Vaid)?

The third group of questions concerns *representation of emotion words and concepts in bi- and multilingual lexicons* and, more specifically, translatability of emotion words and concepts: Are emotion words represented differently from abstract and concrete words in the mental lexicon, and if so, what attributes are specific to emotion words (Altarriba)? Are there meaningful differences between emotion concepts in different languages (Besemeres; Panayiotou; Stepanova Sachs & Coley; see also Pavlenko, 2005; Wierzbicka, 1999)? Do some concepts differ even when they are linked to translation equivalents (Panayiotou; Stepanova Sachs & Coley)? Do bilinguals draw on different concepts in interpreting the 'same' stories in their respective languages (Panayiotou; see also Pavlenko, 2002)? And what is the role of language and emotions in encoding of autobiographic memories (Schrauf & Durazo-Arvizu; see also Marian & Kaushanskaya, 2004)?

It is our hope that these questions appear as exciting to our readers as they do to us and that our readers will find novel ways to pursue them. We also hope that this volume offers both theoretical and methodological support for such future inquiry. Theory-wise, the contributors draw on a wide range of theoretical paradigms, from Bakhtin's (1981, 1986) ideas about language and Foucault's (1977, 1980) notions of power to spreading-activation theory by Collins and Loftus (1975) and the connectionist framework (Rumelhart & McClelland, 1986). More importantly, we are now seeing an emergence of theories intrinsic to the field, created specifically to explain the multifaceted relationship between multilingualism and emotions. To date, representation theories include Altarriba's (2003) theory of multiple traces advanced to explain the representation of emotion words in the mental lexicon and Schrauf's theory of language and emotions in autobiographic memory (Schrauf & Durazo-Arvizu; see also Schrauf & Rubin, 2004). Age- and context-of-learning theories include the emotional contexts of learning theory articulated by Harris and associates in this volume, and Pavlenko's (2005) theory of affective linguistic conditioning and language embodiment, both of which aim to explain differential perceptions of languages learned in different contexts and at different points in life.

Methodological approaches developed to study multilingualism and emotions are equally diverse and often appeal to triangulation of different types of data. The first among these are *introspective data*, such as interviews (Koven; Panayiotou), self-reports and ratings collected through written and web-based questionnaires and surveys (Dewaele; Pavlenko; Vaid), and autobiographic literary texts (Besemeres; Pavlenko). The second type are *experimental data* that come from rating and categorization tasks (Altarriba; Harris *et al.*; Stepanova Sachs & Coley), recall tasks (Schrauf & Durazo-Arvizu), and electrodermal recordings of skin conductance amplitudes (Harris *et al.*). The third type are *performance data*, such as conversations, oral narratives (Koven), interviews (Panayiotou; Piller & Takahashi), and literary texts (Besemeres). The fourth type are *ethnographic data*, that is, a combination of direct observations, field notes, e-mails, telephone conversations, interviews, and media and web-based texts, used to arrive at a deeper understanding of local ideologies of language, multilingualism, and emotions (Piller & Takahashi). The fifth and final type, not illustrated in this volume but abundant in the literature on bilingual psychoanalysis, are *clinical data*, that is, data from case histories and sessions with patients who speak more than one language (e.g. Amati-Mehler *et al.*, 1993).

Scholars also appeal to diverse analytical approaches to understand the collected evidence. The approaches illustrated in the present volume range from different types of thematic (Panayiotou; Pavlenko) and discourse and text analysis (Besemeres; Koven; Pavlenko; Piller & Takahashi) to descriptive statistics (Dewale; Harris *et al.*; Koven; Pavlenko; Vaid), to a variety of parametric and non-parametric statistical analyses (Dewaele; Harris *et al.*; Schrauf & Durazo-Arvizu; Vaid). They also address a wide range of emotions, variably approached as concepts, states, relationships, or affective repertoires: anger (Dewaele; Koven), desire (Piller & Takahashi), guilt and shame (Panayiotou), envy and jealousy (Stepanova Sachs & Coley), and fear, anxiety, sadness, sorrow, and grief (Besemeres).

This brief overview makes visible both achievements of the present research and its limitations. Emerging theories of encoding of emotion words and autobiographic memories and of emotional contexts of language learning are undoubtedly a sign of healthy development in a new field. What the field needs in the future, however, are not only explanatory theories, but also new models of the bi- and multilingual mental lexicon that would incorporate affective dimensions of word and concept representation, cross-linguistic differences in emotion concepts, and differences in language emotionality, and make testable predictions about ways in which these properties might function in language learning and use.

From an empirical and methodological viewpoint, studies in the present volume offer a rich array of directions to follow and to expand to a wider range of languages, speakers, and contexts. At the same time, existing approaches have several limitations, in particular lack of attention to affective socialization and to affect performance in conversation. We hope that future studies in the field will undertake conversational and interactional analyses of multilingual affect performance. We also hope that the new generation of researchers will engage in longitudinal ethnographic studies of affective socialization of multilingual children and of adults who make a transition to a new linguistic and cultural environment.

Despite the unavoidable limitations of approaches represented in this volume, we believe that the new field is off to a good and productive start. In the words of Harris and associates, the contributors to the volume are no longer willing to see the inquiry into multilingualism and emotions 'as inherently indeterminate'. Instead, they offer a model example of scholarly creativity and interdisciplinarity in devising approaches that illuminate physiological, cognitive, affective, and linguistic processes taking place in bi- and multilingual minds and bodies. We also persevere in our attempts to capture in words – and oftentimes in words of one language, English – the elusive and dynamic interaction between emotions and language learning and use.

References

Altarriba, J. (2003) Does *cariño* equal 'liking'? A theoretical approach to conceptual nonequivalence between languages. *International Journal of Bilingualism* 7(3), 305–22.

Amati–Mehler, J., Argentieri, S. and J. Canestri (1993) *The Babel of the Unconscious: Mother Tongue and Foreign Languages in the Psychoanalytic Dimension.* (J. Whitelaw-Cucco, trans.). Madison, CT: International Universities Press.

Bakhtin, M. (1981) *The Dialogic Imagination: Four Essays by M. Bakhtin.* (M. Holquist, trans.). Austin, TX: University of Texas Press.

Bakhtin, M. (1986) *Speech Genres and Other Late Essays.* (V. McGee, trans.). Austin, TX: University of Texas Press.

Collins, A. and Loftus, E. (1975) A spreading-activation theory of semantic processing. *Psychological Review* 82, 407–28.

Foucault, M. (1977) *Discipline and Punish: The Birth of the Prison*. New York: Pantheon.

Foucault, M. (1980) *Power/Knowledge: Selected Interviews and Other Writings, 1972–1977*. New York: Pantheon.

Hoffman, E. (1989) *Lost in Translation. A Life in a New Language*. New York: Penguin Books.

Kellman, S. (2000) *The Translingual Imagination*. Lincoln/London: University of Nebraska Press.

Kinginger, C. (2004a) Alice doesn't live here anymore: Foreign language learning and identity reconstruction. In A. Pavlenko and A. Blackledge (eds) *Negotiation of Identities in Multilingual Contexts* (pp. 219–42). Clevedon, UK: Multilingual Matters.

Kinginger, C. (2004b) Bilingualism and emotion in the autobiographical works of Nancy Huston. *Journal of Multilingual and Multicultural Development* 25(2/3), 159–78.

Marian, V. and Kaushanskaya, M. (2004) Self-construal and emotion in bicultural bilinguals. *Journal of Memory and Language* 51, 190–201.

Panayiotou, A. (2004) Bilingual emotions: The untranslatable self. *Estudios de Sociolingüística* 5(1), 1–19.

Pavlenko, A. (2002) Bilingualism and emotions. *Multilingua* 21(1), 45–78.

Pavlenko, A. (2005) *Emotions and Multilingualism*. New York: Cambridge University Press.

Pérez Firmat, G. (2003) *Tongue Ties: Logo-Eroticism in Anglo-Hispanic Literature*. New York: Palgrave Macmillan.

Piller, I. (2002) *Bilingual Couples Talk: The Discursive Construction of Hybridity*. Amsterdam/Philadelphia: John Benjamins.

Piller, I. (in press) 'I always wanted to marry a cowboy': Bilingual couples, language, and desire. In T. Karis and K. Killian (eds) *Cross-Cultural Couples: Transborder Relationships in the Twenty-First Century*. Binghamton, NY: Haworth.

Rumelhart, D. and McClelland, J. (1986) *Parallel Distributed Processing: Explorations in the Microstructure of Cognition* (Vol. 1). Cambridge, MA: MIT Press.

Schmid, M. (2002) *First Language Attrition, Use and Maintenance: The Case of German Jews in Anglophone Countries*. Amsterdam/Philadelphia: John Benjamins.

Schrauf, R. and Rubin, D. (2004) The 'language' and 'feel' of bilingual memory: Mnemonic traces. *Estudios de Sociolingüística* 5(1), 21–39.

Wierzbicka, A. (1999) *Emotions Across Languages and Cultures: Diversity and Universals*. Cambridge: Cambridge University Press.

Index

Authors

Subjects